JOURNEY ON A BUMPY ROAD

ELLEN PATRICIA

ISBN 978-1-955156-83-7 (paperback)
ISBN 978-1-955156-84-4 (hardcover)
ISBN 978-1-955156-85-1 (digital)

Copyright © 2021 by Ellen Patricia

All rights reserved. No part of this publication may be reproduced, distributed, or transmitted in any form or by any means, including photocopying, recording, or other electronic or mechanical methods without the prior written permission of the publisher. For permission requests, solicit the publisher via the address below.

Rushmore Press LLC
1 800 460 9188
www.rushmorepress.com

Printed in the United States of America

CONTENTS

Acknowledgements v
Introduction vii

Chapter 1:   My Early Childhood 1
Chapter 2:   Early Traumas 4
Chapter 3:   Living with My Aunt. 27
Chapter 4:   Living at Bushy Pen. 32
Chapter 5:   Life with the Lens 34
Chapter 6:   Escape from Bushy Pen 39
Chapter 7:   Visit to Miss Brown. 46
Chapter 8:   No Bed Of Roses. 50
Chapter 9:   From The Pot to the Fire. 59
Chapter 10: Surprise in the Bushes 62
Chapter 11: Home Sweet Home. 67
Chapter 12: A Period of Turmoil. 76
Chapter 13: Life with My Mother. 80
Chapter 14: The Stranger. 84
Chapter 15: Life in the Children's Home 90
Chapter 16: Return to Windsor 98
Chapter 17: Searching for My Mother 105
Chapter 18: The Betrayal 113
Chapter 19: Condition Got Worst 117
Chapter 20: Visit to My father 122
Chapter 21: My Eldest Son's birth. 128
Chapter 22: The Bishop's Advice 131
Chapter 23: Sojourn to Town 137

Chapter 24: Living at Ferry. 147
Chapter 25: Unfortunate Course of Events. 161
Chapter 26: In Search for My Cousin Tiny. 177
Chapter 27: Launching Out 185
Chapter 28: Journey to an Unknown Land. 201
Chapter 29: Costa Rica. 212
Chapter 30: On Route to Mexico 242
Chapter 31: Tijuana 254
Chapter 32: Landed in America 261
Chapter 33: Arrived in Florida 267
Chapter 34: Trip to Tennessee. 288
Chapter 35: Return from Tennessee 302
Chapter 36: Vale. 311
Chapter 37: Travel Up North to Pick Fruits 319
Chapter 38: Living at the Camps 329
Chapter 39: A Change Must Come. 333
Chapter 40: Return to Live with Jack and Jill 369

ACKNOWLEDGEMENTS

Through it all I give thanks to Divine Providence, who brought me thus far, despite my many trials. With the efforts that it took, and the time and patience involved, I want to identify and acknowledge a few wonderful people who have contributed in countless ways.

First let me acknowledge my husband for his support. He by his willingness; allow me to pursue my dream laid an unhindered path which allowed me to reach the final stage of my biographical work.

I am more than grateful to express my thanks to Bill my good friend for the help and motivation which encouraged me to complete this autobiography. It was a struggle to get pass the many obstacles, but I was determined to accomplish this task. I had to pay an ultimate price.

Lastly, it would be remiss of me if I did not mention my friend and confidant Adam. It was often through his moral support that I took heart to press on in the face of my difficulties.

May this book prove to be not only a testament to my effort, but also the efforts of those who have stood by me through the many years which helped me to make it a reality.

My gratitude and thanks goes to everyone.

INTRODUCTION

Ellen Patricia's purpose in this book is to primarily address her families and friends from a position that she had not had the opportunity to do before.

The author of this book is not seeking to direct any animosity towards anyone for past unpleasant events. Instead by her unabashed reporting of her life experiences, she is hoping to open a window to those who have a need to know her better.

The traumas which she experience were the reason for the pain and unhappiness which have plagued her all these many years. Traumas brought about in her early and later years as a result of her inability to gain acceptance from her parents, siblings, families and friends.

This testimony of her life's experience should be a treasure trove for her family; it will also be therapeutic for the author, and has done much to heal many emotional wounds which have marred her life for many years.

It is the Author's desire that this autobiography will be therapeutic for her; because of her abusive life, and rejection.

She found it difficult to communicate with her mother. Even to report incident of child molestation's was difficult for Ellen Patricia to do; as her mother rarely listen to her words over that of her perpetrators. Even when her vigilance would have protected Ellen Patricia's chastity, she chooses to remain silent, so as not to offend her daughter's molester.

Her mother primarily goal was to protect her social position in the community.

The author's maternal influence was such that the memories often left her recoiling at the thought of her mother's austere attitude.

Her early years formed the template on which the course of her later life had built.

Ellen Patricia became an early recipient of the most insidious forms of child abuse. This abuse was perpetrated by none other than the individuals who should have offered guidance and protection, but instead only caused her pain.

So much so, that at the tender age of four, child molestation seemed normal to her.

During her youthful years she did not experience any love at home from her mother and father.

At the behest of her mother, Ellen Patricia was sent to various foster homes where she often was made to work incessantly. This continued up to her adolescence years.

Because they lived in a rural setting, chores were always plentiful at home.

Her parent's cavalier attitude about the importance of her attending school caused her attendance to be anything but regular. They placed more importance on her domestic chores than her academic pursuits. The net result was that she was deprived of needed schooling in her formative years. As a result of her experience she is now equipped with wisdom to impart to parents and kids alike about the importance of a good education.

I found it was a surprise to some of Ellen Patricia family members to learn that for most part of her life she was regarded as the 'black sheep' of the family.

The lack of normal amenities was always the hallmark of her life, but the author's adolescence years saw her life beset with 'abject poverty.' Her indigent state was compounded by the fact that she was supporting a growing family as a single mother.

It would appear that her fortune was not to be gleaned from the association with the opposite sex.

Broken promises and unfulfilled expectation were the markers that appeared time and time again so she became knowledgeable and mindful in the dispensing of her emotions.

As a close person of Ellen Patricia I can attest to the fact that her children had been her primary focus over these many years, as many of her life changing decisions were made with them in mind. That became her main focus. She wanted to sojourn to other countries in search for a better life to help her children.

She reported to me that her life at Windsor, Ferry and many other places brought back very few memories of happiness.

As she was never a gregarious person by nature, her solitare lifestyle usually brought out an insensitive attitude towards her from the members of the community.

And from time to time and stemming from very trivial circumstances she often became an object of ridicule.

Through all her trials the safe harbor that she remembered was her grandparents. They became the 'safety net' which kept her going in moments of despair. Her encounter with love of a family came by way of her grandparents. Their guidance and affection should stand as a testimony to the importance of grandparents in many families. I have no hesitation in stating that Ellen Patrice's Grandma and Grandpa will be placed on a pedestal in her heart, a position which they so richly deserve. Had it not been for both of her grandparents in many instances she would not be able to fend off many of the storms life sent her way.

Their encouraging words and loving smiles will always remain with her.

As Christians and God-fearing people, they, by their simple way of life ushered her into a life of religious observance. During her difficult times, she inquired about migration to another country, hoping to find a better life. As she migrated through other countries she was faced with hardships, and terribly abusive conditions on each leg of her journey. Still her determination was to push ahead, and not look back.

Ellen Patricia's faith in God was her main support in dealing with the many vicissitudes of her life. Just like an 'ugly duckling,' through her belief in the saving power of 'Jesus Christ' she will be transformed into a 'beautiful swan'.

In some ways I compare the parallel of the author's life to that of Joseph who was despised and rejected by his brothers. Nevertheless,

Divine intervention will make the stone that the builders refused become the chief building block.

God has placed His anointing on her life through his son Jesus Christ, and she is a living manifestation of that anointing today.

It is my hope that all who read this manuscript will come to the realization that despite their many trials, God has brought us back to Him through Christ's death and resurrection. It is with great hope that many will discover the path to redemption, especially the young when it is advantageous at this time in their life to accept Jesus Christ.

It is only by an unreserved acceptance of His Divine invitation that we will access God's promises and be a light to all men so that we can be truly conquerors and manifest the Divine victory

This book has been written with love by Ellen Patricia. Negative experience made known, sometime, becomes the gateway to healing. So by way of this book the author exposes her life to the light, but primarily to her children. Her aim is to set the wheels of love in motion between herself and her family.

The author has communicated to me that she was divinely inspired to write this book to free her from the abused she had experienced in her life, which caused her recoiling memories; and it is by obeying God's command that he will give her release from the bondage of her psychological traumas. By 'Divine Providence,' her greatest desire, for the first time, through all her traumas; she would like to refer with great love to herself and her siblings as 'a family.'

- Vincent.

CHAPTER ONE

My Early Childhood

Windsor is a small town close to Wildwood. One of my earliest memories was of my grandmother telling me that as a baby I came from Locket to Windsor, on the mail bus which was the public transportation at that time.

I remember one night as a little girl we were experiencing what my grandmother called 'bad weather.' There were heavy rains and unusually strong winds, and I recalled everybody saying that a hurricane was 'coming.' I later learned it was the infamous Hurricane. At that time I was almost four years old. My family at that time consisted of my mother and father, my grandparents, my brother George and myself.

That night everyone seemed to be in a state of panic. Even the neighbors sounded very excited, and people were running to and fro.

The church was located close to our house, so my grandmother took me and my brother across the fence to seek refuge there. She put my brother George to lie on a bench, but I, being a little scared, and 'hid' under a table she had brought from our house. The church was now a designated storm shelter, so many people from the community came there through the night.

I fell asleep early that night, sleeping through the worst of the storm, so I was not privy to the natural devastation which ensued throughout the night.

I was awakened in the morning by the noises of the people in the church and the community. Everyone seemed to be expressing their shock at the extent of damage that was done by the hurricane.

Looking from the church across to our house brought to me a very stark reality.

Our house was leaning precariously to one side. There were fruits, broken tree branches, and zinc sheets that were scattered all over the entire yard. Outside looked literally 'torn up.' I had never seen anything like that before. Even the pig pen had blown away and my grandfather had to go in search of the pigs.

The flora of the area was in a mangled state, and the entire area was also in a state of desolation. My father, who was a carpenter, assisted my grandfather in repairing the house, including some of the other houses in the community.

The house we lived in; belonged to my grandmother. She told me that it was built originally in Ferry but on the insistence of my grandfather she sold her land there and physically moved the house to Windsor where it was reassembled. This then resulted in the migration of her entire family.

My relationship with my grandmother was an endearing one as long as I could remember. She reminded me that at three years old I was eating a star apple and told her that I would like to plant the seed. She told me that it would be a good idea, and helped me to do it. Years later I had the pleasure of eating many succulent fruits from the first tree I had planted.

As time passed, and I got older my mother and my father soon rented a house on a hill nearby to where my grandparents were from a lady named Miss Hula. This house was occupied by my parent's, my brother George, and myself. My grandparents were now living on their own.

To my knowledge, my grandparents' relationship did not appear as amiable as it should because they lived in separate rooms.

Unfortunately, I was about four years of age when I was being molested by my father; which continued as I got older.

My father was employed as a headman by The Ministry of Agriculture and Land, at the district of Fountain in Wildwood. His means of transportation to work was to ride on his bicycle each day which was a long way from home. My parents would have regular arguments; particularly about my father alleged 'womanizing.' One day in plain view, I remember seeing my mother confront another lady, questioning her loudly about her 'relationship' with my father. My mother started beating the woman severely, and pushing her repeatedly on a nearby barbed wire fence leaving her with her clothes torn and bloody from the cuts she had received. I don't recall ever seeing that woman again. After a while when I was approximately five years old my parents moved from Windsor to live at Fountain.

CHAPTER TWO

Early Traumas

My earliest memories of Fountain were of my family living at Fountain in a house they rented from the Martin's. Fountain is historically known for the famous mineral spring which is located there. This 'healing spring' is said to have been discovered by a slave in the 1600's who used its water to heal his wound. This legend made the area very popular and a large park, and garden was established there.

Fountain was the center of much of the activity filtering in from adjoining cities. As a result, it assumed the position of one the social center. In the 1950's, I remember as a child, most of the bigger grocery stores were owned and operated by people of different races.

My father was a handsome man of Indian descent. I loved him very much and always wanted to go everywhere with him. Unfortunately my father started molesting me at four years old, which continued through my teenage years.

While living at the Martin's, my cousin Joe who was my father's nephew came to live with us. My father soon took a dislike for Joe. This stemmed from the fact that my father; which later discovered that I was also being molested by his nephew Joe. My father responded to the situation by meeting out severe corporal punishment on Joe for the slightest infraction by tying him by his two hands to a breadfruit tree. Joe would always sit and cry daily, and was afraid to enter the house when my father was home. His sleeping quarters were under the cellar of the house.

After some time the situation became unbearable for Joe. He made his escape during my father tirade and was never seen at the house again.

This took place during the year which my mother gave birth to my brother Roy.

Mr. Martin was an alcoholic. On weekends both Mr. Martin and my father would drink together at the bar. I remember as a child; when they came home being a drunken stupor, they got belligerent, and abused their wives. As time passed, father purchased land, not far from Martin's house. He subsequently built a wooden house on that land which was some distance from the road, in a valley, and in close proximity to a river. We were also fortunate to have a spring which cascaded from the hills behind and above our house that flowed into the river not far from our house. The only stove we had at the time was a coal stove which my mother used on Sundays or whenever it rained. Normally we used wood for fuel. The wood fireplace consisted of five stones on which were laid old machetes to support the pots. The toilet was a pit toilet. It was constructed from bamboo, board, and zinc, was located behind the house, and close to the river. On a regular basis, my mother would put Jeyes and ashes into the toilet to disinfect it. This was done to suppress the obnoxious odors which came from it. On Saturdays, one of my chores was to put dye on the toilet floor, polish and shine on my knees using a coconut brush with burnt coconut, or candle wax. The finished job was such that the brilliance of the toilet flooring could be compared to that of the house.

I attended an infant centre at the corner of Fountain cross road at the Garden Park. The school was located beside a church which had a large bell house beside it. After school was dismissed in the afternoons, I would sit inside the 'bell house' accompanied with other children and wait for my father to pick me up on his way from his job. The journey in the morning was much easier as my father rode his bicycle downhill. Returning home, we had to dismount from the bicycle and walk most of the way. This made the journey seem so much longer.

Somehow, I still enjoyed being with my father.

Ellen Patricia

My parents would frequently quarrel and fight. This went on for many years. As a child, I had no idea what the problem was. They would regularly shout at each other, always using profane language. During those times my father would chase me away from the house, sometimes accompanied by a swift kick. I had to seek shelter in the cellar under the house where I would sometimes have to lay all night in the dirt like an animal with neither nothing to lay on or cover.

My grandmother at the time was living with us. The problem did not get any better; but worsened. My father showed no respect for her. Her efforts to calm his tantrums were always unsuccessful.

On one occasion, during a brawling altercation, my grandmother took my brother and me to shelter in the cellar under the house. While there we felt a copious dousing of water. We realized it was my father when he shouted, "Wet up the dirty bitches, wet up their asses."

My grandmother immediately took us from the cellar, hid us beside the banana trees and ran quickly into the house to get dry clothes for us. When we got dressed she said she was going to take us away from this unpleasant situation. As we were going through the gate, I heard my father's voice, as he came out shouting profanity and running towards us, obviously in disapproval of our grandmother taking us away. He and my grandmother had a physical tussle, and then my father slipped and fell down an escarpment, giving us the opportunity to escape.

It was very late that night, and there was no one around.

My grandmother wrapped our clothes in a bundle, held our hands and dragged us. She told us that we have to run very fast because she was taking us to Windsor to escape from my father before he killed us.

The road was dark and lonely and the journey was very long, but my grandmother did not care about that, she kept dragging us three children along with her, because it was like we were running to save our lives.

It was late that night when we arrived at Windsor. We all stayed there for quite a while.

Time passes. One day my grandmother told us that she had gotten words from my mother that the situation had changed between her and my father so she would be taking us back. My grandfather was very displeased about us going back to the same problems but he was not financially able to help us.

On returning back to my father's house things had 'cooled off' for some time. After a few weeks went by the problem started again, this time, it only got worse. My father would wrestle with me, and dragged me through the coffee field and down to the river bank, when I tried to resist him he fought hard and molested me, and then I was being bludgeoned by him. I told my mother about it. She accosted him about the incident but a fight ensued. My mother tried to escape but was unsuccessful, as my father caught up with her running some distance from the house down the road where she ended being bludgeoned. She had to run quickly to the neighbor's house for safety. After staying there for a number of days, she returned home. One day she told me to pack my clothes as she was going to take me away because, "She did not want my father to kill me." I had no idea where my mother was taking me, and I knew there was no point asking.

She took me down the street where we lived to her friend, Miss Day. When we reached Miss Day's house she told me to wait outside while she went in to talk to her. I tried to hear what they were saying but they spoke so softly. Not long after my mother came outside and told me that Miss Day would be taking me somewhere and that I should behave myself. My mother then left and returned home. I was very frightened.

As memory serves me, I was about six years old then.

After waiting a long time, I saw Miss Day come out from her house, well dressed and told me to take my grip case and come with her, because we were going to catch the bus. I asked her where she was taking me, and she said that we were already late but would tell me when we got on the bus. We had to run most of the way and luckily we made it just in time to catch the bus.

Before I got on the bus, I noticed the sign on the bus that said, 'TO Rosehill.' We boarded the bus and sat together. I asked if we were going to Rosehill and she said yes. I asked her why I was going there with her, and to whom I was going. She said to me that my parents were not getting along well with me at home so she was taking me to stay with one of my mother's friends.

It was late that night when we arrived at Rosehill, and as a result I was unable to observe very much. Miss Day then said she was going to stop at her house first before going to my mother's friend. When we arrived at the lady's house, she had already retired for the night. Miss Day knocked on the door and a lady voice answered asking, "Who is it." Miss Day replied, "I bring the little girl from Miss Polly." She told Miss Day to give her a chance to put some clothes on. When she opened the door, she had a kerosene lamp in her hand which shone brightly so that it lit up the area outside. She invited us in., but on seeing the lady, I took a sudden dislike to her. She was dark skinned, with a very unpleasant countenance. Notwithstanding, I felt no attraction towards her. Anyway, I went inside her house. Miss Day did not come into the house, but told the lady she wanted to speak to her in private. They stayed outside and talked quietly for a while. I could not hear what they were saying but I overheard Miss Day telling the lady that she had to leave, but had five shillings to give her which came from my mother. Miss Day then came to the doorway and told me she was leaving and I should behave myself.

After Miss Day left, the lady asked me if I was hungry. I was, and told her, "Yes."

She took a plate from under her bed and handed it to me. The plate had food on it, but I could not tell what kind of food it was. I took the plate from her and told her "Thanks." But before I started eating, I looked at the plate, it was so black, and the food was just as black as the plate. I was afraid to eat it, but the lady kept watching me. I tried tasting the food but it did not taste good, so I gave the plate back to her. Just looking at the plate and the colour of the food, made me felt bad in my stomach. I had noticed when she took the plate from under the bed and gave it to me a cat ran from under the bed, but I did not think anything about it, until after I gave the plate back to her. When I gave the plate back to her, she appeared disgruntled. She told me to put my night clothes on and go and lie in the corner of the bed.

My mother and grandmother had always taught me to say my prayers before going to sleep, so I knelt beside the bed and said my prayers. When I told her good-night she did not respond to me in a pleasant way, her voice was almost an inaudible grumble.

The following morning, I watched her take the plate from under the bed and put in the doorway outside. When I looked at the plate again it was empty. A cat soon came and ate the food from the plate. The lady did not seem alarmed by this. I was now convinced that she had given me the cat's food the night before and I was relieved that I had not eaten it. This made me develop an increasing dislike for her and hated the thought that I would have to stay with her. Being only six years old, there was nothing I could do.

I wanted to leave this lady, but because we had arrived there at night, I was unable to see the route we had taken to get there. She went to the kitchen to fix breakfast. She soon served me green bananas in a sardine can and an unusually tasting black tea, which she gave me into a rusty milk can. The containers were so dirty, that although I was hungry, I very boldly told her I did not want any food from her and that I wanted to go back home. I told her that if she did not allow me to leave, I would run away. I reminded her that she had given me the cat's food to eat the night before and now she was giving me food in dirty utensils. She responded, "If you ever tell anyone that I gave you the cat's food to eat I will fix your business and mash you up." She then told me to put my things together because Miss Day would be coming to get me to take me back to my mother and father. I was so happy to hear this.

After packing my clothes she locked her door and told me to sit outside under the tree in front of the yard. Before she left for work I saw her give the neighbor the five shillings which my mother sent to her to give Miss Day.

While sitting there, I tried mentally to remember my way back to Miss Day's house. I did not remember the approximate distance and direction to Miss Day's house from the lady's. However I had to get the five shillings to run away, but I had to do it without arousing too much suspicion. In an attempt to secure money for my intending escape.

I first pretended to walk down the road as if I was going to Miss Day's house and stayed in the vicinity for a while. I came back running to the yard as if I was running an errand. With a sense of urgency, I went to the neighbor's daughter and told her that I had gone to Miss Day and she said she would not be able come here herself, so she was asking her mother to give me the money, so I could take it to her. The neighbor did not suspect anything because she didn't know that I knew she had the money. As soon as she gave me the money, I hastily took my little grip case and ran as fast as I could, primarily to avoid detection by Miss Day, which would mean a return to my mother's home.

Later on as the years went by I was informed that this same lady whose name I don't recall was known to work witchcraft, which she used and hindered many people who lived in Rosehill from succeeding in their life.

I did not remember the way to the bus stop, but I remembered that we came from the same direction to which I was running, so I knew I would have to ask someone for directions.

While running along, I saw a shabbily dressed, old lady who was sitting at the side of the road. She seemed very surprised when I greeted her and said "Good-morning." She replied by saying, "Do you know that the children never stop to talk to me, when they see me, they call me dirty names, and throw stones at me, you must be a God sent child." I told her that I did not know that, but I loved my grand-parents very much because she reminds me of them. I told her that it has always been a pleasure for me to help my grandmother while she was doing chores around the house, and anything else that needed to be done.

The old lady said to me, "God is going to bless you one day; you are going to have lots of children. You will travel away. Life will be very rough for a long time, just the way it is now, but as you get older it will get better, and you will have a little money as you get older. Your children would make good of their lives." She said to me. "Don't be too trusting to friends and family as they will hurt you."

I stood there patiently listening to all her advice and predictions. She was very perceptive and asked me if I was running away. I thought it was obvious that she already knew, so I did not answer. She said I had a long way to get to the bus, but I had strong feet and I would get to the bus-stop in time. Before walking away, she told me I would not see her again but that God would always bless and protect me.

As I was leaving, I thanked her and said good-bye. I stood there watching her until she was completely out of sight. I wondered who she was, because she looked so shabby, but spoke so intelligently. "Could she be one of those fairies or witches that I had read about in school?" I was not afraid of her though as strange as she seemed, because she was so real to me.

Suddenly, remembering where I was. I ran hastily along to catch the bus. I made it just in time. Quickly, I got inside and took a seat.

While sitting, I was approached by a tall slim dark skinned young man who announced to me that he was the bus conductor, he inquired of my destination. He then told me that my fare would be nine pence. I took out the five shilling note, gave it to him and told him to take the fare from it. The other passengers were staring at me because five shillings was a lot of money for a child to have in those days, unless you were from a very wealthy family. The bus was not ready to leave so I asked the conductor if I could go and get something to eat. He said yes but I should hurry back. I walked for a while until I found a shop. I was very hungry, because I had not eaten the day before. I bought two patties and a bottle of grape soda and ran back to the bus. The passengers continued to stare at me because I guess it was unusual to see a child as small as I was eating two patties. I felt so strange but I did not care, I was happy because no one knew me.

The bus had to travel through Fountain to get to Windsor. I held my head down because I did not want to be seen by anyone who knew me. Peeping out at one time, I saw my father standing at the cross-road of Fountain and Garden Park. I held my head down fearing if he saw me he would take me off. The bus did not make its scheduled stop there that day as no one was getting off, so there was no chance of him seeing me. I had previously asked the conductor to announce when the bus reached the church at Windsor which would be my stop.

Just after the bus went across the bridge that runs across a big river, I saw a sign that read, 3 miles to Windsor. Before the bus reached the church, the conductor called and told me to get ready because my stop was next.

The bus-stop was immediately in front of the church and close to my grandfather's house. I quickly got off the bus and ran across to my grandfather's house. I did not see him when I went into the yard, but apparently he saw me coming because I heard him call out asking me, "What did your father do to you this time." I explained what had happened and told him that my mother had sent me to Rosehill. I went on to explain to him why I had to run away. He asked me if I was hungry and I said I was. Even if I was not hungry, whenever I went to my grandfather's house I was always ready to eat. He immediately sent me to the shop to buy a loaf of bread, a can of corned beef and two bottles of soda. When I came back, he opened the corned beef, and put it on a plate, gave me a bottle of soda, broke the bread into several pieces and told me to eat whatever I wanted.

We sat around the old wooden table and ate together. It felt so good to be with him. After eating and talking for a while, it was late so my grandfather told me it was time for us to retire to bed.

He had a big wooden bed, but having no mattress he used old clothes, dried banana leaves, cardboard boxes, and crocus bags in place for a mattress. I went to bed and slept well because I was happy and comfortable to be in his company.

I stayed with my grandfather for a while.

Somehow, my mother found out that I had ran away from Rosehill and went to Windsor. There she found me at my usual place of safety with my grandfather.

She became very furious. I explained to her what had happened to me but she was not sensitive to my plight. She only expressed her dissatisfaction about what I had done by saying repeatedly that "I am sick and tired of you," and that I was the reason for all the problems she had in her life. She also expressed dissatisfaction at my grandfather for keeping me there. She grabbed me by my hand and told me she was taking me back with her. I cried and begged her not to take me back to Fountain, but that was in vain. She insisted and took me with her.

My father's behavior was tolerable for a while, but after a few weeks went by, at nights while my mother and grandmother were at church, or otherwise absent from the home, he started molesting me again. I told my mother explicitly about my father's lecherous behavior. This caused their relationship to digress again to a very contentious state, which caused constant quarrels and fights.

During one of these fights, my father threw me out of the house, with an explicit command, and said. "You are a damn big woman now, so you can go look for a man." I was not yet seven years old. I was deeply hurt on hearing that coming from my father. It got to the place where my mother started becoming very abusive to me. The only person I had to turn to who always gave me a listening ear was my grandmother. Whenever I was not in school, and at home my grandmother would take me wherever she went, just to keep me out of harm's way. Fearing that my father would hurt or molest me.

My father was sometimes intoxicated in the evenings when he came from work. This caused his behavior to be very disgusting.

He would then approach me making sexual gestures in front of me, I felt both anger towards him and confusion as to what to do. I suppose getting no response from me made him enraged.

He would then commence by hitting me several times, and then throw me on the floor and trample me with his feet all over my small body.

His 'onslaught' would not be complete until he stood in my chest and stomach. When this was over, I would lie there, in so much pain unable to move. Everyone else in the home had a morbid fear of my father so no one tried to help me.

I was now attending Fountain Elementary School. My teacher name was Miss Brown and my principal name was Mr. Edwards. He was a tall light skin man; he was a very good and caring teacher. As time passed and I got older I remember hearing that he had health problems, and died.

I was now older, so I started walking to school with my friends, who lived in my community, some were also my neighbors. On the way to school, we had to pass by a big tree that was located at a dark corner. We were all afraid of this tree. The tree was so big that its branches hung over the road, and also provided adequate shade for passers-by.

It was reported that under the cotton tree was a venue for ghosts, so we had a sense of foreboding whenever we had to pass by the tree.

Hence, when it was possible, we made sure we had a large party. If unfortunately I was alone, I ran very fast, just to get away from the area.

My friends and I were always happy when mango and apple season came along. We would endeavor to leave for school very early in the morning, so that we would have enough time to pick as many fruits as we could. Our stomachs were already full when we got to school in the morning and on returning home in the evening.

These were some of the happiest times of my childhood.

As memory serves me; I remember that my parents got married. The wedding was conducted by Elder Allen, and the ceremony was held at home, and behind the door of the dining room, which was draped off by a white sheet. It was behind that door my parents took their secret wedding vows. Later on I realized that my mother was pregnant with my sister Lorie. I was not privy as to what was happening with my mother during her state of pregnancy, but I remember the morning in question she was acting very strangely, unable to walk straight, and shouting loudly, saying that she was experiencing terrible pain.

Not long after I saw two ladies entering the yard. One whose name was Mother Dora who was known as the midwife, accompanied by another lady not known to me. I heard when my grandmother instructed my mother to go inside her bedroom and lay down because the midwife was there.

Shortly after, I then saw when my grandmother went to the kitchen and placed a large pot of water on the fire. She took the same pot with the hot water inside the bedroom.

It seems as if my mother was having difficulty giving birth, because I overheard when the midwife told my grandmother to call my father to the house immediately. When my father came inside, I overheard Mother Dora telling my father that he had to lay with my mother in order for the delivery to be made easy.

At that time I hid behind the door in the dining room, peeping and listened, so I was able to observe everything that took place. The moment my father entered the bedroom my grandmother including the two ladies went outside. I quickly ran from behind the door fearing that my grandmother would see me.

Not long after, my grandmother told me that an airplane would be coming soon with my baby sister.

Soon after my grandmother left and went inside the bedroom room. I went back and continued peeping. I saw when my father and grandmother started pulling the wardrobe to and fro, and at the same time they were both shouting, "The plane is coming with the baby."

Then at that moment when my mother was giving birth they also shouted louder so that I would not be able to hear my mother's cries.

It was not very long after my grandmother came outside and told me that the plane had just brought my mother and father a baby girl.

As the years went by, my parents built a spiritual revival church in the yard. It was constructed with bamboo, but the flooring was natural ground. Red, blue purple and white flags were flown high which symbolize the nature of the religion. My mother held service on Sundays. On Mondays, a fasting was held followed by a healing service. Services were conducted on special evenings. These services sometime lasted until very late at night. The Elder of the church name was Brother John. Our church attire consisted of red, white and blue and, red and white headdress. All the female members wore white headdresses. The church was well attended, because the services proved to be spiritually uplifting.

The services were patterned in a deep spiritual pocomania style. Drums and tambourines accompanied the proceedings which were followed by shouting, chanting and myal.

At times, members of the congregation would become so spiritually engaged that they would jump in the air, and then lay prostrate on the ground, remaining in this state for hours. They were said to be 'in the spirit' at that time. This always fascinated me as a child.

Because of this my mother spent most of her time in the church, leaving my grandmother to take care of domestic chores at home. My father was very displeased about this arrangement. He was not 'spiritually inclined,' so he did not attend the services. His leisure time was spent drinking, smoking, and cursing.

Because I was the eldest it was my duty to prepare the table for dinner. We had two white tablecloths, one used for covering the table and the other for covering the meal when it was placed on the table. There were times when the whole family, including my father would sit together for dinner. This was among the rare occasion, when he was in a pleasant disposition.

My father being an alcoholic. When under the influence he became very loud and boisterous, always shouting, especially at my mother and myself, and spoke to my mother in a derogatory manner. When he was like this, we became afraid, so everyone tried to stay out of his way.

It got to the place where he would regularly come home and acted like an insane person. Moments like those he became loud and abusive for the simplest things, especially to me.

One evening while having dinner, my father gave me five scotch bonnet peppers and told me to eat them. I was shocked and told him they were very hot and I couldn't eat them. Angrily, he started shouting and cursing at me. I was afraid and did not want to make him angrier, so I took a small bite of one of the peppers. When he realized I would not eat the pepper to his satisfaction, he grabbed me, threw me one the floor, stood in my stomach, and then kicked me in my private parts. No one tried to help me. My mother and grandmother started screaming, and ran away from the house fearing he would hit them too. Leaving me alone with him, I thought he would kill me.

On other occasions, my father came home and saw me, he would tell me to get out of his yard and go and wash my dirty ass. Having no place to go, I would sit by the roadside until things at home seemed to calm down. Most of the time, he did not want me to eat any of the food that he provided. Times, and times again when he came home and saw me eating, he cursed and told me to go and look for work or, "To get a man to look after me." Being so afraid of him, I usually hid in the bushes. My grandmother would always hide food and bring it to me where I was hiding in the bushes.

We had a lot of coffee trees at the back of the house, and close to the back verandah. During my father's belligerent outbursts, he would throw the dinner from the table, across the verandah, into the area of the coffee trees. My brothers and I got used to my father's evening 'routine' and prepared for him.

We would spread clean banana leaves at the roots of the coffee trees which would act like catchments for the edible missiles that were thrown there. This would ensure us our evening meal which we would collect and run quickly down to the river bank where we sat and enjoyed it. Unfortunately, after throwing away his meal, he became rebellious and began shouting, and cursing at my mother, and they would invariably end up fighting. These were frightening times for us as we usually had to stay away from the house until he decided to go to sleep.

One evening when my father came home in his usual intoxicated state, my mother was leading the church service and most of the people were very high in the 'Spirit.' My mother did not prepare dinner for him. I overheard my father loudly shouting profanities, using every curse word imaginable. He disrupted the service and said. "Where is my damn dinner?" He continued his 'desecration' of the church by kicking down the pulpit and the tables. He angrily shouted repeatedly, "Where is my damn dinner?" This immediately brought the service to an abrupt end. The church was immediately brought to an irreverent silence, and the only sound which could be heard was my father's voice. All the church members became frightened by his actions, and ran hastily from the church. That marked the swansong of my mother's church services.

My parent's domestic affairs became a scandal at Fountain. Although my mother was afraid of him, there were times when he would come home from work very drunk and would fall from his bicycle, sometimes down an escarpment, and ending up into the river, or he would be lying by the roadside, or in a gully. My mother would be notified by passersby. On these occasions my mother would get someone to go with her to rescue, and help him home. It was not unusual for him to abuse her after she had rescued, and took him home.

On one of my father's drunken nights, while my brother's and I were sleeping, he woke us and told us to come and sit with him on the bench around the dining table.

My mother was already warming his dinner and when it was ready, she placed it in front of him at the table. He then told everyone to sit down because he had something to say. He told my mother to sit her 'ass' down. Disrespectfully he told me that I should tell my mother about her ass and he would give me all the meat on his plate. I was very 'put off' by this and refused to carry out his request.

Not receiving the satisfaction he was seeking, he told my brother George to do the same thing, but like me he did not acquiesce. Finally, he then told my brother Roy that he was his boy and if he cursed his mother loud and clear he would give him all the meat on his plate. This time, to my amazement, my brother did exactly as he was asked. My father then extolled him by saying 'he was his boy and everything he wanted he would give to him.'

After my brother Roy compliance, my father then vented his fury on me, grabbing me by the hands and shouting at me, "You stink," and at the same time, ordering me to take my clothes off. Seeing his anger I became fearful and immediately took my clothes off. He then proceeded to place his hands all over my naked body in full view of my mother, my grandmother and my brothers. Everyone was in morbid fear of him and no one would intervene. He told my mother to give him a brand new towel and a new bar of soap as he was going to give this 'stinker' meaning to me a bath like she never had in her life.

It was very late, but my mother obeyed immediately. My father then continued his 'onslaught' by dragging me from the house and down to the river. After prolonged molestation, he dragged me along the bank to the deeper part of the river. I got frightened and started screaming that he was going to kill me. This made him angrier and he threw me into the deep part of the river. While struggling, I felt somebody holding me and pulling me from the water, soon I realized it was my grandmother; she said that she followed him and hid in the bushes. She came to rescue me at the nick of time.

My grandmother then told me she was taking me to Brother John. I had to go in my wet clothes as my grandmother was afraid to go back to the house. We arrived at Brother John's house very late that night so my grandmother explained what had happened, and he agreed to let me stay there temporarily. She told him that my mother would come in the morning to speak with him and then she left.

Brother John's wife took off my wet clothes and gave me some of her underwear and a dress to put on. There were no available beds in the house, so my sleeping quarters were made on the floor from a crocus bag.

The following morning, after my father left for work, my mother came and spoke to Brother John and his wife and they agreed that I should stay with them for a while.

I was unable to attend school because everyone was afraid of what my father would have done if he saw me. After staying there for a while, my mother came and told them that the situation at home had improved and it was alright for me to return.

I soon started attending school again. School was not exciting to me anymore. It was hard for me to focus on school work as I was always thinking of the problems that I had to endure at home. As a result, I was not achieving passing grades like I used to. Instead of being placed at the front of the class, my teacher moved me to the back of the class. My classmates would ridicule me by calling me unkind names. This was so depressing for me so I felt as if I belonged nowhere.

Because the school was located below a hill, which was surrounded with lots of trees and bushes, I spent most of my breaktime sitting in the bushes by myself.

I was always comfortable with the friends who were my neighbors as they knew everything that was happening with me at my home, so they always empathized with me.

One Saturday, both my mother and grandmother were out. I was sitting on the front verandah reading a book while my father was sitting on the back verandah reading the newspaper. My father suddenly appeared and called me and said I should follow him to the river to check and see if he had caught any fish in the fish pots that had been set.

At that time I believed and trusted him. Not knowing what his plans were I would never have gone with him. Furthermore, things had been going fairly well at home, so I did not expect my father to molest me again.

I followed him to the river and when we got there he told me he was going to take a bath and I should take one also. I started feeling very scared. It now became obvious that my father had not come to check on the fish pots.

I started getting nervous and thought of running away, but I knew if I did he would catch me. I asked him if he was going to hurt me and he said no.

We always kept our soap, washed rags and towels on a tree by the river, so I took my clothes off and had a bath.

When I was finished taking my bath I put my dress back on and ran quickly inside the house. I did not hear when my father's came into the house. Suddenly I saw his bedroom door open. My father immediately grabbed hold of my hand, pulled me into his room and then threw me on his bed. Before I could scream, he slapped my mouth and told me he would kill me.

I was frightened because I did not know what he was going to do. He immediately took out his private part and started to approach me. That made me very scared as I had never seen it before. I wanted so badly to get away before he hurt me.

A thought suddenly came to me which I was not sure would work. I grabbed hold of his private in my hands and pulled it very hard. He immediately let go of me because it seemed to hurt him a lot. I jumped up and ran out into the yard. Suddenly he grabbed hold of my hand, and began dragging me under the cellar. Before I could scream he slapped my mouth and told me he would kill my ass. Trying to get away, but he caught me running before I could, and pulled me into the kitchen. He used a rope to tie my hands and neck then he hung me up in the kitchen. I felt as if he was going to kill me. I was hanging there for some time, trying to scream as loudly as I could.

After what seemed like forever, I saw my grandmother coming into the kitchen. She appeared frightened but did not say anything to me, but covered her mouth with her hands. I saw when she immediately approached me with a kitchen knife which she used to cut the rope and took me down.

While my grandmother was talking to me in the kitchen, we heard when my father took his bicycle and left the yard, shouting from the top of the road, "I want to kill your ass."

At that time I was almost nine years old.

It was very late when my mother returned home. My grandmother told her what had transpired. My mother told me to pack my things because she did not want my father to return and find me at home. She directed me to walk along a pathway by the river that would take me to the main road to Fountain, which then led me to my grandfather's house at Windsor.

I was overcome with so much anguish, and cried all the way. When I got there, I told him what my father had done. My grandfather immediately went into a rage. I spent some time at his home and felt so much safer there.

One day; my grandfather decided that it was time to go back to my mother. I became naturally reluctant to go, but he assured me that he would give my father a stern warning and a beating if necessary and pursue the matter in court if it came to that.

My father was there when we arrived and as promised, my grandfather accosted him, and told him that if he put his hands on me again, he would kill him and 'face the judgment.'

My father's response was anything but calm. He took up a machete and brandished it at my grandfather and threatened to use it. In anger, my grandfather removed his hat and threw it to the ground while reiterating his oath to kill my father if he tried to use the machete.

My father's mood changed from one of anger to one of surprise. I guess he did not expect my grandfather to stand up to him like that. My father then walked away and sat alone on his back verandah. My grandfather stayed and talked with my mother and brothers for a while. He then left, as he had a far way to walk because he did not want to miss the bus to return home.

Things improved at home again for a while. My father was much calmer than he had been for a long time. My cousin Dean came to visit my mother and grandmother. They told him about my father's behaviour. My cousin got very angry. He confronted my father, who told him that whatever he heard was not his business. My father accused him of being a "Dam sojourn traveler," who was hardly ever around. This caused them to start fighting, and my father who used a knife and attacked my cousin Dean, and told him that if he ever came back to his home again, and interfered into his domestic affairs; he would stab him to death.

My cousin Dean explicitly told my father that if he tried to put his hands on me again to molest me he would be back there to kill his "Indian backside," and go to prison.

After cousin Dean left, apparently fearing the involvement of the law my father's behaviour was generally much improved.

My father, obviously cognizant of the sincerity of the threats of both my grandfather and my cousin, and did not take them lightly.

As a result, after their intervention, our relationship improved and there were no more incidences of molestation. I was nine now years old, life with my father was a little more 'normal.' At night he would go fishing at the river, taking my brother George and I to accompany him and assisted by holding the bottle torch for him to see. We were all proud to see the bountiful catch he was rewarded with at the end of the night.

It later became very stressful at home for me again. Time passed and my cousin came to live with us; I caught my father molesting her on the river bank. I reported it to my grandmother. Soon she went back home to my aunt. This time though, it had to do with my mother. For some reason, she had become very abusive towards me, cursing me and beating. She would dispense corporal punishment for the most trivial reasons. She often chooses to compound the punishment by not giving me anything to eat. It was my grandmother who had to come to rescue me again by secretly giving me food in an empty milk can. On my grandmother's instruction, I had to take my meals down to the river bank as not to be seen.

One morning, I forgot to wash the chamber pot before going to school. When I came home from school that evening, my mother told me that there was no dinner left in the kitchen for me, but I should look for my dinner in the dirty chamber pot I left on the stone heap before I went to school. When I went outside and looked, I was horrified to find that my mother had really put my dinner into the dirty chamber pot.

I stood there and cried uncontrollably. My grandmother heard me crying and asked me what was wrong. When I told my grandmother, she comforted me by telling me not to worry and that as soon as my mother was out of sight she would leave my dinner under a banana leaf, down by the river, and said I should leave the plate there because she would collect it later that evening. My grandmother consoled me further by saying that my mother would experience retribution for her deeds.

My mother's forms of punishment for 'disobedience,' seemed to get increasingly worse.

Apart from her regularly holding my meals, she would sometimes tie me into a crocus bag and leave me outside in the sun for the whole day or be tethered to the foot of an iron bed for as long as she thought necessary. On these occasions, it was always my grandmother who came to rescue me with food and water, and a welcome from the inhumane incarceration.

One day, one of my school friends came to visit me. We went to bathe at the mineral spring which was a very short distance from home. During that time my mother was visiting with Mrs. Bern who was one of her friends. When we came back home, we went to the river by the house, to bathe again. After bathing in the river, my friend and I went into the house to get dressed.

My mother came and asked me if I did not hear her calling me. I told her I did not because not only were we playing and making noise but also because of the sound of the river we did not hear. Obviously angry, she grabbed me, and pushed me into a crocus bag, and then started dragging me in the bag and through the yard. I screamed for help, but she continued.

Not being able to see, I had no idea where she was taking me to. Suddenly I heard the sound of the river and realized where I was. This made me even more scared and screamed loudly begging her to stop, and also crying loudly hoping that someone would hear and come to help me. Unfortunately, no one came. She continued to drag the bag until I finally realized that I was down to the bank of the river, and then pulled me into the water. My mother then shouted. "I wanted to kill you, because I am damn tired of you, all the problem in my life is because I have you." She then placed me in the river then I heard her walk away.

My mother left me to drown. I felt so terrified and helpless. My grandmother was not around to rescue me, so I had to save myself. I struggled, by pushing onto the top of the bag until the tie became loose. I pulled myself out of the bag and was relieved when I realized that I was very close to being washed into the deeper section of the river, where my chances of survival would be very slim. When I walked into the house, my mother did not only appear surprised, but displayed anger towards me. She was clearly disappointed to see me alive, and cursed me even more.

Later that night, she came into the room that I shared with my brothers. I was alone, getting ready for bed. She approached me in a fit of anger, grabbed my hair and banged my head against the wall. This left me in excruciating pain. I felt weak and started having trembling spells. Some days after, my mother had to take me to see a doctor. I was ten years old and already felt as if I was carrying the world on my little shoulders.

The doctor diagnosed the problem as a 'neurological condition.' The doctor who was a lady asked my mother if she knew of anything going on in my life that would trigger this condition. Surprisingly, my mother appeared oblivious as to what could be causing this problem.

I continued living with my parents. Unfortunately, my illness did not curb their abusive treatment towards me. As the days went by my condition worsened to the point where I was unable to get out of bed. Repeated trips to the doctor did not help. At nights I would experience apparitions and feel a sense of foreboding in my bedroom. This made it hard for me to sleep. My only recourse was to cry out to my parents for help. The times when my mother slept with me, there was abatement in the 'ghostly specters' which I usually experienced in my room. Nevertheless, my physical condition however, continued to deteriorate.

One day, Brother John came to visit. He was well known in the community as a spiritual healer. After 'examining' me, he told my mother that my condition was caused by an evil, 'Indian spirit' and that I needed to be exorcised. He performed a ritual exorcism himself. My feelings only improved for a while but the malady soon came upon me again.

On seeing this, my father decided to have a spiritual feast. With a view to perform a more extensive cleansing ritual. Family members were called from far and wide and a festive Indian séance was held. This lasted for quite a few days. During the proceedings, there were those who actually manifested the visual aspect of some kind of spiritual possession. It seemed as if this elaborate ritual of exorcism was worthwhile because after this my general health was quickly improved, and I got back my health.

Since I was feeling much better, I went to visit my friends. One day I went and sat with them by the roadside in front of their home. While there, a car with two white men drove up in front of us. As the car stopped, the men quickly jumped out and ran towards us. They did not seem friendly at all but tried to grab us. Now being afraid, we got up quickly and ran up the hill into the bushes, screaming while throwing stones at them.

Some of the children hid in the bushes and some frantically climbed trees to escape.

Days later, we told some of the neighbors what had happened to us. They told us we were lucky because they were 'Black Heart' men who catch children to kill them. After this, whenever I visited my friends we made sure not to sit by the roadside anymore.

Because of this experience, we were always afraid whenever we saw any car that was driven by white men only.

It was good to be feeling better and on my feet again. I was now able to go back to school.

On weekends, we would go fishing, and catching shrimp. Sometimes we would make a fire to roast shrimp and breadfruit, enjoying a delicious meal before going home. Most times though we would take our 'catch' home to our parents to prepare for a family meal.

The acts of molestation by my father had subsided for some time and I was feeling much better at home.

However, one day he met me on the way from school and asked me to go with him to the river. Immediately I became frightened and told him no. Another time, he met me on the way home and asked me to go with him to collect some coconuts from a friend. Wanting to get out of this dilemma, I told him that I had to hide my books in a safe place first. He did not want to hear this and insisted that I take the books with me which I refused. He probably thought that if he allowed me to leave his presence, I would run away and not come back. I reluctantly went with him and we eventually ended up at the river.

While I was there waiting for him, I saw him coming towards me, and then exposed himself to me. It was very frightening. I tried getting away from him before he grabbed hold of me, but he caught up with me and slapped me in my face, and then gave me a swift kick in my stomach, then trampled me like a rug. I got away and ran all the way home in total fear and told my mother what he had done. He did not come home until late that night. When he came home he was in a fit of rage, shouting my name loudly, and cursing badly at me.

That night, he came into my room, grabbed and then pulled me off the bed threw me onto the floor. After that, I was unable to walk and actually had to be confined to bed. My mother and grandmother became aware of what was happening on hearing my cries. My grandmother bathes me with hot water and salt. She then applied a warm poultice made from tuna and castor oil, to my stomach. This 'medication' was administered daily until my condition improved. I was then sent to live with my aunt at Mount Ridge.

CHAPTER THREE

Living with My Aunt

Aunt Gale lived in a small town by the name of Mount Ridge located about twenty miles from the major town. I was approximately eleven years old when my mother took me to live with her.

On one occasion when my mother was visiting my aunt, she took me to accompany her while she was visiting a short brown complexion man. While they were talking I overheard when the man said to my mother, "Don't you already give the child to another man, him is the father" I saw when my mother looked around at me. She immediately ran me away angrily, saying, "Go to the front of the yard, because she did not want me to hear of her conversation."

Living there with my aunt was very unpleasant for me, because the place was in a bucolic setting, which gets dark very early. There were not many vehicles around. The only means of transportation were bicycles, horses and donkeys. Once weekly the market truck came to take market vendors to Town.

There was no electricity, so everyone used kerosene lamps. Water was supplied by a community tank which was filled and secured. The tanks were opened twice daily, to allow residents to collect water.

At about 7 o'clock in the morning, the people in the community who relied on this water supply formed a line with their containers. Some people who lived far away came by donkey. This allowed them to transport larger amount and more containers by placing them in hampers which were saddled on the donkey. Those without donkeys had to carry a bucket on their head. I was one of those people.

I had to walk a long way to the tank, making several trips back home, with a bucket on my head. I did this every morning and evening. Sometimes I made more than a dozen trips because my aunt had three large drums that had to be filled to supply the home. One was kept in the kitchen that stored water for cooking and drinking and the others were placed under the gutters alongside the house to catch water when rain fell. That water was used for washing and bathing.

My aunt was a stout, black woman with long thick black hair. Her husband's name was Ken. She had eight children, most of them were grown and living away from home, leaving only the youngest Lela, at home. My aunt was very poor and lived in a two room house. The roof was made of coconut logs and zinc sheets and the sides were made from dilapidated pieces of board. The room, in which she lived, was the only one that had proper flooring. The ground formed the flooring in the other room. The only 'decent' bed was the one my aunt and her husband slept on. The other beds were constructed from bamboo.

My cousin Lela and her children slept on one of the bamboo beds, but I had to make my bed on the ground. This was very uncomfortable for me to endure, but as a child, there was nothing I could do about it.

The kitchen was a frail structure, constructed from coconut limbs. Because of the poor construction the roof leaked whenever it rained.

There was no stove, just a stone fire pit, and wood was used for fuel. My aunt had no dining table or chairs; we had to sit on large stones and wood blocks that my aunt's husband cut and made from tree trunks.

When their friends came over to visit, they were accommodated by sitting on the blocks.

My aunt had no toilet, the field at the back served as an open lavatory. Whenever there was toilet paper at home, my aunt kept it for herself, leaving the rest of the family to use green leaves or whatever could be found to serve the purpose. There was always a lingering unpleasant smell of feces around the house, which worsened whenever the wind blew. This meant that we always encountered problems with flies. This was not unique to my aunt's home though, but the condition was a general problem with most of the neighbors. Although living conditions at Mount Ridge were so unpleasant, I still had a morbid fear of returning to my parent's home at Fountain.

Many of the residents of Mount Ridge made a living by rearing livestock, cash crop farming or selling stones to the local quarry.

On Saturday mornings, most people went to the market to sell produce and livestock. Some people sold their livestock to the local butcher who in turn supplied meat to the community. My aunt's sole source of earning was from the stones she supplied for building roads. This was really hard work for us to do.

We had to search for stones in the field and bushes; the larger ones we had to roll down a hill, and to the roadside, using a hammer to break them into small pieces, which we had to pile into large or small heaps waiting to be picked by a local vehicle. Those stones were used to build roads.

It took approximately three full weeks to break enough stones to be considered a load to be picked up.

Although it was such hard work to do, I always tried to help my aunt. But I ended up hurting my fingers whenever I hit the stones to break them with the hammer; as a result I stuck to searching for them.

After a long day, it was always good when my aunt cooked; she made sure there was always a lot to eat. I ensured that my leftovers were securely covered because of the presence of flies.

My aunt always took her chamber pot in late at night.

Unfortunately I was the one she would send outside to retrieve it. To my disgust, one night in particular, I remember having a strange feeling when I was about to go outside. I told my aunt I was afraid to go alone. She could not understand why I was afraid to go on that night and I was not afraid to go on other nights. I told her I did not know what it was but I was having a very strange feeling. Upset, she told me to, "Shut up my damn mouth and stop talking foolishness." She insisted again that I go and collect the chamber pot.

Not wanting to seem rude, I opened the door and went outside. My head suddenly felt as if it was swelling, almost ready to burst.

I tried talking but could not. I did not know what to do because I would surely get a flogging if I did not get the chamber pot.

I looked towards the kitchen and saw the chamber pot on the stone heap where it was placed every morning. To my surprise, I saw a woman sitting on the block beside the kitchen. I was very frightened because I did not know who she was or what she was doing there. I turned and ran back into the house. My aunt asked me why I did not bring the chamber pot. I was unable to talk. A few minutes after, I found myself shouting, "Lord God, Lord God." My aunt reprimanded me telling me to stop the noise before I called the crowd on her saying she is murdering me.

I tried to explain what happened when I went outside and why I was so scared. She did not believe me when I told her that I had seen a woman sitting on the block beside the kitchen. She kept on insisting I was lying and sent me to my bed.

Everyone went to bed. But I was afraid to go to sleep. While I was lying there, I heard my aunt saying to her husband that, "She can see ghosts, because from Miss Sissy died she never leave us." I pretended as if I didn't hear what they were talking about.

From that night, my aunt never sent me for the chamber pot again. In fact, she made sure that it was taken inside very early in the evening.

I was still afraid that the 'ghost' would hurt me, so life became very uncomfortable for me there; I decided to run away to my grandfather.

I secretly wrapped all my things in a bundle and hid them under the fence close to the road where there could not be seen. One morning, I got up very early, pretended to be going to use the lavatory in the back yard and put my clothes on. I took up my bundle and ran as fast as I could away from my aunt's yard.

I had to get away before anyone saw me. Down the road, I saw a lady by the name of Flying Saucer. She was mentally ill and lived about half mile from my aunt's house. I saw her sitting by the roadside. She seemed to be in my direct 'path to freedom.' I was perplexed with ideas as to how I could avoid her without being seen. She was known to throw urine and other obnoxious things at people. My fears were however unrealized, as our encounter was quite uneventful.

The distance to Windsor was about six miles, but most of the journey was downhill. This made the distance seem shorter so I ran most of the way because I was anxious to get there.

When I got to my grandfather's house, he was just coming from the field. It was on a 'banana day,' so he had cut his bananas and sent them to the wharf to be sold. When he saw me, he immediately asked what was wrong. I told him what had happened at my aunt's house and that I was afraid the 'ghost' would hurt me. I told him I wanted to stay with him, and he said it would be okay. He complained that every time my mother kept sending me away to different places allowing bad things to always happen to me. He said it would be better if she allowed me to stay with him to assist him, and also attend school as well.

I stayed with my grandfather for a long time. Soon my mother came and took me to Ferry to live with Mia.

Mia was my mother's cousin. She took me to visit her when I was almost eleven years old. Our visits to Mia soon became quite regular. Mia had a lot of children. This gave me many childhood companions. They had a big yard in which we played, and many different fruit trees, so we were always able to find something to eat.

Our games sometimes lasted late at night; or until it was the time for us children to wash up and retire for the night.

The house was very small and sleeping space was very limited, so we all had to fit into very cramped quarters. Nevertheless, because of the amicable family relationship no one complained.

In the mornings, one of our chores was to go to the standpipe to collect water for our domestic needs. While we were gone, Mia would prepare breakfast which was usually ready by the time we were finished filling the drums and other containers.

All of us would then sit in the yard on stones or wood blocks and enjoy our meal. Mia's husband was very strict and we had to be on our best behavior when he was around.

Despite the obvious social hardships which I had to undergo while staying with Mia and the other families, I enjoyed the time I spent there. I was very sad when the time ended for me to return back to my mother. The fond memories of my time spent with Mia and her families. These memories became repressed even after my mother took me to live with her in Bushy Pen.

CHAPTER FOUR

Living at Bushy Pen

Bushy Pen is a small district on a hill above Cambridge and located between Dowey and Brookville. Aunt Gale and her husband used to live there.

I was eleven years old when my mother took my two brothers, my sister Lorie and I with her to visit. After an extended stay, my mother decided to live there. This was where my brother Joe was born.

She rented a house behind my aunt's house which was located in a gully, and surrounded by a banana field. This became our new home. It was a shaky old house with two bedrooms. It had two windows and two doors and was built on a number of wooden posts. The structure was so unsound that when we walked the floor squeaked, and the house literally shook when the wind blew hard.

Sleeping conditions were very bad. My mother only had an old iron bed which was infested with bugs. Whenever anyone lay on it, it would squeak and the bedsprings would sometimes break loose.

My brothers and I slept on the floor. Because we had no sheets we had to use crocus bags and old clothes for bedding. We had no chairs or table; we had to sit on the floor. In the yard, we sat on stones or wooden blocks.

Because the house was surrounded by many banana trees, when evening came, it appeared dark even before night came. This made me afraid to go outside. There was no kitchen, so we had to cook outside using wood fire. Fortunately, for us the house was built on stilts, so whenever it rained, we made fire under the house to cook.

The toilet was located in the banana field behind the house. It was constructed from bamboo, board, and rusty zinc sheets. The roofing was inadequate so it leaked whenever it rained. Our privacy from passersby was enhanced by the surrounding banana trees. When the wind blew there was a strong smell of feces, because there was no proper sanitary convenience.

We had no running or well water at home, and the rain did not fall very often, so I had to walk a long way to the standpipe to get water.

My mother like everyone else had to put a drum under the gutter beside the house to catch water whenever the rain fell. Whenever I went to the pipe in the morning, there was always a big crowd and a long line of people waiting. The water sometimes came from the pipe very slowly, so it took a long time to fill the buckets. During these times there were always disputes concerning one's position in the line. To avoid these disputes, I usually arrived very early at the pipe in the mornings, and was able to get my containers filled very quickly as I was not unimpeded by others.

Aunt Gale was employed as a domestic worker, by a long red-haired mulatto woman by the name of Mrs. Len. Her husband was of Chinese descent. They both had seven children. The oldest ones were grown and live with other families away from home. The four youngest lived with their parents. My mother was also employed by Mrs. Len in the capacity as a domestic worker.

To my understanding, my mother also supplemented her income by accepting money and gifts from a man who had a church in the community with whom she had a clandestine affair. Each week, the pastor made sure she was the recipient of his church benevolence. During this time, I would visit Mrs. Len's home to play with the children. She took a liking to me and allowed me to spend several nights there. After some infrequent visits to the Lens house, their home ultimately became my permanent place of abode.

CHAPTER FIVE

Life with the Lens

I was not afforded the opportunity to see my mother, my brothers and sister, nor my aunt on a regular basis, because I was now domiciled at the Len's home, and became a part of their family.

After living at home with the Len's, Mrs. Len's had a daughter who lived in America. On one occasion, she came to visit her family. While I was there she showed a strong liking for me, and was very kind to me. One day while sitting out in the backyard I heard when she asked her mother if it would be ok for her to take me back with her to America to live with her mother-in-law who lives alone. Mrs. Len said she would speak to my mother about it.

Few days went by. One day I saw my mother when she came to visit with Mrs. Len and her daughter. They were all seated in the dining room, where the discussion took place.

I was sitting on the verandah which was located beside a window and the dining room, so I was able to hear the conversation that took place between the ladies.

I heard both Mrs. Len and her daughter asked my mother to let me get the opportunity to go to America, because I was a nice looking girl. My mother told them emphatically that she would never send me to live in America. She told Mrs. Len boldly that if she was not able to go, then I could not go either.

From that day I never saw my mother, my brothers or my sister again. I lost communication with her, and also my aunt. My search for them was unsuccessful in finding their whereabouts. I later learned that we as children were scattered, and live with different people at different homes.

Mrs. Len and her husband were both owners of a bar and grocery store, which was the main retail distributor of groceries in the community. On Saturday mornings, I was sent to purchase goods for the store. The distance was a long way for me. I had to walk down the precariously steep slope of Cambridge Hill. Coming uphill in the evening, with the load on my head, was an even more arduous encounter. Fridays and Saturdays were the busiest days in the town. Almost everyone came out to shop, and drink at the bar, or to meet with friends.

The Len's home was located at the back of the grocery store. There was also a big tent that was used for recreation. On Friday and Saturday nights, a dance was held. People gathered and played dominoes and were entertained by music from the sound system. Food was cooked and provided, which include, curried goat, rice, green bananas and goat head soup. Patrons had to pay an entrance fee at the gate. The food and drinks were on sale.

The music was very loud and could be heard from many miles away. I was not allowed to take part in the activities since I was only about twelve years old. Although I had to go to bed, it was hard to sleep because the music was very loud.

At first, I was happy living with the Lens, but as time went by I realized that I was required to perform the duties of a maid servant. Mrs. Len was much nicer to me than her husband, although she was not as nice as she used to be when I first started living with them. Sometimes she asked me to comb her hair, pick out her grey hairs and oil her scalp. I did not really enjoy doing this, as her hair had a bad smell, but I had no choice. In return though, she would give me extra food to eat and make clothes for me. Nevertheless, Mrs. Len always gave me an inordinate amount of work to do.

Mr. Len behaved miserably towards me. Nothing I did satisfied him. He fussed with me and would call me "Dirty negro," and sometimes threw clean or dirty water on me, pretending not to see me.

Whenever he cooked, he gave everyone food except me. Because of that I was totally afraid of him. Whenever Mrs. Len was away from home, I would hide in the banana field until her return, because as long as he saw me around, he would curse me, in the process, he would spit on me, and also threw water wetting me up. Because of this, I did my best to stay out of his way.

During that time I attended an elementary school; the distance was a long walk to and from school daily. The journey seemed easier because I would meet with friends and play along the way.

It was even more fun when it was mango and apple season. We always raced, to see who could get to the tree first. I really enjoyed the time I spent at that elementary school, especially because I loved my friends and we had so much fun together.

My chores were plentiful before I went to school in the mornings.

The Lens had six big dogs, and a big yard. The dogs usually defecate all over it. Unfortunately, it became my laborious task to clean it up, which took more than one hour for me to do every morning.

After cleaning up, I would have to deodorize the yard with Jeyes to make sure the smell was all gone. Mr. Len refused to let me use the water hose, but insisted that I draw buckets of water to wash the pavement. This made the job so much harder. When I was finished I had to take a good bath. Most times, there was no soap so I had to use limes or sour oranges to bathe.

My breakfast consisted of a cup of cerassee tea and a slice of hard dough bread, after which I had to get ready for school.

On my way home in the evening, I became very worried about the chores that would be awaiting me when I got home.

Mr. Len cooked on a wood fire which made the pots very 'black.' I would have to clean the kitchen thoroughly and scour the pots to a glossy finish. If not, Mrs. Len would have me repeat this chore. I became very tired and sad, that I used my blackened hands to wipe my tears; this gave my face a blackened camouflaged appearance. I was not allowed to have any meals until all my chores, including feeding the dogs were finished, and the Lens were satisfied that they were done.

Sometimes when I became hungry I would help myself to some of the dogs' food, especially since they were better fed than I was. After thoroughly inspecting the pots, Mrs. Len would call me and give me my dinner, which was sometimes kept in the store. The food consisted mainly of white rice and pork. The pork was so fatty that it sometimes made me feel sick in my stomach. I had to make sure not to show dissatisfaction since I knew I would get nothing else to eat unless I stole it.

After eating and took a bath, I went to the grocery store to help sell kerosene oil, cut up codfish and clean up the store. This made me tired and hungry. My fingers were always blistered and swollen.

For supper, everyone else was allowed to have crackers and cheese, or bread and sardine and soda. But for me I had to steal bread and cheese, and hide it in my underwear and then go outside to eat it, or steal ripe bananas from the banana field. If I requested food it would not be given to me. In reality, I had to steal food just not to go hungry.

I was always fearful of the arrival of Saturday mornings. This was because I had to launder the clothes for the entire family. I did the washing and starching on Saturdays and ironing and Sundays. Some of the clothes were of coarse cotton fabric and were sometimes soiled even with feces. This made my job not only arduous but unpleasant as well.

Most times, my clothes were usually left unlaundered. I always tried to start washing before daylight to avoid sitting in the sun all day.

I had to hurry with the washing because Mrs. Len needed to prepare the place for the evening's activities.

I was given one bar of canon soap to wash the white clothes and a bar of brown soap for the darker clothes. I washed until my hands became tired and numb, and also became very weak and hungry.

Usually, Mr. Len would be cooking while I was washing, and as a result, I took the opportunity to steal from the pot whenever he left the kitchen. I would secure the stolen food in my dress and move as briskly as I could to avoid detection.

One day Mr. Len caught me stealing from the pot. He angrily hit me on my head with the hot pot cover, cursed me and then spat in my face. When I reported it to Mrs. Len he denied it and fabricated a story saying I injured myself accidentally, or it was the froth from the pot that he threw out the window that caught me. Although I cried,

Mrs. Len did not show any compassion. I had to go along with the situation because I had no one to help me, or no place to go.

I was not allowed the opportunity to sit at the table with the family; I had to sit on a stool in the kitchen. On Sundays, Mrs. Len made ice-cream which she sold to the community. All I ever got was the empty container which Mrs. Len gave me to wash. I took the container to the back of the house and scraped out what was left. I could not understand why the Lens was so mean to me. I really had no problems with the children, because we always played together when I was lucky enough not having any work to do, which was not very often.

I became tired of the bad treatment I received from the Lens, so I decided to find an escape route and run away to my grandparents in Windsor. My options to escape this inhumane treatment were few.

As I did not know the way to my grandparent's home, I decided to ask someone for directions from Bushy Pen to Windsor.

CHAPTER SIX

Escape from Bushy Pen

This flight from Bushy Pen which I had decided to embark on was filled with a sense of trepidation, and I was also ignorant about the direction to take to.

It took a few weeks for me to get the directions, because I had to be careful in asking, I had to do it without the Lens getting suspicious. When I got the directions and was sure they were right, I started planning my escape.

Each night, while I was selling kerosene oil in the shop, and planning to run away; I stole a loaf of bread, cans of sardine, candies, and large pieces of cheese. I hid them under my clothes, and took them outside to my usual hiding place.

I was told that it was a long journey so I had to ensure as much food that was possible to take with me to eat.

After I was finished cleaning the store, without being noticed, I wrapped the food and my clothes in a bundle and hid them under my bed. At about four o' clock the following morning I got up and tried to open the door as quietly as I could. I did not want Mrs. Len to hear me, but she heard me anyway, because the door always squeaked whenever it opened.

The moment Mrs. Len heard the door open, she got up and came to my room and asked me what was wrong. I lied and told her that I was having a stomach ache and was going to the toilet. Mrs. Len said, "Oh."

My things were already outside so she did not observe anything unusual. She then went back to bed.

Soon as she went back to her room, I went outside immediately, collected my bundle and ran towards the direction of the toilet. Fortunately, there was no light in the yard that night so even if anyone had looked outside they would not be able to see what I was doing.

The toilet was located in the banana field.

To get to the main road, I had to go through the banana field which was located at the back of the house.

I ran as fast as I could in the dark to get to the main road before Mrs. Len became aware of my absence. I kept running, and as soon as I reached the big wire fence which overlooked the main road, I quickly slid under it and started running down the road which led to the district of Dowey.

It was very early and dark in the morning, and there were no vehicles driving on the road during that time. Although I had been given the directions to Windsor, I was not exactly sure how to get there. I was told that when I went through Dowey, the next district would be Catshill; there I would make a left turn, using a landmark, a prominent shop which had an upstairs display.

After walking for some time, I finally made it to Catshill. The moment I saw the shop I did not hesitate, and quickly made the left turn and continued on my journey. It was now approaching daylight, but I did not care, because I was not known to anyone in the area.

As I continued walking, I saw a man riding a bicycle. I stopped to ask him if he could give me directions to Pen, because I knew if I got to Pen; I would be able to find my way to Windsor. He immediately asked me if I was running away. I lied and told him "No," I heard that my mother had died so I was going to see her. Appearing sympathetic, he told me to go down to the corner, keep right and go up the hill to a little shop then make another right turn. I told him thanks, and ran along to see how quickly I could get there. Quickly I got to the shop and made a right.

It was a long walk from there. I was so tired and hungry. Some of the bread, sardine, and cheese were almost finished.

I kept on walking, looking to see if I could find a standpipe or a spring to get some water, but there were none to be found.

The road was very lonely; there were no houses in sight. 'Such a long journey.' I kept wondering if I was going to die, because I very thirsty and weak and thought I was going to faint. Finally I came to a big shade tree, I was so happy. I stopped and rested for a while. When I felt that I had rested enough I got up and started on my journey again.

I was still hungry and thirsty. I would have done anything just to get a little water to drink.

While traveling along I saw several coco trees. I knew that dewdrops always settled on coco leaves in the morning. I looked and what I saw was just enough to wet my tongue. I felt so glad; I started licking the water off the coco leaves until my mouth started itching terribly. At this point I got scared because I had never done this before and had no idea if it could poison me.

My mouth itches so badly, I kept it wide open, and continued walking in fear.

As I got further along the road. Just as I turned the corner I saw a big cow pasture with lots of cows. I immediately entered the pasture looking to see if there was any container with water left for the cows by their owners, but there was none to be found. I saw a large pond that I thought the cows might have drunk from. The water was murky; I was afraid that if I drank from the pond I would die. But I was so thirsty. I just wanted a drop to quench my thirst. I could not pray, and did not know how to talk to God, but immediately I turned my eyes towards the heavens and said, "God don't let me die."

Surprisingly, one of the cows immediately came to the pond and started drinking water. As soon as I saw the cow drinking, immediately I dipped both hands into the water and drank. The water did not taste palatable. I felt even worse; and weaker after drinking. It was very difficult for me to walk out from the pasture. When I got to the road, I sat on the bank for a while hoping that if someone came along they would help me. Soon after I felt better I got up and started walking again.

Further along the road I met a man riding on a donkey. I started smiling to make myself look good. He stopped and said "Pickney where you coming from, you a runaway." I lied again and told him my mother had died and I was going to Pen. He asked how far I had come from; again I lied and told him Catshill.

I did not want to tell him exactly where I had come from in case someone met him and asked about me. He seemed to feel sorry for me and immediately asked if I was hungry. I told him yes; because my cousin had only given me a cup of tea and sent me earlier, as she wanted me to get there before the sun got very hot.

Of course this was another lie I told him. He went into his hamper and handed me a cake. I was so happy to get it that my body started itching me. I thanked him and asked if he had any water. He gave a full cup of water then rode off telling me, "God go with you." I was so happy and thankful for the bulla cake that I tried to eat without letting a crumb fell to the ground.

Further along the road, I saw a water pipe. I was so glad and also getting more thankful. I drank so much water; I thought I was going to suck the pipe dry, because I was extremely thirsty. I then continued on my journey, feeling much happier.

The distance to Pen was still a long way, but I felt more at ease and full of confidence and cheerful that I was going the right way, and also knowing that I was getting closer to Windsor. I wanted to reach Windsor before night came.

Finally I reached Pen, which was close to Mount Ridge where my aunt Gale lived. I had to pass by her house, because it was located close to the road.

I tried to be very careful that no one who knew me told my aunt, who probably would let the children catch me.

This would give her the opportunity to take me back to Mrs. Len.

When I got to my Aunt Gale house, I did not try to stop. I proceeded with caution, and ran as fast as I could, and made sure no one recognized me. I kept running until I was distant away, then I stopped, rested and started walking again.

It was a long and lonely road, but I knew where I was, so I was no longer afraid.

I was getting closer to a big River. I knew there used to be lots of rose apple trees hanging over the river bearing plenty of apples. I was hoping that when I got down to the river I would be lucky to get some.

Fortunately for me, when I got there, so many apples were laying on the ground, under the trees. I was so glad. It seemed like a Fairy Godmother had them waiting for me. I picked up so many apples and held them in my dress; then washed them into the river, sat on a stone and ate until my stomach was full.

I felt so good after eating the rose apples, and was feeling much better because I was getting closer to my grandparents.

I started running along and singing because I wanted to get there before nightfall.

The road was steep. It meandered up and down the hilly countryside. Each time I came to the top of a hill, I would run down very fast, so that I could get to where I was going more quickly. My feet were so tired, but that did not matter to me anymore because I knew it would not be much longer before I would finish my journey.

I kept walking until I came to the road which led to Windsor. I was so ashamed because it had become my practice to keep coming back with my bundle on head, or in my hands. The people there would stand and stare at me, sometimes they laughed at me, but I ignored them and kept walking.

Finally I got to my grandparent's home. I opened the gate and went inside. My grandfather saw me coming, because as usual, he would sit on the verandah so he could observe whatever taking place. Surprised, he immediately asked,

"What happen to you again pickney." As I had gotten used to running away and coming back to him over the years, I relayed to him the bad treatment I received from the Lens. Stating that; Mrs. Len worked me very hard, and whenever I was hungry I had to steal food, or sometimes I ate the dog's food, also because of Mr. Len's dislike for me, I was oftentimes abused by him. I expressed to my grandfather that whenever I report these incidents to his wife she totally ignores my cries.

My grandfather showed such sadness on his face; then he asked me if I was hungry, and I told him yes, and at what time I left Bushy Pen. I told him four o'clock in the morning, I saw tears immediately running down his face. He gave me money and told me to buy a can of herring, a loaf of bread and two bottles of soda. When I returned, I asked him for my grandmother and he told me she was in the backyard. I went and found her digging for yams. I called out to her; she looked around. When she saw me, she immediately stopped what she was doing and came over and asked what had happened. I told her. Her reply to me was 'not to worry because I was growing up, and one day I would have a better life'.

My grandmother told me that if she died before I did, she was sure the "Ants would come to her grave and give her the news about me."

She washed her hands and came around to the verandah, and fixed the food; we all sat down to a meal. I felt so much better being with my grandparents. My wishes were if I could stay with them all the time. But as a child I was not allowed to make decisions.

My mother soon found out where I was and came and took me back to the Len's. I hated this so much. Because I was taken back to the same abusive treatment I had run away from, but I had no choice. As the moments went by I became very weary and unhappy living with the Len's. Because of that I always sat and cried, and cursed profane language very loudly to myself.

As I continued living with the Lens, Mr. Lens and I started arguing and fighting. That made me very unhappy, that I would go to the bar and steal white rum, drink a large amount, lay in the banana field wishing that after drinking I would die, but it only made me intoxicated.

One day after drinking some white rum and got intoxicated, I went to the banana field as usual and fell asleep. I was awakened by Mr. Len who held me down and sexually abused me. Mrs. Len was not home at the time. When she returned, I told her what her husband had done. Mr. Len immediately fabricated a rebuttal. I got to the point where I felt so ashamed. By this I was no longer attending school, and there was also some abatement of the hard work I had to do.

It was only stealing from Len's pot while it was simmering on the fire that I was able to secure food and meat to eat.

Mrs. Len had a friend who lived in Town by the name of Miss Brown. She told me that Miss Brown was a nice lady, and she was going to take me to stay with her for a while. I asked Mrs. Len if I would have to work hard being there with Miss Brown, and she said no I would not.

I felt so frustrated about going from place to place, and also more disgusted because my mother kept sending me away like a cat to different homes. I felt as if I was an unwanted child.

Quite a few weeks passed. One Monday morning, Mrs. Len told me to get ready because we would have to catch the eleven o' clock market truck that would be going to Town, to see Miss Brown. It was in 1959 I was almost twelve years old. She took me to Town to visit Miss Brown, and I never saw her again.

CHAPTER SEVEN

Visit to Miss Brown

The 'visit' to Miss Brown, lasted the entire day.

During the visit, I overheard Miss Brown and Mrs. Len discussing the possibility of me staying. Mrs. Lens recounted the incident when I had been raped by her husband, and was fearful of possible involvement with the law. Miss Brown suddenly came and looked in my direction, she immediately indicated to Mrs. Len by putting her finger across her lips that they should be more discreet in their conversation, and should not speak as loudly, not wanting me to hear. I pretended that I had not heard or seen anything.

Mrs. Len was now ready to leave. She called and told me that after talking with Miss Brown, they both decided that it would be in my best interest to spend a few weeks with Miss Brown, so she could get to know more about me, and then possibly I could stay with her permanently.

I felt a sense of uncertain apprehension about the prospect of staying with Miss Brown who was a complete stranger, as my life with Mrs. Len previously had been so difficult. I was a child, and my mother did not seem to care about my welfare.

Mrs. Len's bus would be coming by four o'clock, so it was time for her to leave. I felt so sad, I started crying. I walked with her to the bus-stop and waited until her bus came. Before she left, she told me that I should behave myself because Miss Brown was a very nice lady who would take care of me. This made me cry even more because; I had heard things like this being said before that someone would be nice, which had turned out to be such unhappiness and disappointment. I became so tired of living here and there with different strangers.

Miss Brown was a stout, brown-skinned lady with a broad nose. She was well known because she had one of the best homes and was considered to be one of the wealthiest persons in the community. Her husband was a sailor who travelled to different countries. Because of that he was always away from home, but would return every three months.

Miss Brown did not go to the grocery store like everyone else did, because her husband always brought her everything that she needed.

It was getting late that evening and I wanted to take a bath but did not have any clothes to change into, only the ones which I had worn there. I went to Miss Brown and told her that I would like to take a bath, but I did not have anything to put on. She said that Mrs. Len had not brought any clothes for me because she was not certain if I was going to stay. Miss Brown said she had seen me briefly on a few occasions but did not have the opportunity to interact with me over an extended period of time. Anyway, Miss Brown told me she would get me something to wear.

I heard her talking to someone, asking the person to give her two pants and a shirt, because there is a little girl here who has no clothes to wear.

In a few minutes Miss Brown came back and gave me two boy's pants, two shirts and two pairs of her large torn crotch less panties. She said I should wear them until Mrs. Len sent my clothes or when she was able to get some for me. I did not feel happy at all about this situation, but because I did not know anything about Town I could not run away.

Miss Brown had a large house which contained several bedrooms. There was also a house in the back of the yard that she rented to other people. It was now very late and time to go to bed. I was not allowed to sleep in any of the bedrooms; instead, she gave me a sheet and a crocus bag and told me to make a bed on the floor in the passageway. This was very uncomfortable for me. I cried all night. When I woke up the next morning, Miss Brown told me that my clothes would be coming on the bus and I should go to the bus-stop to receive them. This I did, but the clothes did not arrive, and even subsequent visits to the bus-stop proved fruitless. As my clothes did not arrive I was forced to continue wearing boys' clothing.

I became very conspicuous because no other young girls in the community were attired in that way.

This made me feel very embarrassed, as I was the object of ridicule.

One day, when Miss Brown was not home, a lady came to visit her. The lady called me from where I was sitting under a coconut tree. Afraid that anyone would see me, because my clothes were so dilapidated. I was very reluctant to go to the gate to give the lady access; fearing that if she saw me she would become skeptic and laughed at me. The lady was obviously moved by my unsightly appearance and said, "Every time Miss Brown gets good children she treats them so badly."

She told me that she would give me some good clothing but had to get Miss Brown's approval so as not to upset their friendship. My response to this news was tears of joy, but when the lady departed I went back to my melancholy mood.

One day Miss Brown told me she was getting some clothes for me. Being privy to its source, I did not say anything. When the clothes finally came, I had to perform the role of a mannequin, fitting on all the clothes, but only one dress was given to me to wear along with the boy's clothes I was already wearing. The rest were packed away by Miss Brown. She admonished me that good behavior would give me access to the rest of the clothes.

As time passed. On one occasion Miss Brown started to express some act of kindness to me. She would take me with her to visit her friend who gave me the clothes. She also registered me at Leeward Road Elementary School. I began feeling happy, but wondered if all the things I had heard about her were true. When I remembered how good Mrs. Len had been to me at first, I did not get my hopes up too much.

Miss Brown had a tenant who rented a room at the back of the house. Her name was Miss Whitney. One day I was sitting on the back verandah eating. I heard the telephone ring. Miss Brown went and answered. Miss Whitney immediately took the opportunity and came and whispered to me. She told me that Miss Brown was only pretending to be nice, but in time she was going to start working me like a slave.

Miss Whitney told me that I should be discreet about this information. She also indicated that I could depend on her for food, as Miss Brown would severely ration my meals.

After being with Miss Brown for a few months, it was fast approaching the time for me to begin attending school. Surprisingly, Miss Brown was still very nice to me, and I started to wonder if she could really be of an unsavory character.

My only discomfort was that I had to sleep on the floor, but I made myself happy as much as I possibly could.

CHAPTER EIGHT

No Bed Of Roses

The Monday morning finally came for me to start school. I was very excited. I got up early, and folded my 'bed.' Miss Brown had bought material and made me a uniform. I took my bath and got dressed for school with great anticipation. Miss Brown immediately came to me with instruction to water the garden. I reminded her that this chore was done the night before as I was told. She was not satisfied, and insisted that the garden had to be watered both mornings and evenings.

It was already eight o'clock and I reminded Miss Brown that this was the commencement of school, she appeared very nonchalant about this, and told me that there was bread and tea in the kitchen on the stove for me, and she would give me bus fare to go to school. After doing all my chores, my uniform was now soiled. I pointed this to Miss Brown, but her response was, "I should be damn lucky to have a uniform, because when I first came to her I did not even have a good panty." This caused me to attend my first day in school in a very melancholy mood.

Unfortunately, when I got to school, the Principal noticed my unkempt condition. He was very concerned as to why I had come to school looking like that. I recounted to him all that had happened at home that morning. I told him that the lady who I lived with was not my mother; I was given to her from another lady. He did not appear pleased with the situation, but nevertheless, he sent me to my class. My first day at school was not a pleasant experience.

The disparaging looks and comments from other kids made the day almost unbearable. When school was dismissed I was relieved to get out quickly, so I would escape the critical glances. When I got home, I told Miss Brown that if I had to do so many chores before going to school, I would have to get up earlier. She agreed.

Getting up earlier in the morning did not make the work any easier for me. Miss Brown had a lot of birds in the backyard that I had to take care of. Looking after the ducks was very hard because I had to let them all out, then catch them and put them back into the pen. Every time I tried to catch one, the others would fly over the fence into the neighbor's yard. There were more than a dozen. After securing the ducks in the pen, I had to feed the chickens and turkeys, sweep the yard, and then water the garden. In addition to all this, I had to dust and polish the furniture, then get down on my knees to polish and shine the floor. The yard now had to be attended to, and it had to be thoroughly swept. After doing all these duties I was very tired and would point this out to Miss Brown, but her unsympathetic response was, "You were a damn little woman at Mrs. Len's house, but here you will have to work like hell." That made me feel so sad and miserable.

The work was even harder when I was not going to school. When my duties ended it would be late in the evenings, and I was famished and feeling very weak. I would have to take a bath before getting anything to eat. On sitting at the table for dinner, I was very dissatisfied with the minute amount of food that was placed before me. My plate consisted of one finger of banana, one dumpling, and a thumb-sized piece of chicken. At the end of this repast I was in tears. Miss Brown saw me crying and asked me what the matter was. I boldly told her that I was still hungry. She showed no compassion towards me, or willingness to give me any more food, but instead, she shouted at me saying, "If I was not satisfied with what I was getting to eat, I should go and steal." That made me cry even more, but remembering Miss Whitney's words, made me gain composure. These grievous conditions continued.

One day Miss Whitney called me and said that as promised, she would have dinner prepared for me in the evenings, and when it was ready she would come and indicated to me by pointing her finger. Miss Whitney kept her assistance to me a secret by inviting Miss Brown for a walk in the evenings. By her doing so, I was alone at home to enjoy the meal Miss Whitney had prepared for me. At the onset of the ladies evening stroll, Miss Brown reminded me of my chores, and demanded that all had to be completed before she returned.

The first evening the ladies left, I watched until they were at a safe distance away, and then I went to Miss Whitney's room. I was pleasantly surprised to find a copious amount of food neatly covered and waiting for me. After eating hurriedly, I washed the utensils, and replaced them, got water to drink, and then went immediately to my evening duties.

Remembering what Miss Brown had told me about my duties on her return, I started to work assiduously, and with renewed strength, as my stomach was now full and I was feeling happier.

When the ladies returned I would signal to Miss Whitney by singing to let her know that everything was ok.

Oftentimes, because my countenance and disposition had changed, and not wanting Miss Brown to recognize the difference, I would hide myself away in the toilet to be out of her sight.

One evening, Miss Brown called me and said she would like to speak to me. I suddenly became fearful, as I did not know if she had discovered the assistance I was getting. I stayed in the toilet for a while, trying to regain my composure before going to her. She told me to sit at the table because she was going to fix us something for us to eat. I sat and waited. Shortly after, she brought two plates with food, one she placed in front of me and the other she placed before herself at the table. She brought two forks. Surprisingly, there was a copious amount of food on my plate. We began eating. This display of domestic concern on her part was not what I was used to.

During our meal she told me that I had caused her embarrassment in the eyes of the tenant, because the tenant had heard me crying for food, after which she said, in the future I would get enough food to eat. She also told me that the clothes she gave me to wear when I came there the first day were from a young man who had boarded with her. I asked her where he was and she told me he went home to his family for the holiday the following morning after I came there.

Things did not really improve except that I now got an extra banana and dumpling on my plate but my belly was never full. I was still dependent on the generous meals from Miss Whitney.

My morning chores were quite numerous, but Miss Brown kept assigning more duties to me. This made it difficult for me to complete my tasks and arrive at school on time. To worsen the situation, Miss Brown told me she was no longer able to provide me with bus fare to go to school; as a result I had to walk to school. Every morning I would arrive at school late and receive a reprimand from the principal.

The summer season brought the ripening of plums and cherries. Luckily these trees were along my pathway to school. On my way home from school, I would stop and have a feast of plums and cherries. This was good for me, as I knew I would not be given dinner until very late at night.

One evening, after engorging myself with plums and cherries I became very sick, but I could not reveal the cause of my illness to Miss Brown.

Miss Brown's male boarder, by the name of Eric, had now returned. In the evening, after preparing his meal, she would put it in a covered container and place it on the shelf under the stove. On a number of occasions, one or both of the cats which lived with us would go to the stove and push the lid from the container and eat some of the boarder's meal. Although I was an eyewitness to this, I was hesitant to make this known, fearing Miss Brown would not believe me.

One evening while the cats were eating from the boarder's meal, I saw Miss Brown chase the cat away. To my dismay, she rearranged the food that was left on the plate as if nothing happened. The incident caused me some uneasiness as I wanted to tell Eric, but I was afraid to offend Miss Brown. As a solution to my dilemma I sought out Miss Whitney as a mediator and confidant. She told me that she would make it her responsibility to update Eric as to what was happening.

Miss Whitney's room was situated close to, and in sight of the kitchen. One evening when Eric arrived from school, she called him into her room and gave him a vantage lookout post. Eric had the opportunity to witness first hand Miss Brown chasing away the cat and rearranging his food as if nothing had happened. Eric became very angry but somewhat abated when Miss Whitney suggested that henceforth she would provide him with meals in the future.

After some time, Miss Brown became aware that Eric was not having his meals. She asked him about it, he told her he was not satisfied with the way in which his food was kept as it was not safe from the cat. Not very long after Eric returned to his home.

Miss Brown used to go to market very early on Saturday mornings, to get fresh fruits and vegetables. She would wake me up at four o'clock to accompany her to the bus stop. I had to walk with her in the dark through the park because she was afraid to go by herself, and waited until the bus arrived, then walked back home by myself in the dark.

Because Miss Brown was so stingy to me with food, I was always happy when Saturday mornings came. That was when I got the chance to eat whatever I wanted. Before she left, she took out a few pieces of liver and green bananas for me to cook. As always, she would count the liver, but this wasn't cause for concern, as I had a way around it. I would remove a small quantity from the liver, and each of the different types of meat that could be founded in the refrigerator. I then put all these meat together in an electric cooker and cook them along with one pound pack of rice.

After preparing this meal, I took it to the park, which was an open field close to the house, where I quickly hid the food, and hurried back home to finish my chores.

My chores would include, cleaning the chicken coop, cleaning the duck and turkey pen, sweeping the yard, and cooking.

There were no houses at the park during that time. It was just an open land which was located behind South Hospital. There had been times the inmates from the hospital could be found wandering off in the vicinity of the park, which made me afraid to go there for walks.

Miss Brown had a large cistern in which she kept water for the ducks to swim in. On Saturday mornings was the day that I had to clean it. I had to get down on my knees with a scrub brush and ashes and scrub it until it looked brand new and fill it with water for the ducks. I also had to clean the outside bathroom that was used by the tenants and myself. When I got finished I had to gather Miss Brown's dirty clothes and put them in a large washing tub with water and soap to soak, which later in the day I had to wash. I had to meet Miss Brown at the bus stop by ten o'clock, so all my chores were performed with a sense of urgency, and had to be completed in time for me to keep my appointment with her.

My appearance after all this was quite unsightly, but I ran the risk of receiving a flogging from Miss Brown if I changed my clothes. So I scamper off with my unkempt appearance. My clothes got so dirty at times that I even scorned myself.

Nevertheless, there I was barefoot and all, making double time across Lee Road to the park to meet Miss Brown. I had to make sure I was standing exactly at the bus door when it stopped, so as she came down the steps of the bus I was right there for her to put the basket on my head. The basket was always so heavy. One Saturday morning when Miss Brown placed the basket on my head, she dropped it so hard on my head that I fell to the ground. At the same time the bus started moving off, I had to depend on some of the passengers to help me while Miss Brown just stood and stared at me disgustingly. Totally unsympathetic, Miss Brown simply replaced the basket on my head and walked away.

I was in so much pain, even though I cried as I walked along, Miss Brown showed no remorse.

With the load on my head, the journey before me involved going across Lee Road, bare feet, and through the ants and bug infested field of the park to where we lived. I could not remove the basket from my head at any time as Miss Brown would not assist me to put it back up. Coupled with this, I ran the risk of getting a flogging for what Miss Brown regarded as my overly lazy attitude.

When we got home I had to struggle to put it down without dropping it. Miss Brown would not help me. It was such a relief. My neck usually felt so numb, and my head dizzy. I sat for a while before I could recover. This was the only time that Miss Brown showed any compassion towards me. Under normal conditions, I could not appear relaxed in her presence; she would find something for me to do, just to occupy my time. To my surprise, she even admitted that the basket had been too heavy for her, as it made her neck hurt.

I rested for a while, and then started packing away the market produce in the proper places. Miss Brown warmed the breakfast I had previously cooked. She soon placed before me a plate containing a half finger of banana with a slice of bread, which was so thin, that it was almost translucent, accompanied by a thumb-sized piece of meat. I was also given a cup of mint tea to go along with this minuscule amount of food.

In contrast to my meals, Miss Brown placed before herself a plate containing five fingers of banana, four slices of bread with a large amount of meat, and a big cup of Ovaltine. Although I was dissatisfied with the obvious disparity in our meals, I took comfort in the fact that at the park, there lay the edible booty which I had previously stashed away.

My many trips to the park to eat became suspicious to Miss Brown, because she began asking questions. I told her I was searching the trees hoping to find cherries and plums.

After eating, there was not even a break to digest my meal, because I had to go immediately and wash the clothes.

My hands became very tender and blistered from the constant scrubbing. Needless to say, this was very arduous.

The highpoint of my weekend was to go to church on Sundays. Miss Brown was a member of a Baptist church, while I attended a different church located close to the park.

Nevertheless, Sunday did not allow me a reprieve from doing my chores, as they had to be done before I got ready for church.

Sometime while doing my duties, the call of nature would cause me to make a request to go to the bathroom. Miss Brown would display insensitivity, by saying that I was lying.

Many times I had no choice but to urinate on myself in full view of her, so it was not unusual for me to wear wet underwear most of the time, with the smell of urine.

Miss Brown would embarrass me by commencing on how unpleasant I smelled.

On Sunday's when Miss Brown cooked dinner, the meal consisted of meat, rice and peas, and green bananas. A piece of codfish tail was cooked with the banana to prevent it from getting a dark color.

My serving was always devoid of any meat, and I had to be content with the banana smothered with pieces of codfish tail.

As I became aware of my fate, I used cunning and stealth to direct my modus-operandi and secured a piece of meat for myself when she was momentarily out of the kitchen. I had to do this carefully, because Miss Brown would always make an inventory of the pieces of meat. Monday morning brought a sense of relief, knowing that I would be at school and away from her. My lunch money was never enough; this only gave me enough to purchase a snow cone. I often asked the other kids for food, or made myself handy at the school canteen in the hopes that I would get some food to eat.

One of Miss Brown's friends was going off to America. This was the lady who had generously given Miss Brown some clothes for me.

They were having a send-off party for her, so Miss Brown took me along for the occasion. The food was served buffet style, and was the first time I had seen so much food at my disposal, and it was also the first time I tasted potato salad, which was so delicious. My first serving of potato salad was not enough; I wanted more but was fearful that I might expose myself to a reprimand from Miss Brown.

When all the entire guests were away from the table, I quickly took a handful of potato salad, wrapped it in my dress and went into the bathroom and ate it.

This was the first time Miss Brown had allowed me access to so much food, but she looked askance at me through the entire function; so much so, that I could not muster up enough courage to pilfer any more food.

As it was necessary to keep my action with the food covert, I went into the bathroom soon after and cleaned the potato salad off my dress. Luckily, there was enough time for my dress to dry before going home.

This was my advantage, as on returning Miss Brown ordered me to remove the dress forthwith, as she only 'lent it to me.'

On returning home from the party, conditions for me went back to what they had been; not enough food and laborious duties.

Miss Whitney still had to assist me with food, or I would sometimes steal from the pot or the refrigerator when Miss Brown was not present.

One Saturday, I felt weak and exhausted and not able to perform my chores. I told Miss Brown, but she would not empathize with my condition. Instead, she got very belligerent and vented her anger by flogging me with a stick. I started to scream loudly hoping that someone would hear and come to my aid. This inflamed her even more; and to silence me, she folded a wet newspaper and stuffed it into my mouth. Somehow I managed to pull the paper out and screamed loudly for 'murder.' She then threw me to the ground and sat on my head. Between the blows she was giving me. She exclaimed repeatedly, "That she was spending money on me and feeding me." The onslaught knew no limit, as she proceeded to drag me on the ground, and for a finale, she kicked me in my mouth.

After being bludgeoned, my mouth was bleeding and my body swollen and sore. I was in so much pain. I found it difficult to sleep that night.

The next day being Sunday found me still with aches and pains. I asked Miss Brown to allow me to go into the bathroom and shower down hopefully as a therapeutic measure. Her response was, "If you want to soak, you should go into the water with the ducks." My thoughts then reflected on how filthy the state of the ducks water was. At this point I made up my mind to run away and defiantly went into the bathroom and took a shower.

This made her very furious, and I decided to remove myself from the situation.

CHAPTER NINE

From The Pot to the Fire

Monday morning brought fresh feelings of hope and upliftment after meeting my school friend. She was my confidant, and I knew she would give me an encouraging ear as she often did, so I was comfortable in revealing my plans to her. This day at school I asked her if it was possible, at least as an interim measure, for me to go with her home. She was hesitant at first, but then agreed as she saw the severity of my situation. That evening, she took me home with her where she and her father lived.

When we got there he was in the kitchen cooking. After hearing my story, he decided that it was best for me to stay the night and in the morning he would accompany me to the police station. He said the authorities would be able to contact my parents and family. After cooking, he served us dinner. I got a copious serving of both rice and chicken. So unlike what I was used to at Miss Brown's. After dinner, my friend's father suggested that she give me a change of clothes so I could wash what I was wearing. He seemed so caring and accommodating.

The family did not have sleeping accommodations for me so I had to sleep on the floor. The events of the evening definitely did not prepare me for what later transpired. During the night, while sleeping on the floor, I became aware that someone was lying beside me. At first, I thought it was my friend, but to my horror it turned out to be her father. He said he was only there to play with me, and that I should not make any noise. He then coerced me by threatening to take me back to Miss Brown if I did not cooperate. This was the last thing I wanted, so I remained passive. As he proceeded to molest me, it was difficult to maintain my composure and to remain silent. I soon felt the painful onslaught of his direct assault on my body. He lunged into me with reckless abandonment. The pain from his actions was almost unbearable. He constantly renewed his previous threat to take me back home. I felt so defenseless, I cried through the whole unpleasant ordeal. I was only twelve years old then.

When he left me that night, I was unable to sleep, because I was in so much pain and discomfort. I tried getting to my feet, but it was difficult. I was only able to get around on my hands and feet. I went to the outside faucet where I allowed the water to run over my body until my feeling was improved. When I felt better, I checked to see if my clothes were dried, and they were.

It was then approaching daylight, and I got dressed and remained sitting in the yard feeling very fearful and confused. When my friend came outside that morning, she saw me sitting in the yard crying, and asked me what was the matter. I refused to disclose to her what had happened. Just at that time her fatter came out of the house, and they both exchanged glances and smiled.

When he left and went back into the house, I went and reminded him of his promise to take me to the police. I told him I would not tell the police anything about him. I said this to him, because I had no idea where the police station was, and I had to depend on him to take me there.

When he took me to the police station I told the police everything that Miss Brown had done to me. I wanted to tell them what my friend's father had done to me, but he was within hearing distance. After he walked away, I immediately told the police that he had raped me the night before, and also what he had done. The police acted on the information I gave to them, because shortly after he was taken into custody. That was the last time I saw him.

The police took all the information concerning Miss Brown. They then sent an officer to fetch her. At the station they asked her about her inhumane treatment towards me. She told the officers I was a bad child. That did not satisfy the police, as the evidence on my body shows that I was badly beaten. They suggested I return to her home, with the proviso that if her treatment towards me did not improve, legal action would be taken against her.

This made me afraid. I did not want to go back to Miss Brown's home, but I had no choice, and I did not have any money to run away to my grandparents. The only changes that took place was that she did not flog me anymore, but I still had arduous tasks to do. As a result of my traumatic molestation I experienced, combined with the beating from Miss Brown, my state of health deteriorated drastically, and I was not able to attend school any longer. This caused me to lose communication with Marie; we did not see each other again.

During the period of my illness and convalescence, the school holidays came around. This was during the summer. My unfortunate situation was compounded by the fact that Miss Whitney had got married and moved away. This eliminated the supply of food she used to give me.

One night I was awakened by Miss Brown. They approached me shouting, and said to me; at the same time she pulled the cover from off my body. Miss Brown took the dog and threw it in the bed with me, and said. "Let the dog sleep with you and breed you little bitch."

Miss Brown continues to show her antagonism towards me by restricting my meals. There were periods in which I would be without food for an entire day. At times like these I would walk to the park and pick ripe and unripe plums from the trees. This would probably be my only source of food for the day. One day Miss Brown told me explicitly that she would make sure that I never come out to be anything good in life. This made me afraid of her, and hates her more.

On many occasions I found the trees at the park sparsely populated with plums, this owed to the summer coming to an end, and the plum season being over.

As a result, there were days when it was difficult to find a satisfying meal. On the very lean days, I would sit under the fruitless trees wallowing in self-pity. As an act of solace, I would bite my fingernails and even resort to eating dirt, crying and pulling my hair. Because of that I always experience excruciating pain in my head.

My hunger was that severe.

CHAPTER TEN

Surprise in the Bushes

There was an ice cream parlor which was located on Lee Road and close to the park where I usually sit under the trees in a very famished state.

One day, I went there to hide from Miss Brown, because as long as she saw me she always found work for me to do. She never liked to see me sitting and doing nothing. One day while I was sitting under the plum trees at the park, I heard something drop over the fence not far from where I was sitting. I got up to see what it was. To my surprise, it was boxes, and containers of ice cream that someone had thrown away. I looked to make sure no one saw me. Fortunately for me no one was there which made me very happy. I got up quickly and grabbed one of the cartons of ice-cream and ran into the bushes.

I made a meal of the ice cream, after which my stomach was full. Every day after that, I made visits to the back of the parlor and enjoyed a feast of different flavors ice cream. It seems after eating the different flavored ice-cream gave me a terrible bowel movement. Unknown to me, my regular vigil to the rear of the ice cream parlor was being observed by the owner and operator. On one occasion, as I was about to pick up the box of ice cream, there was a commanding voice of a woman, saying, "You don't have to eat the rotten ice cream anymore." I was so scared and made an attempt to run at first, but the voice was also gentle and compassionate, I did not run away. She said to me, "Don't run, and take this from me." She then came through the gate and handed me a large bowl of ice cream and one shilling coin, and told me that at the same time every day, she would have more for me, and if I did not see her I should call. She said her name was Miss Cho.

Miss Cho kept her word, and her generosity to me continued on an almost daily basis. We soon became very good friends.

After a while I related to Miss Cho about the abusive treatment which I was receiving from Miss Brown, and my desire to run away to my grandfather. She became very nurturing towards me, and encouraged me to save whatever money she gave me. As the friendship grew between us she told me that there was going to be a Coney Island fair which would be held at the park. She suggested that it would be very rewarding for me to be a part of the preparation crew that would clean up the grounds, which would allow me to earn money to fund my trip to my grandfather.

Although I was fascinated with the idea, I told her that I was sure Miss Brown would not approve of me doing this. Miss Cho said she would take the initiative to speak to her on my behalf as she was one of the persons in charge of the proceedings. Miss Cho also promised not to disclose to her the exact amount of money I would be earning.

After about three weeks, Miss Brown told me that a Coney Island fair would be held at the park. She said she had been asked to assist with the cleaning, and that she would be taking me with her to work. Miss Brown then said to me, 'that she was glad I would be working so I would be able to pay her back the money for taking care of me'. And also said I would not be excused from doing my regular chores.

The following week the job started, I had to go to work. At the end of the week, everyone got paid, but I was not included.

Miss Brown had made arrangements with Miss Cho to receive my pay. What Miss Brown was not aware of, was that Miss Cho and I had made plans to hold back some of my earnings and give half to Miss Brown, so She was not aware how much money I was being paid by Miss Cho.

As the friendship between Miss Cho and myself continued, she told me that people who attended the fair often times lost their money, so when it begin I should go there early in the mornings and look around.

I was happy to hear of this. The friendship between Miss Cho and myself was very secretive. Coney Island started and lasted for two weeks. Miss Brown told me that if I behaved myself she would allow me to go. I was very excited and wanted to experience what a Coney Island fair was all about, because I have read so much about it. When the occasion arrived I became very excited.

Miss Brown took me the first two nights, and told me that in the evenings, after finishing my chores, she would allow me to go. A few days after the job was finished, I asked Miss Brown if she could give me some money to buy ice cream in the afternoons. She told me no, and said, "If I ate ice cream my mouth would strip." She also told me that the money was to reimburse her for all she had done for me. As sadden as I felt I did not say anything because I had my own plans.

Because it was so close to home, I went every night, but I did not pay to enter. Because I was so small, I crept under the fence.

One of the nights after returning from the fair, I tried opening the back gate which I usually entered by, but to my surprise it was locked. I went to the front but that gate was also locked. I jumped over the fence and into the yard and knocked on the doors and windows, Miss Brown did not answer. I kept calling for a long time but still no answer.

I was friends with the neighbor who lived across the street, and in front of Miss Brown house. I went over to her house, woke her up and told her what had happened to me. She invited me in and said I could stay the night. There was no bed for me to sleep on, so I was accommodated by sleeping on a bench in the passageway.

During the night, I was awakened by someone touching my body. When I looked around to see who it was, I was surprised to discover that it was my friend's fiancée. I opened my mouth to call her, but he immediately covered my mouth with his hands, and stuck me in my eyes with his fingers. He held me down and molested me.

After he molested me, he told me that he had been watching me for a long time, and had been waiting for the opportunity to become intimate with me. Although he covered my mouth I was still able to scream. His girlfriend was awakened; she came out to see what was wrong. He tried to fabricate a story but she actually caught him while he was pulling his pyjama pants up. I told her what had happened and luckily she believed me and was very sympathetic to me.

I was unable to sleep for the rest of the night so I laid there until daylight.

I wondered to myself what I had done to deserve all the things I was going through.

When morning came, I went over and knocked on the gate, this time Miss Brown came and opened it for me. She said to me, "I hope you had slept with the chickens last night." I felt so hurt by that especially when I remembered what transpired the previous night. I started crying immediately. I was so astonished; I did not answer her because I was so hurt and felt ashamed. I wanted to go away immediately.

Every morning, I got up early before Miss Brown woke up and went over to the Coney Island to look for money on the grounds. Most times I was successful. The money I found was kept in a secret hiding place at the park which added up to eighteen shillings. One day I told Miss Cho I was preparing to run away to my grandfather. She assured me that she had kept her promise to put the money aside for me. I also asked her to inquire about the bus schedule, which she had done for me.

Every Wednesday morning at 8 o'clock, Miss Brown would go to the Pier to meet the boat owned by the company her husband worked with to receive the things he had sent for her. I decided that the next Wednesday morning when she left, I would use her absence from home as my opportunity to run away.

The day before I left, I told Miss Cho about my final plans, and she told me to meet her behind the ice cream parlor because she had something to give me.

That evening I went to her and she gave me a box and two pounds. I took it from her and told her, "Thanks." With tears running down my face, Miss Cho told me that I was crying now, but later on my life would bring me a lot of laughter. I told her good-bye and left.

I took the box and hid it at my usual hiding place of safety at the park. It was hard for me to sleep that night as I was so anxious to see

Wednesday morning come. I prayed all night, just for the moment to come when I could get away from Miss Brown.

It was now Wednesday morning. How glad was I.

When Miss Brown left home I watched her, and made sure that she had boarded the bus and was gone. I quickly got all my clothes packed into a carton box and took them over to the park, fearing that she might return before her usual time and discover my plans.

After making sure, I got dressed and ran from the house to the park, collected my boxes and went straight to Lee Road to get my bus.

I stopped for a short time at the ice cream parlor to say good-bye to Miss Cho and to thank her for her kindness. As I waited for the bus I became very nervous, fearing Miss Brown would return and caught upon my scheme.

When the bus finally came I was happy as a lark. I boarded and sat down. I felt so relieved to be on my way to Windsor.

CHAPTER ELEVEN

Home Sweet Home

After enduring such horrible conditions in Town with Miss Brown, it was a welcome opportunity to be back at Windsor once again, which proved to be the sun center of my existence.

I explained the problem that I endured at Miss Brown to my grandfather. He was very happy to see me, and happy too that I had brought home money with me. He took some of the money and went to Town and did extensive grocery shopping. At last I felt as if I was somewhere I really belonged.

At the behest of my grandfather, I was now determined to remain at Windsor and to even oppose my mother's efforts to remove me from there.

As the years went by my grandparent's house had fallen into a state of disrepair. My grandmother's room was in the worst state one could imagine. The floorboards were completely gone, so my grandmother and I were practically walking on the bare earth. The room door was nonexistent, there were only a few pieces of board which she hung crocus bags on and placed them in the doorway. There were holes in the walls and all over the house. This gave free passage to lizards and rodents. My grandfather's room was in a much better condition.

Unfortunately, he gave scant attention to my grandmother and her problems in general. There were times, nevertheless, when he displayed an unusual amount of attentiveness towards her; this was done only after spending the night with him. Normally, he was not concerned about her welfare.

My grandmother and I would often use newspapers and magazines to paste over the holes in the walls, but the rats soon ate their way through.

At night one would often hear my grandmother cry out in pain after being bitten by rats. Our sleep at night was often disturbed by the mating calls of lizards. Grandmother soon developed a problem with her feet because she was bitten incessantly by the rats. The problem with her feet was exacerbated, because grandmother was unable to afford medical attention. She had to employ different home remedies. She tried not to let others know of her condition, fearing that she and I might be ridiculed in the community.

Grandmother, like myself, was not neatly dressed. We were also afraid of going to the public faucet and appearing to be a social anomaly. The sneer and innuendoes from the residents of the district were just too much to take.

The kitchen was located about twenty feet from the house, under the star-apple tree which I had planted. It was built with bamboo, coconut logs and a few old sheets of zinc. We did not have a stove, and so we made do and set up a fireplace on the ground. Whenever it rained, we were partially exposed to the elements, as the thatch roof of the kitchen leaked and did not give adequate shelter. My grandmother had to cover the pots on the fire with a piece of zinc to prevent the rain from snuffing out the fire. Thus, we had to keep a sheet of zinc as a contingency measure.

Because of the close proximity of the house and kitchen to the church, anyone attending church could look directly into the kitchen. My grandfather would try to achieve some privacy by placing coconut branches on the sides of the kitchen. This was a temporary solution, because in time the coconut branches would rot away and re-exposed our kitchen.

The pots we used for cooking were very black and battered. So much so, that my grandmother told me that whenever I was washing them to wash only the inside alone. She feared that because they were so dilapidated, washing the outside might cause them to get holes. Our plates, likewise, were all chipped and studded with holes. When we were using them, we had to use the food we were eating to plug the holes to prevent the gravy and soup from leaking out. The only good plates we had were the ones which my grandfather ate from.

On Sundays or when a function was being held at the church, the prying eyes of all and sundry were able to give unsympathetic stares at our kitchen and our general poor lifestyle. This made me feel very uncomfortable.

To gain some semblance of privacy, my grandfather planted a row of croton trees along the fence line between the church and the house. But this hedge was more of a decoration than anything else.

The toilet was located about thirty feet from the house; situated under an orange tree in the banana field. The flooring of the toilet was so shabby and unsound that we had to be very careful where we stepped, fearing the floor might give way. At nights this became an even more difficult exercise. Roaches dominated the enclosure of the toilet. They were such a nuisance.

As time passed, my grandmother was employed as a domestic worker with the John's. They were a wealthy family who lived at Apple Hill. She would always take me with her to work. So it was, the John's became my adopted godparents and I was treated very well by their family.

I would look forward to an opportunity to go there, because of the love and affection my 'godmother' and her husband showed me. At meal times I was allowed to sit at the dining table with the rest of the family. Usually on my visits Mrs. John allowed me to sleep with her, because during that time she and her husband did not occupy the same bedroom, unless my grandmother would be staying. Whenever my grandmother and I were going home, Mrs. John and her husband usually supplied us food and clothes. This was the way my grandmother used to offset her austere lifestyle at home.

I was now attending Windsor Primary School which was held in a church. In later years a new school was built in a different location in Windsor. I had such fond walking to school especially during mango and apple season. I would leave early in the morning, so that I would be in time to glean the choice mangoes and apples which were under the trees.

The school uniform was primarily a blue dress complemented with a white blouse. Unlike most students who had two or three sets of uniforms, I had only one set.

As a result of this I had to launder my uniform every evening for the next day. My grandmother made an effort for me to look tidy, so that when I attended I would look acceptable. Needless to say, I was still a shabby-looking student.

The new school principal's name was Mrs. Benjamin. She had a son who was a singer. Miss Riley was another teacher; she was always encouraging and supportive and had a very profound influence on my life. Miss Riley and my mother became close friends, and because of that I would often go to her house on weekends to wash and do housework for her.

For all my labor, I would be paid a paltry sum of one shilling and sixpence along with personal gifts. My mother would promptly relieve me of my earnings as soon as I got home.

There was a popular male teacher by the name of Mr. Wiles. We all regarded him as a very efficient teacher. He would often conduct the after school classes which were held at the school.

It became an item of gossip that he was having an affair with some of the female students. Two of my friends and I became very curious. We decided to investigate to see if there was any validity to the gossip. Late one evening, just about the time when class would be dismissed, we sneaked back to the school. We positioned ourselves outside Mr. Wile's class, under the classroom window. It was now very dark, and we were careful not to give our position away.

To my amazement, we became witness to Mr. Wiles having sex with a girl named Peck who was a student in his class. Being privy to this knowledge, we were not only astounded, but very scared. As children, we did not want the dissemination of such damaging information to be traced back to us, with the attendant consequences.

My cousin Jack attended school with me. He was a brilliant student and would often assist me with my school work. My grades reflected his help, and I would always feature first, second, and third in regular class tests. He was very kind to me, and would often take things from his parents shop to give me. My good grades soon caused me to be the object of jealousy. One day I was set upon by a number of girls. My defense was to fake an epileptic seizure. I suddenly started to roll on the ground, with eyes open and foaming at the mouth. They all got scared and ran away.

On another occasion, I got attacked by a girl and a boy; the girl grabbed my hair while the boy kicked me in my buttocks. This took place while I was not far from my home, so I ran to my grandfather crying. He abruptly came out with his stick, but as soon as they saw him coming they all ran off. Another time, for no reason, a girl in my class stuck me in my ear with her pencil in an unprovoked incident. These were just some of the unkind things I had to endure as a child at Windsor Primary School.

Nevertheless, I became an active student and started attending evening classes with the hope that I would gain a scholarship. In the fullness of time I was required to go to Bedford to sit an examination. On the morning of the exam, I was feeling very weak and dizzy. I called out to my grandfather and told him what was happening to me. He made some concoction and gave me a curative massage. I lay in bed for a while. I was already late for my exam, because the bus was already gone. I had to wait for another form of transportation to get there.

I was late, but I was glad that the examiner accepted me. While in the examination room, as the test papers were placed in front of me, surprisingly, two wasps fell dead on my test paper. Immediately my feelings deteriorated and so I was unable to sit the exam, so I had to leave.

It was very difficult returning home that day, because due to my illness I had to wait a very long time for the bus to arrive. When I got home and told my grandfather what had happened. He anointed me with an elixir he had prepared, and. after a week, I felt better.

Mrs. McCoy was one of our distant neighbors. One day, surprisingly, her grandson came and told me that she wanted to see me, so I went willingly. She gave me a pair of new white sneakers as a gift, and as a child in my indigent condition, I was happy to receive them. No sooner had I started to wear them, my feet became swollen. And not very long after, I was tending to a lame leg that broke out into a sore. For weeks my grandmother tried her home remedies which did not work so she took me to the hospital where I received treatment, but the wound only got worse, to the point where I was unable to walk. At this stage worms were coming from the wounds.

After days and nights of excruciating pain and frustration I was prepared to try anything to heal myself. I crawled on my hands and knees and went up into the bushes behind my grandfather's house, removed the dressing and took some of my feces and placed it on the wounds. By the next day the pain was not as severe. I continued to make a poultice with my feces. My grandmother soon noticed that the leg was improving and I was able to ambulate, but she thought it was because of her attentiveness. After the visible improvement, everyone was surprised when I told them of the remedy I had used. My grandfather believed me, and encouraged me to continue.

I had three school friends whose name was, Nancy, Ann and Ellen. Nancy lived in a small community which was close to Windsor. She was of Indian descent. She was very kind to me. She lived with her grandmother, at the residence where she was employed. Her grandmother's employees were people of some means, and of Caucasian descent. Whenever I visited there she made sure that her grandmother's employer did not see me, so she would caution me to be very discreet as not to alert anyone.

My visits usually lasted very late in the evenings.

One night a murder took place along the road coming from where Nancy's lived. This fact was always on my mind, so I made sure it was not too dark when I left Nancy's home. Because I was afraid, I made sure my visits ended before night.

My other friend Ann and I had a close resemblance in facial features, she was always someone who I wanted to have as a close friend, but she always acted aloof to me and displayed very snobbish behavior.

That really affected our friendship.

Ellen was a nice friend; she was the product of an affluent father who was living abroad in another country. She was always furnished with most of the physical amenities.

In stark contrast to her, I did not have enough clothes to wear. I had to fashion makeshift panties to wear on my hand.

Most of my clothes were either hand sewn or were gifts, and reflected the condition caused by excess laundering.

On one occasion at school, my hand-sewn underwear waist string gave way. It created the most embarrassing moments for me. I had to employ what measures I could to keep it up and ran to the bathroom.

It was my indigent lifestyle that forced me to swallow my pride and asked Ellen to give me a pair of her panties. She agreed to do so, but told me that I would have to accompany her to the river when she was going to take her bath. The only way she could give me a pair of her panties was the one she was wearing. The reason for this was because her grandmother always checked on her clothes, so Ellen had to have a convincing reason for losing her panties. Her grandmother was taken by excuse that she sent Ellen back to the river to look for the panties. She gave me a second pair on another occasion. Ellen used the same excuse that her panties had been washed away in the river accidentally while she was bathing. Her grandmother became very furious, and told Ellen that she would never allow her to go to the river to bathe again after losing two panties.

My grandfather was a tenant farmer. The crops he tended were such as coconut, bananas, breadfruit, yams, star apples, apples, ackee, nutmeg, coffee, and chocolate. As with most farm products these were seasonal crops, and likewise; the income from these crops was also seasonal. This had an adverse effect on my schooling.

There were many days when I did not have lunch money for school. When lunch time came I was usually famished. I went around to the other children while they were eating. If it appeared that a few morsels of food would be left on a child's plate, I asked for the opportunity to have what was left. At times, I was driven to steal food from the plates of unsuspecting students. Thus, I was known to be a mendicant in the lunchroom. They gave me the name 'clean up' which was very embarrassing.

We had a neighbor named Mass Henry. He was a frequent visitor to our home, as he and my grandfather often exchanged pleasantries. His wife used to make biscuits which she supplied to the community. She was very kind to me and often gave me some to take home. During my visits to their home as a child, I became good friends with Mass Henry. He was very kind to me, and would regularly give me lunch money. On several occasions when I visited their home, I usually sat and had conversations with Mass Henry. As an elderly man his stories were always funny and interesting.

One particular evening it was getting dark and I was getting ready to leave. As usual, Mass Henry would accompany me part of the journey. To my surprise, one late evening as we were walking along the dark pathway, Mass Henry suddenly grabbed me, forced me to the ground, and started to fondle my vagina. He told me that if I did not let him have his way with me, he would no longer give me lunch money. In my young mind I could only think of the independence his money afforded me at lunch time. Thus Mass Henry started a vicious cycle of raping me, ensuring my silence by continuing to give me lunch money daily. This continuous onslaught on my tender body was soon more than I could physically bear.

I decided that at all cost I had to avoid him. So it was back to begging and foraging for my school lunch. At times, I would run home during lunch time to see if there was anything at home to eat. Oftentimes I would return to school hungry.

Some time had passed and I kept my conviction to stay away from the home of the Henry's. Ironically, his visits to our home also stopped, which was a relief for me.

After this incident, when Mass Henry was passing our home he would only give a greeting in passing to my grandfather, or try to be inconspicuous. Even if he saw my grandfather their conversation would be brief and he would be on his way.

Among the many crops which my grandfather planted were nutmeg and chocolate. These had to be given special attention. When the harvest season came they had to be reaped with care and diligence. The chocolate pods bearing the edible seeds would have to be opened and the seeds extracted, then they are spread on sheets of zinc and are placed in the open air to be slowly sun-dried. There was a high demand for these products so we gave them the highest priority.

My grandfather had a cousin named Betty; she often took some of my grandfather's produce to sell in the market at Bay. Hence, she also acted as the retail outlet for other persons in the district.

Betty lived close to our house. Her relationship with my grandfather seemed to extend further than just business and distant cousins, because my grandfather would be caught leaving her house early mornings. She usually cooked daily meals for my grandfather, although my grandmother was present in the house. I was the one who oftentimes had to go to Betty house to fetch my grandfather's dinner.

The meals were exclusively for my grandfather, and were scarcely shared with the rest of the family. My grandfather's open, and unabashed relationship with Betty, was in contrast to his total neglect and disrespect for my grandmother. This later posed a problem between my grandfather and Betty's husband when he returned home.

Oftentimes when my grandfather was having a sumptuous evening repast, grandmother and myself were rummaging through the garbage bins searching for food. Sometimes grandmother would leave the house, and on her return she would collect an empty can or two. She would also return with a bag containing a stone, to give the appearance that she was returning from the store.

This was done primarily for my grandfather's eyes. She would do anything to appear defiant because his mean-spirited behavior towards her was compounded by his open relationship with Betty.

CHAPTER TWELVE

A Period of Turmoil

Grandfather was a close neighbor to the Willis family. My grandfather and Mr. Willis were constantly in dispute over land rights and the appropriate position of the dividing line between their two properties. Over the years, this led to many court battles between them. Needless to say, my grandfather was opposed to our family having any social interaction with the Willis family. And he made it known in an unequivocal fashion.

Mrs. Willis was of Caucasian descent.

The irony of the situation was that my grandmother and Mrs. Willis had a good social rapport as women, but grandmother always made sure to behave in a covert manner whenever she saw Mrs. Willis at the fence and desired to talk with her. The amicable relationship between the women was enhanced by the fact that Mrs. Willis would often assist us with food. Mrs. Willis realized that we were so destitute, that she often gave us their leftover food that they had partially eaten.

All this had to be hidden from my grandfather. I was often the one who went and secretly collected whatever Mrs. Willis had to give us.

In contrast to the acrimonious relationship between the men of the two families, my grandmother and Mrs. Willis shared a friendship, which involved dependence on my grandmother's part.

As for Mrs. Willis, she condescended by displaying an air of social tolerance for my grandmother and her circumstances. Once, my grandmother was suffering from a lame foot and Mrs. Willis observed that she had difficulty walking. She made a concerned inquiry about it and gave my grandmother a concoction which eventually healed her foot.

There was another family by the name of Lopez. The matriarch of the family was Mrs. Boltz, who was my grandfather's cousin.

When my grandfather was younger, he was very kind to her, and she was also very fond of him. During her twilight years; he became very instrumental in giving her hospice care until the time of her death. Mrs. Boltz was very appreciative of my grandfather's care and attention. She showed her appreciation by bequeathing to my grandfather a substantial portion of property. Mr. Lopez was a relative of Mrs. Boltz and like the rest of her family was miffed over the action of Mrs. Boltz.

Mr. Lopez formed the spearhead of the family's litigious behavior. He sought relentlessly to have Mrs. Boltz nullified. His action was always rebuffed with the perversity for which my grandfather was well known. The Lopez family was not satisfied with legal recourse only, and resorted to also using witchcraft as a modus operandi. My grandfather was however undaunted by this and reciprocated in like manner.

My grandfather was a man of very aggressive temperament. He was unapologetic about forcefully expressing his opinion. Whenever he was threatened or provoked, he would arm himself with his machete or his defensive fighting staff; and would not flinch from using either should the need arise.

He would proudly boast that his aggressive manner came from the 'king bloodline' of the ancestors to whom he was related. He believed and proclaimed, 'death before dishonor.' My grandfather told me that he and his brother David had fought in the Great War of 1914, where his brother died. Despite his belligerence, my grandfather possessed strange shamanistic qualities. This is a trait which runs in the family. Grandfather recalled going with his father to give spiritual assistance to people; a practice he later adopted himself. He related to me one incident in which his grandfather had to go to a cross road late one night to meet and subdue disincarnate spirit entities. My grandfather's treatment of my grandmother was indicative of his vile and aggressive nature.

The citizens of the community, at the time, saw witchcraft as a viable option to carry out reprisals on their perceived enemies. Miss Kitty who lived at Yale was a known practitioner of witchcraft in the community. She once had a liking for Sailor who was my cousin. Because he did not return her affection she cast a spell on him. That was manifested in the form of a lame foot, a condition which the doctor was unable to cure.

Almost every week in the community of Yale there would be a spiritual ritual called kummina, and by the following week the death of someone or something bad would be announced.

The road to Yale was very dark, and because of the infamous reputation of the community I was always afraid to go there alone especially at night. My feeling of foreboding about Yale strengthened whenever I remembered one occasion when I attended a funeral there. I was a member of the funeral party. The pallbearers were carrying the coffin on foot to the burial ground. Suddenly, the pallbearers came to a standstill and the entire procession followed suit. The coffin was placed on the ground and miraculously it started spinning by its own volition. Everyone present was struck with astonishment.

Mr. Ricketts, who was a member of the funeral party and also the member of a local lodge in the district of Fountain went forthwith to the head of the procession and stood in front of the coffin. He turned his back to the coffin, removed his pants and underpants, and then unabashedly brandished his bottom towards the coffin. He proceeded to speak in an unknown language. Immediately, the coffin started vibrating as though it was responding to his command. He then shouted, "Pick up the damn coffin now." The pallbearers obeyed him and the procession continued. On the way, the mourners started singing. Mr. Ricketts then shouted, "Shut up your mouth, I don't want any damn singing from anyone, not a sound." And with that, the procession continued in silence to the graveside. Memories like these about Yale remain in my thoughts even to this day.

Tanny Town was another district close to our home. Some of the residents there were of Indian descent. Some Saturdays, the Indians would have dinner and dance; it was always a pleasure to attend. The way to Tanny Town, however, was a very scary one for me; because I had to pass by a cemetery, and also crossing the river. I always hear the sound of owls hooting. The most treacherous condition was the fact that whenever it rained, the river would become impassable; so for this reason, when I went to Tanny Town I was always concerned about the time of day I was going there, and the weather forecast for that day.

There was a quarry further down the road from our house called Mall Hill. It was rumored that ghosts resided there, and anyone who ventured there at night would be attacked. My friends and I often went up the hill overlooking Mall Hill to gather mangoes, but because of the reputation of the place, I always made sure we were strong in numbers.

About that time we knew a man named Mr. Norton. For some time he and my grandfather had an adversarial relationship. One particular morning, after I had slept at my grandparents' house, I heard a rustling sound coming from the cellar of the house. The height of the house was such that someone could easily be accommodated under there. As my grandfather was an early riser, I first assumed that he was up and about. But to my surprise, I saw my grandfather still asleep in his bed. This made me curious, and discreetly investigated. I peeped through the holes of the flooring in the house. To my surprise, I saw Mr. Norton crouched under the cellar with a machete in his hand. I quickly pulled the wood that was used inside the house that formed a partition and slipped into my grandfather's room and told him what I had seen. Grandfather immediately thought of a plan to flush out the intruder. Grandfather's first plan was to remain in the house for an inordinately long period, thereby frustrating and confusing his predator. The floor of my grandfather's house was wood, which had several holes and cracks. Grandfather executed the next stage of his plan by literally flushing out the intruder. This was done by pouring the overnight urine, collected in his chamber pot, through a crack in the wood flooring into the cellar. This did the trick, as Mr. Norton did not seem to fancy his presence being acknowledged by a copious dousing of urine. Out came the would-be attacker immediately; only to be the recipient of a number of swift and decisive blows delivered by grandfather, who was deft at handling his stick. This was Mr. Norton's opportunity to beat a hasty retreat and since that incident Mr. Norton no longer posed a problem to my grandfather.

CHAPTER THIRTEEN

Life with My Mother

I remember as a child, that Windsor was a small community in a rural area that was serviced by a few grocery shops owned by people in the community; and also the Justice of the Peace. She was an affluent woman in the community, who also was the owner of a number of homes that she rented. Unfortunately one of the shops which were Chinese owned was destroyed by a fire. That shop was never rebuilt.

When I got older, my parents were separated. My mother after residing at different places came to live at Windsor. I was always unhappy whenever she was around. Although I had to work hard at my grand-parents' home, I was very happy being there with them, because the atmosphere was congenial and loving.

My mother later found employment at an infant center. She rented a house above the Willis' house, which was located in a banana field. Overtime I started to live with her, but most of my time was spent with my grand-parents. My mother did not have adequate sleeping quarters for me so I had to sleep on the floor.

My father would regularly send money to my mother for child support. One Friday when my grandmother was visiting us, my mother somehow misplaced the money. Without even looking around carefully or asking if anyone had seen it, she attacked me with a pair of long scissors and accused me of stealing the money. She then pinned me onto the floor with her knees in my chest and the scissors at my throat. She began shouting. "I am going to kill you, because you are a damn blasted thief, give me back the money." I tried to tell her I did not take it and pleaded with her to look more carefully. At my grandmother's insistence, she looked in the drawer of the cabinet of her sewing machine; sure enough, tucked in the top of the drawer was the money. Even with the discovery, my mother did not consider an apology to me. That made my grandmother very upset about the incident and told me to accompany her back home.

When my grandfather heard, he was miffed, and cursed my mother in her absence. Because of this incident I did not return to my mother's home for a long time. Although life with my grandparents was very hard, we made do for the most part on a paltry amount of food from one day to the next, but I preferred to stay with them.

Whenever my mother came to visit, I would hide and pretend that I was not home.

I soon went into puberty and my body started developing. My brassieres were of my own design, fashioned from old clothes. My mother totally ignored the changes I was going through, and even gave me a severe flogging with the strokes of the whip directed at my genital area when she found out I had started menstruating. Needless to say, I was ignorant about what was happening to me and my mother did nothing to help me through these changes. After this needless reproach, my mother not only kept me in the dark as to what was happening, but she did not furnish me sanitary cloths to address my condition, so I was forced to use newspaper and any coarse and discarded material I could find. The ridicule from the girls at school was too much to bear.

One of the girls at school felt sorry for me and demonstrated sympathy towards me. She invited me home with her late one evening after school. When we arrived at her home she made sure her grandmother was not aware of my presence. She gave me some of her sanitary cloths and instructed me how to use them. I was so grateful for this. After my mother realized what my school friend had done for me, the following week, she gave me two white flour bags and a large piece of calico, giving me no instruction as to what I should do. I went to my school friend and asked her for help. She showed me how to prepare and fashion them for the purpose.

Around this time, my grandmother was visiting my aunt who lived at Mount Ridge. When she made these trips, she often stayed for a considerable period of time. I was always very unhappy during these times because I was without the umbrella of my grandmother, and left to the vituperative onslaught of my mother.

My fondest memories of Christmas were to watch and be involved in the Jankunno parade. My mother was always set against me participating in the parade. But usually I would not be 'put off' by her opinion.

Just before the parade was scheduled to pass, I would hide and make my whereabouts unknown, then join my friends in the parade with some amount of stealth. At this stage I was not concerned if I was recognized, as I was moving in joyous tandem with the other children. After the parade I went to my grandfather's house just to be on the safe side.

My mother often received clothes from her cousin Lola who lived at Bay and her cousin Beryl who lived in another country. She never saw to extend the generosity which she received from her cousin. I had to sneak and take what I could, and do the necessary alterations, and then quickly returned them after I had worn them, in a fashion where she, of course, would never find out. My grandfather was an ex-soldier and sometimes received clothes through a program the army had to help the families of the ex-soldiers. I would always accompany him on these trips. This was one of the ways I was furnished with 'decent' clothes.

In time my mother started attending Mother Mayes Spiritual Church in Bedford. On several occasions I went with her and was given spiritual baths and healing. Mother Mayes took a liking to me and would often invite us to stay at her house. These visits continued for a long time.

Over a period of time my mother rented another house from Miss Dawkin in Windsor, which was situated on a hill overlooking my grandparent's home. I had several visits with her at her new residence; and eventually started living with her again. The relationship between my mother and myself was very unpleasant, because I always remember the abusive things she had done to me.

She soon started having an affair with a man named Mr. Otis, who lived in Pen. During this time, she was receiving child support from my father. Coincidentally, Mr. Otis would visit my mother on the day when the child support came. Whenever he came, I was sent to the shop to purchase sardines, bread, beer, a soda, and dragon stout. Later in the evening I was given a piece of the bread end and the empty sardine can. This comprised my evening meal. My mother and Mr. Otis would have dinner and entertain themselves using the beer, dragon stout, and soda to toast for the evening.

At nights I had to sleep on the floor in the same room where my mother and Mr. Otis slept. They were both insensitive to the fact that their nocturnal activities often kept me awake. This made me resentful of my mother and caused our relationship to deteriorate even more.

It soon became obvious that my mother was pregnant. When the time came for her to have the baby, I was not privy to the happenings, or was not allowed to help with anything. Two unannounced female visitors arrived at the house one day and I was later told they were the midwife who came to assisted her. They went straight to my mother's room. Soon after I heard my mother cried out in a loud voice. 'Shadrach, Meshack and Abednego', with repeated intensity. Shortly after, I heard the cry of a baby. This was the birth of my sister Bev.

CHAPTER FOURTEEN

The Stranger

Mass Larry was an elderly man, who was not known to me; came from another town and rented the front room that was adjacent to the verandah of the house which my mother rented for quite a long time. My mother and Mass Larry soon became very good friends. We all shared the same kitchen, so that was an opportunity for them to interact frequently.

Mass Larry was very kind to me and my family, and often sent me to run errands for him. He and my mother would always sit on the verandah and have conversation, but they would stop talking whenever I came along.

As time Passed, one day, my mother and grandmother were away from home; Mass Larry and I were left alone. He had just finished cooking and asked me to fetch him a cup of water and put it on the table in his room as he always did.

When I brought the water, surprisingly he told me to sit down on the stool beside his table. I had no reason to feel afraid or nervous because Mass Larry was a very calm and respectable man in the community. He started talking to me, but the conversation got a bit boring, so I told him that I would be going to my grandfather's home to stay until my parents return home. He then put his hand in his pocket and showed me the outline of a coin that looked like two shilling which he subsequently took and offered to me. As I reached out to take it, he grabbed my hand and held me in his arms. Surprisingly he then asked me if my father had ever molested me. I became astonished and denied it. Mass Harry unexpectedly grabbed hold of my hands. I struggled to get away from him. I was unable to fight him because as a small child he overpowered me and held me firmly. He stated to me that my mother told him I was molested by my father which had caused a lot of problem in the home.

With that he then placed his hand into my underwear. When I threatened to tell my grandfather, he said if I did, he would put 'Obeah' on me, which I was afraid of hearing about.

He pinned me on the floor in his room, so that I was prostrate and at his disposal, then he molested me, which caused me such pain and agony. Before he ended this lecherous encounter, he then exposed himself to me. That was such an embarrassing sight and painful experience for me. I felt so much hatred and anger for my mother. I could not believe she would have told this stranger that my father had molested me. After this incident, I tried the best that I could to stay away from my mother's house in order to avoid seeing Mass Larry.

I took my religious observance very seriously even as a child. I used to attend the church which was adjacent to my grandfather's house and property twice on Sundays. Despite the fact that I did not have adequate clothes to wear, whenever the church was having an outing, my grandfather's always see to it that I attended. Sometimes he accompanied me or he would ensure that I had a chaperone. Nevertheless, the reaction from the members of the church towards me was less than friendly.

My grandfather and the church had a longstanding land dispute, and some of the rancor leveled at my grandfather was also directed towards me. Many times I was forced to stay away from the church because of lack of proper clothing, fearing I would be ridiculed about my clothes.

My grandmother always did her best to furnish me clothes made from flour bags.

There were times when she received clothes from relatives who lived in the Bay and abroad. These she would alter as best as she could to augment my Sunday wear.

My grandfather also provided me with clothes from material he bought from a traveling salesman.

When I was unable to attend church functions, I would climb on the ackee tree which was located in the yard and hang over it so that I could get a clear view of the proceeding taking place at the church.

Even at that young age of my life the church meant a great deal to me. I would often play church by making an enclosure constructed of coconut log and banana limbs. There I would sing and danced while beating my tambourine, all to the 'Glory of God.' During my infantile enactment of the church service preaching and playing my tambourine, passersby would often shout at me. "Mad gal, shut up you damn mouth, you nothing but an idiot."

Even members of the church would ridicule me, saying. "You don't know what you're saying, shut up your mouth fool." Anyhow I was oblivious to their taunts, and kept my service with even greater fervor.

Although I was treated less than friendly by the other members of the church, I continued to attend. Also partly because there was no other church in the community I wanted to attend.

I started taking a more active part in the church, getting involved in several activities. I even started attending baptismal classes. When the time came for me to be baptized, this was one of the most memorable days of my Christian life. The baptismal party had to march in a pious procession to the river, which was about three miles away, to be baptized. My willing involvement in the church activities was noticed by the deacon, who suggested that I should be appointed a Sunday school teacher.

This suggestion was vehemently opposed by a female church member, who was one of my grandfather's 'detractors', and who had some influence in the church. This incident brought home to me the feeling of inadequacy which I always felt. At this juncture I made a decision to withdraw from some activities and to avoid some church members. Nevertheless, I still tried to be a 'good Christian'.

At this time I lived with my mother, and now had the persona of a practicing Christian. This parental overshadowing was required by the church, as I was still a minor. Mass Larry was still living at the house, but I tried to avoid him as much as I possibly could.

At this point he did not make any attempt to interact with me, only with my mother. On the surface he appeared to be a very demure person, almost so 'pious' in manner. He did not socialize very much, and with the exception of my mother, always had a taciturn approach to other people. But for my part, when I remember how monstrous he was to me, I remained very leery of him.

My fears were not misplaced as I was soon to have another traumatic encounter with him. One evening, I went to the side of the house, with a tub of water to take a bath, as there was no bathroom. I did not realize that Mass Larry, being the voyeur he was, had been watching me. I became shockingly aware of this when he grabbed me and covered my mouth with one of his hands. He then dragged me into the toilet and with my mouth still gagged, and said, "So this is where you have been hiding." He kept my mouth gagged and sexually assaulted me.

Another evening, I was in the toilet, just as I had just finished defecating, he surprisingly burst into the toilet and demanded that I clean up right away. This I had to do in full view of his unsympathetic stare. I was hoping that somehow this would distract him. I tried to escape but he kicked me against the toilet wall. I again threatened him to tell my grandfather. He said that if I let my grandfather take him to court, he would 'mash me up with obeah.' This threat always scared me. After this he closed the toilet lid and dragged me onto it and proceeded to rape me in the most vicious manner. When the ordeal was over, I was bleeding profusely and had difficulty getting up to walk. The back fence of the house where my mother lived that she rented from Miss Dawkin, being the dividing line between my grandfather's properties. I quickly used the fence for easy access to get to my grandfather's house immediately.

I went into the bushes of my grandfather's property and employed the dried leaves of the banana tree for hygiene and sanitary purposes. In the wake of the trauma I experienced pain for several days. Telling my mother about what transpired would not have served any purpose; because she did not display any interest in my welfare. She would probably get angry at me anyway.

My grandmother was not around at this time to give me any support, as she was still at Mount Ridge visiting her daughter. Being coldly rejected by my mother and the constant molestation by Mass Larry and not seeming to have anywhere to turn, I decided to run away.

I became very tired and disgust about my situation and wanted to get away, but this situation requires money. There was no one for me to ask for assistance. The thought came to me to ask Mass Larry. I was actually thinking of how I could use my position as a battered child to' extort' some money from my 'molester, without giving him a reason. I asked him to give me one pound. He flatly refused to give me, saying that I was a child and I did not know how to spend money.

This was another hurt perpetrated on me by this man. I was very disappointed and decided that this time he would have to 'pay the piper' even if I had to employ surreptitious methods.

From a vantage on the verandah, I could see through the window and into his room.

One day, after making a discrete observation of his movements, I saw him place some money on his table. Shortly after, he went out of his room and left the yard. I hurriedly entered his room and counted the money on the table. It was exactly three pounds. That money remained there for a couple days. One day, I sneaked and took the money and ran all the way through the bushes to my grandfather's house.

Later that day, my grandfather sent me to the Post Office, which was some distance away. On returning, I saw my grandfather and Mass Larry having a dialogue with a police constable. I overheard the policeman telling my grandfather that he had a warrant for my arrest for stealing Mass Larry's money.

To this point, my grandfather knew nothing of me being molested. Now, faced with the prospect of going to jail, I lost all fear, and was no longer afraid of Mass Larry's threat, so I decided to expose him for what he was. Then and there I made everything known to my grandfather about Mass Larry's attacks. I even recounted to my grandfather about the time when I was unable to walk properly, that it was because I had been molested by him. After hearing my story, my grandfather was livid with rage, grabbed his cutlass and turned on Mass Larry. Mass Larry made good his escape and was not seen for a long time.

My grandfather tried to settle the matter with the police. To avoid me being arrested, he offered to repay the money, but the police officer said it had already been reported to the station at Fountain, so there was nothing he could do about it, as it was out of his hands. This incident where Mass Larry called the police marked the ending of my traumas that I experienced at his hands. This would also set the stage for a new chapter in my life, one which brought new events and circumstances that were much beyond my control, and which I was totally unprepared for.

CHAPTER FIFTEEN

Life in the Children's Home

After the incident which took place with my abuser, my grandfather became very perturbed, and discussed that his only revenge was to put an end to Mass Larry life. My grandfather went to Fountain Police Station and was informed by an officer who encouraged him to address the problem to a probation officer who would be able to help me. A few weeks went by; my grandfather and my mother were visited by a probation officer. She was very nice to me and listened keenly as I relayed the traumatic experiences in my life to her. She told me that we will have to go before a judge, who would decide what would be best for me. I was happy to hear that, although I had no idea what it entailed. It just seemed at the time that it might offer me a long awaited opportunity to get away from my abusive and indigent life at Windsor.

In the courtroom, I again recounted the experiences of my life to the judge. My mother, father and grandfather were present. The judge sent me outside while he made his decision. Soon after the probation officer came and told me that I would be sent to a Children's Home.

In my ignorance, this was such great news for me, because I felt that I was now leaving my miserable childhood behind.

On arriving at the Children's Home, I was surprised to see that there were many other girls living at the home. I had actually thought that I was being sent to live in a family setting. Nevertheless, as I settled in; I realized that life there was not bad and the treatment was good. We had to conform to the strict rules of the home, which includes, participating in prayers both mornings and nights. There was always enough food to eat. Everyone was treated equally and so I felt comfortable, which caused me to get involved with the activities there. Unknown to me, my hard work and dedication were observed by my superiors.

My dedication and participation was foremost in the communal prayers which we had.

Miss Doris was one of my teachers. She was a fervent Christian and was always the person who conducted prayers. As a result, because of this, I was very drawn to her. One Sunday morning, during prayers, I had an encounter with the power of the 'Holy Spirit.'

It seems that my frame of reference touched the 'Divine realm,' and no longer was I aware of my earthly existence.

Miss Doris was the only teacher there who was astutely guided by the spirit, and recognized what was happening to me. She helped me by 'praying me through' my experience. In the wake of this 'heavenly encounter', Miss Doris lovingly guided me through my Christian walk.

To this day I remember those times as the halcyon days of my Christian life. In the following weeks and months, my interaction with the other students brought me to a more mundane way of thinking.

The girls at the children home sometimes were very freckled in their friendship towards each other. At times, and for no apparent reason, allegiances among the girls would change; resulting in angry feuds.

One morning in particular, just before breakfast I was in the yard. I saw Lorna busily pounding a substance which gave off a grinding sound. That morning at breakfast, it was my turn to assist with placing the breakfast on the table. Lorna handed me two cups of chocolate tea, and gave me specific instructions as to who should receive those cups.

Later that day, the two girls who had received the cups of tea, fell ill.

It was later discovered at the hospital that they had ingested pulverized glass. Immediately suspicion was cast in my direction. In my defense, I made it known how I was innocently implicated.

It was later brought to the light of day that Lorna was the culprit. She was in the throes of a feud with the two girls, and this was her way of venting her anger.

I later received an apology from the supervisors in charge of the children's home.

After living there over a period of time, one night I overheard some of the girls in the dorm planning to run away. They persuaded me and I became part of the scheme, that night we all ran away. I went with one of the girls to her parents' home and the following day I found my way back to Windsor.

At first my mother was not aware that I had run away from the children home. My grandfather had a cousin named Mrs. Peters. She was very fond of me, and I used to visit her regularly. It was on one of my visits to Mrs. Peters that I realized my mother learned of my arrival and where I was.

While I was inside Mrs. Peter's house, I heard my mother yelling from outside at me the road in front of Mrs. Peters house. "Get out of Mrs. Peter's house and come go back to the Children's Home." Feeling ashamed; I scampered out the back way and ran through the bushes and went home to my grandfather.

My grandfather was very furious when he heard and had 'strong words' with my mother about her behavior. He told my mother that he would see that I returned to the home, and that she should stay out of it as her interference was not welcome. My grandfather told my mother it was her carelessness why I experience these many problems in my life.

My mother started crying and said, "What you want me to do now, after the father mashes up my life." My mother then walked away. The following day, I put my things together and my grandfather took me to the police station in Bay.

He waited patiently until I was processed by the police and was ready to be taken back to the home. Because of the long processing, my grandfather was forced to take the late bus home.

When the police took me back to the Children's Home, all the children were happy to see me. Everyone questioned me about the other girls, wanting to know where they had gone. I was even interrogated by the superiors. It was then I learned that my untimely departure had forfeited a pending decision to place me with a regular family. I was so disappointed to hear about this. After this incident I endeavored to conduct myself in a way that would attract the approval of my superiors. But that plan was cancelled.

A few months after my return to the Children Home, I was transferred to another Children's Home. The rules at this new home were even more rigid than at the first Children's Home.

Individual privacy was at a minimum, and information about one's action always reaches the ears of those in charge. Recreation was a very ordered affair, as were the other pursuits of the school. My participation in school activities was in the area of home economics, arts and crafts, and music, along with my academic subjects. I particularly excel in singing and was singled out as one of the school soloists. I even sang the signature song 'The Sound of Music' at a pageant attended by the public.

I was approximately seventeen years old and was privileged like the other girls, to visit our families when the school holidays came around.

For me, Mia who lived at Ferry was the only family member who was qualified and accepted me. The reception I now received from Mia's children was less sociable. They would look askance at me and whisper behind my back. They left nothing to the imagination. I was stigmatized because I was attending a juvenile home. When I complained to Mia about her children's behavior, she did nothing and soon made it apparent that it would be best for me to return to the home.

Condition worsened to the stage where I was not being fed.

Mia's family reared pigs, and sometimes to satisfy my hunger I had to steal food from the pig's troughs and hide in the bushes to eat it. My position in the home caused me to be in a state of melancholy.

One day, the family had gone to church and I was alone at home. I took a walk down the road until I came to a big tree. There was a young man by the name of Ray sitting alone. We started talking, and over time we became friends to the point that he invited me to his parent's home. His parents often offered me food which was very welcome as my cousin Mia had stopped feeding me.

On another occasion I was walking down the road late one evening and saw Ray. We were now friends, so I greeted him warmly. Surprisingly, his greeting was not at all pleasant; in fact he appeared hostile towards me. Unexpectedly, he grabbed me by the hand and pulled me into the bushes. He shouted at me, telling me, "I was nothing but a reformatory school gal, and I should come and let him give me a 'dam beating."

He commenced beating me all over, especially in my mouth whenever I tried to scream. The area was bushy and no one was around, so my intermittent cries went unheard. Ray then raped me in the most violent manner. When he was finished, I felt as if I had been physically tortured. I could hardly walk. Physical pain and shame consumed me, and I tried to hide myself from anyone seeing me coming out of the bushes, and on the way back to Mia's house.

I quickly stopped by the standpipe on the way before I reached home and used the running water as a soothing agent for my female genitals. I was happy to see that the family had not returned home when I got there. I was so consumed with shame that then and there I immediately decided to go back to the Children's Home.

I already had my fare in hand, so I packed my things to leave the following morning.

That sleepless night under the cover of darkness, I watched and waited like a sentinel for the first cock crow which was usually about four o'clock in the morning. When I heard nature's reveille, I got myself dressed and made a hasty rush to catch the first bus that would be going to Town.

Removing myself from the area where my perpetrator was, and where the unsympathetic eyes were, was not the end of my woes.

Before the summer came I was told by the head sister that after returning from my holiday visit with my cousin I would be sent to the School of Music for training. That summer at Ferry I had such an unfortunate experience. When I returned to the Children's Home I relayed to the head sister about the terrible ordeal that had transpired with Ray. They seemed sympathetic at first. To my dismay, their attitude towards me was anything but considerate, and I was treated as an object of tacit derision.

That night, as usual I was sent to the dorm with the other girls. The following day, after morning prayers, when the other girls were dismissed, I was held back by the caretaker of the dorm and sent to a room where I sat and waited for a long time, not knowing or understanding what would transpire.

To my bewilderment, the head sister came and started rebuking me about my 'unclean' state and accused me of lascivious behavior. Being a child I was dumbfounded. I could not believe that my mentor had become so hostile towards me.

The head sisters then removed my clothing violently, and gave orders that I should be placed in a crocus bag instead, and remain domiciled by myself in the room. That night and accompanying nights, I was forced to sleep in the crocus bag on the floor. The following morning, I was sent to kneel on the verandah until nightfall.

This 'in-house' incarceration continued for approximately a week. During this time, as punishment, I underwent long bouts of prolonged kneeling. If I was caught not kneeling, my punishment would become more drastic. The modicum of food which I did receive was given in the manner of feeding a household pet. A small bowl along with a cup of water was given to me; this was the treatment that was meted out to me. The proposed plan to send me to the School of Music did not come to fruition. I was deeply hurt.

My involvement in sports was not extensive, and it was limited to my participation in softball.

The most profound aspect of my tenure at the Children's Home was my spiritual life. This meant a lot to me since I was a very young girl. Because of my obviously tractable nature, I was chosen by the sisters at the home to perform certain chores at the convent.

Once, while attending to my chores, I went into one of the rooms in an attempt to take out the garbage. I did not knock before entering. Two sisters became shockingly aware of my unheralded entry. Flushed with embarrassment; I made a hasty departure. Since that day, for whatever reason, the two sisters in question were extraordinarily kind to me and always indicated by their facial expressions that they appreciated my 'silence.'

One of the sisters I did personal chores for was Sister Rose. She was very fond of me. One day, I was summoned by her to the convent. When I arrived, she had a treat waiting for me. The night before, a banquet was held at the convent and she had saved cakes and other 'delicacies' for me to take back to the home. She however entreated me to eat as much as I wanted before returning. Needless to say, I gorged so much that I had such difficulty handling the broom, and was hardly able to do my chores.

My sense of alertness was brought to the fore, when on that same day, while I was cleaning the hallway; I heard a salacious groaning coming from one of the bedrooms. I peeped in and saw two of the nuns in a 'sexual' position. Shocked and embarrassed, I walked away without being seen. My most incredible experience though, was the day I was doing my duties and heard Father Barclay talking softly coming from one of the sister's rooms. This at first struck me as being odd, that a male voice would be coming from a sister's room. The door was ajar, and curiosity got the better of me. My questioning mind made me privy to Father Barclay and Sister Sari in what appeared to be a mutually passionate close encounter. These experiences served to lower the high esteem in which I had held the sisters and ultimately dissuaded me from pursuing a lifelong vocation in the convent, a 'career' I had often given serious thought.

After a while, I became one of the senior girls at the Children's Home. With this came the privilege of not having to share the dorm with the other girls, I was placed in a room on the first floor with the senior girls. There I had some semblance of freedom and could command a little more privacy. As a senior, the home also assisted me to get employment as they did the other girls. I was now gainfully employed at a Pharmacy; and the money I earned from that gave me much more independence.

The time finally came for me to 'part Company' with the Children's Home. That was one of the saddest days in my life. The experience and the friends and acquaintances there I made, which helped me to grow from a shy child to an assertive and confident young woman.

All the teaching that had contributed to building my character, and most of all the mentoring which had come to mean so much to me, which had helped to strengthen me, was all now coming to an end. I was leaving all the friends and acquaintances I made behind.

My heart seemed to sink in despair. As I stood at the top of the steps of the building, with my suitcases and box in hand, knowing that my ascents of these steps were at an end, I started to cry. My departing steps were made with my face turned towards the building. I felt as if I was leaving a part of me there and could not turn my back on it.

It was so hard for me to turn my back and walk away. I sat on the chapel steps and cried uncontrollably.

Before me was laid the decadent and impoverished lifestyle of Windsor, and the pain and discomfort I was going to face again. After crying, what seemed like a deluge of tears and sitting for an undetermined length of time on the chapel steps, I went to Storey Road and board a bus that was bound for Phillip Street. There I boarded the bus which took me home to my grandparents at Windsor.

CHAPTER SIXTEEN

Return to Windsor

Resettling at Windsor with my grandparents was anything but easy. As an eighteen year old young woman, I discovered that my many 'detractors' made no attempt to be subtle with their disparaging remarks towards me. They called me names like 'prison bird' and 'reformatory gal' were open salutations that were regularly used to my face. And that was just the tip of the iceberg. Behind my back, I could imagine my name providing fodder for the most pejorative forms of village gossip.

It was sometimes so hard and painful to go out and face the public. 'It was so bad.' I even contemplated committing suicide. My feelings of frustration and desperation and melancholy caused me once to pen a suicide note which I posted to my family. It must have been my spiritual strength that I changed this course of action why I am alive today during these low points.

Because my grandfather was a war veteran, he was eventually given housing assistance as one of his benefits. This new house gave my grandfather a renewed sense of independence. Unfortunately, his treatment towards my grandmother was still very bad. He saw the new house as an allocation of his own 'sacred space,' and he boastfully told my grandmother as he vacated the old house, "See your dam house here, and keep your damn self away from my new house."

My grandmother was very displeased about the derogatory manner which my grandfather addresses her; but nevertheless, grandmother and I remained living in the old wooden house.

As a young woman, I was always told how attractive I was. But despite this, my relationships with the opposite sex always came to an untimely end. My frustration and bouts of deep thoughts brought to my memory Mr. Porter, who was a dear friend of my grandfather. He had always endeared himself to my family. I made enquiries about him and found out that after all that time while I was in the Children's Home he was still living at the same house in Windsor. When I went to visit him, he was so happy to see me. He was so caring that in the course of our conversation I poured my heart out to him. He told me that all the trouble I was having with the people in Windsor, primarily stemmed from the longstanding and ongoing battles my grandfather had with the church and many parishioners over real estate and religion.

As a result, I was always vicariously vilified by the people around. My stay at the Children's Home just increased fuel to the fire of their vituperative insults towards me.

Mr. Porter said he had on several occasions been privy to gossip that was being circulated about me. Needless to say, he was however very reserved about giving me information as he did not want to be identified as the bearer of gossip. He told me that my 'prospect was blighted' by the fact that Miss Kitty had put 'Obeah' on me since I was a child. He said for all these years, this had cast a shadow over my life like a 'dark curtain'. Nevertheless, he told me I should not despair, as in time I would be a source of help and inspiration to the people that now hated me.

Mr. Porter was a tailor by profession. During our discussion, he was hard at work so I pitched in and assisted him. He was pleased with what I had done and paid me for helping him. He suggested that when I was not busy I could come and help him and he would pay me. I gladly accepted the offer, and so secured a well needed source of income for myself.

Mr. Porter even allowed me the opportunity to make my own clothes on his machine. I could then augment my wardrobe.

I was now in a position, and also felt more confident about my appearance when going out in the public.

In the course of events I met a young man named Neville. He was very attractive and I think we both liked each other from the initial stage of our meeting. Being friends for a while, we entered into a loving relationship. After a period of time, it was obvious that Neville's interest started to wane, and he became few and far between.

Not knowing how to contact him and feeling frustrated and hurt by his rejection, I went to his place of employment to visit him.

When he saw me, he deliberately ignored my presence. I was overcome with consternation. My tears came down in an uncontrollable manner, and I was oblivious of where I was. It was only then that he gave me a modicum of attention. I inquired of him as to the justification for his behavior towards me. He told me that a lady had informed him about my past and as far as he had heard, my character did not meet with his ideals of a lifetime partner. He said he was dissatisfied with my life at the Children's Home and that it would only cause him embarrassment if he associated with someone of such a questionable character.

I responded by telling l him that these things were in my past as a child, and he should not use that to judge me now. I also explained that I did not have a loving and responsible parental guidance, and this was the reason I took the wrong path as a child. He appeared somewhat sympathetic to my 'dysfunctional' childhood, but stated I was a beautiful girl who he would want to take places with, but he did not want this to result in embarrassment to him.

I was so distraught over his response that I left crying without trying to defend myself anymore. I went to the bus stop and took the bus back to my grandfather's house.

When I arrived, my grandfather was sitting on the verandah. He immediately recognized my state of melancholy and asked me what the problem was. I told him Neville had said he had been informed about my wayward past from someone in the community and could not in all conscience have any further association with me.

My grandfather was very upset but tried to console me by saying that, "A person with many years to his credit, he had been a living evidence as to the reward of the wicked." He encouraged me to be optimistic about my future, and not be 'put off' by this singular incident, as, "One swallow does not make a summer." In spite of his encouraging words, I was feeling so frustrated and wanted to leave Windsor there and then.

Just about this time I met and befriended Howie a policeman who was stationed at Fountain Police Station. As time passed, and our friendship grew, we became intimate. Over time our meeting became irregular, and I lost contact with him, and never saw him again.

There was a dress-maker named Miss Teri and her children who were living in a house across the street from my grandfather. In time I established a good rapport with the family, I even assisted Teri with her work for which I was financially rewarded.

My interaction with this family soon became the most pleasant aspect of my life at Windsor. Unfortunately, in time Miss Teri soon migrated to England and my life was once again beset with boredom, loneliness and frustration.

My grandfather's cousin Miss Florence became the new occupant of the house across the street. As time passed, to my amazement I was surprised to discover that my grandfather and Florence had struck up a clandestine affair. I observed him on a few occasions, late at night, route to her house. After a few years, Miss Florence subsequently migrated to Canada and the house was left vacant again.

A few weeks passed, the Greens family became the new occupants of the house. Mr. and Mrs. Green soon became my good friends. My visit to their home was so frequent that it became my second home.

My presence at their dinner was a normal occurrence, almost as frequent. Mrs. Green's had a sister named Avery, she and I became especially close. We established ourselves as a team of two; going places together and being a complement to each other. One day, she asked if I would accompany her to visit some friends in Bamboo Pen, which was a town some distance away from Windsor. I accepted her offer with alacrity, because to me at that time it was an opportunity to get away from Windsor; be it only for a short time. It was expected that we would return on the same day. But when Avery got there she decided to stay longer.

I was very upset I did not agree with the new arrangement, so I decided to return home alone. She however convinced me that it was already too late, and that I would miss the bus, so I should spend the night and return the following morning.

I was 'put out' by Avery's suggestion of staying the night, but conceded that it was getting late, and the bus stop was a long distance away.

I became concerned about where we would spend the night. Avery assured me that I would be staying anywhere she stayed.

That evening at the house where we stayed, I noticed her enter a room, and closed the door behind her, then emerging about two hours later. During this time, I was sitting under a mango tree in the yard.

It was long past dinner time and my hunger forced me to inquire of Avery, as to what and where we would eat. She told me that her friend who lived down the road was cooking and had invited us over. I accompanied her to her friend's house. I was surprised, when we got there and entered the friends' kitchen, to see five young men sitting under a tree in the yard. They greeted me as if they had been expecting me. It became obvious to me, and I realized that Avery had made plans and announced that I was coming with her. One of the young men confirmed my conclusion by saying, "Boy, sister, you are so nice looking." and added that Avery had said good things about me. Needless to say, I did not welcome the voyeuristic gaze of those testosterone 'Driven Male.'

I was not at all happy about the comments they were making. I discreetly asked Avery the whereabouts of her friend, since I did not see any females around. She pointed to the young man cooking in the kitchen, and said that he was the friend to which she had referred. After the initial introduction, we all sat and got more acquainted. Willie, who was her friend, finished cooking and treated us to a sumptuous meal.

Later that night, Avery and I returned to the house where we were staying. Just before going to bed, Avery told me that her friend Willie would be coming over, so the both of them would sleep together in one of the rooms. She then directed me to another small, dimly lit room where she said I would spend the night. I had no knowledge of the place and the people there. I felt a sense of uneasiness about her surreptitious last minute arrangements, especially since I had not planned to stay over-night.

As my options were very few, I retired for the night.

During the course of the night, I became aware that someone else was occupying the bed with me. I asked who it was. My nocturnal intruder, as I later found out because he told me that his name was Ed, one of the young men I had seen at Avery's friend's house. In the darkness he started groping my body. Quite a struggle ensued between us. My resistance to his onslaught only seemed to excite and energize him with more fervor. As I weakened, his insistence afforded him the upper hand, and he tore away my undergarment saying, "I heard about you a long time, and since you arrived I have been waiting to get you." In my state of weakness and frustration he achieved his goal and apparently gratified of his lecherous desire by molesting me. Because when he was finished ravishing my body, he remarked with a sense of accomplishment, "Me get you gal."

After he left the room, I lay there in frustration, and mental anguish thinking about what had transpired, wondering how I had gotten into that situation. I felt angry.

The following morning, I directed my hurt and anger at Avery, as it now became clear to me that the entire proceedings of the preceding day were part of the result of Avery's plan.

My shield of modesty was shattered when Ed my rapist had no qualms about embarrassing me and said loudly in the yard that, "He knew he was going to get some of a nice and pretty woman last night." Everyone knew he was speaking about me. This made me cringe with a sense of shame; I didn't even try to explain.

That morning, when Avery and I were leaving for the bus stop, Ed, unwelcome as he was, came along with us. I was very uncomfortable to be in his company.

It was a long journey on foot to the bus-stop. I made sure that I distanced myself from Avery and Ed by walking briskly, and even running at times, just to get away from their company.

When the bus arrived, Ed boarded with us. He annoyed me with his frivolous conversation, trying to get my attention, I ignored him, but that did not seem to get the message across to him. He behaves as if we were friends for a long time. Changing my seat was useless. Finally, in frustration, I pointing to him, and shouted, "That man raped me last night, and that somebody please call the police." Shocked at my outburst, and because people were staring, he immediately went to the back of the bus.

For the rest of the journey I was unencumbered by his presence. When the bus arrived at Bay, I disembarked and left Ed and Avery behind. I then returned to my grandfather's house at Windsor. I was feeling very displeased and angry with Avery that I did not speak to her for a long time.

After the unfortunate experience in Bamboo Pen, I tried to eradicate the incident from my mind, but in reality it resurfaced and hit me hard when I discovered that I was really pregnant. I was almost nineteen years old and was going to have my first child; so I was hoping that Howie was the cause of my pregnancy, and not Ed my rapist.

Because of the shameful circumstances surrounding my pregnancy, I did not want to stay in Windsor. Fearful about the experience of my pregnancy, I had a strong desire to find my mother. Even if she did not want to see me, I felt that I really needed her.

CHAPTER SEVENTEEN

Searching for My Mother

Bay is a large town located near Wildwood. Because of the popularity of the town, people came from different places to reside there. It became famous because of the revolt of 1865 by a famous hero who was also related to my grandparents. A statue was erected in his honor in the square at Bay. And also a monument erected in honor of the soldiers who fought and died in World War 1.

There is also a big market in the Bay, and on Fridays and Saturdays people come from far and near to buy and sell meat, fruits, and vegetables. I was almost nineteen when I heard that my mother was living in the Bay. Although the relationship between us had not been a good one, up to this point, I still endeavor on finding her with a view to improving our relationship.

My knowledge of her whereabouts was very sketchy. Due to extensive inquiries I was told that she was living somewhere on Mountain Road. After a few weeks passed I took the bus from Windsor to Bay. On the way, I questioned the driver and passengers hoping that they might have some knowledge of my mother's whereabouts.

The driver was very friendly and helpful. Not only did he tell me where to disembark, but also advised the conductor that I should not be charged because of my state of destitution.

As the bus approached Bay, the driver signaled to me to be in a state of readiness, because we were soon approaching Mountain Road where I would disembark.

While walking along Mountain Road, I constantly asked by-standers if they knew my mother, but without success. I soon came upon a shop and went inside. I saw a fair complexioned man who appeared very friendly. After he heard my inquiry, he looked at me and smiled. His response was, "And both of them really resemble each other." He gave me direction to my mother's house, for this I was very thankful for his help.

On arriving at my mother's house, I met her with two pots in her hands coming from the kitchen. I said to her, "Good evening Mama," but she responded angrily asking me, "How the hell I had found her, and what I was doing there." My response was, "You are my mother and that is why I come here." She looked at me disgustingly and walked away, leaving me standing by the kitchen and went upstairs to her room. I followed her and pounded on her room door for a modicum of motherly attention.

She shouted at me angrily, asking, "What the hell I wanted from her." At this point, I was overcome with feelings of loneliness and rejection from my own mother and broke down with uncontrollable crying.

Fearing that my crying might alert the neighbors, she immediately opened the door and told me to come inside because she did not want me to make noise, and bring down any crowd on her.

She expressed how my unexpected appearance was unwelcome. My mother made it clear that my presence made her very uncomfortable, and was a condition she was not forced to endure, as it brought her a degree of unhappiness and sad memories about the life between her and my father. She looked at me and asked if I was pregnant and I told her yes. She asked where the baby's father lived. Trying to avoid any further conversation, and not wanting to relay to her the circumstances that led to my pregnancy; I told her he was a policeman, and I heard that he lived in Bay. My mother went on to say that she did not know why I had come back into her life because having me had destroyed her life and caused her nothing but grief.

I explained to her that I had nowhere to go and that although she did not like me, she was still my mother and that will never change. Her behavior was indicative of the fact that she did not welcome the relationship between us. She insisted that she did not want to have me around her. I was determined to stay although she displayed such rejection towards me.

The room she occupied was very small, and sleeping conditions were not adequate, I was forced to sleep on the floor.

Despite the cramped conditions, I was quite prepared to accommodate the circumstances with a view to ameliorating the relationship between my mother and myself.

It was now morning. She got immediately out of bed and went to make breakfast with a disgruntled look on her face.

My mother was employed as a teacher at an infant center. When she went to work in the days, I would wash her clothes, and cook for her. She ate whatever I prepared but had no verbal communication with me. To my surprise, after a few weeks, one morning she got up and said, "Good morning." Nevertheless, her stoic and indifferent attitude towards me never changed. She demonstrated an air of secrecy whenever she had to communicate with anyone in my presence.

After living with her for a while, she introduced me to a lady by the name of Tiny who she told me was related to us. Tiny lived on the front side of the same house. As time passed she was very kind to me, and soon we became friends. I could always depend on her for meals and other forms of assistance. She had a great sense of humor and would entertain me with many jokes.

We became fond of each other's company. In the evenings, we would walk to the town of Bay to meet friends and hang out together.

As time passed my mother spoke about some family members who lived not very far from the town Bay. Soon I started visiting them. One day I overheard my mother talking to her niece about a man who was a preacher with whom she was having a clandestine relationship. News later reached my ears that the preacher whose name I cannot recall was my brother Joe guardian. Because the last time I saw him he was a baby I wanted to visit with my mother to see him. Each time I asked her to take me with her she always had an excuse. I inquired about the preacher where about, and someone gave me direction. I took it upon myself to see my brother. When I got there I was greeted by the preacher. He asked me who I was. I told him that I came to see my brother Joe. The preacher asked me if my mother knew I was coming there, I told him no. He told me that she is not going to feel very happy to know I visited his home. He called my brother to the front where I could see him. I was very glad to see him, but he was shabbily dressed. I spoke for a short while, then, I hurried away.

One evening while I was in the kitchen, my mother accosted me about my visit to the preacher home. She spoke to me in the most derogatory manner, and told me to get out of her 'dam blasted' business. I was so hurt, and broke down crying.

Every Friday, my mother went to Locket to visit Mr. Wright who she said was related to her, and would return on Sunday evening or Monday morning, bringing with her much needed provisions to replenish the home for the coming week.

Our landlord was a lady by the name of Miss Biggs. She also lived in the same house with her mother and two daughters. Miss Biggs was a nurse who was employed as a receptionist in a doctor's office. She would display a sense of indifference towards me, and whenever I tried to communicate with her she rarely spoke to me. Unlike her mother was very friendly towards me. Miss Biggs did not approve of her mother fraternizing with anyone, and especially me. She would flog her mother if she was caught speaking to me. As a consequence of the landlord's behavior, and attitude towards her, myself, and her mother, I respectfully kept my distance, and had little or no dialogue with her mother.

During my pregnancy I tried to contact Howie at the police station in Bay, but was unsuccessful. Not very long after I met and made friends with a neighbor named Miss Lin who was employed at the police station in Bay. I asked her if she knew Howie, and she told me yes. I sent a letter with Miss Lin to give to Howie; few passed and I got a visit from Howie. After several visits, a few weeks passed and I never heard anything from Howie again. I contacted Miss Lin and asked her if she had seen, or spoken to Howie. Miss Lin told me that Howie told her the reason for him not seeing me anymore. During his last visit to see me my mother accosted him on Mountain Road, and told him he should not return, because he was not the responsible person for my pregnancy. I became so sad, and disappointed, and broke down into uncontrollable tears, realizing that my mother was still the nemesis in my life.

It was fast approaching the time for me to give birth to my first child, so my mother contacted the midwife who came to the house and gave me a physical examination to satisfy herself as to my state of health.

One day, while I was busy in the kitchen, surprisingly, my mother appeared at the door with Ed at her side. She presented him to me with a knowing look of satisfaction, as if she had solved the 'enigma' surrounding my pregnancy. I became very angry remembering that I was raped by him. He and my mother sat in the kitchen and spoke for a while. But I tried my best to ignore their conversation.

At this point I was closer to having my baby.

One evening, my cousin Tiny made dinner. The menu consisted of salt mackerel and dumplings. I was given seven dumplings at my request, salt mackerel and a large can of lemonade. As cornmeal dumpling formed one of my favorite foods, I engorged myself.

After enjoying my meal, I felt a great deal of discomfort which forced me to lie on a bench in the kitchen until I felt some bodily ease, after which I went to bed. At approximately four o'clock am the next morning I was awakened by excruciating abdominal pains. I tried lying down and endure the pains but they became almost unbearable. Feeling scared, I awakened my mother and told her. She appeared more confused than anything else.

Unable to figure out what to do, she woke up my cousin Tiny, who immediately realized that I was experiencing labor pains. She thought 'labor' might have been induced by the many dumplings that I had eaten for dinner the night before.

Tiny seeing I was scared, did her best to cheer me up.

It was soon daylight and the pain continued in all its fury. I screamed uncontrollably but that of course did not help the situation. My mother suggested that walking around the room might quicken the baby's delivery. This suggestion made no sense to me, but I was willing to try anything to alleviate the pain. My mother went to call the midwife who lived about twenty minutes away on foot.

When the midwife came, she asked my mother for some hot water, which she had already prepared. She gave the midwife a white enamel basin with hot water and a clean rag. The midwife kept sapping my tummy with the hot rag. After she continued for some time, I told her that I felt something moving in my tummy. The midwife told me it was the baby. The pain kept getting worse, but the midwife assured me that I would be giving birth soon.

With her physical assistance, I finally gave birth to a healthy girl who I named Lilly. My faithful cousin Tiny was there to comfort and console me through the experience. My mother on the other hand, was too frustrated and unsettled to assist.

The weeks after my delivery seemed to pass very quickly, and my child was increasing in size and demanding attention. This disposed of a special problem for me. I was in need of financial assistance for the baby and myself.

Just about this time my condition worsened, because mother had moved away to live in Locket, and my cousin had moved to live in Cityville. This denied me of any assistance I was receiving for the baby. I now had no one to help me. This displaced me in a dilemma where having no money to employ a baby-sitter, so I had to find someone in order to seek employment.

With my present situation, my options seemed few; but then I remembered that Ed had once taken me to visit his parents who lived at Bamboo Pen. Although I hated him for raping me, and did not like the area, I realized that this was my 'saving grace'. I decided now that I had to ask these people I hardly knew, to get involved in their granddaughter's life, so that I would have time to be gainfully employed.

Bamboo Pen was situated at a very far distance from any civilized township. It was nested far in the hinterland, and boasted few if any modern amenities in Wildwood. When I arrived there after a long arduous journey, my child's grandparents greeted me very warmly. As luck would have it, my arrival coincided with dinner. This for me could not have been timelier as I was very famished.

To my surprise, Ed's family welcome and treatment felt warm and genuine.

After my initial meeting with the family, I was made to feel at ease. My child grandmother, in particular, was most congenial and seemed willing to help, so I never hesitated to ask her to baby-sit for me which would allow me to seek a job, for a while, until I could get myself back on a better financial condition. She promptly agreed on the spot, and this put my mind at rest, but after a few days passed, the decision seemed to be weighing heavily on her, and I feared that she would renege on the agreement. This change of plans was not keeping with my agenda.

One morning while everyone was home, I got my things packed and told the family they had to honor their position, as it was Hobson's choice. Then without any further ado, I left and went back to Bay.

After being at Bay for some time, my condition was still the same so I decided to make friends with people in the community and told them about my situation and that I was seeking their assistance. One day I heard a knock at the door. Being alone and fearful I asked the person to approach the window. To my luck, it was a man who was not known to me, but bore good news.

Sometime ago before my mother had promised to speak to someone on my behalf with a view to securing employment for me. This man bore a message from Mr. Gus a shoemaker who was the husband of my mother's lodge sister. Mr. Gus was requesting that I report to his shop the following day.

My elation was boundless, and although I had made inquiries on my own. As the hog says, 'the first water he gets he washes.' With my level of expectancy, I could hardly sleep that night.

The following morning, I reported to Mr. Gus's business place. He was a prominent shoe-maker in the community, who also worked for the local police and the fire brigade departments.

When I arrived, he was already hard at work. I said, "Good morning Mr. Gus, he said, good morning." He then asked me if I knew how to repair shoes, I said, "No, Mr. Gus." He said, 'Well, you will learn now.' After our introduction, Mr. Gus told me that my salary would be a paltry of fifteen shillings per week with a promise of an increase as I became more skilled. That did not really meet my approval, but I was determined to prove to Mr. Gus that I could make a success of the job. I became more proficient as the weeks went by and I was just as good as the other workers in the shop.

My salary soon increased to three pounds per week. That was still not enough for me because there were times when I had to be a kleptomaniac in order to augment my salary.

One day, a lady came into the store as a customer. She seemed quite cordial and we had an interesting conversation. Her name was Ebony. Over time, we became friends to the point that we became inseparable, and would even dress alike. Because of my association with her my scope of friends became very wide, which brought changes to my life generally.

CHAPTER EIGHTEEN

The Betrayal

My friend Ebony was very popular in the Bay and also participated at different places, and parties. There was an upcoming police party on her schedule, and she invited me to come along with her.

At the party, I made acquaintance with a tall dark and handsome police officer, I was immediately smitten with his charming personality. I asked Ebony if she knew anything about him. She said his name was Karl.

By some stroke of luck the stranger wended his way through the crowd and ended up in the company of my girlfriend and myself. During the course of the evening we engaged in continuous dialogue.

I liked him even more because he had a good sense of humor and spoke articulately. After that evening, we both zealously sought each other's company.

Our friendship grew over time and it culminated in us becoming lovers. The relationship at this point was very blissful, as we both formed the nucleus of each other's world. The time soon came when Karl was called away on duty to return to police training. I had grown so accustomed to his company that my loneliness at times could not be described in words. Letters were my only solace in trying to maintain close contact with him. During his absence, I found out that I was pregnant. The joy of this discovery brought a feeling of further bonding with the love of my life. The joy of breaking the news to him, I thought was best kept until his return; when I would break the joyous news while in his arms.

After a month passed, I was awakened one night by a knocking on the door. I asked who it was and the person said it was Karl. My joy at his arrival knew no bounds, as this moment marked an oasis in my month-long desert of loneliness. I jumped up to let him in. He entered my room with a gift in his hand, as was his usual custom, and a warm, loving smile on his face. During the course of the night, after we both earned for ourselves a needed time of relaxation, I lovingly broke the news about the pregnancy to him. As I expected, he responded very calmly. This did not alarm me at first. After that night he told me he would be leaving the following day. We spent the day together and he left that evening.

Karl did not give me a time period for his return, so when the weeks passed without any correspondence from him, my world slowly crumbled like a building imploding on itself. My constant enquiries about him at the police-station were to no avail.

Like a meteor from the sky, after some weeks, Karl appeared one day at my work-place. He said I should ask my boss for time off as we would be going out together the following day at about two o'clock.

On seeing him, my pit of despair was transformed to a mountain of joy. I told my boss that I would like if he could give me part of the following day off because I had urgent business to attend to. My boss did not hesitate to acquiesce to my request for time.

In anticipation of my date with Karl, I went to Bay with alacrity, to purchase a new outfit for the occasion. I returned from my shopping just in the nick of time as Karl knocked at the door about half an hour after I got home. He had a strange look on his face. He told me that he would be taking me to the doctor to have an initial examination of the baby. I asked him the doctor's name and he said it was Dr. Barker. I mentioned to him that I heard about Dr. Barker's reputation for performing abortions. Karl responded and said not all doctors do that. This response was out of character for him and I immediately became concerned. I asked him if this trip to the doctor was for me to have an abortion. He assured me that this exercise was not the case, and that it was just to secure the good health of both the baby and myself.

On his insistence, I got dressed and accompanied him to the doctor. When we got there, Karl told me to sit and wait for a moment as he was going to pay the doctor. At this point, I was totally oblivious as to what was in store for me. When he ended his conversation with the doctor he gave me money and said he had to leave for work immediately, but assured me that everything would be alright because the doctor was capable to help me and the baby; and had everything under control. All that was new to me, because, although I had a child before; I had never been to a doctor so I was not familiar with the entire procedure.

After waiting for about half an hour the doctor called my name and directed me to his office. In the room there was a surgical looking bed and a chair with a gown draped over it. The doctor told me to remove my clothes and don the gown. He said I should lie on my back until he returned. The doctor soon entered the room carrying an unusual looking instrument.

I did not know what it was, so I asked him what he was going to do. He assured me he was only going to examine me. The doctor placed my legs apart and inserted the instrument. I soon felt a very sharp pain. Frightened, this caused me to ask the doctor what was going on with the baby. To my chagrin, he then said to me, "Didn't your boyfriend told you that he was taking you to have an abortion?" I emphatically said 'no.' the doctor said, "Well, that is what just happened." A feeling of consternation overcame me and I became speechless, and could only break out in tears at this personal betrayal by someone who was so dearly loved.

After the doctor was finished with me, I got dressed and went immediately to Karl's workplace to speak to him about the incident.

When I saw him, he became very evasive, and tried to decline having a conversation, citing that he was very busy at the time. This caused me to become very angry and insisted that I deserved his attention. I asked him what I had done to deserve his betrayal and why he now hated me so much. Karl then confronted me by saying he had gone to Windsor, and Fountain Police Station and made some enquiries about me.

He expressed his dissatisfaction about what he had heard about my childhood at the Children's Home, and the different abused, and molestation I underwent. He told me that I would not qualify for the position as the mother of his child. And coldly said there was really nothing more for us to talk about. He concluded the conversation by saying, "I have found someone who had come from a decent family." I could only walk away in tears.

On returning home, I felt as if both my heart and my stomach were in pain. That night I could not sleep, and my pillow was soaked with tears. The following day I was unable to go to work. In fact, I was not feeling well to return to work for the rest of the week. I sent a message to my employer saying that I was ill. My employer was very understanding because when I returned to work, he paid me for the week I was absent.

Mr. Gus, however, after seeing me he knew there was something amiss, and he expressed his concern towards me. Being so depressed, I explained what had happened. He was very sympathetic and understanding. He felt that my condition needed some kind of therapy; he thought the best thing would be for me to remove away from my present locality for a while, and give myself a 'change of scenery'.

To this end, I made the difficult decision to go and stay with my grandparents in Windsor. After communicating this to Mr. Gus, he was not happy to hear of my decision because he thought he was losing a competent employee. But as usual, he was very understanding. With a plan in the forefront, I worked with Mr. Gus for more than a month, and also stole money from the shop in order to have additional savings.

When the time came, my departure, for me, marked a shedding of the skin of my dark past. I was returning to a very simple and rustic lifestyle with my grandparents at Windsor. After assuming my new lifestyle I decided that I would not attempt to return to Bay, nor would I enquire anymore about Karl. I was determined to leave that chapter of my life behind.

CHAPTER NINETEEN

Condition Got Worst

After returning to Windsor and recuperating for a while, I brought my eldest daughter Lilly to live with me. At that time my grandmother was very instrumental in helping me with her. One day, my grandmother took ill and had to be admitted to the hospital. Everyone was concerned about her state of health, but the doctor assured us that based on his diagnosis, she was suffering from an overdose of a laxative and would soon be alright. He said she was a very strong woman.

My grandmother's nephew by the name of Dean, who was a seaman, was visiting with her at that time. After her illness, I had reason to be away from the house for a while, so I left my daughter in my grandmother's care. During my absence, Dean returned to find my grandmother alone with the baby. When I returned, he told me that this was inadequate parental supervision for the baby; and saw this as a temporary abdication of my parental duties. He was very miffed about the incident. He rebuked me and gave me many slaps for what he regarded as my delinquent behavior.

The reason for my absence did not sound a resonant chord with him. For the education of the reader, it was nevertheless, worthy, stating the reason for my absence from the house that day.

The 'bucolic' condition at Windsor was an 'indigent' lifestyle for me. Ways and means had to be found to eeke out a meager living for myself and my daughter.

I had two trusted friends, in the personage of John and Ebony. They were both employed at the priest's rectory in Bay. At a pre-arranged time when the priest was away, they invited me over and procured me some material benefits that were in store. I would often assist them with the packing to expedite my departure with my booty. When I was leaving, I was always laden with food, clothing and household items. That was where I had gone when I had left the baby, so this is the reason I felt some consternation at Dean behavior because as a member of the family, he also benefited from the 'spoils' I brought home.

He subsequently went back to sea, and life continued at Windsor in its usual vein.

My visit to the rectory continued interspersed with visits to my godmother's family to seek assistance.

The relationship between my grandmother and grandfather left much to be desired, and to gain a semblance of financial independence, she would often steal chocolate and nutmeg from the trees and sell them to gain a paltry income for herself.

My grandmother had to do this secretly as my grandfather would be upset if he knew. At times like these I would go to the river to catch fish and shrimp to augment the meals.

I was now twenty years old. My mother was living at Ferry; having moved from Bay, so I decided to pay her a visit.

One Sunday afternoon, I took the bus and got off at a cross road not far from a high school. From there I had about a mile uphill walk to Ferry. About the same time my brother George and Joe were living with Mr. Wright, who was related to my mother. George was my oldest brother. Both he and Joe were the work-horse and slaves for Mr. Wright.

Their presence in the home was that of an indentured servant. George could be seen in the field from very early in the morning until late in the evening.

His movements were always in unison with the horses, donkey, hogs, and goats, so he was always inaccessible to me whenever I tried to see him.

After reaching Ferry I acted on information I had previously received about my mother's whereabouts. I was told that she had rented a house from a lady by the name of Miss Perry.

On approaching the house I saw my mother sitting on the verandah, I was so happy to see her.

When she saw me coming she got up and turned her back towards me. I called to her to announce my presence and to make sure that she had recognized me. She immediately yelled out, "Why the hell did you have to come here? I don't want to see you." My approach was abruptly halted, and I could only break out in uncontrollable tears.

Dejected and heart-broken, I walked back down the pathway leading away from my mother's house. As I entered the roadway, I met an Indian lady who saw me crying and had compassion on me. She asked me what was wrong and I relayed my traumatic experience with my mother to her. The lady consoled me by telling me, "God will help you one day, and that you should not be so sad." As the bus schedule to take me back to Windsor would soon arrive, I could not converse with her for a long time and left with all haste.

After this traumatic experience with my mother, I did not return to Ferry for some time.

As time went by, I learned that she was now living with Mr. Wright as man and wife, and her social position seemed much improved.

My eldest daughter was getting older, so I decided to find the whereabouts of her supposed to be a father to get financial assistance for her.

He was now living in the town of Cambridge. When I got there, he was at home. This was our first meeting for a long time, and it was not very eventful. He acknowledged his responsibility and gave me money and other supplies to take back home.

On my second visit I saw him in the company of a woman. He then expressed his desire for me to share the same bed with him and his companion, as a precursor to giving me anything towards the assistance of the child.

When I refused to do this he went into a blind rage, started to curse and began beating me. In desperation; in pain I ran aimlessly to get away from him, and found myself into a neighbor's house crying for help, but he would not relent. Finally I escaped and ran into another male tenant house. This man whose name was Don turned out to be more than my 'safe harbor' that day from Ed. He gave me shelter and food that night, and on my departure the next morning he gave me money to cover my expenses back to Windsor and encouraged me to return and visit him after my recuperation.

During my period of recuperation I became acutely aware of Ed's inhumane treatment of me, and his cavalier attitude towards the care and welfare of his child.

I took my daughter to him at his home, but he was absent, so I left her with his female companion. I express my feeling to her about how I felt, seeing that she was privy to what Ed had done to me.

While at Windsor, and a few weeks after the incident, I got a visit at my home from a young man who rode on a motorcycle. To my surprise, it was Don. He decided to visit me since I had not taken up his invitation. We talked for a while then he left.

Few weeks passed, and he visited me again. This time I went riding with him on his motorcycle. We went to Cambridge, where I spent the weekend. A few months after, I became pregnant with my second child.

Don and I began spending a lot of time together at his home. One morning when I was approximately six months pregnant, I was making breakfast. Don suddenly approached me and started striking me on my leg, which I assumed was a playful gesture as he usually did, but his action got more insistent, and his attitude became belligerent.

He repeatedly struck me with blows all over my body with increasing fury. My cries attracted the attention of other tenants and neighbors but they only remained spectators. No one came to my assistance, despite my visible pregnancy and abuse.

After my mauling and enduring this physical punishment, I was in extreme discomfort and pain all over my body. Soon after, I got my things together, and dragged myself to the road, where I took a taxi to Bay. On reaching Bay, I got in touch with a lady I knew who arranged for me to see a doctor right away.

After the doctor examined me, and seeing the way I was beaten, the doctor expressed surprise that in my 'bludgeoned' state I was lucky not to have lost the child. He gave me medication along with instructions. I left and went home to Windsor to my grandfather.

Owning to my pregnancy, I needed assistance, but because of Don brutal treatment towards me, I was afraid and refused to see him; and so I decided to visit my father, and ask him for help

CHAPTER TWENTY

Visit to My father

It had been a long time since I had seen my father. I was informed that my brother Roy was living with him, so I went to visit them. I had not intended to stay, but after several visits, and because my brother was living at home with him I started living with him again. At this time, Ed was working as a farm-worker in the United States.

While living with my father, I helped with the domestic chores and as time passed we developed a good communication. During my visit with my father, I met a handsome looking Indian man named Rodney who came from a decent family; and was popular in the community; but because my father was an Indian, also remembering what he had done to me, I refused to have a friendship, or relationship with him.

There was always conversation between my father, my brother and myself. And because he was a very intelligent man, he always had interesting things to talk about. I learned a lot from him.

Later on as the years went by I discovered that my father was skilled in the art of clairvoyant. He would often read cards and tea leaves, performing these feats in a very spontaneous manner, much to the amazement of my brother and myself. One day while my father was reading the cards he told me that my daughter was not Ed's child. To my chagrin I was surprised.

Because my father was an alcoholic, my brother and I once tried to see if we could get him drunk. One night, we gave him white rum that was chased with red label wine. We sat and drank with him, but we both had very little to drink. My father drank very quickly and soon became drunk. He remained in a drunken state for more than a day. We were hoping this would stop him from drinking, but it only seemed to intensify his craving for alcohol.

Over time my brother and I continue living with him.

Late one night I heard my father calling out to me, saying, "Come and sleep with me, am lonely." I pretended as if I did not hear him.

The following day, my father went to work. A letter arrived from the post office for me. It was from a hospital in England. This English hospital was responding to a recommendation that someone had made on my behalf. That person who was a family member had promised that when she went away she would help me to obtain a job in England. This was the fulfilment of the promise. My dreams were shattered because my father destroyed the letter. It was my desire to study medicine and possibly become a doctor.

An accompanying event, on the same day was the arrival of my daughter's father from America. I was not privy to his time of arrival. When he came to the town of Fountain, he inquired for my father's residence. My father was quite popular in the area. Luckily, Ed met my father in person who gave him directions to the house.

I was very happy to see Ed, and accepted the gifts he brought for me. Ed, my brother, and myself prepared an elaborate meal and waited for my father to get home. To my dismay, when my father arrived, he went into a rage, threw the food away and angrily stated, "No other man must have any affair in his house but him." Ed then insisted that I pack my things right away and come with him. When my father heard that, he calmed down and told us to stay. He apologized, and said that he was drunk. The atmosphere after this became congenial, and a healthy conversation flowed between us. My father even accepted gifts from Ed.

Later that night, Ed and I were sitting having a private conversation; my father verbally made his disapproval apparent. He started to curse us again, and then he returned the gifts, and ordered Ed saying, "Get out of my dam blasted house." At that time, I packed my things and was ready to leave.

When my father saw the seriousness Ed displayed about my leaving, my father immediately calmed himself down again and apologized to Ed this time in tears. We all went to sleep that night.

When morning came, and we had awakened, my father said that he would like to make a preposition to us. He told us that he would love to go and visit his families who lived down the country but his funds were insufficient. Ed told him that he would fund the trip. The next morning we left.

When we got there, my father introduced us to the families. But he was more interested to see his sister. We visited quite a few family members. During our visits I discovered that Ed was missing; which later discovered that he had an affair with my cousin Jean. I became so irate and ashamed about his behavior. Time was fast approaching for us to leave, which I was eager for. Fortunately for me I was so glad our visit lasted only for a short time.

After returning back to Wildwood I saw no progress with my life, so I decided to visit my aunt down the country again, hoping some doors of opportunity would open for me. While I was staying with my aunt I regularly visited my uncle and his wife. After quite a few visits I ended up living with them for a while. The living arrangement did not last very long owing to the fact that I discovered my uncle's wife acts of wrongdoing. I spoke to her about it, which made her very angry with me. Immediately I told her that I was running away back to my aunt. When my aunt saw me come, she asked what had transpired between me and my uncle's wife, I told her about my discovery. My aunt remark was that, "I am glad you find out."

Later that day my uncle's wife visited my aunt. This caused a big uproar between her and my aunt, my aunt insisted that I return to my uncle's home as they were well-off than she was.

Although I did not want to go back I returned for' peace sake'

One night while I was sleeping I was awakened by someone pulling the hair in my head. I woke up just in time to catch my uncle's wife cutting some of my hair out with a scissors. I pretended that I did not see her. I continued lying in bed, but was unable to sleep. This time my decision was to get my belongings and go to my aunt, even if sleeping on her floor or under her house was the only accommodation she could afford me.

After living with my aunt for some time I began experiencing excruciating pain in my head. I was given pain medication from my aunt and other neighbors, but got no relief. It got to the place where I became very disgusted with myself, also smoking marijuana on a regular basis. My aunt would not tolerate my behavior because she had no idea what was wrong with me. She told me to leave because she could no longer tolerate my behavior. I spoke to a neighbor whose name was Mass Tom who lived a few houses away from my aunt about my problem. Mass Tom told me that he would discuss the matter with his wife before agreeing. As luck would have it, his wife agreed that they would accommodate, but I had to hide in the kitchen during the day and sleep in the house at nights. As time passed my aunt discovered my hiding place. Not long after the both families got into an altercation. Mass Tom and his wife told my aunt 'that they were not going to put me on the street because you people have been very wicked to her who is your own family.'

Mass Tom and his wife took my illness into consideration and told me that I needed spiritual help, because they were not pleased with what was happening to me.

They both decided to take me to see a spiritual man. The distance that I would be going was located on a hill. His wife was unable at that time to accompany us, but Mass Tom took me and told me that the spiritualist would tell me everything that was going on with my life, and help me.

The moment I entered through the man's gate, he came out shouting, "They want you to go mad, and eat shit. What a wicked Indian woman". It seems he knew Mass Tom, because he called him by his name, saying, "Tom, bring the gal here."

Mass Tom took me around the back of the man house. He grabbed my both hands, swung me around, he then told me to lay down flat on my stomach. He started breaking branches from a tree, and began beating the ground around where I was laying. After he was finished doing that, he proceeded and got some dry coconut which he broke around me, and then grabbed my hands, pulled me up from the ground and began speaking in unknown tongues.

Immediately he poured a bucket full of water all over me. Seems this did not complete the task. He took another bucket with what seems like a mixture of herbs, threw it all over me, then instructed me not to have any dialogue with anyone for three days. On leaving he told me to run all the way down, and not stop to talk to anyone I meet along the way.

Mass Tom and his wife were very pleased about my daily recovery. I was very happy to do chores for them; I was now living like a member of the family. As time passed I made few friends in the community, and would visit adjoining districts. I later started to become dissatisfied, because I saw no improvement for myself. And remembering what that man told me, I wanted to get away before my uncle's wife found some other ways to damage me again.

Not wanting to make it seem that I was ungrateful I fabricated to my Mass Tom and his wife that my grandmother was very sick, and I would like to go home for a few weeks to help her, and then return. They were very generous to me, because they believed me. With my bags already packed, my plan was to leave very early one morning without being noticed. That's what I did. I went to Windsor, and never returned because I became fearful of what my uncle's wife had done to me.

As time passed I became pregnant with my eldest son and was faced with serious financial hardship. I had no source of income; and I was not being supported by my child father. I needed to get help from somewhere. I knew if I asked my mother I would experience rejection, my grandparents were not in a position to assist financially. Because of the abuse I received from Don, I was fearful to contact him during my pregnancy, so I decided to visit my father at Fountain to ask for help.

After giving things a good thought. One Friday I reluctantly decided to visit my father and seek his assistance. When I arrived and saw him he was in the company with his friends, and associates. He appeared happy to see me and suggested that I come to the back of the bar where he was drinking, for us to discuss whatever problem there is. Obviously he was intoxicated, because he was speaking very loudly. When we sat to talk, his words to me caused me only disgust to hear the things he was saying to me. He approached me with an incestuous proposal for us to become intimate.

Unable to restrain myself, and not caring at that time that he was my father, I erupted with a very 'vituperative' response, forgetting any filial relationship, and cursed him in a 'derogatory' manner. I was overcome with shame; I walked back to Windsor, crying all the way.

When I returned home, I told my grandfather, and he spared no words in describing my father's behavior as being very debased and objectionable. Because of this shameful incident,

I did not visit Fountain for a long time.

CHAPTER TWENTY-ONE

My Eldest Son's birth

The time was fast approaching for me to give birth to my child, so I secured the services of a midwife. When it was time for delivery the midwife was summoned. She came and examined me and said that the birth of the baby would take some time. She asked me for garden herbs which she made into tea and gave me to drink. This she said would speed up the delivery, and would return shortly.

Before she returned, nature took its course, and I gave birth to my second child, which was a boy. My grandfather heard the advent of my son into the world, signaled by his cry. Grandfather stamped the floor in jubilation and joyfully shouted, "Samson, Samson, Samson, you are here."

When the midwife returned she was surprised to see that I had given birth on my own and even severed the umbilical cord myself. She was pleased, nevertheless, that I was able to help myself. Thus Andy, my second child was born on a Sunday.

Shortly after giving birth, I was forced to throw myself back into the domestic chores of the house, and whatever activities allowed gaining some income. My grandfather went about his usual activities of picking coconut and breadfruit. This was my only source of income so I had to ignore my fragile state of health and gave him my usual assistance.

The trips up and down the hill with the bags containing coconut and breadfruit proved too much for my fragile state of health. My body started hemorrhaging, and I grew increasingly weak and fragile. My health deteriorated to the point where I was unable to ambulate, and could only get around by crawling on my knees or dragging along on my bottom. Getting around from one place to another in the house became an arduous journey for me.

My destitute condition would not allow me the privilege of seeing a doctor. My grandfather gave me herbal tea, and prepared a poultice with tuna and warm castor oil, which he placed on my back and stomach.

My efforts had a marginal effect on my condition, but my state of ill-health was exacerbated whenever I had to move about; in particular when going to the open faucet.

Just to avoid the menacing eyes of people, I waited until it was late and no one was around, then I would drag myself, or lumber as best as I could to the standpipe.

As an adjunct to breast milk, I was only able to give my baby herbal teas and porridge.

Being so domiciled, because of my ill-health, only made things more difficult. The care for my child at this critical time in its life was severely restricted. This caused greater pain and mental anguish to me as a mother. I was totally powerless to immediately change my condition. In time I felt better and was able to move about, but remain cognizant of the degree of strenuousness of whatever task I undertook. Few months after I had given birth to Andy, I was visited by his father. He apologized to me, by saying that someone fabricated a lie about me to him, and said he was very sorry for what he had done. Being afraid of his rebellious nature, I told him to leave me alone, because he will do the same things to me again. He then rode away on his motorbike.

The Green family who lived across the street were still my friends; not wanting to solicit their sympathy; I did not want to make my condition known to them.

After some time I took the baby to visit them. Mrs. Green was very pleased to see me and the baby. She encouraged me to visit the family as before, and even expressed her willingness to assist me in any way she could.

She was employed as a domestic worker to the principal of Windsor Primary School. Our mutual friendship became a strong one. Many days would find me at the school cottage where Mrs. Green worked. I usually assisted her with her chores, and so, was able to partake of any meals she prepared. The principal soon took a liking to me.

I became comfortable with the relationship I shared with Mrs. Green, because it proved very beneficial to me. I was very happy to have her as a friend.

CHAPTER TWENTY-TWO

The Bishop's Advice

My presence at the school cottage afforded me the opportunity to interact with many new acquaintances. It was by way of this social exposure, that I met and befriend Lloyd. He was very nice to me, and made me feel comfortable in his company.

Once, when he came to my home to visit, he saw my baby and inquired about the father. I relayed the unfortunate circumstances of my pregnancy, and the reason why I had not registered the child in the biological father name. He empathized with my situation and suggested that since he had never fathered a child, he would be happy to have the child registered in his name. Our relationship to this point was pure platonic, so I was moved by the magnanimity of his suggestion. Soon after this, we went and registered the child in his name.

His behavior towards the child was as if it was his own, and this endeared me to him even more.

He and I soon became intimate friends, and although he was unable to provide me with many material comforts, he displayed a great deal of kindness towards me and the child.

My overt relationship was being observed by many persons. Not least of these was Bishop Hines. He was the bishop of the church which was located close to my home. Bishop stood on the church balcony and from a vantage point, observed Lloyd and myself socializing on many occasions. The bishop was very fond of me, and one day he asked me about the relationship between Lloyd and myself. I told him that we were not engaged, but we were having an intimate relationship.

As a pastor and bishop, it appeared that he was interested in the social decorum of our relationship. Bishop Hines suggested that we should come and have a talk with him to discuss the direction our relationship was taking. He even indicated that he was in a position to help us to migrate to America. I told Lloyd about this, and we agreed on a given date when we would meet with the bishop.

On that day in question we went before Bishop Hines for his pastoral counseling. The bishop extolled the virtues of marriage to us and encouraged us along the path. Lloyd, however, had some reservations, and told the bishop he was not mentally prepared at that time for such a momentous decision. He said he would return at a later date when he had given the matter further thoughts. Lloyd's hesitancy made me quite uneasy, and I was in a quandary as to how he felt about me.

On some occasions, my grandmother would go away to visit relatives. It so happened that Lloyd came to visit me while she was away. We then had grandmother's room to ourselves. This was an opportunity for intimacy that we could not pass up.

To my surprise, while Lloyd and I were being intimate, my brother Roy was the observer of the entire affair. The wooden structure, of which the room composed, showed its age by having a number of cracks and opening in the joints and other areas. These gave access to the gaze of any inquisitive observer, so we were not allowed much privacy unless the room was in a darkened state.

After we exited the room, my brother Roy suddenly attacked me with a large piece of stick. He struck me on my back, sending me to the ground, writhing in pain. Lloyd accosted him about what he had done to me, but it only drew further indignation from my brother. He proceeded to curse Lloyd and me in the most unabashed manner about our intimate relationship.

My brother had struck me so severely with the stick, which caused me excruciating pain for many days. Lloyd with the help of my grandfather had to administer whatever home remedies they could to alleviate my pains, as I could not afford to go to the doctor.

In time I felt little much better; but over the years I continue to suffer from that injury that I had sustained; to this day.

The matter of our return to see Bishop Hines came up, Lloyd expressed the view that he was now ready to speak to him.

When the day finally came, I was tingling all over with a feeling of expectancy. I thought that at last I would be a woman 'spoken for.' A woman with a semblance of dignity about her relationship, whose trip to the altar was very imminent. Bishop Hines went directly to the question of marriage. Lloyd said in a solemn manner, that he loved me, but I would not prove to be a positive influence on his life. He said I was too poor and uneducated, and that his family would not accept someone from my 'social station.'

After clearly stating his position, he got up and made an untimely departure, leaving Bishop Hines and myself.

In the wake of his statement I was left emotionally drained and speechless. This man, who had brought my feelings to the apex of the mountain of hope, had hurled me down to be smashed on the rocks of despair and heart-break. The bishop saw my pain and held me in his arms and comforted me. He said that God would surely bless me and I should always consider him as a source of help.

Lloyd never came back to see me after that, and tried his best to avoid me.

Despite this, it was difficult to get him out of my mind. In time our infrequent contact led to a resurgence of our friendship. Lloyd was now going to visit his family at Stanford Hill and invited me to go along with him. I gladly accepted the invitation, as I saw this as an opportunity to be with him. I also saw this as a way to improve our strained relationship, with the hope that things between us would improve, and he would consider marrying me as a viable option. I told Bishop Hines that Lloyd wanted me to visit with him to meet his family. The bishop met with my grandmother. He encouraged me to visit for a few weeks, which would probably allow Lloyd to change his mind, and marry me. The bishop promised that in my absence he would assist my grandmother with whatever was needed for my son. I welcomed the opportunity and went with Lloyd.

In Stanford Hill, I stayed at his aunt's house. This was because there was not adequate space at his grandparent's house where he lived, and because his grandparents were Christians he did not want to incense them with an overt display of his sordid affair.

The first couple of days, my stay at his aunt's house went well. Soon after, I was made into a work-horse. I was given chores from sunrise to sunset, washing, ironing, cooking, cleaning, fetching water, gathering wood, and making fire. Work seemed unending from day to day.

The family included Lloyd's aunt, her husband and her children. The children obviously approached manual work with a sense of disdain; so I was actually living out the Cinderella story.

Over time Lloyd showed disinterest in me, and his visits to his aunt's house became quite infrequent. He showed no concern or compassion for the inhumane way in which I was treated. I decided somehow that I have to get away from this life of servitude.

One day when I went to the stores, I asked everyone I met about finding a job, or a place to stay. A Rasta man I met told me he knew of a man who needed a domestic worker. He gave me direction to the house. I went and had a meeting with him. He appears very mannerly and intelligent. I was in a desperate situation so offered my service. I was very fortunate because he hired me immediately. The job only lasted for a few weeks, but that would give enough money to fund my bus fare and other expenses back to Windsor.

While on the job, Lloyd had come to pay one of his rare visits to me at his aunt's house. Not finding me there, he made inquiries and was directed to the house where I was working. He came to my new place of employment displaying a very bellicose attitude and accused me of infidelity.

He obviously was not privy to the fact that I was now employed. I told him, and repeated it several times that it was my place of employment. I even expressed to him that it became necessary for me to find a job because of the drudgery with no income from his aunt. His response was that I was willing to clean other people's houses and wash their dirty clothes, as opposed to doing these things for his family.

His fury was further kindled, as he apparently found my story to be incredible, and proceeded to beat me with a piece of board, and kick me in my stomach, then and there. My cries and pleading made him even more belligerent. He even ignored the presence of on-lookers who had gathered. It was only on the arrival of my employer, who attested to the truth of my story that he desisted.

After the mauling I received at Lloyd's hand, I refused to remain at his aunt's house. I begged my employer to give me temporary lodging.

Through the kind nature of my employer, in answering my plea, I got lodging at his house. I continue working for two more weeks. I then discreetly put my things together and took the bus back to Windsor. This was the last time I saw Lloyd for quite a few years.

When I return to Windsor, the paltry amount of money I had lasted for a short time. My economic condition became grave again, because I was unable to maintain myself and my family. I went to Bishop Hines and explained what had happened. He offered me words of comfort, and also offered food and clothing. He said that these clothes were part of the benevolence which the church received from abroad, so he would have to make it known to Sister Rena, as she was the one who would dispense the clothes to me.

On the bishop's instruction I went to Sister Rena and made her aware of what the bishop had said, but she made no effort, and refused to give the bag of clothes to me.

On a later occasion the bishop asked me if I had received the bag of clothes. I told him that Sister Rena had not given them to me. On another visit to the church I saw the same bag of clothes lying idly on the floor, so I took it.

No sooner had I started to wear the clothes, I was labeled as a, "Church Rat." It was intimated that I had stolen the clothes, so I became the object of ridicule from the church and community.

With the passage of time, I met and became friends with Jordon. He was employed as a salesman for a local dairy industry. Our friendship, although it was only platonic, was a strong one. He would visit me regularly, and always brought me gifts of some kind. It was apparent that he was very fond of me, because he always tells me that I was 'beautiful.' On one particular occasion he came to my home and I was not there, so he had no idea as to my whereabouts.

Because I had told him that my father lived at, the town of Fountain he went there and inquired for me. Fortunately for him, the search took him to a local bar, and to where my father was. He made my father privy to his reason for being there. My father being a drunken stupor; practically exploded to Jordon's face in a derogatory manner, telling him that he was quite capable of taking care of his own daughter. Jordon was shocked about what he heard, and repelled by my father's belligerence and overtly incestuous statement. Jordon immediately got into his car and drove off. This marked the cessation of his visits.

All this was later relayed to me by my girlfriend Daisy Moore, who happened to be in the shop at the time and was close to hear everything.

My observation that something was wrong came by way of me not seeing Jordon. When he drove past my gate he would not stop, and totally ignored me whenever he saw me. This caused me to fall into a state of depression.

I was very angry with my father for what he had done.

I had lost such a good friend.

CHAPTER TWENTY-THREE

Sojourn to Town

During this time my grandmother, as usual, went to visit other members of the families. After my grandmother's return I related to her the extent of my frustration, and told her about my decision to look for a job in Town. My grandmother agreed and prayed for me before leaving; and told me that my son would be alright.

My sojourn to Town first had me staying with Grace, who was a friend I had made acquaintance with, by way of her brother, after I left the Children's Home. Grace could not provide me with any lengthy accommodation, so I decided that I would have to seek help. I struck up other alliances as soon as I could.

This was how I met John and Lacy. They invited me to their home and agreed to help me find a job. The sleeping accommodation was satisfactory. I tried to make myself domestically useful in the home, as I was not contributing financially. Things went well for a while, but soon John started making advances towards me. He made it clear by his overtures that gratuitous intimacy had to be a condition of my remaining at the house. My rejection of his advances causes him to start displaying open hostility towards me. Eventually he convinced his girlfriend that I was no longer welcome at the house. At night they began locking me out of the house, and I was forced to sleep on the verandah. Even this did not satisfy them, so I was chased from the verandah as if I was a stray animal.

Having nowhere to go, I was forced to sleep in an abandoned car which was parked on the side of the road, and close to a mechanic shop.

This uncomfortable lifestyle was something I decided to endure, as I had hopes of getting a job in Town, because returning to the dormant lifestyle at Windsor was not an option at that time.

During the days, I utilized the washroom of a nearby gas station to clean up. I was forced to ask favors from strangers as much as I could without appearing to be a mendicant. My self-esteem was at its lowest point. It was only my belief in God which caused me to maintain my sanity.

Through my social interaction, I soon discovered that John and Lacy neighbors ran a packing and shipping business. This seemed to be an act of Providence for me, because I was immediately employed as a filing clerk the moment I approached them about a job.

This job started out quite well for me, but I had to conceal the vagabond lifestyle that I secretly maintained. On the job I found out that my employer had a vacant room on the premises. I asked him if it was possible for me to rent this room; giving him an erroneous reason for my wanting to change where I presently resided. He agreed, and I was so happy to have my own living quarters and bathroom facilities.

My social status was much improved and I could display some amount of financial independence. Not only was I able to go shopping for myself, but I was able to visit my grandparents and my son with whatever I was able to garner for them.

My fortune later took a downward turn when my boss started to make sexual approaches to me. Since I was living on his premises, whenever I went out he would be there waiting for me when I returned, expecting 'sexual favors.' His response to my rejection of him made him stop paying me a salary. Because my job gave me access to cash I started to steal from him. This led to a downward spiral, and he eventually fired me. My position again became one of destitution.

Not knowing what to do, I went back to my friend Grace. Fortunately, her brother got a job for me at a local club name 'The Palms'. The club had an arrangement where the female workers could sleep over, but the accommodation provided only a single bed.

This posed a problem at time, especially when more than one worker needed to use the facility.

One worker in particular, compounded the problem by inviting her male companion to sleep over with her. I was often relegated to sleeping on the chair since I had no other options. This condition left much to be desired.

The job at The Palms had its benefit. It gave me the opportunity to meet many influential people, persons in the military, the police force, and the political arena. Nevertheless, the sleeping accommodation made things intolerable for me. I was always getting into an altercation with the worker who invited her male friend to sleep over. The other girls agreed with my stance on the matter. This however caused me frustration and after time I left the job.

Although I was now jobless, I was still living with Grace. To give some semblance of support in the home, I went to Windsor regularly and brought back fruits and provision for her family.

With time on my hand, and not much to do, I often visited Miss Brown who had been my guardian when I was a child. My period with Miss Brown and the help I offered her, only secured me a meal. I asked Miss Brown to see if she could use her influence in the community to get a job for me, including the friends I met, and made. Miss Brown's response was that I should go back to the country and sit down. It was during that period of social uncertainty in my life that I met and became friends with Bill. We became close friends, so he took me to meet his family. Our friendship, although it was an endearing one, was purely platonic.

After a while my fortune in the job market saw me getting a job at a commercial school in Town. Although I made it known to my employer from the outset that I did not possess the adequate qualifications for the job, he nevertheless accepted me and said he would help me. There was another female teacher at the school, and it soon became apparent to me that the boss was having an affair with her. It was not long before he expressed his desire to give me his promised assistance 'behind closed doors.'

My refusal to go along with his program cost me my job.

Being unemployed again, and after making many inquiries directed my path to a job as a domestic worker in the town of Reveria.

This family consisted of a man and his two sons. My new boss proved to be a very kind and respectful man. My employment at their home developed into a family-type arrangement, and I was soon regarded as a quasi-family member. My employer, Mr. Samuel, had a friend who was the proprietor of a hardware store in Town. It was this channel that got me a job with a hardware store as a sales clerk, and also gave me the opportunity of meeting and befriending politicians.

Although my employer Mr. Samuel had secured a job for me, I continued to live at his home, and continued the servitude as a domestic worker. His manner and attitude towards me was always one of consideration, but he expressed a desire to be intimate with me.

He was of Indian descent like my father, and my thoughts of accepting his advances conjured up in my mind the memories of the abuse I had experienced at the hands of my father. For this reason, I could not allow myself to get involved with him.

During my tenure at the hardware store, I met and became friends with Nora who was employed there. I made Nora aware of the condition that I was experiencing while living and working with Mr. Samuel. She expressed sympathy towards me, and invited me to come and stay with her. Nora and her cousin lived in a single room with one bed in Colleyville Gardens. Sleeping accommodating was inadequate, but we made do.

As time passed, I met and befriend Roger.

He was employed as a driver with a local construction company. He had his own transportation, and also owned a house in Colleyville Garden.

After communicating with him for a period of time he told me that he was married, but his wife was living abroad.

He had the bearing of a decent and clean cut person. I later found out that Roger was once intimate with Nora. When I asked her about the situation she expressed disinterest in him, stating he was too old and ugly for her. The friendship between Nora and myself strengthened. Soon we both decided to get a bigger place since my income could now afford somewhere more commodious and dispense with the cramped room we occupied. I was then able to buy my own furniture.

Roger and I started to date in earnest. He was very loving and attentive to me. Nora's attitude then changed. She became jealous of our relationship and suddenly decided that she wanted Roger back. The relationship between Nora and myself changed; and the once harmonious nature of our interaction changed to an abrasive one.

After a time, I became very sick, and was unable to stay in good health. One day during my period of ill-health I stood by the gate, and by chance I became involved in a conversation with a young man who was passing by. I told him about my state of constant ill-health. He told me that his father was a spiritual healer and I should accompany him to see him. As I had my misgivings about the young man and his story, I told him to relay my story to his father and return with a response.

In a few days, the man returned with an elixir in a bottle which he said his father had prepared for me. At this point, I decided not to appear gullible, and refused the concoction. To prove he was sincere, he drank some in my presence. This allayed some of my doubts and caused me to taste the mixture, but I would not relinquish all my apprehension. He then took the bottle from me, saying, "Give it to me," and he drank the remaining balance. He suggested that we both go to the father, intimating that he would not be vindicated.

At this time it was against my better judgment to go with the young man.

The father lived in the country, and when I met him, all my doubts were removed. The elderly man showed in a glass of water that revealed who was responsible for my constant ill-health. There before my eyes was Nora's picture in the glass of water. He told me that her nefarious act got its leverage from her using my underwear as a source of contact with me. This was why I was feeling so sick, and that her intent was to hasten my demise. This he said was of course due to jealousy. This was the straw that broke the camel's back.

After this the relationship with Nora and myself got unbearable, and I was forced to move out with my furniture which I placed in a storage by some of my friends; and I rented a furnished room just to get away from her.

Because of my poor health I was unable to work, and was behind on paying my bills. One day while at my new apartment, I heard a knock on my door. When I inquired who it was, someone responded that they were a crew from the furniture store, and forthrightly made me aware of the purpose of their visit. They had come to repossess my furniture as I was in arrears in my payments. It was highly unlikely that these people could not have known of my new address if they had not been directed. Naturally, I suspected that Nora was responsible because we both lived in the same subdivision.

Because Roger's job was distant, he only came to see me every two weeks, so I was without any help to offset the repercussions. Ashamed and distraught, I went to Windsor for a few days, and stayed until the time when Roger would come to visit me.

After this experience, I took whatever furniture and belongings I had on the bus to Windsor.

Due to age, and also ill-health, my mother took my grandmother to Ferry to live with her. I was now without the assistance she gave me with my child, so it became very difficult for me.

Although my grandfather had the best of intentions, he could not offer the support I needed, so I decided to take my son to my mother in Ferry. Trying to find means and ways to survive, my movements now were between Windsor, Ferry, Bay, and Town.

Each time I re-visited Windsor the house appeared dilapidated, as the ravages of time had taken their toll on the wood hovel which had sheltered us all those years. Despite that, there was always the warmth of my grandfather's welcome, and the love and happiness I felt being at that old house.

With the slow denuding of its structure, the old house became a hospitable habitat for roaches, rats, and lizards. These vermin, although present in daytime, came into their own at night.

There were always lizards on the rafters issuing their mating calls; rats running around under the bed, and on the floor. And if this was not enough to keep me awake, my annoyance was ensured by the sensation of roaches and bedbugs crawling on my body and on my bed linen.

Because of the fecundity of these vermin, most efforts to control then were not effective. A friend suggested that I used kerosene oil in a spray can; this seemed to have a measurable effect.

My old bed was now falling apart. At nights it offered me very little comfort. What took the place of a mattress were old clothes, newspapers, and sheets of cardboard boxes. The metal framework of the bed was constantly falling apart. I had to make temporary adjustments by binding the springs with wire each time one came loose. There was always a risk of the bed falling apart whenever I lay on it.

One day, I went in search for wire to effect some repairs to my bed. While walking along the street, as luck would have it, I came upon some men who were working with the telephone company. They were in process of laying cables. They had a large amount of wire with them. On asking for some of the wire, I was happy to be given more than I needed.

When I returned with the wire, my grandfather who was sitting on his verandah said laughingly, "Now you could fix up your bed properly." He lent me a pair of pliers and I effected the needed repairs to the bed. After that I slept with a feeling of assurance about the stability of the bed, although still enduring the rigor of my makeshift mattress, and a patchwork spread which I fashioned from old clothes.

The desire to better my conditions caused me to return to Town to get a job. I assumed occupancy of the previously furnished room in Colleyville Gardens, as my tenancy of the room had not been relinquished. I got a job at the Cove Inn on Fox Hills Road.

During this time Roger and I were still friends. There were times I did him favor by baby-sitting his youngest daughter some evenings when the helper left before he came home.

Roger and I were in constant contact, and soon I got pregnant with my third child. The pregnancy adversely affected my health, and I was forced to leave my job. There was no other alternative for me, so I went back to Windsor.

The thought that I had to face my detractors in Windsor, placed me again under a canopy of shame and humiliation. As a result of this, I secured as much food and provisions as I could before I returned home, so that I could remain domiciled indoors as long as it was humanly possible, just to avoid the critical onlookers.

The faucet which we used was situated on our adjoining property, but belonged to the church. Whenever my grandfather and I went to the pipe, there would always be disparaging remarks made about us. Sometimes the church members would throw water at us from the church balcony accompanied by pejorative remarks, to express their disdain. As a result of their overt display of rancor, I made sure that all visits to the pipe were made late at nights.

During this time Roger became noticeably absent from my life. It became quite apparent that he was avoiding me. One morning, very early I boarded a bus bound for Town. I arrived at Roger's place at work quite early; and was conspicuously present when he drove in for work that morning.

On seeing me, his countenance changed to one of anger and disgust; and he initially ignored me and went directly to his job. It was only by my pleading with the security guard at the jobsite to contact Roger that I finally saw him reluctantly approaching me.

He made it unequivocally clear to me that he did not want me to visit him at his work-place. He grudgingly gave me money and told me to, "Leave right now."

Although I was ashamed and angered by his attitude, I was compelled to take the money because I didn't even have money for my bus fare to return home.

When I returned to Windsor, I felt so ashamed and depressed. I broke down into a state of sorrow and despair; and poured out my grief to my grandfather. He was very displeased at what he heard and told me that I needed a spiritual bath.

Later that evening my grandfather went to the hills and collected different herbs. He made a fire and placed a large pot with water and the herbs to boil. He instructed me to fetch the large wash tub and place it in my room.

After divesting all my clothes, grandfather administered the bath himself.

At the end of my 'spiritual cleansing, my grandfather quite confidently, and with assurance, told me that I should not worry because Roger would be coming back soon.

About a week later, I observed a familiar car coming up the street, and sure enough, it was Roger. When I told my grandfather that Roger was present, he told me not to be argumentative with him, but to welcome him instead.

I introduced Roger to my grandfather and they both sat and had a long talk.

Roger had brought a box with him, and he encouraged me to open it. I did, and was pleasantly surprised to see clothing, chicken, fish, and other foodstuff. I prepared a meal of chicken and rice, and fried fish for the following day's meal. We all sat down to a sumptuous meal. After dinner, Roger took me to the mineral bath. He stayed over that night, and I made breakfast for him in the morning.

When he was preparing to leave that morning he invited me to accompany him with my daughter Lilly to Town; I immediately accepted his offer. He then said that he was appalled at the dilapidated condition of the house, and the emaciated state of the bed. He had no reservations in telling me that it was the worst bed he had ever slept on in his life, and also the shabbiest house he has ever been in; and the poorest girl, and living condition he had ever gotten himself involved with.

A few weeks went by. One day I saw Roger car coming up the road with a mattress on the top. This drew the attention of a lot of people, but I felt very pleased with my 'gift.' Roger started laughing when he saw me, and my grandfather too was pleasantly surprised. Grandfather also was very happy, and thanked Roger, then told him that he was a good man. Roger expressed to me that he would not let the village folks scared him away with their malicious gossip.

Roger continued to visit me.

One day he invited me to go for a drive with him because he had something to talk to me about. It was unclear to me what was on his mind. While we were driving along, he stopped the car under the shade of an apple tree, which was located between Windsor, and Fountain and began talking to me in a loving way; then he told me that it would be best for me to have an abortion because he did not think it would be suitable for his child to be born in my poor economic condition under which I lived. I was shocked at his suggestion, but remained adamant that I was going to have the child. He then drove me back home and left.

After a few weeks, he returned and said he had consulted a doctor, and the professional opinion was that as the pregnancy was already six months, having an abortion at that time would definitely be a life's threatening exercise.

I became very 'irate' to hear this, and asked him, "Do you want to kill me." I told Roger that I was quite prepared to go the full term of my pregnancy and give my grandfather whatever help I could with his bananas, coconuts, and breadfruits. I told him that I was tricked once into having an abortion for the same reason, and I was not going to let it happen again.

He looked at me disgustingly; he then left but said that he would be back. Even then I still believe that he would be true to his words.

The time was fast approaching for the birth of my child. I decided to go to my mother and explained about my prevailing circumstances. She then invited me to come to Ferry because she had adequate accommodation there. I got in touch with Roger, and told him of my plans. He was willing to take me, as this was not the first time he would be meeting my mother.

My grandfather was saddened by my departure, but conceded that I needed help with the baby; because I had no help when Andy was born.

CHAPTER TWENTY FOUR

Living at Ferry

Ferry is a small town close to Locket located on a hill overlooking the Sea. The climate is always refreshing because it is always bathed by the winds coming from the sea.

Locket is noted for its lush flora. It also provides rafting on the River, which is second to none as a tourist attraction. It is also renowned for, 'Jerk Pork.'

H.K. Williams, who lived in East Locket, not very far from Ferry, was reportedly the wealthiest man in the community, and he was second cousin to my grandmother. As a planter, Mr. Williams employed a large number of skilled and unskilled workers on his banana plantation. After his death, the succession of his business was continued by his relatives. The size of his business also provided a large amount of clerical work at his office. In later years my brother Roy and others were employed there.

There were other farmers who provided employment for some people, but these farmers were clearly not on the scale of Mr. Williams.

Most people in the community were self-employed. They were mostly engaged in rearing pigs, goats and chickens, or the purchase of coconuts for the production of oil, along with tenant farming.

The livestock farmers sold their produce to the local butcher. Those who were engaged in the production of coconut oil and farming sold their produce at the market in Town. It was by and large a self-reliant community.

During my stay there, I became acquainted with some of my cousins for the first time. The Indian lady whose name I found out to be Mrs. Singh who I had met and consoled me was also living there. She was an endearing family friend, and after some time my brother Roy ended up living with her. My sister Lorie was also living at Ferry with a lady by the name of Miss Lee.

As my stay at Ferry lengthened, my mother and I soon got re-acquainted and became friends. It was about this time I was pregnant with my third child.

As the facilities at Windsor with my grandfather were not at all that conductive to taking care of my baby I asked my mother if I could come and stay with her for some time until I have my baby; she agreed.

I was six months pregnant. I took Andy who was two years of age with me and made the exodus to Ferry.

My mother had now taken up residence with Mr. Wright who she had an intimate relationship with, but still maintained the house she rented from Miss Perry, so when I moved to Ferry with my son it was her old house that we occupied.

The flora around the area of the house was very lush, and there were always a number of fruit trees to be seen.

My mother's new companion, Mr. Wright, was a farmer by profession. He owned two houses on the property on which they lived.

The larger one was made of concrete; this was where he lived with my mother. The smaller was a wooden house, which was occupied by my grandmother, and my brother Joe.

Life at Ferry was no easy feat for me. The amicable relationship between me and my mother would vary frequently. My lack of income also put me in a dire financial straits, often to the point where there was not enough to eat, and I would go hungry on many occasions as my mother refused to help. These times I would depend on my grandmother who would always come to my aid, or steal meat from the pickle barrel in my mother's kitchen.

Grandmother would often wait until my mother and Mr. Wright were not at home, and artfully sneak food from the house and kitchen to give to me. She would sometimes cook herself to supply me with food. I can remember her coming through the bushes with a closed container of food. The precious meals I needed so much caused me to be reliant on her.

After living at Ferry for a while, I made a number of friends in the community. The most treasured of these was Mr. Covey. He was tall in stature and of dark complexion. He was born in one of the Caribbean Islands and grew up where I lived. Mr. Covey was like a surrogate father, a mentor, a confidant, and a friend, all in one. To this day, thoughts of him instill' a feeling of euphoria in me.

His goodness towards me far exceeded any kindness ever shown to me by my family members. He displayed a paternal concern for my children, and always made sure they had food to eat. He would place his feelings in tandem with joys and sorrows; he was an exceptional person.

Mr. Covey was another father figure to me. I could always depend on him, and be greeted warmly, he made sure I never left his home hungry, or in need, even if he had to seek help from his neighbors to assist me.

Because he was advanced in age, he imparted a great amount of knowledge to me. I enjoyed being a friend to him, and doing whatever domestic chores he needed me to do. Gwen was a friend who I met through my association with Mr. Covey. My friendship with Gwen graduated further than a casual relationship. I was welcome at her home at any time, and my visits always coincide with her daily meal preparation.

Her mother would always grumble in disgust when I arrived at meal time, but I ignored her, as I had no other place to go when I was faced with hunger. Gwen was always happy to see me.

While living at Ferry, and to overcome boredom, I pursued my education by enrolling in evening classes at the high school, where I sat my exams. It was an arduous walk, being pregnant, going up and down the hill to classes daily, but I stuck with it and was successful.

When the time came to have my baby, my mother's attitude towards me was less than pleasant. I sent my brother George and Roy to inform her that I was in labor.

After a long wait, Mr. Wright arrived with her in his car. She bore a disgusted look on her face and begrudgingly invited me into the car.

On the way to the hospital she openly displayed so much unkindness and impatience towards me because I was groaning in pain. She became disgusted with my cries and stuffed a handkerchief in my mouth, because I would not 'shut up' on her insistence. In such pain, my only concern was to get to the hospital.

When we arrived there, I was registered and checked into the delivery room, and was directed to a rectangular metal table which was used for the delivery bed.

It did not contain any bedding material so the table was very cold to the touch, and also uncomfortable to lie on. Nevertheless, this is where I gave birth to my son Marsh. The nurse was not present during the birth process, but came into the room soon after. She was upset with me for not calling her. To me that was not practical, as I was in such excruciating pain.

After the birth of my son, I stayed in the hospital for a few days. My sister Lorie came to visit, she helped me pack my things to go home. The following week Roger came to visit me. He expressed his satisfaction that the child was his because of the many similarities he identified in body features which existed between the baby and himself. He was very happy. After that, he visited me every two weeks, and brought me diapers, Cow and Gate formula and other needed things. As the days went by I realized that the baby formula was finishing very fast, but I couldn't understand; and I was afraid to accuse any of my two brothers. That caused me not to have sufficient feeding for the baby. Times like these I had to make do.

There were times when Roger visited he would take me and the baby for a drive, that made me felt very special.

The baby was getting bigger and I wanted to be gainfully employed but there were no jobs to be had, so I remained totally dependent on Roger.

As his visits grew infrequent, the support dwindled.

My mother was an elementary school teacher at Ferry Primary School, and although she was well respected in the community, I faced her displeasure whenever I had to depend on her for assistance.

I would go to her house and wash, cook and clean for her to secure a meal, and justify any support she gave me.

Whenever Roger was very supportive and I was more independent, the relationship between my mother and myself improved.

Things got worse and I had to start weighing the options before me again. I knew for sure that Mia was not a possible source, because of how she had treated me in the past. Bart was another cousin, along with his wife, they displayed kindness towards me, but he was very poor and had to eeke out a living as a fisherman and hamper maker. His good heart and shallow pocket just allowed him to give me a meal, on occasion, whenever it was possible.

Despite his problems as being an alcoholic and a pot smoker, he had the uncanny ability of being clairvoyant and could see spirits.

My mother was living with a fairly affluent man in Ferry at the time, and was a professional herself, but the support and attention she gave to her children, especially me, was woefully inadequate.

Whenever she cooked meat, she would remove the flesh from the bone, securing the meat for her and Mr. Wright, and then leaving the bone to my brother Roy, Joe, and myself. Luckily I did the cooking sometimes, and so was able to steal food from the pot without her knowing. Her treatment to me was bad, but to Roy it was worse. It was like he was not her child at all. He was treated as a street urchin.

On rare occasions when she gave me a piece of meat from the pot, it was done with the charge that I should not say anything to Roy.

Roy would often use a footpath through the bushes that led from the neighbor's house to the back of Mr. Wright's kitchen. This made his approach un-noticed. Roy would then get into a crouching position at the back of the kitchen and remain in hiding until he could seize upon the opportunity to steal food from the boiling pot. There were also times when he would remove the entire pot from the fire just to secure a meal, even if it was partially cooked.

Roy attended school regular, but he was not furnished with proper clothes in comparison to the other students.

On the night before Roy graduated, he was so lacking in clothes that my cousin Bart had to give him a white shirt and a pair of cufflinks to wear to the function.

My mother again reverted to her malevolent ways, telling me to vacate the house so that she could put an end to paying the rent. Although I offered to pay the rent myself, she refused and insisted that I vacate, so I packed my things and left.

My cousin Bart provided me with the sparest accommodation he was able to afford. The bed I got to sleep on was falling apart from age and over use. I had to secure it with wire.

On hearing this, Mr. Covey was peeved, and went and had words with my mother about the situation. After their conversation, my mother recanted and told me to return home. Our relationship was marginally improved.

Owing to my past of having been in the juvenile home, which was common knowledge in the area, I remain quite reticent in the community. Nevertheless, I got to know a young lady named Sally, and we became very good friends. She later introduced me to her cousin Julie, who lived close to Bay. We both became friends. There were times I visited Julie and spent one or two days with her at her parent's home. She took me many places with her, and also introduced me to her friends. Julie was a very nice person to me.

As luck would have it. The Indian lady Mrs. Singh had lost her husband, so she vacated the house and moved away to live in Wildwood. This event encouraged my mother to return to her former stance of ordering me to move out of her house. She suggested that I occupy the lady's former house instead. This time she was relentless, especially since Roy and George were already living there. On her insistence I moved into the house with my two brothers.

One day just trying to overcome boredom, I went and sat on the verandah with a needle and straw and started to make a hat. I showed Mr. Covey the finished products, and he suggested to me that my efforts could be commercially viable. He offered to be my sole agent. I was now making an income by selling hats. This did not last for a very long time, but for its profitable duration, I was able to purchase articles I needed, and reward Mr. Covey some return for his efforts.

After this business venture ended, I returned to spending days engulfed with boredom and frustration. To get over these feelings,

I soon decided to continue my studies and registered to do more academic subjects.

All through these lean times, Mr. Covey's support was evident, providing me with food from time to time, and encouraging words. My grandmothers also remain a tower of strength to me.

I sometimes secured a meager income by doing chores for Mr. Oso, who was a sick and disabled elderly man, and a very prominent and respectable member of the community. As time passed my mother had also rented a house from him. My brothers and I were still living in the house where our mother placed us.

The room I occupied had been the former bedroom of Mrs. Singh's husband who had died. After living there for some time, I got very sick, unable to diagnose what the problem was. Whenever I retire to bed at night, I always feel as if someone was lying on top of me. One night, my son Roger visited me and stayed overnight. In the morning he told me that he felt as if someone was moving in the bed, and at one time the bed got unusually hot.

My sickness progressed, until one morning I was unable to move. I sent a number of messages to my mother asking her to come, but she never responded to my call. My brother Roy eventually got very angry with her behavior and went to her house and admonished her in the most expressive language. This caused her to give heed to my calling, and she came and saw the pitiful state I was in. She did not know what to do but call Brother Todd. When Brother Todd came and saw my condition, he explained to my mother that my sickness was an evil spell. I then heard him telling my mother that he would return very quickly.

When Brother Todd returned, he gave me a steamed bath which did not seem to make any improvement in my condition. My mother then suggested that I should go back to Miss Perry house, but I was so weak and unable to walk. It was my brother Roy who had to assist by lifting me.

I was totally unable to ambulate on my own. This change of residence did not improve my condition in any way. Actually, I got weaker and lost my appetite. When I tried to eat, mastication was very difficult. My mother finally accepted that my illness was not from natural causes.

One night I was alone lying in bed, I heard approaching footsteps on the verandah, but the door was never opened, and no one came into the house. Because of my constant nightmares of dead people interacting with me, I realized it was a 'ghost.' And so I was prepared to 'give up the ghost.' Not long after my sister Lorie came and brought me dinner. I asked her if she had entered the verandah previously that night, she said she did not. This confirmed my suspicion that it must have been a 'ghost.' I immediately broke out in uncontrollable tears. My sister asked me what the matter was. I could not respond to her because it might appear incredible. After my sister visited for a while, she told me goodnight, and left.

Later that night my mother came and asked me if Lorie had brought me dinner, I said 'yes.'

She then went into the adjoining room and started praying. I could hear her 'speaking in unknown tongues.' That night, unusually, my brother Roy was not home early. Later I heard him, Cousin Bart, and his wife Terry speaking in the yard. Bart came inside my room very upset, and reprimanded me for not informing him of my sickness. He said, "We are blood and despite our differences we are blood, and when it comes to sickness we should put all our differences aside." All through Bart's dialogue with me my mother was still praying and speaking in 'unknown tongues' in the adjoining room.

Bart then went about to diagnose my condition. He asked for a measuring tape, luckily Terry was wearing one. He then performed some arcane practices then concluded that, 'it was an Indian spirit that was causing the problem.' The man was actually the owner of the house I lived in. Bart said the only reason I was alive was because my spirit was a few percentage stronger than that of the Indian man's Mr. Singh. Bart then sent Roy to the back of the house where a lime tree was located to pick some limes that he needed to do an exorcism.

When my brother returned he was shouting and appeared frightened. He reported that on approaching the tree he had mysteriously received a blow on his forehead. There was a visible contusion on his forehead; Bart immediately used a cut lime to treat Roy injury. Bart then instructed my mother and Terry to sponge my body using lime juice, and then anoint me with a prepared elixir which he added to olive oil.

After they were finished I was able to get up, as I felt better immediately, after being unable to walk for a number of weeks.

That night Bart and his wife observed me walking around and were surprised that my gait was just like that of the Indian man Mr. Singh. Bart took the machete and said to my mother, "Come with me." He apparently was going to do some 'spiritual investigation' and he needed her support.

I could hear them going off in the distance; my mother speaking in 'unknown tongues' and Bart rebuking and admonishing the spirit while wielding his machete.

When they returned, Bart reported that the spirit was angry with me because I was sleeping in his bed and had also cut his banana down.

In reality, the bed I was sleeping on was mine, but it was in the same position of that of the deceased, so the spirit would always come and lie on top of me. I then recalled that one day while I was living at that house I went to a banana tree and attempted to cut a bunch of bananas, but strangely the tree and bunch of bananas fell and all the banana fingers were broken up.

My sickness manifested a strange bodily function. My feces were goat like appearance, and also my period became viscous to the point where it appeared granular in texture.

As the days passed my health began to improve. Bart suggested that I should drink chicken soup made with a rooster that never lay with a hen. When he brought the soup, he told me that I should drink all of it because that's what I needed to gain my strength.

During my illness I had lost a great deal of weight, this was exacerbated by the fact that I was unable to feed myself. Fortunately my mother continued to supply me with food which really helped me to recover.

My strength had returned, and I was able to walk around, so I started doing my laundry again.

During my illness, and on Mr. Covey insistence, my mother had taken my son Marsh. Gwen was hired as the baby-sitter while my mother had to work. After I got better and it came time for me to take the child, my mother was not very accommodating to the idea, so I left the child in her care.

My mother had gone back to her old sinister ways, and our relationship took a downward turn again. I was still living at Miss Perry house and things got very bad for me financially.

Oftentimes, I would sit and cry very loudly with the hope that someone, especially those persons that traveled regularly to Town would hear my cries and display some compassion towards me. I was hoping that someone would try to get a job for me in Town, or any other place for the matter, but no one showed pity.

When I walked on the road people would ridicule me as a mad person. As a result of this I tended to remain domiciled at home for the most part.

My grandmother was now living at the house which my mother rented from Mr. Oso; I would sometimes hide and go there to visit her, and seek refuge.

One day I was walking down the road and met a lady by the name of Kelly. As she saw me, she immediately became verbally abusive and said "You damn blasted mad gal, what the hell you doing on the road, how the hell you not dead yet, you need to be in the blasted madhouse." Kelly angrily grabbed me and expressed her dislike for me. She continued to abuse me by saying 'I should not be alive at this time, because I am only taking up space.' She then started to beat me in a violent manner. Despite my loud cries for help, no one came to my assistance.

It was reported to me by Mr. Covey that my mother heard about the incident. When I later related the incident to her, she was totally unsympathetic. She said I was an embarrassment to her professionally, and it would be best that I went away. I told Cousin Bart what my mother had said, and he offered to give me some accommodation in his house. As he was a person of very modest means. I was appreciative of his kind gesture.

One day I was on my way to visit my grandmother, when I was approaching a Hill I heard a beckoning whistle. I looked to see who it was, and saw a tall light-complexion young man, quite tall in stature. He had an unusual accent when he spoke. He asked me my name and said his name was Sims, and wanted to know if I was from the area. We then started having a conversation. His remarked to me was that a 'good looking intelligent girl' like me should be in a foreign country or somewhere making good for myself. I agreed with him, but said that I did not have any means of assistance to make that a reality.

Before we parted that day, he encouraged me to come and talk with him again.

As a young woman, I had misgiving about strangers, and was also fearful that someone in the community might relay some of the sordid aspect of my past to this stranger, so on subsequent visits to my grandmother I took another route to avoid meeting Sims again.

My constant visit to my grandmother belied the fact that I was really living there.

During the days, I would appear to be making casual visits, but when night came and everyone had retired I hid my belongings which I sneaked under my grandmother's bed and spent the night there. Apart from my grandmother and myself, Bart and Mr. Covey were the only persons who knew my secret.

My grandmother would also place food, or whatever else she had for me at the foot of the bed; it would be there until I could retrieve it.

My mother's rancor was only directed to me, as she only accepted my children living there with my grandmother. She would not knowingly allow me to visit my children even to offer them support.

One night while sleeping under the bed, I woke up to find my clothing soaking wet. I realized that my movement during sleep caused me to knock over the chamber pot, and I was inundated with urine. I woke up my grandmother and she accompanied me outside to get cleaned up. Luckily no one heard, and my mother was not at the house at that time, as she was living at her own quarters.

This situation with me continued for some time, until I got tired of the second class status which I had to assume.

I decided that it was unimportant if my mother found out where I was staying, because I did not think I deserved that kind of treatment.

When my mother heard of my living arrangements, her anger knew no bounds, as she verbally expressed her dissatisfaction in no uncertain manner. It was Mr. Covey again, who had to come to my rescue, because he was so 'put out' by her behavior that he had words with her.

He reminded her that her behavior was not befitting someone of her social standing, and she should not allow the family's 'dirty linen' to be hung in public.

This seemed to have some positive effect on her, as she relented. After this our relationship took a somewhat upward turn.

Sims lived close to where my grandmother lived. Soon we became platonic friends.

Sims, at the time had a girlfriend named Gil, but shortly after we became friends their relationship ended, and our relationship became much more than a platonic one. Sims would display his affection for me by giving me gifts. I suppose he also saw the dire financial condition under which I lived and knew I was in need.

There was a large boulder in front of my house. Whenever he had anything for me, and was passing by, I would be heralded by the sound of a pebble on the verandah to alert me that there was something out there for me. So whenever I knew he was gone at Bay, or Town I would eagerly await his return. His support was very welcome, especially because it helped me to support my children.

Notwithstanding the fact that Sims and I had an intimate relationship, I endeavored to behave with some propriety in public and before my children, as I did not want everyone to know the nature of the relationship between Sims and myself.

We made sure that the visits to my home were very late at night, and when we spoke to each other in public it was always in passing or for a very short duration. Sims had a car, and as time passed, at nights he would take me driving and also crab-hunting on the highway.

I was not aware that my mother had 'gotten wind' of my covert affair. On one of our nocturnal rendezvous, as Sims was about to leave, I felt a sense of uneasiness, as if we were being watched. I looked around to make sure the path was clear. It was about two o'clock by then and I did not expect anyone else to be around.

Suddenly my mother emerged from under the house. She accosted Sims in a violent tone and said to him, "What the hell are you doing at my house?" and shouting that he should not come back there again. He did not respond to her outburst, but became moved when he saw that I was in tears. He asked me repeatedly if I was okay; and I assured him that I was. He then said that as a man he was very embarrassed at the incident and he would not be coming back there. My mother coldly stood her ground and watched until he left.

This was the pattern of behavior my mother had come to adopted with me in any relationship I had with the opposite sex. She never desists from meddling in my private life although I was twenty-four years of age.

Overcome with grief and embarrassment, I was crying after he left, I tried not to awaken my children or anyone in the house. My grandmother, who was really my best friend, heard me crying and came to console me, and said, "One day God will send you a man that no one will be able to chase away." She also said that in time my mother would have to seek my support, as things would change for me. She also said that even if she is not alive to see this, 'ants would carry the news in her grave.' I went to bed that night, but sleep was far from my eyes. I cried all night, which caused my face to be swollen. Luckily my children were too young to understand what was happening. The next morning I visited Bart and related what had happened. He was miffed, and agreed that my mother should stop meddling in my private life.

Bart knew though that my mother did not regard him as having an equal social standing to her, so it was unlikely that he would get an audience with her to discuss my situation.

Mr. Covey quietly boldly spoke up for me again. He was very supportive and disheartened by my mother's behavior.

My mother's domineering behavior was evident in all aspects of my life. I was literally tormented by her.

Whenever she was at the house where I lived, I would avoid going there until she left, and if I was there and she came I would find a reason to leave. Not even respond to nature's call on my bodily function, would cause me to remain at the house, I would gladly take the chamber pot to the bushes and leave it there if the toilet was occupied.

Mr. Covey would be my companion night after night. We would sit by the roadside and talk until very late, just to put my mind at ease.

There was not much more he could do about my situation. Being frustrated, I concluded that the only solution was to get away from my mother. I contacted my friend Sally and told her what I had decided to do. She told me about a guy she had met who was visiting from Rio, who had information about a prospective job. Sally arranged for me to meet him.

When we met, he seemed pleased with my appearance and said that the lady who needed the help would also be pleased with me as I was a fine looking young woman.

Although I was prepared to leave then and there, I did not have the money for the fare to Rio. I told Mr. Covey of my predicament, and he suggested that I ask Sims to help me, but I was too embarrassed to face Sims.

Mr. Covey knew how I felt, so he offered to act as my mediator. He met with Sims and arranged for the both of us to meet. Sims relayed to me the plans he was making with a friend for me to go abroad so that I could enjoy a better life. Plans he said, that my mother's behavior had shattered. He nevertheless, gave me fifty dollars towards my trip and wished me all future success.

Mr. Covey then gave me five dollars.

I contacted Sally's friend and told him I was ready to leave.

I told my grandmother my plans, and she wished me good luck and said, "God go with you." She allayed my fears by assuring me that she would help the best way that she could with the children while I was away.

CHAPTER TWENTY-FIVE

Unfortunate Course of Events

The day finally came, and I was on my way to Rio escorted by a friend. When we arrived there, he took me directly to my prospective employer. She was a 'well to do' lady, living with all the comforts the time offered.

Her husband was a sea-man who came home periodically. Practically speaking, she lived alone with her two children. Meeting her, she explained to me that my job was to be in charge of the children and do all the domestic chores that were needed, but declined to offer me a salary. My presence there would be that of an additional family member, where I would share meals and enjoy free occupancy. This arrangement did not meet with my approval, but I, nevertheless, decided to stick with it, as returning home to Ferry was not an option.

I then settled into the arrangement, performing the household chores, and caring for the children. There was plenty to eat. I also was given my own room.

After living there for some time, we developed an amicable relationship. She would often come to my room at night just to talk. Sometimes after chatting, she would fall asleep and ended up spending the night.

On this particular night after our 'chit-chat' she fell asleep in my bed. I woke up to find her hand groping and fondling my body. With surprise and anger, I said to her, "What the hell are you doing." She only smiled at me and asked me if I was vexed about the situation. The next morning I made an effort to hide my scorn and disgust I was feeling towards her. In the ensuing days I did my best to avoid her.

Needless to say, our relationship took a downward turn, as she obviously was not happy with my attitude.

It got to the place that whenever she cooked I was not offered anything to eat, and also removed the toiletry from the bathroom.

Things got real bad for me, and I became very uncomfortable. My desire was to get away from her house.

As I was a stranger in the community I did not know anyone around. I started befriending everyone I could with the hope that an avenue of escape would be opened.

One day while walking down the road in the vicinity of Jacks Hill, I saw a group of people in a yard standing and talking. My instinct drove me to enter the yard and approach the group of people. I introduced myself, and quickly relayed my plight to these strangers, explaining to them what had happened between me and my employer. They empathized with me and immediately right there and then offered me living accommodation.

That same day I returned to the lady's place and collected my things.

The living accommodation with this new family was not anywhere near as comfortable as where I was coming from, in fact the family was a poor working class, and the house was small, so things were quite cramped for the most part.

There were six people living there after I came, which include three females and three males. I was forced to share a room with Bill and his niece, which I was very uncomfortable about. Still I made do because it was 'Hobson's choice.' I paid for my 'keep' by doing the household chores. We all had a good relationship.

As the days dragged on by, I remembered that once while I was visiting my family and friends in Stanford, I had met two men who had told me they lived in Rio. Their names were Randy and Carl, so I set about making inquiries of their whereabouts to see if I could find anyone who knew them. I got in touch with Carl first, and he took me to Randy. We soon became friends again. My association with these guys enhanced my social life a great deal.

Carl had a motorcycle and at times he would take me for a ride in the town of Rio. Randy had a glass bottom boat, in which he took the tourists on sight-seeing excursions, and also did deep sea fishing, which enabled him to supply the hotels with seafood. Oftentimes, he would take me on many excursions in his boat to view the underwater flora and fauna. Because of my increased social life the times I spent at my new home was much less.

To my dismay, Bill, who was one of the men who lived at the house started behaving in a very unseemly way towards me. It soon became apparent that I could no longer stay at the house. I told Randy about my situation and he invited me to come and stay on his boat until I found a place.

One morning very early I packed my clothes and was in the process of leaving.

Suddenly stones were hurled in my direction. I realized it was Bill showing his angry response to my departure. I had to make a retreat in a desultory manner to avoid being hit.

After settling on the boat, I started seeking employment. Randy inquired around and got a job for me in a bar. This job included living accommodation.

The proprietor was an Indian lady. We got along fairly well. After working for a while a problem soon arose when one of the regular customers displayed an interest in me. I did not know that this customer was having an affair with my boss, as she was married.

Her actions towards me became progressively unfriendly, and then openly hostile. It soon became clear that she found my company objectionable. Finally she told me that the living space was getting crowded and I would have to leave.

While working at the bar I had met kitty. She was an exotic dancer at a club. We later became friends. Our friendship strengthened, and on many occasions I visited the club to watch her perform. This was such an entertainment for me. At about this time I became acquainted with a local tailor, and whenever I could, I would go to his shop and assist him. This was a welcome source of income for me.

My association with this tailor came at an opportune time. He valued our friendship so much, and on many occasions I would spend the night at his shop. Soon after, he offered me accommodation to live at the adjoining living quarters to his shop.

In spite of his generosity I did not reveal to him that I was homeless at the time. My new residence was established, the tailor made it apparent that he accepted my gratitude to take the form of intimate favors. Upon rejected his advances he promptly evicted me.

As time passed I heard about another job which involves working at another bar. This new job gave me some stability, and in time the owner whose name was Jerry came to trust me. I used my own initiative and introduced the selling of cooked food, which he was pleased about, as he had not done so before. This venture turned out to be quite lucrative. Because of this he came to demonstrate confidence in my abilities. While I was working at the bar I received an unexpected visit from Roger. He told me that he was on his way from Trumpet, but heard that I was living in Rio. We dialogue for a short while, and then he left.

The job gave me the opportunity to save money and rented a room in Mayfield, which was an upscale neighborhood in Rio, and also bought new furniture.

After some time my boss died, which caused me to be very sad. His friends and families were very appreciative of everything I had done, and rewarded me with money and gifts.

Because of my notoriety in the business, a prominent business man named Victor Bell offered me a job at his club and restaurant. I did not accept the offer immediately because I had some things to sort out, and needed some time. I told him to give me two weeks to respond. He was favorable to this arrangement.

Because of my friendship with Carl and Randy, my social life expanded, and also widened my circle of friends.

I became a regular visitor to quite a few hotels, where I met and became friends with a musical band, and also a famous singer; who were popular musicians at that time.

Around this time Sally came from Ferry to visit me in Rio. Sally, Kitty and myself enjoyed social life together. I even got a job for Sally in Rio.

At one point, my dire economic state caused me much embarrassment in dealing with my landlord. At every opportunity

Journey on a Bumpy Road

I would try to avoid any face to face contact with her. Some of my actions to remain inconspicuous took the form of getting up early in the mornings to cook; being away from the house for a long period of time; and even using water from a pail to flush the toilet so as not to draw any attention. During my down time, it was Randy and his wife who supported me financially.

On one occasion I went visiting Short rock with a male friend and his friends. We were at a beach club having drinks and socializing. My companion and I went and sat some way off by the seaside. During the course of the night, the sea, the winds and the rocks seemed to have a captivating effect on us.

After a while, my friend left me alone and went to talk with his friends. After sitting there alone for some time, I was approached by one of his friends who started to make advances to me. I rejected him, and a struggle ensued. Suddenly two more of his friends came over. The three men worked unison and forcibly held me down. They pinned me to the rock leaving my body in an exposed and defenseless posture. I was now totally helpless. They started raping me. Each taking their turn, and trying to penetrate and ravished my body mercilessly. They each performed the act with a sense of reckless abandonment.

After they were finished their countenances all displayed an expression of accomplishment and satisfaction with what they had done, totally oblivious to the pain I was experiencing.

My suffering came from my body lying on the rocks, and the bludgeoned onslaught my body had to endure internally.

I was unable to walk properly, and I was left on the rocks lying like a rag doll.

With my body writhing in pain, I tried to stumble and dragged myself from the beech to the roadway. The car I had come in was not parked at the spot it was left. My attackers had already boarded and removed the car to a different parking spot further up the road.

There I stood dazed with pain and anguish. There was no one around, so I waved to them to see if they would help me, but it was to no avail, as they pretended as if they never saw me. I then noticed on a hill overlooking the road there was a lady standing seemingly observing the scene. It could be that the men were cognizant of the presence of the lady on the hill, and that she may have seen what had transpired, because they soon reversed the car to where I was standing.

My male friend came out of the car and angrily grabbed me by my hands, and while pulling me, ordered me into the car, shouting. "Get your ass in the dam car." I was shocked to experience the total change in his attitude towards me.

It was very hard for me to endure when I realized that my male friend was party to this conspiracy. They also showed disdain for me by letting me out of the car a good distance from my home. I had to walk and endure the painful journey home.

Sally was home when I arrived, but I got myself ready for bed.

During the night and subsequent days, I experienced a lot of pain and discomfort but I just kept it to myself.

The physical trauma I had endured made it difficult for me to urinate and have bowel actions. I made no one privy to my dilemma, fearing that I would be vilified and ridiculed in the eyes of my friends.

In the ensuing days and nights, I administered hot water to my body until I was better.

After such a traumatic experience my thoughts at the time led me to believe that soup would strengthen and aid my recovery; so I invited Kitty, and Sally to accompany me to the market to purchase some barracuda fish.

After returning home I meticulously prepared 'the soup' which we all enjoyed.

To our misfortune, we later discovered that we had a case of food poisoning. This condition was one of possible hazard of eating barracuda fish at certain time of the year; which was not known to me at the time.

Sally was the worst hit, as she did not regurgitate any of the food we ate; she had to seek medical help. As nature would have it, Kitty and I did a copious amount of regurgitation which expelled the poison from our system.

We soon realized that the extensive vomiting was also partially due to the fact that we were both pregnant and were experiencing symptoms of morning sickness.

The poison was still in us and we thought it would be prudent for us to return home at that time. Sally was exhibiting more symptoms than I was, so I made all haste to return home with her.

We boarded a bus to get back to Ferry with only our bus fares in hand.

The trip was an arduous and lengthy journey, because it required a number of transfers between buses over many hours of travel. We soon got very exhausted and hungry.

When the bus reached to Terry Town, it made one of its scheduled stops. Luckily, it was parked just across the street from the police station.

By this time Sally and I were famished, with cracked lips, as we had nothing to eat, or any money to purchase food. I suggested to Sally that I would go to the police station and ask for some assistant. She was not all together in favor of the idea, but her hunger made her less resistant to my proposal.

I went inside and started a conversation with a tall dark skinned officer at the front desk. It would appear that he found me quite congenial, and my story very credible, because he gave me enough money to purchase food to last us for the rest of our journey.

It was late that night when we reached to Ferry. Our first stop was at Sally mother's house, as I was concerned about the fact that she had left Ferry on my account.

Her mother was distraught over her condition, and proceeded to vent her fury on me, and said I was responsible. She cursed me in the most rancorous fashion for most of the night, but still gave us both bissy tea which is known as an antidote for poison. In the morning we both felt much better. I stayed on at Sally's house for a few days, and then I went to visit my cousin Bart. I was petrified about the prospect of speaking to my mother.

Soon after, my son's father Roger came to visit me. Not knowing where to find me he had gone and asked my mother if she was privy as to my whereabouts. When he saw me he did not seem very pleasant, and told me that he had a revealing conversation with my mother concerning me, and was very disturbed. Disgust looking, he then said that if he had spoken to my mother before we met, he would never have proceeded with any relationship with me. I interjected, and told him that my mother had artfully contrived a story for him, but in reality she was responsible for many of the woes I had experienced in my life, as I was rejected by her since I was a child. And not seeing him, and unable to gain employment in the community I was left no choice but to accept help from other sources.

My suggestion to him was to speak with Mr. Covey and other residents in the community rather than rely on the demeaning picture which my mother painted of me. Roger did not appear convinced, and said that I will want to see him in the future but it might be too late. And with that I will get a red white and blue envelope from him. He then drove off.

My random visits to my grandmother's house started again, until after a few weeks I eventually took up residence there much to the consternation of my grandmother.

Her attention and love once again was very evident.

It was now 1972, and apart from having to readjust myself to life at Ferry, I was pregnant with my fourth child.

My problem was compounded by the fact that I told Roger that my pregnancy was due to our relationship. He immediately denied it by saying, 'no not you again a dam.' I felt rejected, also remembering how he had degraded me in the past due to my indigent condition. In my mind I thought that if he was not the father for the child I was pregnant with then it may probably be another person who I met shortly after the affair I had with him. I felt worthless, and was left in a state of frustration. I told the family a story that the man who got me pregnant was married but belongs to a prominent family whose name I gave them, but died recently.

It was my hope that this story would cause my family to display some semblance of acceptance for me due to my situation, but this was not to be.

This did not overshadow the fact that I was having financial problems and was forced to go from house to house in the community begging, just to secure something to eat. My 'visits' to some of these people would be deliberately made to coincide with dinner time. Mr. Covey was again appalled at my condition, especially seeing that I was also pregnant. He decided to speak to my mother.

As usual, whatever he said always had a positive effect on her. It was not long after she came to see me and gave me money for the impending birth of the child. These again, mark another trend in our dubious relationship. This caused me to feel a little more settled, and again decided to register at the high school for an exam.

The birth of my child was quite imminent, so I started going to the clinic and made sure to engage the service of a midwife beforehand. I had to take the arduous walk up and down the hill to visit the clinic.

When the time came for me to give birth, I sent a messenger on foot to fetch the midwife. My grandmother was by my side administering any help she could.

The time it took for the midwife to be alerted and reach the home took a long time. My baby came into the world with my grandmother's assistance. She cut the umbilical cord with a pair of rusty scissors. It was through 'Divine Providence' that the birth was successful. I gave birth to my baby girl Jewel.

My mother was still living in a common-law relationship with Mr. Wright. My daughter was getting older. Oftentimes I would go to the house and help my mother with domestic chores.

It soon became apparent to me that Mr. Wright's interest in me was more than that of a step-father. My fears were realized one night when I was visiting his home. I was sitting on the verandah, and my mother was in the kitchen preparing dinner. He suddenly approached me and placed his hand on my leg and started to massage my thighs, and said that he wanted to get close to me. I tried to capitalize on the situation by telling him that he had no right to touch me like that, and if he did not give me some money I was going to let it be known to my mother. He did not appear daunted by my threat and boldly told me to do whatever I 'damn' well please.

I decided that one way or another he would have to pay for his indiscretion. Some of the pimento that he harvested was kept in his house. As usual, I went to the house under the pretext that I was doing laundry. I took a large wash pan, and conspicuously went into the house and put bags of pimento into the 'wash pan.' My exit was usually executed with the same level of stealth as before. I took the 'booty' to my Cousin Bart house for safe-keeping. We later sold the pimento and shared the proceeds between Bart and myself.

This gave me a personal sense of satisfaction after the sordid encounter with Mr. Wright.

My baby Jewel was getting bigger and I was still experiencing hardship in fending for myself in Ferry. I was not loved and appreciated by the residents in the community, owing to the fact that my mother propagated the negative aspects of my life.

My cousin Mia had a small grocery shop which was located in front of our yard. Whenever she saw me, she would look at me in disdain, as she thought her position was superior to mine. She often makes unsupported claims that her shop was broken into, intimating that I was the perpetrator.

Mr. Nick, the assistant principal of the high school, was one of my Cousin Bart's friends. Bart told me about him, and suggested that he wanted to introduce me to him; hoping he would help me out of my difficulties. One day Cousin Bart took me to the high school to meet with Mr. Nick. Cousin Bart boldly told Mr. Nick that I was his beautiful cousin, and would like to introduce the both of us. Mr. Nick's response was. "As a matter of fact she is really good looking." As time passed by Mr. Nick and I later became platonic friends. This was during the time I was studying for my exam. Mr. Nick was non-judgmental in his interaction with me, and admired the progressive attitude I displayed. Because of my association with him, I met a lot of new and interesting people; many of them were from different countries who displayed an interest in knowing more about me.

It was always pleasant for me to visit Mr. Nick and socialized with him. Mr. Nick was also very fond of my brother Roy. He was my teacher and mentor, and willingly gave me invaluable help with my studies. The contact between us gained momentum over the months, and our relationship blossomed into an intimate one.

Mr. Nick was very kind to me. As a result I was able to take care of my children and myself. One day he said that he had something to say to me which I might not find very pleasing. He appeared very hesitant at first, and then he told me that he was married. I was totally distraught, and felt like my entire world was crumbling one more time. I now became scared of the possibility of his wife visiting.

He assured me that their relationship was such, and that she would not be visiting.

Mr. Nick's kindness towards me continued; he even allowed me to take my baby Jewel with me whenever I visited him.

The news of his marriage made me stay away for a while.

One day I re-visited Mr. Nick's house, I saw two men, Larry and Mr. Brown. These two men were not very affable towards me. I was very frightened thinking that they might be a harbinger of bad news for Mr. Nick. When they saw me coming it seemed as if my presence made them start stuttering and then left suddenly. Mr. Nick was very evasive when I asked him what they were talking about. That evening we socialized together, but I did not spend the night just to avoid any contentious moment.

I later found out that Larry and Mr. Brown were social drinking partners of Mr. Nick. Apparently, my relationship with Mr. Nick had caused him to be absent from their company and made him a teetotaler temporarily. Missing the comradeship with him, they had made a visit to find out what was the problem. Apparently, they used that opportunity to vilify me to Mr. Nick. From that time our relationship started to 'peter out.' We then only met on occasions that I needed help with my studies.

At about this time my mother was separated from Mr. Wright and moved in with my grandmother, my sister Lorie, my brother Roy, my children, and myself. My brother Joe at the time lived in Laneville with a family member, but was present for most of the time. The house was quite large, so there was enough room to accommodate her. Not very long after, she became very contentious. It appeared that her attitude was sparked off by my presence at the house, because she was always ill at ease whenever I was around her.

The relationship between Mr. Nick and myself had been smothered, so I lost the support that I so desperately needed, therefore I became dependent on my mother again, or back to begging in the community.

Things got very bad again. One day I was very destitute, and had no food to eat. I knew that asking my mother for money would only inflame her, so I thought the next best thing to do was to take what I needed from her purse. Although I stole the paltry amount of two dollars from my mother's purse, her violent reaction on discovering the money was missing, brought home to me the severity of my action. Immediately after the money was missing she made an accusation that I was at fault, and that the money belonged to my sister Lorie. I denied anything to do with the alleged theft.

A resolution of the matter could not be arrived at, and my mother was not prepared to let the matter rest just like that.

That night my mother, my brother Roy, and my sister Lorie decided to perform a spiritual ritual to ascertain who the culprit was. The ritual involved using a Bible, a gold ring, a piece of thread, and a clear glass of water.

After the apparatus was set in place, the names of the prospective thieves were called. If the name called was indeed the perpetrator, the ring would indicate this by moving on its own volition.

A clarion call was given to the spirits with the name of each family member in turn.

The ring remained motionless in every case, but when my name was uttered, suddenly there was an involuntary movement of the ring, indicating my guilt. This exercise was done repeatedly to prove the validity of the result.

Armed with new knowledge, my mother, brother and sister cursed me in the most vituperative manner, in the presence of my children. My grandmother was the only voice which tried to abate the situation. She reminded them that we were all family and should display a more loving attitude towards each other. My brother Roy angrily rebuffed my grandmother, and told her that her presence was only taking up space.

Well, I finally went to bed that night. I felt as if I was covered with a cloud of shame. In the morning, my grandmother came and told me that she overheard Lorie talking with my mother. Grandmother told me that Lorie had said she was going to tell Mr. Nick about the incident. When Lorie left the house on her mission, my grandmother instructed me to follow her. I trailed some distance behind her and took an alternative route, getting there, so I would not be seen.

I arrived at Mr. Nick's house shortly after Lorie got there, and secured myself outside under his window. Lorie left nothing to the imagination in describing the incident and the entire negative occurrence in my past life to Mr. Nick. She did all she could to totally debase me in his eyes.

As soon as she left, I went around to talk with Mr. Nick. He was very surprised to see me. I made every effort I could to reverse in his mind any bad picture he might now be harboring about me.

He said he did not think I was a bad person, but that he perceived there was a problem in my family. Mr. Nick said that if he was not a married man he would marry me and take me away from them; so he thought it would be best for me to get away from them. I reported the incident pertaining to what my sister Lorie had done to Mr. Covey. He said that Lories is my sister, but she had always been vindictive of me; also she was very wicked for going to such an extreme to take bread from me and the children's mouth. Mr. Covey was very miffed about it; and said that it was 'family matter.'

My sister Lorie made sure that the incident about the two dollars was common knowledge all-over in Ferry.

Feeling so ashamed, and uncomfortable, I avoided going back to see Mr. Nick or even to go out in the public unnecessarily.

Feeling frustrated about my condition, one day I took a trip to Grove. I met a young man by the name of Kirk who was employed at Factory in Bay. He kindly offered me a listening ear, which I really needed at that time. We talked for a while and I expressed the desire to leave Ferry to try and improve my life. He was taken by my sincerity and gave me five dollars for my fare back home. We maintained a correspondence and soon became friends. Our relationship was such that he soon took on the persona of a brother to me.

One occasion he came to the house in Ferry to visit me. Our house, like the rest of Ferry, was nested in a bucolic setting. We sat on the verandah and talked for a while. My mother suddenly appeared and declared loudly that she did not want any man visiting me at her place, that he should take me to his mother's place.

Embarrassed at her outburst, Kirk and I got up and went and stood in the yard. He was obviously turned off by the incident and left shortly.

When I went back into the house, my mother continued to express her anger towards me. At this point I could not contain my disgust and disappointment at her years of bad treatments towards me. I was twenty-five years old and I thought the way she chooses to deal with me was totally insensitive and uncalled for. I finally vented my fury towards her and told her that, 'whatever I did she had never been supportive of me, and whenever I meet someone who is willing to help me with my children, you as a mother will not protect my dignity as others have done in Ferry.' I told her that I was sick and tired of her 'dam blasted' treatment.

Despite my outburst in claiming my independence and rights as an adult, my economic circumstances still remained very grave. I was now forced, despite my better judgment to call Kirk and ask him for assistance. He agreed and arranged to meet me at the grocery store in Grove the following evening. He generously gave me the full run of the store. I was allowed the freedom to buy whatever I needed, prompted by his accommodating suggestion.

He seemed to be acquainted with the store owner, and some of the customers who were there spoke very highly of him.

Kirk offered to take me home on his motor-cycle. This made me very uneasy, as I feared another unpleasant incident with my mother. Nevertheless, I relented and agreed.

When we got home he took the large box of groceries and placed it on the dining table. My fears were realized when my mother came in at that moment. 'She abruptly ordered me to, "Get the damn box of food off her table and get out of her house." Kirk then confronted her and said, "Woman you are crazy. Your daughter came to me for help, and that is why I am here. If I was not married myself, with the qualities your daughter possesses, I would marry her just to get her away from you and this bad family life." After saying all that, he left and went outside. I then burst out into uncontrollable tears.

We talked for a while, and he told me clearly that he would not return because this was the second time my mother was disrespectful to him; but told me that if I needed help in the future I should come and visit him at his place of employment. Before he left, he promised that he would continue helping me because he cares for me very much.

My mother's unsavory attitude towards me continued. This was exacerbated by the conflict between my brother, my sister and I. They had clandestine discussions where I was always ridiculed and treated as the family mascot, which continued all through my adult age. There was a case in point when my brother Roy joined the army. As memory serves me, he was on leave and came home to visit. He was in the company of my mother and my sister Lorie, all speaking in muffled tones so that I would not be aware of the fact that he had returned with money. Wanting to hear what they were talking about, I hid under the house cellar and overheard my mother telling my brother to talk quietly because she did not want me to hear that he had brought money back and beg for some, or maybe come and steal it. That night I felt so dejected that I took a crocus bag and went back under the cellar of the house to sleep. In time, my brother got married and was domiciled in Town.

As the years passed, my grandmother got advanced in age and was no longer able to bathe herself. She now needed individualized attention. This responsibility fell on me as my mother thought that kind of thing was beneath her. This was a duty that I, nevertheless, accepted with alacrity, as my grandmother had always shown me so much love and been a source of comfort and strength throughout my life. She always wore a bright smile and would look on the bright side of any situation. I considered myself truly blessed for having her around, and especially when she played her harmonica to entertain me. I was very happy to take care of her.

Nellie was my very good friend in Ferry. Her boyfriend was employed at a meat storage in Town. Every week-end she would visit him and return home laden with meat. As I was always seeking avenues to help myself, I asked her if she would allow me to accompany her the next time she went to Town, and she agreed. I soon started making regular trips to Town and eventually became friends with the workers at the warehouse. Through this I was able to secure meat to last me for a week. My main reason for socializing with the workers there was to secure a job, directly or through a third party contact, wherever, or however it came about, I was desperate.

The friendship between Nellie and myself lasted for some time. Whenever we went to the warehouse I had very little contact with her, so I did not pay very much attention to her liaisons.

One night she sent word that she wanted to speak to me. It seemed unusual and I thought it must be an urgent message from a male friend from the warehouse. When I got to her house she said that I should come closer to hear what she had to say.

To my amazement, she hit me on the side of my neck with a bottle, accusing me of revealing to her boyfriend that she was having an affair. This came as a shock to me hearing this, as I had no idea what she was talking about, because maintaining her trust in me was also to my benefit.

A loss of her friendship would also cause me to lose my free supply of meat bones and the friends I made at the warehouse. I was not that stupid, because that would cause me to lose the opportunity of going to Town.

The blow I had received from Nellie, has affected me until this day.

During that same week I was home and received a message that Nellie had come to see me. When I looked outside she was nowhere to be found, so I went to my gate to gain a panoramic view. To my horror, coming up the road like a charging bull was Nellie armed with a machete. She was accompanied by a few of her belligerent friends, obviously just as angry as she was, and all directing their venom at me. She shouted at me from a distance to, 'come out there and let her whisper in my ears with my machete.' Her command was of course punctuated with profanities. I asked her what it was that she had against me, and what it was that I had done her. And with that I made a hasty retreat into my house just to be in safety.

Our relationship waned from then on. I subsequently learned that someone had maliciously told a lie about me which she had acted on. This marked the swansong of my visit to the meat storage warehouse.

There was a lady in the community by the name of Sister Dee. For some strange reason she took an utter dislike to me. One day she saw me walking on the road. She came up to me and pronounced what seemed like a curse on me, saying, "You will not amount to anything good in life, you will just go from man to man and have fatherless children, and will never get a husband." From that day on I saw her as my nemesis, and tried my best to avoid her at all costs.

As time passed I was feeling very despondent about Ferry, and this incident only caused me much more fear and frustration, I refused to be domicile there any longer. I was soon packing my things, and removed myself from that locality and went to my grandfather's home in Windsor.

CHAPTER TWENTY-SIX

In Search for My Cousin Tiny

Cityville is located between Bay and Town. After quite a few inquiries I heard that my cousin Tiny was living there.

Living at Ferry with my poor economic condition, I had four children and was unable to support them because there were no jobs to be had there, or Windsor, apart from working in the banana, or sugar plantation, or at the coconut factory. These jobs were all physical and extremely strenuous, and were outside the scope of my physical ability.

Due to my situation, I was feeling desperate; so I decided to take a trip to Cityville to see if I could find my cousin Tiny. She had always been very nice to me, and I thought finding her she would help me. I did not have much money, but what I had could sustain me for about one week at the most, with hopes that I would be able to find her by then.

I pondered on this for a while, but although I was experiencing some trepidation, I decided, nevertheless, to take the trip. I told my grandfather that I was going to Cityville to see if I could get a job. He told me that if things didn't work out, I could always come back.

On the appointed day I boarded a minibus which was on route to Town via Cityville. I knew the route to Cityville because I had driven that way before, but I was not familiar with the town. When the van reached my destination in Cityville, I got off.

Because it was a popular town, a lot of people lived there. I was not aware though that I was not very far from where Tiny lived.

Ellen Patricia

I started to walk around inquiring as to the whereabouts of my cousin, but no one was able to help me. I looked across the street and saw a parked van with the driver sitting inside. On approaching the vehicle, to my pleasant surprise, I discovered that the driver was Tiny's boyfriend Dud. He was just as surprised to see me, and jokingly asked me, "What breeze blew you into Cityville." I told him that I had come trying to find Tiny. He said she would be very elated to see me, because she had recently been talking about me, and expressed the desire to know my whereabouts. He even said that he knew she would be willing to help me if things were not going well. I told Dud that I was in need and had no one else to assist me. Dud was ready to go home, and invited me to accompany him.

When the van drove into my cousin's yard our eyes met and there were tears of joy coming from both of us, the feeling was overwhelming. Tiny said she had been very worried about me because we had not seen each other since we separated in the Bay; and was concerned about the poor treatment I was receiving from my mother. She asked Dud where he had met me. Dud told Tiny that he was sitting in the van contemplating, and undecided as to whether he should leave for home or continue working for some time.

My sudden appearance brought home to him the reason for his ambivalence; he said he was very shocked to see me.

Tiny complimented me about how good I looked. She asked me how my mother was. She asked me what the reason was for my visit. I told her about my difficulties of having to eeke out a living in the harsh conditions at Ferry, and Windsor, having four children to support. And job opportunities were almost non-existent, and that I was always ridiculed by the people in the community about my past which hindered my success. I explained to her that my meager income would only come from helping my grandfather with cultivations of his crops, or by assisting with domestic chores.

Tiny was very understanding and accommodating, and said although she was not affluent I was welcome at her home and could sleep in the children's quarters. She told me of the regular Saturday and Sunday night parties at the beach club which was close by, and suggested that I could attend these parties with the hopes of meeting a prospective mate or getting information about a job prospect. My cousin invited me to put my things away and come into the kitchen to get something to eat.

Tiny and Dud had six children, and they all lived in one big room. Seeing this arrangement, I knew that my sleeping quarters would be on the floor along with the children. Nevertheless, when I considered the austere conditions at Windsor, this arrangement was very acceptable to me.

When I arrived there, the children were all in school. She introduced a lady to me as her step-mother.

Soon after, the children came home. Cathy, who was the eldest, was not known to me and came home first. The other children did not recognize me; because when I last saw Tiny they were very young and so they did not remember my features. Tiny said she always told them stories about me. After the introductions, Tiny sent the children to take their bath, and then come and have dinner.

All the children could not be accommodated at the dining table, so some had to sit on the floor to eat. To add to the cramped living condition, the domestic sanitation left much to be desired. The house was infested with flies, and this was especially apparent at dinner time. This was one of the discomforts of Tiny's home which I found hard to endure.

Despite all this, dinner was quite satisfying. It consisted of chicken, yellow yam, dumpling and green bananas. For me, the yellow yam was a welcome fare, as it was not part of my regular diets.

The kitchen and bathroom was detached from the house. The toilet exudes a very foul odor which could be detected from far away. Tiny had a chicken coop which was located in the general area of the bath and toilet. Its obnoxious smell resonated with that of the toilet. It must be said that Tiny made every effort to sanitize these areas of her home, but there was very little she could do to eliminate the lingering odor, because her attempt seemed futile.

When I retired for bed that first night, I huddled among the children. I awoke the next morning to find myself and the mattress inundated with urine, and my clothing infested with bedbugs. Tiny did not seem very perturbed about this, and admitted to me that this was a situation which she had to deal with on a regular basis. Her solution was to put the mattress in the sun to dry and be disinfected.

Ellen Patricia

The next night Tiny gave me some loose sheets and clothing to make my bed on the floor. This I did every night. Cathy and Tiny's step-mother shared the same room. On the nights when her step-mother was absent I would spend the night with Cathy.

Cathy was attending high school. Her mother told her to invite me to the beach club on her next visit.

One Saturday night there was a party being held at the beach club and Cathy invited me to go along with her. Although Cathy was much younger than I, my appearance was so youthful that you could not tell the difference in our ages.

On our way to the club Cathy told me about the club owner, and that his name was Mr. Thomas. She recounted how much of a father figure to her he was. Mr. Thomas maintained a motel which facilitated guests. She told me about Kelly who worked for Mr. Thomas and lived on the premises. He was the cook and caretaker and officiated at the parties. Cathy informed me that her good standing with Mr. Thomas provided us with access to free meals and other amenities at the party. This made me very anxious to reach our destination, and I quickened our pace.

When we arrived, Mr. Thomas was already there and Cathy introduced me as her cousin. Her notoriety gave me immediate acceptance.

These parties were attended by many well-known and influential people from Town and adjoining communities. The menu at the party usually consisted of curried goat, rice, green bananas and goat-head soup. The beverages were mostly red stripe beer, white rum and an assortment of other potent liquor. After my introduction to Mr. Thomas, we engaged in a short period of chit-chat, but my mind was focused on the food in the kitchen which was now pervading the air with smells and had an effect on my appetite.

We went forthwith to the kitchen, but on our way I heard an admiring whistle which seemed to be continuously directed at me. Not to appear less than coy, I ignored it and went to the kitchen. We collected our food, and on our way back I realized that my admirer was no less insistent.

We secured a table under a tree which was some distance away from the throng. While we were eating, a young man came over and handed me a note. It read, 'Hi good-looking, be my guest.' After reading the note I displayed an attitude of nonchalance. Cathy noticed my lack of response and said, "Aren't you going to look around to see who sent you the note? Don't you see he is staring and making signals?" I jokingly said to her, "One should be in a hurry to catch a flea."

I was aware though that my admirer was some way off 'giving me the eye.'

Most of the guests at the party were members of the police force, and their friends. Remembering the painful experience I had with a police officer, I was scared to even look around to face my suitor.

When the music started playing, everyone seemed to be on the dance floor except me. While sitting there, a tall light complexioned young man came over to where I was sitting and introduced himself to me. He told me that his name was, and that he was stationed at a Police Station in Town. I told him my name. He asked me why I did not look to see who was whistling, I told him I did not want to appear less than modest. We talked and laughed for a while, and then he asked me to the dance floor. Everyone's eyes were watching us as we glided across the floor. After we stopped dancing, he offered me drink which I gladly accepted. We continue talking for a while, and then he told me he had to leave because he was on duty that night. He gave me his telephone number and told me to call him. After he left I remained at the party until Cathy was ready to leave.

I did not take the initiative and call Brown because of my prior bad experience with a police officer.

One day, about three weeks after the party, I was at home with Tiny and a red car came and stopped in front of our gate. To my surprise, it was Brown who alighted from the car. I explained to Tiny that he was the man I had met at the party a few weeks ago. Tiny was obviously very excited about him visiting me and said, "Why don't you go meet him?" She was immediately impressed with his debonair appearance. I timidly went out and meet him halfway along the gate, as he was on the way in. He asked me why I had not called him. I told him quite honestly that I was afraid of policemen. He said to me that not all policemen are the same, and that I should not 'use someone else's fat to fry him.' His financial gift to me was very substantial. He gave me thirty dollars for which I was very grateful, because it had some spending power to it in those days. Tiny encouraged me not to let this man slip away through my fingers. I gave her ten dollars and she was very appreciative.

Even after the visit I could not bring myself around to call Brown because I was still afraid. Months went by and still I did not contact him. He continued to visit me and would bring me gifts of clothing and money. But on each occasion he came I sought to remain elusive, first by hiding myself, or second by or telling the neighbor to relay the message that I was not home.

On one occasion when he visited I decided to assume an intrepid posture and confronted him head on. I made it known to him that my distrust of men of his profession would make it impossible for us to have a relationship. He was obviously saddened by what I told him, and when he left on that occasion he never came back.

My sojourn at Tiny's house took an uncomfortable turn after a while. Her boyfriend Dud started to make improper advances towards me. This first started when he told me that I would have to pay for food and lodging, although he knew that I was not working at the time.

One night while I had retired to my sleeping quarters on the floor, Dud suddenly appeared beside me in a very amorous manner. Out of respect for myself and Tiny, I got up immediately with the excuse that I had to go to the toilet. This incident obviously did not seem to deter him from his course of action. On another night I was awakened to find Dud lying beside me with his hand probing my internal private parts. I rejected his advances in a very violent manner, and pushed him away from me.

The relationship at home became strange as Dud's attitude towards me became less friendly. Tiny soon noticed his change in attitude and inquired what the problem was. To which he replied very hostile, "She should go look for work."

On occasion when I asked him to give me a ride into Town, Dud would tell me explicitly that he was operating a taxi. This caused an even further denuding of the relationship. Because of this strange relationship between Dud and myself, whenever I had to go to Town I would walk, as the distance was not very far.

During this inhospitable period with Tiny, my fortune took a turn for the better as Tim came into my life. Tim came from a 'well off' family in Cityville. We first struck up a casual acquaintance, and then our friendship strengthened and we became lovers. My visits to Tim's house became very frequent, as he was living alone.

After some time Tim saw the need to have me around him constantly and asked me to move in with him. Although I was flattered by his suggestion, I told him that I would have to discuss it with Tiny first as I always valued her opinion, and I also was glad, because I wanted to get away from Dud.

Tiny advice to me was, "If you love him, go for it and don't let another good man slip through your fingers."

With this encouragement, I became the lady of Tim's house.

Tim promised to take me to meet his mother, but because he was a hard-working man and the opportunity just did not present itself.

One day Tim's mother made an unheralded visit to his house. She was very critical of my presence and expressed her anger by saying, "You are here and don't even come to my house to see if you could assist in washing my clothes, or cleaning my house." She added, "I don't think I like you, as you seem too proud." I tried to explain to her that Tim had promised to take me to visit her but he had been very busy.

I did not mention this incident about his mother for about two weeks.

Sometime later she appeared at the home again, and this time she displayed how much she held me in derision by saying angrily to me, "You are still here with my son, you don't leave yet." She then told me that the house belonged to her, and she wanted her son to have a woman that would help her at home. My defiant response was, "Lady, I will do whatever I can for my in-laws, but I was no monkey." I made the decision to tell Tim about these incidents with his mother and myself, but when I did he gave no response to me.

His mother continued to make visits to the house. On these visits she behaved very contentiously, and speaks to me in a very derogatory manner, and also treated me with impunity.

On one of her visits she got several buckets of water, and while making vituperative attacks on me she symbolically washed me out of the house by tossing the water to every area outside of the house, and washing the place as much as she could. Her symbolic ritual was not complete until she entered inside the house with a large pail of water to which she added dirt from the roadside, this she tossed into the house angrily, and at the same time cursing me. It got to the point where I could not endure her behavior any longer and told Tim that I would be going back to Tiny's house. He did not seem to be moved by my decision.

One day when he was not home I packed my things and returned to Tiny.

In spite of it all, Tim was still very kind to me and would visit me. He asked me to return back to the house, but I refused. He admitted that this was the behavior of his mother with every woman who came into his life, and added that if I was more docile and condescending to his mother things would be much improved.

I told him that he should have informed me about his mother's attitudes, and I would be more prepared to deal with her, also maybe we could have had a better relationship. Tim said that he could not afford a place for himself, so that was the reason why he lived at his mother's house.

I did not take kindly to some of the things he said in defense of his mother, and decided then not to return.

Because of Tim's generosity while living with him, on my visits to Tiny I was able to give her money in gratitude for her kindness, and I also gave her some to put aside for me.

I was now living at Tiny's house again, but having money saved I could enjoy a greater sense of independence; with the hope of finding my own place to live, and getting a job.

CHAPTER TWENTY-SEVEN

Launching Out

During my sojourn I met and became friends with a young lady named Beth. She was very popular in the community; my association with her brought me a lot of new acquaintances, and up-to-date information about news and gossip.

As time passed I learned that the town Of Cityville needed workers to do community-based jobs. I went there and inquired and was told that the duties involved cleaning the streets, and the coastline of the town. I applied and was immediately hired. I asked if they needed more workers, as I knew that my cousin Tiny was also in need of a job. I asked the presiding person if her name could be affixed to the list to be employed. The lady told me that it would still be necessary for Tiny to be there by seven o'clock that evening, as she would have to meet her in person. Tiny was overjoyed when I told her about the job that afternoon, and actually found my story incredible that I had such good fortune.

Nevertheless, Tiny accompanied me back that evening to meet the lady. She told us that the job would only last for a few weeks, depending on the weather. On our way back, Tiny expressed how fortuitous my arrival at Cityville had been for her, and that she had wanted to add another room for some time to alleviate the congestion of her family in the one-room flat. She expressed with such enthusiasm that she would now be able to do that.

After two weeks of working I was able to rent a room for myself.

I had only my clothes and two sheets which I possessed. Tiny was not able to assist me in any way because she was faced with her own circumstances. My sleeping accommodation was on the floor, and the window curtain was fashioned from my clothes. My job continued, and in time I was able to purchase a bed, two chairs and fabric from which I fashioned curtains made with my hand for my windows. Pots and pans were my next acquisition; the following week I bought a stove, including pots and pans for the kitchen. In time, my room took on an 'acceptable' appearance as new pieces of furniture were added to the space. This gave me a feeling of pride and accomplishment; I was now able to entertain visitors.

The weekends were my days off, so those days I visited my mother, and grandfather with a gift. When returning to Cityville I would be laden with food like, breadfruit, bananas, ackee, and whatever fruits were in season. This I always shared with Tiny. After a few months of working the job ended and I became very sad.

Knowing the tentative nature of the job I had employed very frugal money management.

Anticipating this downtime, I had purchased a good deal of fabric because I had the ability to sew my own clothes. Fortunately too, all the furnishing in my room, together with six months' rent, was already paid for in advance.

After a while, with no job it became increasingly difficult to pay my rent and other overhead expenses. I had to find a way to offset this problem. This came by the way of establishing a good rapport with my landlord. He had previously shown that he had an infinity for me, so I decided to capitalize on this penchant he had for me. We soon struck up an intimate association, which was to his satisfaction. For my part I got a reprieve from paying my rent. My landlord, Mr. Green also extended his generosity by giving me gifts and money.

He was a fisherman, and I would secretly meet him on the beach when the boat came in and collect some of his catch. This became less than modest means.

As a young woman I soon got very disgusted with the association.

He was married and fairly advanced in age and wanted me only for 'intimate gratification.'

My financial conditions still remained grave to the point where the stress from this situation started affecting me mentally. I was now unable to visit my children and grandparents, because I could not afford the bus fare for the trips. I had to fashion my clothes by hand because of my dire economic condition.

My creation often drew a ludicrous response from some of the individuals in the town, but I tried to ignore their negative criticism.

Mr. Green had a lot of mango trees on his property, and during the harvest season and at nights, I would steal mangoes from the trees and secure them in my room. When they were ripe enough for market I sold them to a vendor. Despite all my efforts life showed me its most uncomfortable side. My resolve now was to get help by any means possible.

During that time I met and became friends with Carol, who was younger than I was. She and I spent time together, and would travel to different places. We had a lot of fun together. Later she became unkind, and cruel to me. After a while we went separate ways because things were not working out very well with us. Life continued with me in all its fury.

Friends and admirers would always comment that I was a charming and attractive young woman, so I decided that since nature was kind to me I should use my natural abilities to my best advantage.

On my visit to the town I had struck up a casual acquaintance with a man named Bill. He was a very popular person in the area and always seemed to have a visible presence.

He said that he had always admired me, and that it seemed unusual to him how I always appeared by myself, as opposed to the other young ladies who had male companions. In the midst of my frustration, Bill seemed like someone I could confide in. We spoke extensively and I poured out to him the problems which I was facing. He suggested that it was possible that my life was being negatively dragged down and effective by witchcraft. Bill suggested that I should go to see Mother Rhoda, who was a spiritual healer and visionary. It now became apparent to me that spiritual cleansing was the only way to 'free' myself.

He cautioned me that this should be kept as a secret, and also expressed that he was a very private man.

After our conversation we parted, but somehow I realized that my visits to Mother Rhoda were always being postponed, although she lived only a few miles from my house.

When I saw Bill again he asked me if I had seen Mother Rhoda, and I told him I had not. He said that my reluctance to seek spiritual help was definitely an evidence that I was under a spell. He insisted that I should go to her because she was very good at what she did. He even tried to convince me that he had experienced her ability firsthand.

Her charge was only twenty-five cents, but my position was so destitute that this paltry amount was not readily at hand on most occasions.

After making the resolve to visit Mother Rhoda I was faced with the problem of obtaining money. There was a police sergeant in the town who was an acquaintance of mine. At that time he seemed to be my only option. I went to the sergeant as a platonic friend and asked him for ten dollars. He promptly suggested that it would be a sexual trade off. I became indignant at his salacious comment, and admonished him for seeing me 'less than a lady.' Embarrassed at my reaction to his offer, he quickly retracted his words, and gave me the money, saying it was okay because he valued our friendship.

The next day I decided to make the trip to Mother Rhoda. The distance was daunting, but nevertheless, I did it on foot.

I knocked at Mother Rhoda's gate and she came out to me. When I made it known what my purpose was, she refused to see me because I was wearing pants at the time. Not put off by her principles, I went home and donned a dress and made the laborious trip back to her house.

When I arrived she invited me into her work-room. There was a table in the center of the room with a glass of water on it. She instructed me to put twenty-five cents in the glass of water and it would reveal to her and become visible to me my problem.

To my utter astonishment, there appeared a picture of three women in the water. The women at that time were not known to me.

Mother Rhoda said that at the age of ten I had been tampered with by witchcraft. She said the 'curse' was meant for me to wander aimlessly through the world, without a place of abode. She continued to say that at the age of twelve I had again been set upon by people who had directed malevolent 'curse' on me which had been intended for my mother.

Mother Rhoda prided herself on operating on a clean spiritual level. She did not entertain clients who harbored evil intentions. She would even chase off such prospective clients from her home. She concluded by telling me that the remedy for my solution would include five spiritual baths.

One should be taken each week at the cost of thirty-five cents.

Mother Rhoda encouraged me that I should trust in God for my deliverance.

I made all the necessary sacrifices and took the five baths as she ordered.

By the third bath I noticed an improvement, but after the fifth bath I felt a sense of freedom.

At the end of these baths my luck seemed to take an upward turn.

The next day there was no kerosene oil in the home, and there was none to be had in Cityville. I had no choice but to go to Town to get some.

While standing on Lee Road, and waiting for the bus to return home. A car came and stopped beside me, the drive inquired as to my destination. He did not find me very responsive. To assure me of his sincerity, he gave me information about himself, and gave me a number to call to make inquiries about him. Being curious, I went forthwith to the near-by phone booth, and after making a call I was surprised to confirm that his information was true.

He offered to take me home to Cityville, although he was still on the job. We had an interesting conversation on the way home; and I found him to be very intelligent and quite charming. Before we parted he gave me his work number and I promised to call him. His name was Mike. The next day I called him, he sounded very happy to hear from me, he was very kind and accommodating. He promised to visit me the following day.

At this point I was beside myself with anticipation about his visit. I thought my room needed a lift to make it somewhat more presentable for his visit. With this in mind I went to cousin Tiny and asked her to lend me some flowers to decorate my room. She not only gave me a bouquet of flowers, but she also lent me a spread for my bed.

Armed with these things to improve the décor of my room, I now set about cleaning and polishing the floor to an impeccable finish.

After the appearance of my room met with my satisfaction, I took a bath and donned the best dress I could find.

My wait was not in vain, as just about the time Mike was expected I saw his car come and stopped at my gate. He greeted me very warmly and handed me a package. I took the package inside my room and opened it. The package contained a blouse and a pair of pants. There was also a sealed envelope which I did not open. When he came inside, I thanked him for the presents, but the envelope was still unopened. He suggested that I open the envelope. On seeing fifty dollars that was in the envelope I was overwhelmed by his generosity.

This became the genesis of an intense love relationship.

Over the ensuing months, Mike came to visit me regularly, and for me, he became the center of my universe. He was very thoughtful and generous.

We would often go out to dinner and attend social events together. On one occasion we went to a very salubrious restaurant. It was the first time I had the occasion to enter this restaurant. There was a young man there who knew me and started to question my presence there. I boastingly told him that, "You will have to get used to seeing me at this place."

As I was living alone it became a concern to me that Mike would not stay the night, but would always leave at around eleven o'clock.

Despite my efforts to entreat him to stay he would always go. This heightened my concern, as he would not give a reason for his untimely departure.

After a while the tree of our love blossomed into my pregnancy with my fifth child. This event brought us closer, as Mike was happy to hear about the coming baby.

Marriage was now being discussed between us and this brought me a sense of fulfillment as a woman. The only fly in the ointment of our love was Mike's early departure at night. The topic kept arising and eventually culminated in argument. It was at this point that he shattered my world by admitting to me that he was already married.

Our relationship took a downward turn from this point on.

This troubling information was now causing me many sleepless nights on a saturated pillow.

Mike's visit not only became less regular, but he would arrive late at nights armed with excuses as to why his arrival was so late, and why his stay had to be brief.

One of the reasons was that he had relatives who lived in Cityville, who knew his wife. Hence, unlike before I became pregnant, he suddenly became concerned about us keeping our relationship clandestine.

During the period of my pregnancy, Mike's attention towards me became less, and he became very disagreeable. His financial support for me also took a downward plunge. As he was my only means of support, my bills started mounting. My constant pleading to him for even a modicum of support seemed to fall on deaf ears.

I was now faced with the prospect of having to visit him at his work-place in Town.

My arrival at his work-place would often cause him to behave in a belligerent manner.

My state of pregnancy causes him to treat me with the greatest impudence. Despite my importunities he would often send me away with only the bus fare to return home. For some reason he displayed hatred towards me.

As my back was now against the wall, I resorted to stealing from the cash register in his office whenever I went there, and eyes were not watching me.

My pregnancy got more advanced. Jane, who was my good friend, asked her to visit him in my stead. She was very nice, and quite happy to do this for me. I would plan a lie for her to impress on him that there was urgency or catastrophe in my life. Nevertheless, despite Jane pleading; he only gave her five or sometimes ten dollars to give me.

With the imminent birth of my child, I was faced with the prospect of engaging the services of a midwife to assist me when I was ready to deliver my baby. Fortunately, there was a lady by the name of Granny, a practicing midwife who lived about four houses away from me. I acquaint myself with her and over time we became friends. There was a young lady who occupied a room in the same house where I lived named Jean who previously had an altercation with Granny. To avoid any contact with Jean, Granny suggested that I come to her house for the delivery of my baby.

As she, Granny, was spiritually attuned, she said that she would know when the time came for the delivery of the baby, and would make herself available.

Because of the friendship between Granny, she took me and my daughter Lilly in to stay with her for a while before the birth of the baby.

Granny's warm and accommodating personality was in sharp contrast to the conditions in which she lived. Her single room was sparsely furnished.

The small bed did not have a proper mattress. Having offered me a comfortable bed, she and my daughter slept on the floor. She had a make-shift kitchen at one side of the room, with a sheet of zinc on which a coal stove was placed. The kitchen utensils were unsightly and reflected years of consistent use.

Granny told me that I would need a cleaning elixir of local herbs which she would prepare. She emphasized that it was necessary, as evil spirits would be warded off me and the baby. During the few weeks I stayed with Granny; I faced the stark reality of the level of poverty in which she lived. The delivery went through quite well, and I gave birth to my son who was born with a caul over his face. I named my son Peter. Granny encouraged me to stay at her house an additional week so that she could perform a ritual to protect the baby, and give me a spiritual bath which would help me to regain my strength.

When I returned home, after a period of about two weeks I called Mike and told him that I had given birth to his son. He came, and surprisingly, displayed a great deal of joy and immediate acceptance of his son. He gave me money to pay the midwife and to purchase things for the baby. Although thankful for his help, I still remain apprehensive about his behavior.

After the birth of my baby, Mike's attention towards me continued to dwindle. My problem was also exacerbated by the fact that the lady who was living in the house, for some reason, showed a dislike for me.

My friendship with Granny may have been the cause, as she for some time maintained an acrimonious relationship with Granny.

It was getting increasingly difficult to behave in a civil manner towards her. At every opportunity she would seek to become contentious with me. It became unbearable to live there. As a result I rented a room some distance away and moved out.

My new apartment was situated on a hill and further from the town of Cityville. Because of the elevation of the land, securing water from the faucet was always a problem. This new location imposed a further inconvenience, as getting around from there was an arduous journey, as the home was so remotely situated.

In time I found the lifestyle was not to my liking, and was forced to change my place of residence. The new location, being more central, allowed me greater access to all social amenities. Despite this, my economic situation was still not improved as I was not employed, and found it difficult to survive.

On one occasion, in Cityville, and while passing a factory, I noticed that there was a great deal of discarded foam. This sparked my interest and I inquired of the security guard on duty if the foam were available to the public. He not only said yes, but was very accommodating and directed me to the back of the building and told me that there was more foam to be had.

This was a blessing to me. That day I brought the foam home and proceeded to make pillows by hand with the help of my younger sister Fay who was living with me at that time.

The next day I was busy at the job of making pillows. A young man was passing, when he saw me, he asked me if the pillows were for sale. My entrepreneurial zeal was immediately awakened, and I told him yes. He promised to purchase some of the pillows the next day, and was true to his word. This small sale gave me enough capital to go to Town the following day to purchase material to manufacture more pillows.

As the foam was easily available, I sought to secure prospective customers at the police station and local business places.

Not long after I had a thriving pillow business and expanded into making cushions as well.

There was a lady by the name of Sheila who lived close to me. She and I became friends. It was a stroke of luck on my part that Sheila's mother had a sewing machine which she had not used for some time. She agreed to sell it to me for fifteen dollars. After securing the machine my business took off, so to speak. The production of pillows and cushions increased dramatically, and I also extended my manufacturing to the making of men's shirts.

Through friendship with Sheila I was informed that there was going to be a religious meeting in an open air lot which was located near to where I was living. I attended the meeting, and during the proceedings I was smitten by the Holy Spirit.

My memory of all that happened was very sketchy, and I awoke in my bed not knowing how I got there.

I soon became a regular visitor to the meetings.

The group came from a church in Town, and was attempting to build another church on the lot. I decided to become a part of this bold venture. Each day I would go to the building site and take my youngest son Peter with me. My participation was always rewarded with a meal for my input. At the end of the day, there would also be food left over for me to take home for my sister Bev, myself and my son Peter.

One day at the site I injured myself by stepping on a protruding nail. This caused me to be immobilized for a few agonizing weeks.

Nevertheless, after my recovery, I returned to the site.

By this time my entrepreneurial venture in the making of pillows and cushions had taken a downward spiral, and my income had dwindled to almost nothing. As a result the daily meals I received from my involvement at the church site were more than welcome.

At about this time my landlord and his wife started behaving hostile towards me. His wife would often direct disparaging innuendoes at me. Her husband also started the practice of washing the area in front of my room each morning. I realized this was symbolic of washing me away from the house. I finally learned what the reason was because of my landlord and his wife's malevolence towards me. On confiding in Sheila about the problem, she told me that the relationship with her mother and the landlord had gone sour. Their display of rancor towards me was because of my continued association with Sheila and her mother.

Just about this time I pen a letter to my mother informing her that I was facing difficulties, and was unable to take care of my sister Bev, and sending her to another person's home will not solve the problem. A few weeks after my sister Bev had gone to live with my mother and I was now alone with my son Peter.

The landlord made life increasingly difficult for me, so for my peace of mind I moved away from that house. My new residence was located further down the street.

The rent was cheaper as the house was not in a state of completion.

There was no door to my room; I had to use a hanging curtain in place of a door. Things were very difficult for me economically at that time. My business venture had concluded and I was unemployed.

All my efforts to find employment proved futile. My frustration now led me into a relationship with a married man. It never lasted, because he soon left me and returned to his wife. I was left alone again.

After a period of time this man died and at nights I would experience the presence of a poltergeist in my room.

Not knowing what to do, I related my nocturnal experience to my friend Sheila; she suggested to consult a friend of hers who was able to help me.

Sheila's friend said that I was actually experiencing 'spiritual visitations' from the deceased man I was once intimate with.

He made some suggestions, and gave me instructions to follow. After this, the nightly 'specter' was no more, and I could sleep peacefully at night.

Miss Tilly, who was my landlord, took a liking to me, and we became friends. I became her tutor as she was not literate. When she received letters from her relatives, it was my job to read them to her. Miss Tilly saw my financial plight and suggested that I do washing for a local butcher in the area. The butcher was well in need of my services, and after a while he asked me to prepare his meals.

As fate would have it, the butcher started to make amorous advances towards me. It was not long before we were into a relationship.

This covert affair provided me not only with 'meat' for the table, but financial support way beyond my salary.

To remain discreet about my relationship with him, I would go down to the market to receive my cuts of meat with the pretense that I was making a purchase.

My point of concern was his hygiene. He would visit me at night coming directly from the abattoir, wearing clothes that were blood-stained and smelly. He was oblivious to his unkempt appearance.

This lifestyle was not to my liking, but as my son's father, Mike, was not assisting me at the time I had to make do.

It got to the point where I decided to throw my fortunes to the wind and move to a place called Utep, which was some distance off. I first occupied the back room of the house. But there was a lady who lived at the front in the same house, and as luck would have it, she took a dislike to me. I soon found some of my washed clothes which had been hung on the line came up missing. I made inquiries and found a soothsayer in the area who told me that the lady was the one responsible. I reported this to the landlord; who was very friendly with me. Not very long this lady moved away. Soon after the front room of the house was vacant, so I rented it.

My only means of financial support was again going to Town to my son's father Mike to get money.

On one of these visits I discovered that his support was not forthcoming, and again I had to resort to stealing from the cash register at his office.

One day as he left the office momentarily; I opened the cash register, and with unbridled haste, grabbed a handful of twenty dollars and quickly assumed a demure posture. When I left his office that afternoon I went to the market and purchased a copious amount of household articles and food.

I justified this act with the thought that I should not have to reduce myself to a mendicant to get support for his child. After a while I struck up an acquaintance with yet another married man. This man worked at a local bauxite company; and appeared to be a man of some means.

He was very fond of me, and treated me quite well, but he was very committed to his marriage. This relationship, like all the others did not last very long, it was a passing fancy.

I was getting weary of the financial difficulties that I encountered, also the abused, and my promiscuous lifestyle. My children were now getting older, and I was unable to support them. Somehow things started to turn around in my favor. I met and got to know a number of prominent people. I was successful in passing the examination to enter the police force. I then found a very lucrative job at that time. While at this new job I heard about the rewarding prospects of traveling to other countries.

One day I spoke to my neighbor about this, and he told me he had a friend who lived in another country who would be coming to visit very soon. 'Serendipitously,' his friend did arrive in a few weeks.

On the day we were to be introduced I made sure that my appearance was as alluring as it could be.

His name was Fred, and he invited me out to have a drink with him. We had a warm conversation, and he seemed to be smitten with me from the start.

During his sojourn we saw each other a number of times. Before his departure, he told me to get my passport, and make arrangements to come and visit with him, and also promised to receive me when I arrived.

My son Peter was getting bigger and there was no future for Mike and myself, so I decided to look in another direction.

He would give me money to pay my rent, but that was all he did. Life continued to be very challenging. I was unable to dress myself. Because of my destitute state I had to ignore my pride and asked my friends to assist me with clothing.

There were times when after showing generosity, my friends would change, and revert to a contemptuous attack on me, and request me to return the clothes. Despite all my efforts, a job could not be found. I was now forced against my morals to have a relationship with men just to provide for myself and my children.

I loved living in Cityville, also the friends I had. But after the many bad experiences, and with the plans to travel aboard, I decided to pack all my belongings and return to Ferry.

My mother as usual, we did not get along very well, but because the children were there with her, I thought it would be better to move my things there.

During this period at Ferry, I established contact with new friends who gave me more information which spearheaded my resolve to travel abroad.

My previous plans with Fred had gotten more definite. And the friendship between him and myself became stronger. I was now resolute in my decision.

Having no money, I had to find ways of acquiring some as I need to see this materialized. I went to my friends and begged for money. Some I had to sleep with. I asked Mike for help, and informed him about my plans. He degraded me by saying that someone like me could never go abroad. I could only break out in uncontrollable tears on hearing this coming from my child's father.

I wanted very badly to go to a foreign country like others to make a better life, and be able to help my children, my family; because life for me was very 'hard.'

I approached my mother and told her about my plans to leave the country. Surprisingly, she gave me money towards my trip, which I welcome very much. I visited my father, and also told him about my plans. Without hesitation, father gave me a contribution to fund my trip. I contacted my cousin Dean who lived in another country; he sent me two hundred dollars.

After my mother's kind gesture I settled down at Ferry with hope that I would remain there until I left the country. This was not destined to be the turn of events, as my mother digressed into her old antisocial behavior towards me.

This for me was the last straw, and I decided to pack my furniture and return to Windsor.

I made my plans known to my grandmother. She was very tearful and wished me all the luck and blessing she had to give. She said that my departure would mark the last she would see of me, and if she died before I did her spirit would always be with me. She also said that if anything happened to me, that 'ants' would bring the news to her grave.

After this emotional parting with my grandmother, with my face bathed in tears, I packed my furniture for the trip to Windsor. Unlike Lots wife, I did not have a second thought about looking back to where I was coming from.

I was convinced that although I was leaving my children behind with my mother, they would be in safe hands.

I returned to Windsor with my eldest and youngest son Peter and Andy.

My sister Lorie was already living there with my grandfather.

Although this marked my final sojourn at Windsor, I still maintained my job in Town. While in Town, I stayed with my cousin Harold and on my days off I returned to Windsor.

Harold opened his door, and his heart to me at the time of my greatest need. This was during the time I was making plans to migrate abroad in search for a better life. All that he did for me was done in a selfless manner, and without condition. He empathized with my situation, and unlike the other family members, he did not question me about my past, but just loved and accepted me.

The magnanimity of his heart was what endeared me to him.

The time finally came for me to leave, and I remember talking to my grandfather on the morning of my departure. He 'prophetically' stated, just like my grandmother had, that I would not return to see him alive again. He warned me that wherever I went I should always be weary of 'my own kind of, people,' and especially my own country's people.

It was so hard for me to say good-bye to my grandfather especially after he had told me that I would not return to see him alive again.

My eyes were filled with tears. I tried my best holding them back. My eldest son Andy gave me a pair of his dirty pants to wipe my tears.

We all got ready to go to the airport. Everyone came with me except my grandfather. I sadly told him good-bye and boarded the van that took us to the airport.

Ellen Patricia

Sitting in the van, I kept looking back at my grandfather's house, and at my grandfather who was sitting on the step at the front door.

With a feeling of ambivalence I asked God to take care of him, and to keep me alive so I would be able to return and see him alive.

I kept looking back until he was completely out of sight.

The memories of the receding vision of my grandfather left an indelible memory in my mind, even to this day.

When we arrived at the airport, I hugged my sister Lorie, and my two sons. We said our good-byes, and I left and boarded the 'Flight' that would take me away from the shame and humiliation I had experienced and flew away.

I knew what I was leaving behind, but I had no idea what was laid ahead for me. I was going to a foreign land, a strange place I knew nothing about. I said a prayer asking for guidance and protection on my journey, for the wisdom to make the right choices and decisions when I got there, and for strength to do what I needed to do for myself and my family.

CHAPTER TWENTY-EIGHT

Journey to an Unknown Land

My eyes opened from a period of slumber, to reveal to me the upper cargo bay of the plane, and a feeling of trepidation overcame me at the realization that I was thousands of feet above ground.

My immediate response was to issue a prayer for protection and guidance, on this unknown quest, on which I was embarking. I became so excited getting on the plane for the very first time. On an invitation I boarded the Flight. My seat was located next to the window. I was so excited looking down and beholding nature's beauty.

Soon I landed in another country.

On my arrival there Fred who sent the invitation to me was there to meet me, and gave me a very warm welcome.

This welcome was not indicative of the coming hardship I was yet to face.

Life in my country was very difficult for me, which caused me much frustration about my indigent condition, because I was unable to provide for my children.

Going abroad was my greatest desire, but I had no one to help me. I came to the realization that I had to do whatever possible to help myself.

During my trip I met a lady named Millie. We both were going to the same country, but we got lost among each other in the crowd at the airport.

Fred took me home with him. We were both happy to see each other.

The immigration gave me a few months to stay in the country.

Fred told me I should not worry, because I can always go back and get an extension.

Fred lived in a small quiet one bedroom apartment. We both now got very intimate. As always, he was very kind to me.

When I met Fred, he told me that he was the owner of a Tailor shop and had few men working for him. I did not question him about that, because at that time it was not important to me when I was at my home.

Living with Fred and getting intimate I wanted to know more about him.

One day he took me with him to work, no one was there. I asked him what happened to the guys he told me were working for him; he said it was their day off.

Each time he took me to the shop no one was there. Still I did not question him.

On one of my visits to the shop with him, he took me to a small convenient store which was located next to his shop. The owner's name was Mary. He introduced me to her. She came from my country, so we both got into a dialogue.

Somehow Fred could not stay with us, because his shop was open, so he told me that whenever I was finished talking I could return.

Mary asked how long I have known Fred, I told her I met him in my country a few months ago.

She said that she would like to say some things to me, but I would have to remain silent.

Mary gave me her phone number, and told me to hide it from Fred.

I did not stay with Mary very long, as I did not want Fred to become suspicious. I left and went back to him.

During the days I would visit and spend actually the entire day at the tailor shop with him.

Because I was able to make my own clothes, on my visit in the town I found a store, and bought several yards of materials and began making clothes for myself.

The workers at the shop were men; we later became very good friends.

On most days when I visited the shop I was asked to do the hand work for them, which I was paid for.

I now started to meet other people and made several friends.

I made friends especially with Mary and Eric who owned the convenient store next door to where Fred worked.

During the friendship between myself and Mary, she reported to me that Fred was not a merchant tailor, or the owner of the shop; he was just an ordinary tailor who was employed to the owner whose name was Burke.

At this point after several conversations with Mary I started to distrust Fred, but I kept very cool, fearing if I said anything to him about what I had discovered things would blow up in my face and I would be forced to return to my country which I was not prepared to do. It became difficult for me to relate to Fred like I used to because I found out that he was a pathological liar, and he was not able to help me, but I remain very calm.

I told Mary that I was not prepared to continue living with Fred, but I had no place to stay. She told me that I could come and stay with her, but requested that living with her she would like for me to do the domestic chores for her and Eric, which I agreed.

As the days went by I became very weary and wanted to move away from Fred home. I became very frustrated, and would curse myself. Days when I was alone I sat and cried, feeling hurt and betrayed. Even though Mary told me that I could come and live at her home, I was mentally trying to plan my escape route to get away from Fred.

One day I met and became friends with a young man named Triny who came from another country. He told me that he was living in the same yard I lived in, but on the other side of the building he has always been on the go, because of his job. I informed him about the situation between Fred and myself, also that I wanted to leave him, but fearing if he caught me leaving he would try to hurt me.

Triny told me that I have to be careful if I plan to leave Fred, because I was not the first lady who he had invited from other countries to live with him, but as soon as they found out he was a liar they always ended up leaving him. Each time they tried to leave him he abused them badly, and then ended up sending them back home. Triny told me that he would help plan my escape but I would have to go to bed with him. As there was no other way out for me, I did not question my integrity because I saw that as an opportunity for me getting away from Fred. Triny was true to his promise.

The next day he told me to open the window and give him my things to hide at his home for me, which I did.

During the course of the night Fred wanted to become intimate with me, but I told him that I was not feeling well; this made him very angry at me.

He said to me that, "If I was having a period he could understand, but it's just the week before it stopped, so it seems that you have found another man." I said no. He said, "What the hell is wrong." I told him I just don't feel well in my stomach. Fred went to the kitchen and got the Dutch pot. He began hitting me in my head, and at the same time using profanities to me. It was at that moment that I told him I found out that he was a lair, and that he was not the owner of the shop, or a merchant tailor, but just a tailor boy who was employed by Burke. He got into a vicious rage, at this point he told me to get my "Wretched ass out of his place and go walk up and down and eat shit." I quickly got away from him and found my way to Triny's place. Luckily Triny told me where he would hide the key when I was ready to leave and he is not at home.

When I left and went inside Triny's home, it seems Fred realized that I was not there. I heard Fred voice in the yard shouting my name, and addressing me in the most derogatory manners. It Seemed like Triny had just come home from work, because I heard someone talking to him. When Triny came inside his apartment and saw me he realized why Fred was upset. He told me that Fred's behavior reminded him about the same way he treated the other ladies. I soon went to sleep.

The next morning I sent Triny to Mary to tell her what Fred had done to me; she told Triny I must get away and come and live with her and Eric. I spent the day with Triny. I was blistered in my face and arms, and experiencing excruciating headaches. Triny bought a bottle of Anacin for me, and took hot water and salt which he used to bathe my wounds.

I waited until it was late that night when I knew that Mary and Eric would be home. Triny helped to carry my things as I was in so much pain and unable to lift them.

When I got to Mary and Eric's home, they were already gone to bed, but Eric opened the door when he heard me knocking as they were expecting me. I told Triny thanks, he then left, and I went inside the house. Eric was very questionable as to the reason for me to appear the way I was. I told him what Fred had done to me. His remark was, "That why Fred can never have any good woman, because every time he bring one from another country he ill-treat then." Eric told me to wait for him to let Mary know I was there.

When Mary saw me, she was miffed about my condition, she directed me to the bedroom, and ask me if I was in pain, I told her that Triny had given me some Anacin, she said that would help my pain, but I should use hot water and salt until the swelling was gone. As the days went by I was feeling better. Mary provided food for me during my illness. After I was much better she boldly told me she would not be able to provide food and lodging for me together. Mary expresses that she and Eric eat from the restaurant daily but the days when she is home and cook, l would be more than welcome to eat.

After listening to Mary I realized that I had to fend for myself. I had very little money, plus I did not have any work permit to help me find any employment. I had to find ways and means for my survival. I decided to walk and beg whoever I met. That gave me the opportunity to meet and make friends. I began visiting several clubs hoping to meet someone to help me, but each time I met someone they wanted to use me as a courtesan, which I refused. I decided to position myself at different business places, including the bank and waited; there I fabricated stories about negative things occurring with me, and my families. This worked out very well, as I was successful.

I had female friends, but they resented me, by calling me a fool because I refused to hang out with them at night. I told them that I would rather be a mendicant. They addressed me as being an idiot, which did not matter to me. I started losing my friends. I continue my mendicant lifestyle, because actually each person I met was very kind to me. That was my modus operandi; and I was very successful.

Next door to where Eric and Mary lived was a construction company; I decided to make friends with the employees and employers. I got dressed and stood by the gate which was located in front of Eric and Mary's home. This gave me the opportunity to meet other people and also have conversation with the workers.

One day in tears I relayed to one of the employees that I had a death in my family but I had no money to fund my fare, or send to help with the funeral. I also informed that worker that I did not receive my work permit as yet, but was expecting it any time soon. That employee, including others, was very kind and considerate to me.

One night I visited a club and met Larry. After talking with him I found out that he was the owner for music that was being played, and was quite popular at different places. As time passed we became platonic friends. Because he was married he was unable to extend a vast amount of generosity to me, but he was very kind.

It was not my intention to return home, having nothing to offer my children, and families. I was informed that if I travel from where I was to another country I would get close to America. The help that I received from Larry was not enough for me to send to my mother for the kids, so I resorted to my mendicant lifestyle.

While living with Mary she told me about her friend who was a police officer, who she would like to introduce to me. Soon after our introduction he seems to be smitten by me.

As time passed, one day he asked me how long I was going to remain in the country. I told him not very long, he said that would like to get an extension for me so that I could get a job, which he did. This made me feel better about the plans I had to travel.

Somehow Fred became very angry and wanted to get back at me, so he reported that my time was expired and I was hiding. He did not know that I had gotten an extension to remain in the country. Not long after I got myself together and planned to travel to another country.

Journey on a Bumpy Road

On my arrival at the airport, after checking in I was stopped by an officer who told me that I could not travel to another country because my stay there was expired. The officer's name was Mr. Roberts, he told me that I should return to the airport the following day and he would get me on the flight to my country. I told Mr. Robert that I had gotten extension to remain for another month; he said my extension did not show up in the record. I could do nothing but walk away in tears.

The next day while I was home, in the afternoon I heard a rushing sound, I looked outside to see what was wrong. To my surprise I saw two officers rushing towards the house. I was wondering what was happening, and if they were looking for me due to the fact that the night before I was stopped by an officer at the airport. I started getting scared and wanted to get away, but they were coming very close to the house where I lived. I decided that somehow I was going to run from the house fearing the officers would force their way in the house and got me. I ran from the house to the back yard, and through the bushes. While in the backyard there was hardly any place for me to escape.

I looked across the back yard and remembered that there was a swamp that's located not very far from where I lived. I was very scared and did not want to be captured and be deported. I ran quickly towards the swamp. The closer I got to the swamp I could hear the sound and voices coming towards me. Not knowing what to do, I quickly emerge myself into the swamp at the shallow end and lie flat on my stomach. It was so hard for me to hold my breath because each time I try to breathe I inhale water.

After being in the swamp for a little while I listened until the sound was gone. I quickly lifted my head up from the swamp and looked around to make sure no one was there. I ran from the swamp and back to the house. When I got out from the swamp my body started burning me. I became afraid that maybe I have caught some germs, or a disease, due to the fact that this swamp was known to have alligators, and it was a place where most people dump their garbage.

I went to the bathroom and took a shower, but taking a shower did not stop my body from burning. It got worse. I did not have any medicine for that problem, also Mary or Eric was not home. I took some petroleum jelly and applied it to my body, but the burning did not cease. I came down with a temperature and did not know what to do, because I was scared that if I went outside someone would be there to catch me.

The owner of the business that was located next to the house and I had become friends, I looked across through the window to see if he was still there in his office, he was not there but there was someone else who I was friends with. I started to experience a feeling of weakness in my body. I got out of the house and sneakily crawled through the fencing to their office. My friend whose name was Bob saw me coming and asked me what was wrong, and why I was walking like that. I did not want to tell him the exact truth, so I fabricated a story that I was feeling bored and decided to go to the swamp and take a bath. Bob looked at me surprisingly and said." You crazy, that swamp has germs in it." He said that I had to go to the hospital immediately.

He asked me if anyone at my home I told him no. Bob told me that he was about to take care of some business, but my condition looked very grave, so he would take me to the hospital immediately. Bob took me to the hospital, and told them what was wrong with me; he waited until I was treated. I was given an injection and medication, after which, Bob took me home.

I was apprehensive that somehow the officers would come back. Mr. Rivers who was a very prominent and popular man in the community and I were friends. After staying home for two days and felt recuperated I set out to get in touch with him. I told Mr. Rivers what had transpired the night I was boarding the flight at the airport, also what took place at my home. Mr. Rivers told me that I have not committed any crime and I should be free to travel. He informed me about his friendship with the chief officer, and that he would give me a letter to take to him the next morning. Mr. Rivers took me in his car to his office and prepared the letter and gave me. Mr. Rivers was a very good friend; he was someone I would go to and ask for favors. He told me that on my next trip I should not return, because I was a nice looking lady who needed a better life.

The next morning I took the letter to the Chief Officer. After he read the letter he told me to have a seat and wait until he returned. Not long after waiting I saw him come back to his office accompanied by the officer who had stopped me from taking my flight. The Chief told the officer that he had no right interfering with me during my travel, and that he should not interrupt me during the next time I travel. The officer looked at me angrily, and then he told the chief ok, and left.

The chief told me that I should be careful of those guys, because at times they do things that are not instructed by him. The Chief told me to go and travel, and then try and get to America to better myself, because I was a nice looking lady.

I went back home feeling happy that things worked out in my favor. I went back to my mendicant life because I was more determined not to return to home having nothing, but to keep travelling even though I knew no one, or where my destination would be. One late afternoon I was home and got a visit from the same officer who stopped me from traveling. His approach to me was friendly.

He asked me if I had got a job yet, because if I did not he would get a work permit for me. I told him that it would be very appreciative.

Mr. Roberts apologized to me for what he had done. He said it was because of the report he received from Fred about me; and due to the fact that he was the main officer for deportation that gave him the opportunity to come after me. The conversation went on for a long time, and then he asked me if I was hungry, I told him yes, because really I had not yet prepared anything to eat. He offered to take me out for dinner where he would not be recognized.

I accepted his offer as he appeared so genuine, especially when he told me he was sorry, and the reason why he and the other officer came after me. I took his offer and went with him. As we drove along, I noticed that his countenance was not as pleasant as when we first began talking. I asked him if he was mad with me, he said no. But as we drove along I realized he drove past quite a few restaurants, and then took a lonely road that led down to the beach. I had feelings of apprehension, wondering why he was driving down to the beach. I asked Mr. Roberts if we were still going out to eat, but he did

Ellen Patricia

not reply. This got me more scared. As he drove along I tried to get out of the car, but he got into a rage with me, and grabbed my hands. As a matter of fact there was no place for me to run away from him, because it was late in the evening and there was no home close around.

The moment he got down to the beach he stopped the car and dragged me by my hands from the passenger side towards the driver side and outside where I was thrown on the sand. He cursed me in the most derogatory ways, and told me that if I ever report him to the chief again and about this incident and let him lose his job he would kill me.

Mr. Roberts forced me to the ground, tore my clothes and abused me, and assaulted me in the most unabashed manner; at the same time holding me to the ground with one of his feet into my chest and plastered my face with his body fluid. He then drove off at such a speed causing the car to throw sand in my face and body. I was left alone. It was a dark and lonely road, and a long way to walk to get home. I went into the ocean and washed myself clean. My clothes which were torn off, I had to tie them together to wear.

It took me a long time to get home. My body was writhing in pain, which made it more difficult for me to walk, but I had no choice. When I got home that night, Eric and Mary were already home and retired to bed. I went to bed. I was unable to sleep thinking about what had happened to me. The following morning Mary saw me crying and asked what was wrong, I told her that she would have to promise not to reveal what I told her to anyone as it may caused me my life. I told Mary what had happened to me, also what the officer threatened to do to me. Mary told me the sooner I get my money together I should go away. My only source for getting money was by being a mendicant. I wanted to have enough money that would last me until I was able to gain employment, or found someone to help.

As time went by I found out that Mary would accuse Eric for taking money to drink with friends, or giving to other women. Somehow a thought came to my mind. As I had access to the home I decided to search hoping to discover where she had hid the money. This search took me a few days, as I had to be careful not to get caught in action. I found a package hidden with enough money to help me to travel.

Mary asked some of her friends to help me and was successful.

The next day after, I took all the money I had and went to the bank and made an exchange, and then purchased my ticket.

As the flight would leave out on Thursdays, I had to wait for the next week to travel.

The time finally came for me to leave.

That night when I went to the airport, the first person I saw was Mr. Roberts, the officer who raped and abused me, he gave me such a disparaging look.

It was now time for me to check in and board my flight.

As I checked in, he said to me. "You are traveling again tonight, I said yes". He said to me, "Good luck, and don't come back here, because his promise to me still stands."

I boarded my flight and left that country.

CHAPTER TWENTY-NINE

Costa Rica

After enduring such bad experiences I was happy to be on my way to Costa Rica.

When I boarded the flight I realized that the passenger sitting beside me was a Jamaican lady. During the flight we got acquainted with each other. She told me her name was Sarah, and I also discovered that we both were destined for Costa Rica. That gave me a feeling of euphoria. The flight took much longer than when I flew from my country. During the night we experienced several air pockets, which caused the passengers including myself to become afraid.

The plane arrived at the airport in Costa Rica late that night. Not being able to communicate in Spanish made me become very nervous, and fearing that going through the immigration I would be denied entrance into the country.

I tried to communicate with the passengers but I got very little response because no one understood my accent. Sarah also experienced a similar problem. I watched the other passengers as they formed a line so I followed through with them, even though I was scared. The moment I realized that I was the next person to face the immigration I got into a tantrum, and began to perspire and shiver. It was so difficult staying calm. There was a man standing behind me. All of a sudden I felt when he kicked me on the back of my foot. I immediately looked around. The man who spoke a little English said to me, 'calm yourself down, it's going to be alright.' I was now facing the immigration. I looked around to the man who had kicked me, he smiled at me and said again, 'it'll be alright.'

The immigration officer asked me several questions in Spanish, being unable to communicate the Spanish language; I could not give the proper answer. The immigration then asked me in English if I had money to shop in 'his' country. In reply, I asked him how much money I was allowed to have, he told me $1000.00 US dollars. In response I told him I had the required amount. The officer then said to me, "If you didn't have any money I would not allow you into my country because you don't know any blasted Spanish, and I don't know how the hell you are going to manage here. They need to rob your ass and send you back to my home naked." He stamped my passport, spoke something to me in Spanish, and angrily gave it to me. I watched the other passengers as they walked away when their passport was given back to them, I did the same.

Sarah was not yet processed by the immigration, she took a longer time, but I waited for her. Soon after, we both got our baggage and left. We bonded together, because neither of us spoke Spanish. It was night and we wanted to find a hotel. We had difficulty getting a taxi, as we were afraid of being robbed. The suitcases were very heavy, to carry, but we dragged them along with us.

We began asking questions until we met a man who was bilingual to direct us to a taxi driver. It was then I saw a policeman come driving by. I shouted out, the police stopped and inquired what the problem was. After explaining to the police he took us to the taxi stand. The police did not leave until we were both safe in a taxi. He informed the taxi driver where we wanted to go, and where the taxi driver should take us in the morning.

As we were driving along in the taxi, the driver informed us that after we checked into our room we should be careful not to leave the door open, and if anyone knocked we should not open it for fear of being robbed, or killed. The taxi driver told us that this has been a practice in the city of Dixy. We paid him and told him thanks. He then helped us with our baggage inside the hotel and reminded us that he would be there to take us to the bus that would take us to the county in the morning.

The hotel was located beside a restaurant. The moment we entered inside the hotel we were stared at, by bystanders. Looking across the hotel, I saw a man standing at the counter who seems to be the receptionist. We approached the counter and asked him for a room, but he did not understand us, so he immediately got someone to help us. We paid for one night. After we settled in our room we took a bath and went out to the find a restaurant to get something to eat. Returning we decided to watch TV. While we were watching TV, we heard a knock on the door. I asked who it was; it was a man voice who spoke Spanish, saying 'open the door,' sounding very domineering, and remembering what the taxi driver told us, we both got scared and refused to answer. The knocking went on for a long time. We made sure that the door was locked and secured properly. After that was over, we started discussing about our destination. I told her I was going to country, and also my refusal to go back to my home, because I was tired of the shame and humiliation that I faced constantly, so I was in search for opportunities to make my life better to help my children. I then remember a lady who I met when I lived in the other country who told me she had plans to go to Ranch which was a city in Costa Rica. I told Sarah that I was also planning to go there hoping to meet her. Sarah informed me that someone told her if she got to Ranch there would be no problem, because there were many people including blacks who reside there and spoke English. Sarah asked me to describe the lady who told me about Ranch, I told her. Coincidentally; Sarah knew her, and told me that her intention was traveling to Costa Rica to get in touch with her. After talking and finalizing our plans, I tried closing my eyes to sleep but could not as I was afraid that someone would return and knock again. The next morning the taxi driver came and woke us up; we got ready and left the hotel. The taxi driver took us and help us to board the bus that would take us to country. This time Sarah and I had separate seats so we were unable to communicate with each other. I did not know the place so I tried to talk to some of the passengers. I was being ignored because I was unable to speak Spanish, but I was not discouraged. There were some people who cursed and spit at me when I tried talking to them. Finally a lady was very nice and approached me. She asked me where I was going, I told her to Ranch. She told me that there are other places that the bus will stop before reaching Ranch, but the driver will announce the name of the place, so I should listen for the name of my destination. That lady was so nice to me. I started crying because I had a feeling of ambivalence, not knowing what lies ahead for me. She wiped my tears, then hugged me and walked back to her seat. It was a long drive to Ranch.

Sarah was now acting very skeptic with me. My decision was to find a better life, comes what may. The bus arrived at Ranch late that evening. Not knowing anyone I inquired about finding a hotel. One was located close to where the bus stop was. The cost for the room was 115 colon weekly. I paid one month's rent, and settled in. It became obvious to me that Sarah's plan was to separate herself from me the moment she got the direction to Ranch. I was very disappointed about her, but I had faith that I would be okay.

While in Ranch I inquired about Liz, the lady who I met before I came to Costa Rica. In approximately two weeks after living in Ranch I was told that she lives there. Sarah displayed a selfish attitude towards me. I tried not to let it interfere with me, because I was meeting and making new friends. I had to be frugal with my spending because I was not sure how quickly I would find a job. After living in Ranch for approximately three weeks I was hired at a cook shop. The job was very difficult for me, but I needed to earn in order to maintain myself. I was not making enough money, because I had to work a whole month before I was paid a salary of 400 colon, but because I had access to the money it became my modus operandi to steal from my employer daily. My inability to communicate Spanish caused me to be ridiculed by the customers. But because I was favored by my employer whose Name was Steve, he made sure that I was respected.

After working at the cook shop for some time, it gave me the opportunity to meet people who displayed a great likeness. I did not have to worry about my meals, because Steve provided meals for his employees, but the days that I did not work I had was to provide my own. I tried to be frugal with my money because I did not plan to remain in Costa Rica, but continue to travel until I got to the United States. On my days off I had very little to eat, which usually consisted of a cup of coffee and two slices of bread. Some days I eat both sardine and bread, a soda, or I drink water. But most days I was a mendicant to my friends.

My hotel room was located upstairs above a bar and restaurant. To my surprise, late one night after the restaurant was closed I saw the employers throw the leftover food to the back of the restaurant for the dogs. This was done constantly. I became interested because I saw it as an opportunity to feed myself. At nights I would position myself there to get some of the food before the dogs got it.

I became very tired of eating with the dogs so I made friends with Jim, an elderly man who was an employee at the restaurant, and who was responsible for doing that chore at night. Jim and I became good friends, my wish was granted because he secured a meal for me each night. As the friendship between Jim and myself grew, he requested sexual favors from me in exchange of food and money. I did not like Jim very much, but the salary that I was paid at the cook shop was not enough unless I stole. As time passed Jim got a job for me at the same restaurant working with him late at nights. I then started a saving. I kept my job at the cook shop, and continue to steal from my employer. My scope of friends grew enormously. I met and associated with bank managers, business owners, immigration officers, and other affluent people.

Coincidently I found out that Liz rented a room from the same hotel where I lived but spent most of her time away in the country with her fiancée. Finally I got the chance to meet with her. The days when she was home we would spend some time together. Being friends with her I met and became friends with a man name was Henry who lived in the country close to where his fiancee lived. Liz told me he was a coffee and chocolate farmer who was able to support me just like her fiancée did. I decided to meet with Henry. As time passed we became friends. Henry would visit me on weekends when he was not busy. I was not very fond of Henry, he was very kind to me, and because he had money which I needed to fund my trip to whatever destination I would travel I got into an intimate relationship with him.

While working at the cook shop, one day I asked my employer if he could allow me to fry fish after he closed the shop at night. His response to me was yes. I went ahead and bought enough fish that would last for a few days. The first night I began frying fish passerby found out because they caught the smell. They inquired if this would be done constantly. I was surprised, because I only wanted to fry just a few fishes for myself and also if my employer wanted some. I looked at my employer, he looked back at me, and then he gave me a wink from his eyes, while bowing his head, meaning I should tell them yes, which I did. All the fish were sold that night. I made more money than what I had bought them for. The next day I went to the fish market and purchased more fish.

Frying fish became regular at night, both for me and my employer. After frying fish for a few nights, my employer Steve got very excited about the idea and started spreading the news. This time he provided the fish himself. The money we made was divided between the both of us. I was having a lot of fun at nights during the fish fry, and was complimented as being a good cook. This caused my scope of friends to increase.

As time passed Steve took a liking for me and wanted the both of us to become romantically involved. On a few occasions he displayed his generosity by giving me money. Oftentimes I refuse his offer, but he was very insistent, so I accepted the gifts. It got to the place where I became very uncomfortable working with him. I like and respected him, and was grateful for his kindness to me, but I did not want to become intimate with him because he was an older man, and remembering the experience I had with older men in my younger years made me afraid. I still maintained my job; also continued frying fish at nights when I was feeling well.

Steve continues to offer me gifts. There were times I would hear a knock on my room door, when I opened to see who it was, there was no one, but on the floor under my door was an envelope laying there containing money. One day, to my surprise he made it known to me that he had been the person who had been putting money under my door.

Steve occupied a room at the same hotel where I was living. The shop was located across the street from the hotel, and because we close the shop late at nights we usually walk home together. One night on our way home from the shop Steve told me that he would like to talk to me. There was a stairway which led to our rooms. As soon as we approached the stairs, surprisingly he held my hand and pulled me down the step. I started to scream, but he told me that he was not going to hurt me, because I was a lovely young lady and whatever it took from him, he wanted to have me, even though he knew he was married, and that he was an older man. I did not respond to what he was saying, I was full of fear because he had strong arms, so I just sat quietly and listened to what he was saying to me. Soon after he let go of my hands and I went to my room.

One night after work I went downstairs to the bar to have a drink with my friends. After that I went back to my room. To my surprise, when I opened my door I saw Steve sitting on my bed. I was so astonished; and became extremely nervous; I thought I was seeing a ghost. I asked him how he got inside my room. His response was, "I am a very smart man." He then spoke the rest in Spanish.

I told him that he should leave, because we did not make any plans for this occasion. When I looked at his face he had a disgusted look, also his eyes had an unusual reddish color.

Steve then grabbed me by my hand and threw me to the bed, and said that he wanted to make love to me, and if I refused to give him, he would take it from me, and also fill my belly with baking soda. Steve held me down in the bed, and then dragged me to the floor, at the same time speaking in Spanish which I did not understand.

He was a large man, so he threw his big body on top of me with his feet towards my head while pressing himself very hard against my body.

I felt his hands fondling my private area, but I did not know what he was doing. Immediately I saw him take something like a syringe from his pants pocket. He held me down to the floor. I tried to scream but he took his foot and kicked me in my mouth, and face. This made me even more scared.

I was unable to escape.

Steve wrestled with me while holding the syringe in his hand. I felt when he inserted it into my private and began pumping, because I felt a pressure going inside my belly, and also like my belly was being blown up.

Normally he spoke to me in English, but that time he spoke only Spanish, which he knew I did not understand, and at each repetition he displayed aggressiveness towards me. Not long after he released me and left my room.

I was in such excruciating pains. I tried getting up and going to the bathroom, but was unable to walk, because I felt like my belly was torn apart.

I had an electric pot. I tried going to the bathroom to fill it with water along with a pail I had. After the water had boiled I put some into a cup along with salt and drank the rest I poured into the pail and sap my belly and private area.

About less than an hour after drinking the hot water and applying a hot towel to my belly I began to pass air like gas, and fluid from my belly. That alleviated the pain somewhat, but I was still in agony. I had difficulties sleeping that night because I was experiencing a lot of pain, and fearing that Steve would return.

I prayed that I made it through that night so I could get in touch with my friend the next morning who was a pharmacist, and relay my condition to him, hoping he would help me.

In the morning when I was awakened I was still in pain, and unable to walk. The pharmacy was not close to the hotel, but I had to make the effort, even in my painful condition.

On my way to the pharmacy I met a few people who knew me; they inquired of me as to why I was walking the way I was. I replied that I had a terrible pain in my belly and was on my way to the pharmacy.

When I got to the pharmacy my friend the pharmacist was there.

He was very glad to see me, but was wondering what the cause was for me being there so early in the morning.

I told him that I wanted to talk to him privately; he told me to have a seat until he was finished with the customers. Soon after he invited me to come inside and have a seat. He inquired of me what the problem was; I told him what had happened to me in confidence. He was very upset and also sympathetic about my condition. He gave me medicine and told me that it would help my condition, and also gave me instructions about what I should do.

After talking with him for a while I left and went home.

On my way I stopped at the store and got a few cans of food, bread, crackers and soda, also other things that I could eat, because the pharmacist instructed me to stay off my feet for a few days. I also went to the hardware store and bought an extra latch, a hammer, and nails, to put on my door.

Later that day when I realized that no one was around I quickly nailed the latch to my door. I then felt more safely, because no one was able to enter my room even if they had a key. I took a shower, had something to eat, took my medication and went to bed. The following morning when I got up I was much improved. I took a bath, filled my pot with water and went back to my room. I made porridge, and bread for breakfast; took my medication and went to bed because the medicine made me drowsy. Somehow my friends started missing me and wondering why I haven't showed up for work.

One day, while I was asleep I was awakened by a knock on my door, when I inquired; it was two of my female friends. On seeing me they were very disheartened that I was ill, and offered me their assistant. They did not ask if I had money. They went and bought cooked food for me and also gave me money to help with my rent. I did not ask them for it, but they knew that I had not worked for a while. As the days went by my condition improved. I wanted to return to work, but I was afraid, ashamed, and so hurt because of what Steve had done to me. One day I met Tim who was employed by Steve. He asked me why I was absent from work, I was very reluctant to relay the reason to him, but I took the risk and told him what Steve had done to me. Tim was in a state of shock. He said that he wished I had told him about the night when Steve first attacked me by the stairs, because he would have informed me about Steve's temperament.

Tim told me that I was not the first woman that he had done things like that too. Tim also told me how badly Steve has treated his wife. I got more scared about returning to work. I asked Tim about Steve where about, and if he was still in Ranch, because usually you would hear his voice when he entered the hotel. Tim told me that Steve informed him that he needed to get away because he was tired so he went home to be with his family and placed him in charge of the shop until he returned. After Tim's advice and encouragement I decided to return to work.

It was not my intention to continue working there, but because I had access to money and wanted to pay the piper. I made sure I stole enough money to pay my rent for up to three month and to take care of my other needs. Tim knew that I was stealing. One day he said to me, "Girl you better help yourself real good." During that time I bought things that I needed, and secured a large enough savings.

Tim promised that he would keep me informed as to the exact time when Steve would return, and he would create a situation to make it seem as if there was a problem which caused me to be terminated. I was in a state of readiness for that moment. Steve did not return until more than three weeks. I was now out of a job, and was ready to face whatever difficulties was ahead for me, because returning to my country was not my intention, I was willing to do whatever it took for me to fend my way until I was able to help my children and families.

Liz had returned from the country and started spending more time in Ranch where I was. She told me that Sarah said she did not like living in Ranch because the place was not what she expected, due to that she had planned on returning home. Sarah usually acts very strangely. At times she would lock herself in her room, and came out only when using the bathroom, or going to the restaurant. She hardly ever dialogue with anyone. Soon after I found out that she had moved away.

On one of Liz's visits to the country to see her fiancée she invited me to visit with her to see Henry. Over time my trips to the countryside became very arduous and for me, accompanied by the fact that the sanitary convenience was inadequate. I had to fabricate a story as not to create any animosity between Liz and myself.

As I continue living in the city of Ranch, my popularity allowed me to have many acquaintances. I became friends with one of the local tailors. Some days I would visit him at his shop and assist with his unfinished work. I was paid a paltry sum, but I was grateful, because he provided me with lunch or dinner. Before I met the tailor I made my clothes by my hands, but after he and I became friends, with his permission, he allowed me to use his sewing machine. I was so happy. Because my hand made clothes would sometimes tear apart, because they were made in a hurry. I would cut and pin together several outfits which I took to the shop and made. Because of that my wardrobe increased.

Being in Costa Rica I begin a thorough investigation about finding a way to migrate from Costa Rica to America. I did not have any visa but that did not discourage me from investigating. As time passed Liz met and became friends with three brothers who spoke Spanish, she introduced me to them. As the friendship grew I started getting information because they were also planning to migrate to America. My association with Liz and her friends became stronger, because I saw them as an opportunity for me to obtain information due to the fact that they spoke Spanish and I was not conversant with the language. In the meantime I was seeking other help for myself. My main goal was to obtain enough money by any means to fund my trip.

After my job ended at the cook shop I became dependent on Henry for financial support. It so happened that Henry farm was not providing him much money, so he was unable to help me financially. Things took a downward turn for me. I was now forced to renew my friendship with Jim who worked at the restaurant. I had money put aside but I was unable to spend it just in case an opportunity presented itself to me to travel to America. I decided I would rather become a mendicant, and if I had to also live the life of a kleptomaniac; because my main goal was to go to America by any means necessary.

I had a friend whose name was Jose. He was the owner of a store. I told him about my difficulties and my plan to migrate to America. Jose offered me employment, and told me that he would be able to help me, but suggested that he wanted to have a relationship with me even one time. Jose stated that he 'loves Island women.' I was surprised. I like Jose because he was so handsome, but I was afraid because of my experience with Steve. I decided to have a talk with Jose and explain to him about my fears in relation to Steve. He understood, and was very honest with me by letting me know that he was married, but because I was such a clean and nice looking woman he wanted to have an affair with me and do whatever he could to help me. He told me that he would not make any promises to me. I respected and loved Jose because of his honesty. Jose and I became intimate friends. This was a situation when they say, "A drowning man catches after a straw." This was a straw that came to my refuge, because returning to my country was the last thing I wanted to do. With Jose financial help I was able to support myself, including the meals that were provided for me from Jim.

As time went by the relationship between Jose and myself took a downward turn, because he was married and was unable to see me on a regular basis. I started to feel rejected but I continue to maintain my job at his store. Soon after his wife got privy to our relationship so Jose had me terminated. I was now without a job.

One day Liz informed me that they had found a passage to migrate to America. I became so excited and decided that I would avoid any spending so as not to miss out on the opportunity. One week I decided not to pay my rent. The caretaker and watchman was the person to whom I paid my rent. I told him a lie that I had a death in my country and I had to send money to my mother. He told me that in order for me to continue living there; he requested an affair with him, I told him no. John began to curse me in Spanish because he knew I did not understand, he called me a fool, and spit on me.

John had keys for all the rooms. That same night as I was sleeping I was awakened by him fondling my private area, this got me into a rage. He then slapped me in my face and began cursing me, also spitting in my face and on me. I got out of my room and went and sat on the balcony, he followed me and kept spitting on me. Because I was crying out loud one of the other tenants were awakened and came to see what was wrong with me. That made him get more belligerent and gave me a swift kick in my belly. That same male tenants who were also Spanish wanted to know what my problems were, I explained to him. He told me not to worry because he would help me to pay my rent until I got help. He was very kind to me, he gave me money, and I was able to provide for myself. This tenant was a farmer in the country, and was absent during the week, but would return on weekends. This condition continues with me for a while.

I willfully made my decision not to pay any rent, so I was locked out of my room. Having no place to go, I slept on the sidewalk bench with other drunken men. All my belongings were still locked in my room; I had no access to them unless the rent was paid. Because of non-payment my things were all thrown in the street.

Liz moved away and lived some distance from me. When I was not able to feed myself I visited her. Some nights I slept on her floor because by the time I walked back I became hungry. Having no direct place of abode I always sit in the park, or on the hotel balcony and sleep on the chair, but I was always fearful of John, because even after that incident whenever he saw me he would spit on me.

A few days after visiting Liz and her Spanish friends, she told me that she was hoping I came to see them so they could inform me about the place in Costa Rica where we could get visas to travel through several countries until we get to the border, so we have to hustle whatever money we could. Liz told me that with this plan, as long as money was available we could pay someone to take us across the border to America. That was like music to my ears. I decided that I was going to sleep in the park or on the benches at the street corners and starve myself to save whatever money I could.

My friend who was the pharmacist was someone I could talk to so I told him about my plans. His response to me was, 'that's a good move which needs money.' He told me that he would help me the best way he could. He was very genuine.

I visited the Tailor also, and informed him about my plans, also my condition. He had a small cot at the back of his shop, he told me that I should stop sleeping in the street and park, and come and sleep there. I accepted his offer. But that was not exactly what I expected. I told him that I would gladly secure my things there. To this point I started asking for help.

I was still hanging out at the hotel and other places. The man who I bought fish from while I was working with Steve was someone who was very kind, so we talk on many occasions. One day I visited him at the market, he appeared very glad to see me, and he asked me why I was not working with Steve any longer, because I was one of his best customers. I told him that things were not working out very well. He offered me fish, which I refused because I had no place to cook them. He then gave me 100 colon and told me that he missed talking with me, so he would stop by one day to see me. That money came in just in time.

Journey on a Bumpy Road

One evening I was sitting on the hotel balcony, surprisingly I was visited by the fish man. He greeted me and came and sat on the chair beside me.

He began talking to me, and said he had been wondering what had happened to me, because he had not seen me for some time, and asked if I was working I told him no. He questioned me about how my rent was paid. I got angry because I did not want him to know that I was homeless. I told him I pay my rent from the money I saved. He said that he would help me until I got on my feet. He then took money from his pocket and gave me to pay my rent and said that I should visit him at the market sometime. I was very thankful and appreciative. As the friendship between him and I continue his generosity increased. But in my mind I was afraid because of my bad experiences.

As time passed Liz moved back to the hotel, so I decided to live there again, because of our plans to migrate, and that the hotel was closer to all transportations.

One week the fish man paid my rent without informing me. John came and said to me, "So you don't have to sleep on the street again because your man paid your rent." I did not know who would have done that.

I continue living at the hotel, but also was considering moving away and occupying the Tailor's quarters in order to save money.

The fish man would stop by to talk with me, and was always kind to Liz and myself.

One day Liz and I had a conversation about the fish man's generosity to me, she said he was working his way to me. I said to Liz, 'This is crazy.' One Friday while Liz and I were seated on the hotel balcony he visited us and gave me money and fruits, he also told me the room number he would be spending the night in. I said to him, "Ok." I was very puzzled, because he and I had no conversation in relation to us having any sort of relationship.

That night I went out, had a few beers, and came home very late, and went to my room. The next morning I was awakened by a knock on my door. I thought it was Liz. To my surprise, when I opened the door to see, it was the fish man in a rage. He got very boisterous, saying I was only using him so I told him I don't understand what he meant by using. He got more furious, and began to curse me and said that, "I am going to wreck your life, I am going to wreck your life."

I said to him. "You did not let me know that you had any interest in becoming intimately involved with me, I am not a mind reader, and furthermore you told me that you would be spending the night at the hotel, but you did not invite me to visit you."

He said that from the moment he told he would be spending the night at the hotel he did not have to invite I should realize that he wanted me to be with him. I told him that I did not understand what he meant.

Luckily Liz was there, she talked with him. Soon after they ended their conversation he came to where I was sitting on the balcony and said to me, "I am very sorry about how I acted with you. I should tell you my intention." He asked me not to hold it against him, and if I needed anything I should not be afraid to ask him, but he would like for us to become intimate. Immediately I lashed out and told him I was afraid because he might do the same things that Steve did to me.

He asked me what it was, I told him one day I would tell him.

I was very mad about the fisherman's action towards me, so I tried to stay away from him. After such a bad experience I decided that it's best for me to begin reading the bible. I would lock myself in my room and read my bible and pray. My friends could not understand how I suddenly became quiet and locked myself away. I refused to tell anyone about what had happened to me.

Liz and her friends began to ignore me; because I did not speak Spanish properly I experience such feelings of loneliness.

I prayed when everyone was running to and fro, because I did not know what else to do, because I was experiencing so many problems in my life, but after reading the bible and prayed God made ways for me.

One day during my search for work and financial help I met a man who migrated from an Island for many years by the name of Bill. We became a very good friend who was very kind to me. Being friends with Bill I met an elderly in his late 80's whose name was Mr. Brown who lived very far in the country but would occasionally visit the Ranch to see his friends, and go shopping. After several conversations with Mr. Brown; and as I shared information about my families in my country with him, he told me he knew my grandfather, and that they were related.

That moment I found out that we were related gave me such a feeling of euphoria. After our meeting his visits to Ranch became more regular. He was very kind and supportive to me.

Mr. Brown told me that he wanted to take me to see a lady to help me spiritually so that things could change for me. I informed him about the plans I had to migrate to America. He told me that I should be very careful.

One Wednesday he took me to a spiritual lady to help me to be successful. When I went to her she gave me a talisman along with prayers and instruction. Mr. Brown paid her 1000 colon for her service. The days that I read the prayers I was granted favors from actually each person I met. I could always prepare myself for those days, knowing that my prayers always bring me many blessings. Because Mr. Brown was a farmer and lived on his farm further in the country, the time was fast approaching for his departure. It was a sad occasion for the both of us. I hated to see him go, but it was a situation that I had to face. He left; so I was back out in the cold with my eyes full of tears. Having no choice I had to find a way back to start association with Liz and her friends, because I had an' axe to grind.'

Liz and her friends were getting ready to go to the embassies to get visas. I became desperate and needed help from any possible source. I decided to get back in touch with my friend Jose. I told him about my plans and the cost for the visas. He said that with the ability and determination I have he would help me. Jose gave me money to go to Dixy to pay for the visas.

I was still in need of $3.000 American dollars for traveling. As I did not want to lose the opportunity I made the necessary effort to scavenge from old and newly made friends. The scariest thing that came to my mind, was to visit Steve and told him that I needed a job, and if he refused I would threaten to report him to the police.

I paid him a visit. When he saw me came, he was so excited, and immediately said to me, "Your job is still here, come to work anytime." I was astonished. But my intention was to steal from him which was easy for me to do. Soon after I started working; Steve told his employees that he would be going home to be with his family for a while, so Tim and I would take care of the shop, and I would be frying fish again.

I was completely shocked as to what I heard, because in no time I would have all the money that I needed to fund my trip. In my mind I felt that somehow Steve was ashamed of what he had done to me.

Tim was extremely happy because we were on our own. I was glad for the opportunity of frying fish, being a kleptomania again. Within two weeks I collected enough money for my trip. I got in touch with Liz and the friends and inquired as to what time they would be leaving. They tried ignoring me, which made me so uncomfortable, but I was prepared to communicate with them by their terms. It so happened that one of the friends wanted to have an affair with me but I refused. Because I did not acquiesce Liz friends ran me away and told me they are going to leave me behind right there in Ranch. I realized that it was a serious threat so I decided somehow to maintain the friendship. One day I visited their home, they were all smoking pot, I was turned off by what I saw, but I decided that whatever it took I was not going to let them leave me out of the trip to America. Liz was among the group. I sat down with them. I was offered a very large joint by one of the friends. I wanted to refuse because I did not believe that I was able to handle such a large joint, but needing the help from them I decided to do whatever I had to do. That day I smoked with them and got so high until I became scared of myself.

We had a very good conversation, and as the days went by the friendship was improved. Some evenings on their way to the park they would stop and invite me to come with them. I realize that their main purpose was to smoke. I was afraid to accompany them, because the park was often checked by police. One evening while visiting with them I refused to smoke. Because of that they got into a vicious rage and cursed me in such derogatory manners. I wanted to run away but fearing if I made an attempt due to the fact it was dark they would run after me, so I pretended I was having a headache. This somehow turned them off so they left.

One evening I took a walk to the park by myself. There was no one there when I arrived, so I sat down on a bench, opened my bible and began reading. While sitting I felt a hand grab and pulled me back over the bench, and dragged me into the bushes. When I looked around I saw two men standing over me. I started screaming, but one of the men kicked me in my face, and tried to rape me while the other held me to the ground. Luckily a couple came walking by just in time. When they saw the couple, they both ran and left me lying on the ground. The couples were very sympathetic, and rendered alms to me. This was the first time I ever saw them. They help me to get up and dress myself. They wanted to know where I lived so they could take me home. I did not want them to know exactly where, I told them I was new to the city of Ranch, and did not remember the name of the street I lived on only the direction, so I told them if they took me to the pharmacy I would be able to find my way home from there. I never saw either the two men or the couple again.

One day while I was sleeping in my hotel room I heard a knock on the door. I inquired who it was. They were male voices who responded as being immigration officers. I became so frightened, because I knew my time had not yet expired; also I had my visas in hand to depart the country. Opening the door I was approached by two officers, one was dark while the other one was white. They asked me to present my passport so they could examine it. I gladly gave it to them. After examining my passport the officers said to me, "So you still have more time remaining to stay in Costa Rica. The white officer told me that it seems that someone doesn't like me, because they were given confidential information that I had no visa, and that was the reason why they came looking for me. One of the officers said to me, "So you are going to be traveling to get to America?" I replied yes. "He said to me, good luck." The dark skinned officer asked me if I wanted to remain in Costa Rica, because I was a nice looking lady, and he would take me for his wife. I told him I did not want to stay because of the bad experiences I had with men. He said, "Ok." My passport was given back to me, and then they both left. Later that evening I regretted refusing the officer's offer, because he was a nice looking young man, who appeared to be genuine. I inquired among the people about who that officer was about, but no one was able to give me any information.

Because of how I was treated by Liz and her friends, I had a feeling that they were responsible for reporting me to the immigration; but I remained calm.

Few days before we were ready to travel Liz showed resentment towards me, but as usual I ignored her. We had planned to take the bus the next morning. The night before I knelt down and prayed. I said, "Lord I have to prove you now, you cannot disappoint me because my children need help in my country." I read Psalms 23 and 27, but somehow my spirit told me to write Psalm 23 and wear it on my chest and Psalms 27 on my back. In the morning when I was awake I heard a voice say to me clearly, "Get up, you are not alone, someone is waiting for you, you will see."

I was so astonished on hearing that voice. I had never heard a voice so loudly unless someone was literally talking to me. Being afraid I got nervous and was unable to get up. But then as I lay there I heard the voice again, "What are you waiting for." I opened my eyes and looked around, I realized it was daylight. I thought that maybe they were gone and I missed the bus. Somehow I felt like a force came upon me and immediately I got dressed, and took my things. I went and knocked on their door, but they were already gone. Luckily I was not late for the bus.

When I got to the bus station they were all there. They laughed at me when they saw me coming, they turn their backs to me but I ignored the whole scenario because I was not prepared to lose sight of them. As soon as the bus arrived I took my things and rushed to the bus door. Unexpectedly I felt someone grab me in my back and pulled me. I was thrown to the ground. When I looked up I saw Liz, she stepped right on me and then into the bus, the other friends also did the same to me. A man called out and said, "Don't kill the woman, stop it." That same man came and helped me to get up, and took into the bus and got me a seat in the middle. After sitting down I realized that he was the bus driver. I was so hurt and ashamed for the way my friends treated me.

It was early in the afternoon when the bus arrived in Dixy. My friends quickly exited the bus and started to run away from me, but

I was determined like hell that I would not let them get away from me by the, "Hook and the crook," I was not prepared to lose the opportunity of going to America. I took my bags in hand and ran after them as fast as I could. It seems they realized no matter what they did, they could not get away from me, so they ceased from running.

Soon after we caught up with each other. Liz's fiancé said to me, "It seems as if you are a damn witch, because no matter what they do they cannot get rid of me." In response I said, l read my bible, which I took from my pocket and showed to him, but I did not reveal what I was wearing on my body. He looked at me with eyes wide open.

They all began discussing getting a hotel for a few days until we were ready to leave Costa Rica. Liz then turned around and asked me where I was going to sleep. I told her that wherever she slept I would, even if I had to make my bed on the floor. Liz said to me, 'okay then.' We kept on walking until they found a cheap hotel. The company included three brothers, Liz and myself. Together we rented two rooms.

While in Dixy I met a nice young dark skinned lady by the name of Sylvia who was visiting Costa Rica. She told me that she came from the Islands. As time passed she and I became very good friends. Sylvia would take me places with her. I had to be frugal with my money because I was entering to another country. In Mexico a certain amount was required by the immigration; because of that I was unable to provide food for myself. Sylvia had association with opulent friends who she introduced me to. She made me very happy.

One night Sylvia told me that she had a friend by the name of Mario who was the owner of a restaurant, who invited her out to eat. She told me that I should come with her. I was very excited, also very hungry. It was very late that evening. We sat in the back dining area to have our meal. Mario told us we should order what we need and also take some home with us. I was so glad because I had not eaten a good meal for a few days. While we were having dinner we saw when a young lady took a large pot from the kitchen to the bathroom. The door was ajar so we could observe what she was doing, mainly because our seat was located very close. She took the pot and filled it with water, not long after we saw her take a bath from that same pot.

When she came out from the bathroom Sylvia told Mario what she had seen. Mario had a surprised look on his face. He told another employee that he wanted to talk with that girl, whose name I can't think of. When she came he asked her nicely. Did you bathe in the pot? She said 'yes,' I do it all the time," she then walked away. We all looked at each other. Mario said that he knows that people are nasty, but that's past the limit. Mario thanked Sylvia for being so kind to reveal to him what was happening. Mario then said, "I wonder if they put their urine into the food also." We had already eaten so it made no sense getting upset. We told Mario that we had to leave, but would return the next day. We left the restaurant. Sylvia told me that I should not worry, because she was friends with other guys who were restaurant owners, but because Mario had invited her over for dinner she accepted his offer. Mario accompanied us as we walked home.

After Mario took us home and left, Sylvia took me to another restaurant to meet her friend. We stayed out very late that night, had dinner again and drank a few glasses of scotch and tonic. I took dinner home for my friends.

That night when I went home they were all sleeping. I woke Liz and gave her dinner. After she had eaten she went back to sleep. I went to bed. The next morning when I was awakened I told them about my friend Sylvia. They had a disgruntled look on their faces. Still I remained calm, as I saw no reason to get upset. I told them I have to make friends because the most information and connection I got would be helpful for us. The main problem was because the friends that I met and chose were opposite to them so they did not like that. Each time they would get mad with me but I ignored them. They cursed and acted demeaning towards me, still I was nice to them.

The time was fast approaching for us to leave Costa Rica and go to another country; which was Nicaragua. I told Sylvia that we would have to end our friendship because I would be leaving the next morning. We were very sad. She was the best friend I met during my travels. We both broke down in uncontrollable tears. We spent that night together. We Walked and talked about so many things hoping that night would never come to an end. Later we said goodbye and parted. 'I was so sad.'

I went to my hotel room and packed my things. Being filled with anxiety I was unable to sleep that night. In the morning when I woke up and got myself ready, I did not look to see if my friends were still in their room. I got dressed and knocked on their room door, but got no answer. I was now in a state of panic, because I did not know the exact direction to the bus station. Quickly, I got my things and left the hotel; with the expectation that I would catch them, I started running. While I was running along I stopped and asked a few people for the direction to the bus station. I also described my friends' to them, and the color clothes they were wearing, because I knew from the day before how they would be dressed. Not having much luck; I stop at a cook shop where we always eat. But before I asked any question, one of the guys who work there immediately said to me, 'Your friends just left, if you run fast enough you will catch them crossing the street.' I was so glad when he told me, because I was just about to ask him about them. I quickly bought something to eat; luckily he was the person who served me, so he was very fast preparing the meal for me. As soon as I got the food I ran as fast as I could to catch them. When I got to the street that the guy told me, I was just in time to see them after they had crossover and was about to make a left turn. If I did not run as fast as I did I would not have caught upon them.

After seeing them I did not let them know that I was coming behind, and watching them. They were now approaching the bus station in Dixy. At that time I cared less if they saw me because within myself I felt positive that once I got to the station I would meet someone to help me. It was then I saw Liz when she looked around and saw me. Quickly she turned her head away. Immediately I saw the others looking around at me.

I was almost to the bus station. When I walked inside the bus station, Liz and her friends gave a disparaging look; and her friends began to curse me in Spanish, and then spit at me. I was so hurt, especially knowing that Liz and I were from the same country. At the bus station I sat down and cried, everyone was looking at me.

I saw my friends as they went to the counter and bought their tickets. Soon after they left I got up and went to the counter. I did not speak Spanish, but the clerk who was a man was bilingual so he helped me with the purchase of my ticket, and my documents. I told him how reluctant I was because of my inability to communicate with the Immigrants. He said that the visas in my passport were legitimate and someone would assist me. I told him thanks. He hurried me to board the bus which would be departing in a few minutes.

When I boarded the bus all the seats were taken except one that was located in the front beside a light skinned lady. I greeted her and sat down. Her answer to me was in English. I became so astonished when I realized that she spoke English, and had a feeling of euphoria, which caused me to experience chills all over my body. I gladly introduced myself. Her name was Mia. We talk for a short time. At that moment she did not seem interested in talking to me, but because I realized she spoke English, I was determined to communicate with her until we made friends.

As the bus drove along I took out my New Testament bible and began reading. I saw Mia look at me from the corner of my eyes and smile. She then said to me, "You are reading the bible in English, God bless you." I then held the bible close to my chest. Then I said to her, 'Yes because it is my friend.' Immediately tears ran down my eyes to my face. Mia then started talking to me. She told me that she was visiting a friend in Dixy, but lived in another country. She told me that she was a Christian and had great faith and trust in God. This made me so happy meeting someone like her. Immediately my sadness was changed to joy.

As we traveled along and communicated I told Mia about my friends and their treatment towards me. I described them to her, also letting her know that they were passengers on the same bus we were traveling on. Mia told me that I should not worry because God was with me and God will take care of me. Mia encouraged me about God's love for me. She told me that she was sorry her destination was only a short one traveling with me, but she would help me get myself straightened out with the immigration when we got to Nicaragua.

Along the way the bus driver stopped for us to take a break. My friends came to where Mia and I sat and began to ridicule me in Spanish and English. Surprisingly, Mia did not just sit there, but responded to them. They got very angry because they did not like what Mia told them. One of the male friends stretched his hands and hit me so hard on the top of my head I almost fainted, and then they all walked away. Mia then told me that she spoke to them in Spanish that they need to leave me alone, because I read my bible and all the bad things that they have done to me will return to them. After the break was over we all boarded the bus. Mia was much nicer to me.

When the bus reached Nicaragua; we had to be inspected by the immigration, Mia was such a great help to me. She took my passport and told me she would take it to the immigration herself fearing I would encounter difficulties because I did not speak Spanish fluently. Mia did what she told me and got everything straight. She told me that the same God who provided her to and helped me in Nicaragua, that God would send someone else to help me the rest of my journey.

After leaving from the immigration Mia reminded me what time the same bus would be leaving in the morning. The driver had announced before we arrived in Nicaragua the departure time, but I did not remember, I was so frustrated and confused. My gratefulness for Mia's help had me so tearful. I was feeling so sad, because I knew that soon we would have to go our separate ways.

The passengers were scheduled to spend the night in the city of Nicaragua, and then board the bus the following morning. I told Mia that if I had a choice I would not spend the night with the friends because I was afraid they would hurt me. She told me to come with her because she would be spending some time with her male friend who she had an intimate relationship with, and had his own home, but rented two rooms as a motel, and would make sure I got to the bus station in time. I went with Mia because I trusted her. She was such a nice person to me. My friends saw me leaving with Mia. I saw then as they stood and looked at me, but I held my head straight before me.

Mia and I got into a taxi which took us to her friend. When Mia got there she introduced me to him, and then showed me the room which she occupies on her visits.

After we had settled down Mia invited me to join her for dinner. Both she and her friend treated me very nicely. After dinner that evening Mia told me that she would be going to the bar to have a drink. I was very surprised because Mia was not very young, but you could not recognize her age, because she was all dressed up and looked so charming. I accompanied them to the bar. We drank liquor, and also ate. After all the festivity we went home. Mia made sure the bed was very clean and comfortable for me to sleep on. That night I went to bed and slept like a baby. I guess it was because I was so intoxicated from having so much to drink the night before.

It was now morning. Mia woke me up and reminded me to get ready to catch the bus that would be taking me to British Honduras. She prepared breakfast for me, and also made me a few large sandwiches and gave me some sodas to take with me.

After I got dress; Mia got a friend to take me to the bus station. This was the moment I was not prepared to face, but I had no choice. It was time for me and Mia to say goodbye. That was such a sad time for me, because parting with Mia made me feel very sad. I wanted to stay with her, but it was not possible. Furthermore my plans were already made for America. We both hugged, we cried and kissed each other. It was so difficult for us to say goodbye. She was so nice to me. I could only walk away in tears, hoping the moments with her never ended.

When I got into the car, I kept gazing back at Mia until she was out of my sight. On my way to the bus station I cried till my eyes were swollen and my face became red. The driver who was one of Mia's friends was so nice; he talked to me, and encouraged me as we drove along.

On my way to the bus station I informed the driver about my friend's behavior towards me, so he was aware of what might transpire. When we got to the bus station the bus was not there yet; but my friends were already there, so I showed them to the driver.

When the driver and myself arrived to the station and got my things from the car, he hugged me immediately and whisper in my ears saying, "Don't push me away because I am going to let your friends believe I am your man, so just let me kiss you." When they saw me come at first, I saw them throwing up their hands in the air, and also pointing their finger at me. It was at that moment the driver hugged and kissed me for the longest. Seeing that they all walked away.

The driver told me that he would stay with me until the bus came and made sure that I was seated safely before he left me. I asked the driver to give me his name and address so that I could write to him. That seems to make him happy. He immediately took a piece of paper from his pocket, wrote it and gave it to me.

Just before the bus drove away the driver hugged and kissed me again, and then took money from his pocket and gave it to me. I did not look to see how much it was, as this all surprised me. That seems to intensify my friend's fury. The driver then told me goodbye and left.

I was so sad, because he and Mia were the two nicest people I had met. I was now on my own and on my way to British Honduras hoping that God would send another angel to assist me.

After the bus traveled through the countryside of Nicaragua the driver finally came to a rest stop. Everyone exited the bus, but I sat down because I wanted to see how much money the man gave me. It was 500 colons. I was so glad and surprised, but fearing that I could not spend it because I was in another country, I took a chance and succeeded.

I saw my friends eating and laughing, but I kept away because I did not want them to hurt me again.

I remember having sandwiches that Mia had given to me, so I went back to the bus to get them, but the door was locked, so I sat down under a tree by myself.

I looked across from where I was sitting and saw a large box that was located besides the building where the bus stopped. I went and looked to see what it was. The box contained a lot of mangoes. I looked around to see if there was anyone watching. When I realized that no one saw me, I quickly got quite a few good ones and placed them into my handbag, which was large enough to carry more than one dozen and ran back to where I was sitting. Luckily a water pipe was not far from where I sat so I was able to wash the mangoes which I wrapped into my towels and secured into my bag. Not long after the bus driver returned and started calling out to the passengers that he was ready to leave. I went and joined the line and boarded the bus for the rest of my journey.

I kept admiring the pristine nature of the flora; yet I was surprised to see the abject poverty which existed in that country. This was borne out by the fact that there were many houses that were constructed by thatch roofs and wood. The women who were more visible displayed a picture of natural beauty by having their long flowing hair, visible for all to admire; nevertheless, my attention was again fixed on them when I saw that they were transporting loads and logs on their heads like beast of burden. The bus was expected to arrive in British Honduras the next day.

Realizing that I would be arriving in British Honduras I became very scared and nervous.

Just as we got off the bus; I was startled when I heard the same inner voice that spoke to me in Costa Rica; saying, "You are not alone." It was at that moment that my fears and trepidation was assuaged, and a sense of peace overtook me. So I followed through with the other passengers to the immigration.

Clearing immigration was scary for me, but remembering that voice gave me a sense of peace, and assurance.

That time it was not difficult for me facing the immigration in British Honduras. The officer who interviewed me was very inviting and polite. It appeared that during the interview he became smitten with me, and expressed a desire to see me in the future. To that end he gave me his address. After I left the immigration Officer, I went to the bus and got my baggage which was required to be searched. This proved to be the worst part of my trip. My baggage were searched pell-mell by the custom officers who commandeered part of my baggage with the greatest sense of impunity. He told me that I was a black gal who did not deserve such nice thing. I felt so ashamed and humiliated.

After receiving the remains of my baggage I saw an older couple who was also getting their baggage waving their hands to me, and told me to wait for them.

When they came and spoke to me I realize that they were bilingual. I felt very happy, because now I could communicate with someone again. On remembering the Voice, I then whispered a prayer and said, "Lord you told me that every step of the way you would help me, and you have done it again." The couple introduced themselves to me and told me that they came from Nicaragua and were going to America. They told me that the reason why I was harassed by the immigration was because I did not speak Spanish, but promised that when I got to El Salvador they would help me to get through the immigration.

I was glad that I made it through British Honduras.

The couple informed me where the bus was parked and the time it would be leaving. I had one sandwich left from which Mia gave me and three mangoes. I tried to save them as I did not know what lies ahead for the remainder of my journey.

The couple then signaled to me letting me know it was time to board the bus for El Salvador.

Luckily we were seated in the front section and close to each other's, so we were able to communicate.

It was a long drive and the food I had was finished. I became very famished. The bus made a stop along the way for us to eat; I was unable to spend the money I had, because it was for immigration purposes. The only option I had was to drink water.

The couple who I made friends with I did not want them to be privy to my personal life, so I kept my distance.

Looking at the people who were eating only intensified my hunger and to my chagrin not even a crumb fell from the table where they were eating.

As soon as the passengers left the restaurant and went back on the bus, like a scavenger I quickly searched the tables to see if there were any left over. I was lucky to discover a few pieces of hamburger and half cans of soda. I stuff what I could in my mouth and put the rest into my bag, and drank as much soda that I could, then poured the rest filling one can. This became my meal for the afternoon.

During my continued searching the tables for food, I found a purse which contained $65.00 American dollars. I took the money from the purse and stuffed it into my bosom. Immediately I left the restaurant and boarded the bus.

I did not hear anyone complain about losing money, and I was not about to reveal that I had found any, because I needed all that I could.

It was a long drive. I was experiencing pain and numbness in my bottom and back, also getting hungry; but remembering that I had a few half of sandwiches in my handbag, I started eating.

Most of the passengers had bought food with them. I did not have extra money at the time when the bus stopped at the restaurant, because it was just about the same time when the bus was departing I found the money.

Signs were posted along the road which displayed the name of places, so I knew when the bus would be reaching El Salvador.

On reaching El Salvador, as usual I felt scared having to go through immigration, hoping I would not have to experience the same situation. Even though my friends told me they would help me, I did not want to depend on them. Everyone exited the bus.

Liz and the friends were all traveling on the same bus, but I was not focused on them, I had to fend my own way. The couple I met were standing right behind me.

I did not have to remind them that I might have difficulties facing the immigration. Immediately they dragged, and placed me to stand between them in the line. When we approached the immigration, the husband took my passport and handed it to the immigration officer who was a man and spoke to him in Spanish. I saw the immigration officer look at me with a smile, then he stamped the passport and gave it back to me. I stood behind the friends and waited until they were processed. We all went to claim our baggage. This time I was successful.

We were now on our way to Guatemala.

This was the final stop for the bus we traveled on, so we had to change to another.

The driver told us that we would be waiting four hour. The bus terminal had a large restaurant. I was still unable to buy anything, because I had Mexico ahead of me.

My friend who I travel with from Costa Rica, seems very happy, but I was unhappy due to the fact that I was unable to eat and drink like they did.

Because the bus stop for a long time, that gave me the chance to get acquainted with other people.

As I sat in the restaurant there was a group of people who were eating on the table next to me. I watched them carefully as they ate. Seeing that they had lots of left over on their plates. I asked if I could have it because I did not have enough money to buy food. One of the ladies told me yes. Two of the ladies put the food into one plate and gave it to me. One of the men gave me $10 American dollars, and wished me good luck. Then they all left.

I sat down and enjoyed a sumptuous meal, but I was still hungry because I had not eaten much after leaving Nicaragua. I watched to see if anyone was looking at me. Again, like a scavenger I searched the garbage can and found three half sandwiches. I quickly grabbed them and sat around a different table. While sitting I kept praying that someone would show up and display kindness to me again. I was not neatly dressed like the other passengers. While sitting for a while I saw some passengers who were traveling on the same bus come and sit at the table next to me. We all were in the restaurant for a long time. Watching them eat intensifies my hunger. Suddenly a feeling of sadness came over me that I burst out crying loudly. To my Surprise I saw when one of the lady passengers waved her hands to me. She then came and handed me a sandwich. I was so glad. I took it and told her thanks. After eating the sandwich I went to the bathroom and drank water.

After waiting for a long time, the bus was ready to take us to Mexico. We got on board. I became excited, but also scared because it was such a long drive; I had never driven so long before. I became very tired and uncomfortable. I prayed for that moment when I would be able to buy something to eat freely instead of being a scavenger

CHAPTER THIRTY

On Route to Mexico

The bus was not ready to depart for Mexico, so we had to stand in a line with our travel document in hand and wait for our names to be called.

After an exhausting wait we boarded the bus. The driver later announces that the next stop would be in Tapachula Mexico where we would be inspected by the Mexican Immigration. On hearing this news I felt a sense of trepidation.

It was a long and tiring drive to Tapachula. During the extensive journey my legs and bottom became very numb and painful. I was hungry but I could not venture to spend any of the money I had which was primarily for immigration purposes. As a result I had no choice but to endure my hunger.

The couples who I met earlier on were traveling on the same bus. I was surprised to find that their attitude towards me became distant, and cold. Liz who came from my country traveling on the same bus with me did not change her negative attitude; and was even colder than the strangers were.

Despite the unfriendly attitude I had to undergo from the couple and Liz; I had to direct my thoughts at reaching Tapachula. The driver soon announced that the bus would be reaching Tapachula in the next few minutes, and all travelers should have their documents ready.

That moment brought to me a feeling of foreboding, and nervousness accompanied by stomach cramps. Nevertheless, I was

Journey on a Bumpy Road

eager to go through the immigration and enter Mexico as that was the last round on the ladder to enter America. In Mexico I would have the freedom to spend what money I had, and grace myself with a decent meal.

When we arrived at the immigration checkpoint I felt an unusual amount of fear, with a feeling of flight that I found it difficult to maintain my position in the line.

That feeling increased so much that I literally was seeking somewhere to escape, but found that I was in a secure environment and there was nowhere to go. The immigration area was made of concrete, which was quite impenetrable. Faced with Hobson's choice I decided to feign an attitude of calm. The passengers were now being inspected by the immigration.

Not long after I saw Liz and her friends standing in the line ahead of me with their documents in hand. I realized that soon I would have to face my worst fears.

To my surprise I thought they had their own money, but I realize that they did not. I was startled to discover that an act of substitute was conducted mainly by Liz and her friends. This took the form of each one who after seeing the immigration officer, and declared the allowed amount of money to enter the country. To my amazement each person who was cleared by the immigration officer performed a slight of hand trick and passed the money to the next person behind them. It was done with such skill, that the immigration officer was oblivious to what was happening right in his presence.

When it became my turn to go to the immigration officer and I observed the scant method in which the officer dealt with the previous clients I felt somewhat assured that I would be successful.

When I found myself standing before the Immigration officer his demeanor was not the same. Maybe because of the way I approached him. His questions became very intrusive. He asked my purpose for traveling from my country to Mexico. I told the officer my reason was for Agricultural Research, he looked at me askance, and asked me to declare the amount of money I had on my person. I acquiesced to his demand and he counted the money, and said. "You have enough money to do lots of research." I said to the officer,

"Thank you Sir." With that he hastily stamped my passport and gave it back to me. I felt a sense of ease and walked away.

To my surprise, just as I walked out from the immigration building, one of Liz friends accosted me and said, "You wretch, that's why you did not want me because you were a big courtesan why you got all that money." I ignored him, but this behavior confirmed to me how much I was despised by them. Without saying anything, I took up my luggage and walked away.

When I went to the parking lot I discovered that my bus was not among the number of buses that were present in the terminal. There were many passengers who were standing in line. Nevertheless; I joined the other passengers.

While waiting in line I became aware of a tall white man who was standing immediately before me. After a while we exchanged pleasantries, and an in-depth conversation later ensued. An unusual attraction which was mutually developed between us. He gave me some information about himself, mainly that his wife had died some years ago, and that he was an American from Orange Hill; but came on a bus trip with others to visit Mexico for agricultural purposes.

After a long conversation it became apparent that he was smitten by me, and I also felt myself enamored towards him, because he was a very intelligent man. The virtues about myself which he explained caused his attraction for me was that I was a very attractive and intelligent girl, and would love to take me back with him. In the short time we conversed he developed such an attraction for me that he was prepared to plan a ruse to get me on his bus unnoticed by the drive. I felt a sense of eagerness to go along with his plan because he was an American, and his country was where I wanted to be.

The driver was now calling the names of the passengers who were supposed to board his bus. My luggage was distant from the bus so I had to go and get them. I tried to get my luggage as fast as I could. My friend stood at the bus door waving for me to come.

When I got them and ran to the bus it was late because the driver had already closed the door.

I stood there with a sense of chagrin looking at the bus with tears running down my face. On seeing me standing at the terminal he expressed his disappointment, because he kept waving his hand at me, making gestures like he was very disheartened.

That made me cry even worse; and made me think that the possible answer to my prayer was leaving my life along with the bus.

My friend continued to wave his hands and also blew kisses towards me.

After that brief heartfelt encounter with the American stranger, I could only stand, transfixed with tearful eyes and watched as the bus got smaller in the distance.

To this day no one has affected me so deeply in such a short period of time.

My only option was to look at the situation as, "Ships passing in the night."

After the bus was gone, I then realized that the people who were standing and waiting were all watching me. They all looked at me with such beautiful smiles on their faces.

I was very sad because I had not met anyone with such love and compassion since I parted company with Mia in Nicaragua.

When my bus arrived, I boarded it for the city of Tapachula.

On arriving in Tapachula I realized that Liz and her friends were already there. While in Tapachula, I was in the act of boarding the bus, and connected to another bus that would take me to Mazatlan; I went to the ticket counter to purchase a ticket.

Because my luggage was heavy and I was unable to hold them in my hands, I had to put them down.

While purchasing the ticket I was a witness to Liz rifling through my luggage removing my jacket and the large towel I had to keep me warm and ran away. Under the circumstances I was unable to pursue her because I was in the act of purchasing my ticket, and the crowded nature of the terminal made my pursuit somewhat difficult.

I was so hurt, having to face the bitter cold with nothing to keep me warm.

I boarded the bus and was on my way. The couple who I had met were not on this leg of the journey so I had to fend by myself.

It was night when I boarded the bus; my seat was located in the middle. After travelling for a few hours I was approached by two young men who spoke to me very harshly in Spanish, and then began to spit on me. But I remained quiet, because I could not understand what was being said; also I was afraid they would hurt me. One of the guys grabbed me by my hand and pulled me out of the seat, then threw me to the bus floor. None of the passengers said anything or tried stopping them. They all just stared at me. I was the only colored person on the bus. After I was thrown to the floor I got up and tried to sit in a vacant seat next to someone else, unfortunately that passenger pushed me to the floor. Having nowhere to sit, I sat on the floor; while sitting on the floor they spat on me. It was very uncomfortable sitting on the floor, and especially while the bus was driving, but I had no choice. I was very unhappy, but I was too far to even turn back, and furthermore, that did not even cross my mind. I continue to travel in discomfort. Because even though my body was being abused my mind was focused positively.

It was very late one night when while traveling I was interrupted and stopped by the Mexican Immigration. Everyone was checked for proper documents. Because I did not have the papers that were required I was taken off the bus by the officer who took me to the office and locked away in a room by myself.

While I sat in that room the only thing I could think of was pray. I immediately held my head up and said, "God you have to work a miracle not for me, but for my children's sake." Not long after praying the room door was open. The same officer who took me off the bus entered and asked me if I had any money, I told him yes. He said okay, he will talk to his chief and in return let me know what their decision was.

In a few moments the officer returned and asked me if I could pay him $300.00 American dollar, if not let him know. I told him yes.

The officer looked at me with a pleasing countenance and told me to get myself ready until he returned from his chief. After returning in a few minutes he asked for the money, which I gave to him. I saw the joy in his face as he took the money from me. When he returned he told me that he was going to put me on the bus himself. He then told me to accompany him to the dining room and showed me the refrigerator, also the food cabinet. The officer told me to get enough of whatever I wanted to eat, and make a few sandwiches to take along with me. I had coffee, made a sandwich and took a few bottles of sodas. The officer gave me a large bag to pack my food in, and then hurried me to get ready because the bus would be there shortly.

He asked me if I was planning to go across the Mexican border to America. I was very reluctant in answering, because I was not sure he was genuine. He said to me without me answering, with his fingers touching his head, "I know you are going there, you will get across, because your English is very good."

In a short time the bus came. He took me to board the bus, but while I was boarding he went and spoke to the driver. After he finished talking to the driver, I saw him looking around in the bus, when he saw me, he came to where I was sitting, he took my hand and shook them, then said to me, "Good luck." I told him, "Thanks."

The officer then left.

My eyes were full of tears, because I could not believe that I escaped from being sent back to my country. The officer was so kind to me.

I was now traveling among a different group of people. My seat was located in the back. I was glad that I got away from those wicked and unkind people I was traveling among.

As the bus drove along the passengers who were sitting behind were two young men accompanied by a couple. One of the young men spoke and told me that they were from EL Salvador. He did not speak English very well. He pointed his brother to me, and told me that the couple who were sitting on the other side were related to him, but did not speak English. He informed me they were all traveling to get across the Mexican border to America. After talking with them; as we drove along we developed a friendship. I was very glad I met them, because I needed their help.

It was a long drive to Mazatlan. I asked them, which was the closest point to get to the border. They told me that I would have to take the Ferry with them from Mazatlan to La Paz. I became interested, and decided to travel along with them. On reaching Mazatlan the bus stop was close to the ocean, where we all exited.

I was so excited when I got off the bus and saw the big ocean of water, I would have done anything to jump in and get a good bath. I was also very hungry, but because of the difficulty I had communicating with the storekeeper I had to ask one of the young men to go shopping for me. Each time I asked him to buy anything for me; he tells me that the money I gave him was not enough. After doing that for a while I realize he was lying to me, but I tried to maintain the friendship because I wanted to get the information from them about the Ferry and the time of the departure.

After I was finish eating I wanted to take a bath. I look across to the ocean and saw some large rocks; I thought that maybe I could go behind there and take a bath without anyone seeing me. That was what I had done. After washing myself I felt like someone was watching me. I looked up, and to my surprise I saw the three men who I traveled with standing looking down at me holding their private in their hands. I was so surprise. I quickly got dress and ran up from the water and to the road. When I got to the road, I saw them walking away. Not long after they came to me and said that they were only making fun, but would not refuse a little pleasure with me. I did not reply, l ignored their behaviors.

Time was fast approaching to board the Ferry to La Paz. I had to let one of my friends purchase the ticket for me. This time he was very dishonest, but I made up my mind to endure the situation, because I know it would come to an end.

The announcement was broadcast on the microphone what time the Ferry would be sailing out. I was very excited, because since I left Nicaragua I have not gotten the chance to lie down and sleep. I started to get myself prepared mentally to take that cruise in the Ferry across the ocean. I was thrilled, but also scared.

It was boarding time. I gathered my things and joined the line just like a tourist, wearing my sunglasses. The moment I got on the ferry I was directed to my room. The Ferry was supposed to reach La Paz the next morning. The first thing I did when I got into my cabin was to kneel down and say a prayer to God asking for protection. Even though I could not find the words to express myself, I poured out my heart to God in tears. I then got up and went to the bathroom and took a good bath. The bathroom was not that large, but it had enough space. I stood under the shower, relaxed and let the water flow all over my body. I made sure that I got a good wash because I did not know how long it would take for me to get another.

Soon after taking my bath I unpacked my things and got clean clothes to wear for the next day.

The clothes that I had worn I washed and wrung them into one of the bath towels so that they would dry very easily. I was feeling sleepy so I decided to go to bed. Before I went to lay down I secured the money I had under my shoe sole, and kept $30.00 in my hand bag. While I was sleeping I was awakened by a knock on my cabin door. I was so frightened, but I did not answer. I then remembered that the Immigration officer had warned me to be careful of robbers. So right there and then I realize it might be one of the friends who I traveled with might have come to interrogate me.

I lay still and listened, it was then I heard them speak and I realized that my vibes were right. Soon after; I heard the footsteps as if they were walking away. I did not hear the footsteps before because I was sleeping. After the footsteps were gone I slowly open my door and walk down the passage, I peeped around the corner, I saw one of the guy holding something long in his hands, and the other had something that resembled a bag, quickly I ran back to my room.

It was difficult for me to sleep after such occurrence, so I got up and took another shower and let the water flow from my head downward. I got under the sheet and somehow I went to bed.

It was by the horn from the Ferry that I was awakened. I got up and got myself ready. The clothes that I had washed were almost dried, so I fold them and put in with my luggage.

Where my cabin was located I was able to see the people while they were leaving the Ferry. I stood by the window and watched. The moment I saw my friends exited the ferry I got my things and left.

I did not know where I was, but the good thing I was among people who spoke English and also Americans. I follow them along. Soon I came to a shed where a few shops were located, and quite a few people who were sitting on the ground. I greeted them, and then I went to the shop and bought something to eat.

I felt good, and excited, because I was getting closer to America, and the friends who I had traveled with on the ferry were nowhere to be seen. I was so afraid of them. I sat down with the new people and had something to eat.

I did not have enough money as before, because I had to buy my way with the friends I had met. While I was eating I met a nice looking guy. We sat and talked for a while, and he told me that he was in the army. We had such difficulty communicating because of the language. Each time he tried talking to me and realized that we had difficulty understanding each other he took his hands and hit himself on his forehead. He was waiting to meet another group of soldiers. We talked for a while, he also gave me his address and told me to write to him in English and he would have the letter interpreted. He was such a handsome guy, but we were on different journeys. Not long after, we both hugged each other and said goodbye. For me it was exciting meeting him, but very sad parting.

As I sat on the ground and waited; I was still not sure which direction to take, I watched as the people were coming and going to different buses. Not long after I saw a couple come off a bus, as they approached the shed where I sat they started talking to me. Immediately I recognized that they were American. I was very glad to meet them. We all spoke and made friends. They told me that they were doing research. They wanted to know about me. I told them about my plans to enter the United States, but I was not sure which direction I should take. The man looked at me and asked, "Where are you really traveling from." I told him Costa Rica. He said, "Huuumm." He then looked at his companion and took his cap off his head and started rubbing it with his hands. The man then directed me where I should take the bus to.

I had plans to travel to the Texas border, due to the fact that I had a pen-pal with whom I had communicated with from when I was in my country. She told me that she would send her brother there to meet me.

I relayed this to the couple. The man said to me that it would be a long way for me to get to the border, so I should try going to Tijuana, which would be easier. He also told me that I would get through very easy because I spoke very good English, but informed me that I need to practice saying, "American Citizen," and let it sound the way he was saying it to me, because when I faced the Immigration that is what they are going to say to me, and I need to repeat it back to them sounding like an American. He told me that if I talk like an American they will let me go through without any problems.

I asked the man to tell me how to talk like an American, he said he would. He and his companion began to teach me. They started in a chant saying, "American Citizen." We kept saying it until they stopped and told me to say it alone. I tried and got it a little. They told me that with continuous practice I would be okay.

I was not sure which bus would take me close to Tijuana, so I asked them. They were very nice to me, and advised to take food with me because it was a long drive, which I did.

They were going in another direction if not I would have traveled with them. 'Just a pity.'

Not long after my bus arrived. There again I was so excited meeting those people. Parting was difficult, but I had no choice. We all hugged and kissed, then we said goodbye. I left in tears.

The bus that I boarded was packed, there were not many seats, but I sat beside two people who were small in body. It was very uncomfortable, but I was getting closer and closer to my destination.

The passengers I sat beside were mother and daughter. The daughter spoke English fluently, but the mother spoke very little.

After talking with them, the daughter told me that they were going to meet someone with a big van who would be taking them across the border to America. I was excited, because I realized more and more that I was going in the right direction. It was a long journey, and it was night so almost everyone was trying to sleep. I could not because I was uncomfortable.

As I sat there I saw when a male passenger got up and stretched his hand under the seat and opened the bag of the lady who was sitting before him. I saw him take out American dollars. As soon as I saw him close the hand bag and was about to put the money in his pocket I stretched my hand and touched him. He became so frightened. I realized that he spoke English. I told him to give me some if not I would tell on him. He gave me $40.00 American dollars and a smile.

As the bus drove along. As usual the driver stopped at a restaurant so we could get something to eat. After waiting for a long time, the driver announced that the bus was unable to start, so we had to wait there overnight until the company sent another bus, or until the problem was resolved.

The restaurant had two large rooms in the back, they did not have any beds, but they were able to provide a few mattresses. That night some of the passengers slept on the mattress while others slept on the floor including myself. The next morning the driver told us that he was still having problems and we would have to spend another night. I was getting weary and started to wonder, if we were brought there to be killed.

My money was almost finished. Serendipitously I caught that man while he was pilfering. During lunch time I went to the man and asked him to buy me lunch. He told me to go to the restaurant and order what I wanted and he would pay for it. He was kind to me. That same day the mother and daughter who I sat beside invited me to come and eat with them.

It was night, so we all went to the room. Almost everyone wanted to talk to me, due to the fact that I was from another country so they wanted to know about spirituality. I became the center of attraction. They all sat and listened to me as I told stories that were true and lies to them. The next morning the bus arrived. We all got on board.

I had no idea where this bus was destined for, but I knew that the passengers were all going to get across the border to America.

After a long drive the bus stop at another restaurant. The people came off the bus and I followed through with them. They all waited, so I waited with them. Not very long a man came driving in a big van. The van stopped in front of us. The man came out and spoke in Spanish. They all responded to him. Immediately I saw them walk to the side of the van and got in. The man then came to me and asked me where I was going. I told him I wanted to go to America, he told me to come with them. He drove a very large and expensive van.

After driving for a while he stopped the van and told the people to come out of the van so he could show them where to go. He directed them to an entrance. He then asked me how much money I had, because if I had enough he would take me across the border with those people. I did not have much money left. I told him the paltry amount I had. He looked at me with such sympathetic eyes and said to me, "You will need more money." He told me that I would not have any problem crossing the border because I spoke English. He also said that as long as I found someone who was walking to America I could go with them, because he could not take the little money I had, but would drive me into Tijuana to a hotel. He asked me where I was traveling from, and I told him. He said to me, "You will find someone to help you because you are very smart and brave."

He drove me to Tijuana and left me there.

CHAPTER THIRTY-ONE

Tijuana

After a long and tiresome journey through Central America I finally reach Tijuana Mexico.

Due to excessive spending despite how frugal I tried to be, I was left with only $20.00 American dollars and 150peso. The weather was very cold, which I was not properly dressed for. I was wearing blue jeans overall, a tee shirt, a light sweater, a straw hat, complemented with sunglasses and my red color hair. In my hands I carried a large straw basket with clothing and my handbag.

The place was very strange to me. But I was prepared to take any chances in order to accomplish my goal.

With that limited amount of money, and my bags, I walked aimlessly looking for affordable lodging. I tried talking to quite a few people but got no response. I began to wonder that maybe I was not dressed properly, or they did not understand my accent. I searched to find a cheap hotel so that I could unload myself with the luggage, because the people whom I saw were not carrying the amount of luggage like I was.

In that search of desperation with my luggage in hand I suddenly felt an unknown force which propelled me forward and I came in contact with a door, and I fell to the ground. While lying on the ground I saw a young woman standing above me; and she was speaking in Spanish. When I responded she discovered that I did not speak Spanish. She then said to me in English, "This is a motel." She asked me if I was in pain, I said no. The young lady asked me what happened to me. I told her that while I was walking along I felt like someone, or something pushed me against the door. I was lying on the floor, flat on my stomach.

Given this knowledge my feeling of alacrity was very apparent as I asked her the question how much do you rent the room for. She said 150peso. I told her all I had was 100peso. She was hesitant but agreed to rent me the room for said amount, but I would have to vacate the room by 8: am the following morning. In my condition as I was faced with Hobson's choice I had to agree. I was very happy.

I paid her; she gave me the key and showed me the room. Soon as I entered the room I knelt down and prayed. I was then feeling more positive than before.

To this point I began making plans about what I was going to do with the money I had, which was 50peso and $20.00 American dollars.

I wanted to take a bath, but the room had only a toilet and a wash basin with cold water. I was afraid to wash myself, fearing I would catch a cold, but somehow I had to wash myself after such a long journey. And having no winter clothes, I had to make do.

I was getting hungry and wanted to get something to eat. I took that 50peso and went out to find a restaurant.

As I walked along I met quite a few people, only this time I did not try to talk to anyone. I sang and skipped along just like Julie Andrews. "I have confidence in confidentiality." The people who I met that time, when they saw me coming looked at me and smiled. That made me feel so happy.

Luckily I found one which was close to the hotel.

Soon as I reached the restaurant I was sitting there for about thirty minutes unnoticed by the waiters. I began waving my hands to the waiter who was a man; he came to me fussing. I knew not what he was talking about because he spoke in Spanish, so I held my head down. The waiter stopped fussing, and said to me, "Do you speak English? I told him yes." He immediately bow to me and said, "I am very, very sorry my American friend."

The cheapest meal on the menu cost 50 peso. Because the menu was listed in Spanish I did not know what it was, but I ordered anyway. It was just a modicum of beans and rice.

The 50 peso secured a paltry meal for me which clearly did not satisfy my hunger.

Before I left the restaurant I saw when one of the other male waiters as he cleared the table he took the leftover food outside the back of the restaurant.

Leaving the restaurant, I decided to walk around to the back to see where he was taking the food. I hurriedly approached him and asked what he was doing with the food. He told me that he was going to feed the dogs in the back of the restaurant. I asked him if I could get some for myself. He told me that I would have to be very quick as the dogs knew the time when the food was put out for them. The dogs and I were now involved in a competition, because although I tried to get as much as I could, the dogs were already there and got the most of it.

I ate what I could and wrapped some into newspaper and went back to the hotel to eat. I felt very sad about my encounter with the dogs, but I was very hungry and did not have enough money to feed myself.

After eating I had a bad feeling in my stomach which caused me to regurgitate, and made me feel weak and faint. I washed my face with cold water, then drank some and lay in the bed hoping to feel better. After regurgitating the fourth time I felt a relief. I drank more water and lay back down for a while.

As I lay in the bed I heard a voice which could not be placed, instructing me how to secure my documents; and then I would find someone who is walking to America to take me. Immediately I got dressed. I knelt down and prayed, "God not for my sake, but for the children's sake, please send someone to walk me across the border to America." After praying and reading a few chapters from the book of psalms for good luck and protection, I got myself ready. I put my red cover New Testament Bible in my pocket, along with documents and the $20.00 American dollars, then put on my sweater, and then I left the hotel wearing one suit of clothing. I had my mind made up, that either dead or alive; I was going to America, because I came too close to my goal.

I began walking along the street. I met quite a few people, who I tried talking to, but I got no response, so I said to myself that probably they did not understand me, that did not discourage me.

Somehow I decided to take another route; it was a very lonesome road, but I had no fear; it felt like someone was leading me.

Further along the journey, as soon as I took the other road I met a tall dark skinned man who was walking toward the direction I was coming from. I did not give him the opportunity to greet me, immediately I greeted him. The man responded by saying, "Wow." We then began talking. He was very polite to me. As we spoke I asked him if he could walk me across the border to American.

The man was totally astonished. He said to me, "Where in hell do you come from." I told him, "One of the Islands." I told him a lie that communist had taken over my country and all my families were killed so I am running for my life. The man placed his two hands to his side and said to me. "What the hell are you saying?" I said to him, "Yes." The man immediately said to me, if you wait until tonight I will have my friends come and drive you across the border.

All of a sudden I felt like a strong force. I Shouted immediately. "Not tonight, it's now I must go." The man shook his head quickly and said to me, "Yea." I said to him, "Yes, yes." That man was going about his business but he immediately made a U turn and came along with me. We began talking. He told me that it was a long walk but we could get there in no time.

I did not ask him for his name, because it was not important to me, I was more interested in him taking me to America. But I remember him telling me that he came from Tennessee and lived in California.

The stranger looked at me with such compassion, and said to me. I will take you across the border to America but I would have to talk, and sound like an American.

We both walked and had lots of conversation. He told me that when I face the Immigration they are going to ask me a question which I should reply to them and sound like an American. I said to him, "Can you please tell me what to say, and how to speak like an American." I told him that I was not illiterate, I only speak with a different accent, but I was a fast learner.

Well! He said, "Okay, I will teach you." I asked him to tell what the question would be. He told me the Immigration will say to me, "American Citizen," which when I reply I should repeat back to the officer sounding like an American with the accent. I said "Ok."

I then realized that the people who I met earlier told me the truth.

It was time for me to begin my training.

As we walked along, he began to tell me. Each step I took I chanted, "American Citizen." It was so funny, because this was done between the both of us, we sounded like little children.

The man then said to me. "God-damn-it, you sound like an American more than I do." Hearing him say that to me gave me more confidence with myself.

He kept reminding me it was a long walk before we got to America. But after walking for quite some time, I asked him how much longer we had to walk. He said to me; America was just around the corner.

Excitement got the better of me, so I started singing and dancing.

Suddenly I started getting nervous, which I did not like. Immediately I started singing again, "I have confident in confidentially." Soon after, I felt a spirit of bravery. At that moment I found myself walking like a soldier, with my grandfather spirit walking with me.

We were now getting very close to the Mexican border and the immigrations, but somehow I had no fear, because I was full of confidence. I continued chanting, "American Citizen," by myself to make sure I had the American accent and was successful. We were now approaching the building that led to the immigration department and through the border from Tijuana to San Diego.

On entering the building the stranger directed me which way to go, with him leading the way. When we got inside I saw two lines formed and several people standing. The stranger told me to follow him because they were checking documents in a line that would not be appropriate for me. He took me and placed me into another line and instructed me to stand behind him.

He went in front of the Immigration officer and spoke. I don't know what he told the officer, but I saw when he pointed his left thumb towards me, and at the same time telling the officer that I was his, 'Old Lady.' When I heard him call me an old lady I became very upset, but remained calm.

It was my turn to speak to the officer. The Officer said to me, "American Citizen." I repeated it back to him and continued walking. But somehow the officer gave me a strange look, but I kept walking along with the stranger and other people.

The moment I came through the immigration and was outside the building, the stranger shouted to me and said, "Shit you are in America; you got some kind of nerves coming from so far, running for your life. Damn it."

I was very astonished realizing that I made it across the border to America.

Not long after the stranger then said to me, "Did you wash your behind before you left Mexico?" I played deaf, and gave him no response. He said to me again, "Come with me to the bathroom." I pretended again not hearing what he said because my mind was only focused on reaching America.

I kept walking until I came to a Greyhound bus station. I went to the receptionist and told her I needed a ticket to go to America, but she replied to me and said, "You are in America." Immediately I caught myself and said to her, I am so sorry, because that man frustrates me so much, and I am very tired after such a long walk.

The receptionist said to me, "You mean you want to go to Los Angeles." I told her yes. The $20.00 I had was more than enough to purchase my ticket. There was no bus available for Los Angeles, but she told me there was a bus leaving for San Diego which I should take and when I get there I should take the bus that would be going to Los Angeles. I bought the bus ticket and got a transfer. After the receptionist sold me the ticket, she told me to hurry, because the bus would be leaving immediately.

I ran as fast as I could. I was so lucky, because the bus driver was just about to close the door. I quickly boarded the bus, and found a vacant seat in the middle where I sat.

I stood and looked from the bus window to see if I saw the stranger, but I never did.

My suspicions were founded, when to my surprise the stranger in question offered to take me to the male bathroom. My refusal was instant as I later found out that the intentions of the stranger were quite sinister.

Nevertheless. It was late in the afternoon when I boarded the Greyhound Bus, as it slowly pulled out of the station on route to San Diego California, and with it America.

My feeling of utter joy was so grandiose that I could hardly contain myself. In my mind it was a culmination of years of hope, desire, and meticulous planning.

I was so happy when I realized that my feet landed on American soil.

CHAPTER THIRTY-TWO

Landed in America

After such a long and arduous journey through the Central American countries, coupled with the fact that my ability to communicate in another language, compounded my problems; and on reaching America made me feel more at ease with myself.

As the bus drove through San Diego California, I glanced through the window and saw the beautiful flora, and fauna, of the countryside, and felt a feeling of tranquility, then came the beautiful scenery of twilight hours while traveling. I became convinced that this was the promise land. My joy was exaggerated to the point that beholding such beauty of America caused my eyes to become watered with tears.

As the bus continued on routes to the city of San Diego, and the closer it got, my feelings of expectation grew.

After reaching San Diego, all the passengers exited and boarded another bus that was going to Los Angeles.

The beauty of San Diego was pale in comparison to what I saw in Los Angeles.

As I alighted from the bus in Los Angeles I was without any sense of direction, because I did not know anyone. A gazed from the police and any passerby only gave a feeling of trepidation. Finally I saw a tall dark skinned man standing alone who was a passenger on the same bus. I approached him, and I entered into a meaningful dialogue with him.

After talking with him for a while, I told him that I saw him sitting at the back of the bus eating, but was afraid to ask him for some. He asked me why I did not come and asked him. In response I told him that I was ashamed. I asked him for his name, and he told me, "Tony." I then told him my name.

After our conversation I felt that I could trust this stranger, so I told him where I came from; all the way through Mexico and would like to go to my cousin and friends who lived in Florida.

Tony wanted to know from me if I knew the friends, I told him yes, because my main friend whose name was Val told me if I get the opportunity to get close enough to America he would send the money for me to come to him in Florida.

Tony showed such compassion towards me, and asked me for my friend's name and telephone number. Immediately Tony called my cousin Val and informed him that I was in Los Angeles at the Greyhound Bus Station and he was calling on my behalf. Tony asked Val if he could wire a ticket for me to come to Florida. Val told Tony that he would, but first Val wanted to talk to me. When Val heard my voice he greeted me by saying, "Rasta, gal, you make it to America to hell. Give the phone back and let me talk to the guy."

After the conversation between Tony and Val ended, Tony told me that Val would be wiring a ticket for me immediately. The ticket came, but I was faced with a problem. The receptionist requested that I present my identification in order to receive the ticket. Tony was already aware of my situation; he did not want me to present my passport because I had it in my sock, and I was being watched by an officer. Tony told the receptionist that I was robbed and my identification was taken by the robbers which were in my handbag. That did not satisfy the receptionist. We both became very frightened, not knowing what to do.

Immediately Tony got back on the telephone and called Val. He explained the circumstances that I was faced with on receiving my bus ticket. Val went back to the bus station in Florida, and told them to release the ticket to me in California without me presenting any identification, also the circumstances.

While Tony waited patiently with me, he was also waiting for his bus to go home, but did not want to leave me before the ticket arrived for me.

Tony was very nice to me. He told me that he was without a companion, and would take me home with him to be his lady, but stated that it would be a big risk, because he lives into a rooming house which was occupied by other single male who he was not acquainted with, and that his job as a truck driver have kept him away from home, but return only for a change of clothing. But Tony said that if the bus ticket did not arrive before his bus came, or if there was still any problem he would have to take me home with him, and make an arrangement for my accommodation.

We kept talking for a while. Not very long after the receptionist called Tony and told him that my ticket had arrived.

It seems like a miracle, because the moment I received my ticket in my hands, Tony bus arrived.

I hate that I could not go home with him, because he was such a nice person. We hugged each other so tight. He wished me good luck and told me to be careful. Just as he mounted the bus step, I saw him turn back and come to me. He gave me his address and telephone number; also took $20.00 from his wallet and gave it to me, then he hugged me again, gave me his blessing, and said goodbye. He then boarded the bus, which shortly drove away.

It was very sad to see him go. "Such a nice person." My tears fell uncontrollable, but I had to go on leaning on the good wishes he gave me.

It was 9: pm so all passengers including myself had to board the bus.

My seat was located in the middle.

After the bus drove off I started having mixed feelings. Even though I was in America, I began wondering if my friends in Florida would be nice to me.

As the bus traveled along, the driver made several stops at different terminals, where he let off and picked up passengers. When the bus arrived in Arizona it was stopped and checked by the United States Border Patrol. I was sitting alone in my seat. The moment I saw the officer approached the bus, I quickly lay down, making myself as small as possible. While I lay there my mind told me to open my New Testament Bible and place it on top of my body with the writing facing towards the top. That's what I did.

To my surprise, every passenger and seats were checked except mine. I continued laying in my seat until the bus drove off, and was a long way off.

Finally I sat up. Everyone looked at me, but said nothing.

I was experiencing such a feeling of uneasiness as I traveled along in the bus.

The bus continued to stop at different terminals, and also made several changes before I got to Florida.

There were other passengers traveling to Florida, but they carried suitcases and bags. I only had my two hands.

As the bus traveled along and made a stop, I observed some of the passengers who went to the bathroom, washed themselves and changed their clothes. I was unable to because I had no clothes, but what I was wearing. I was so dirty that I scorned the smell I carried. After standing for a while, I realized that some of the passengers at the bus station looked at me disparagingly. It was then I realized that my odor became obnoxious to the point where I was recognized by others.

At this point my decision was to go to the bathroom and do whatever necessary to cleanse myself.

I washed my hands and face at the basin, using the hand soap, then collected lots of hand towels. I then entered inside the toilet and closed the door. I remove the lid from the toilet tank, wash my underwear, and squeeze it into some of the hand towels, then flush the tank. After it filled up. I use hand soap with the hand towel to bathe myself from the tank, and then dry myself. Having no other underwear, I neatly wrap the seat of my wet underwear with toilet papers and put it back on, with the expectation that I would not contract a cold.

I left the bathroom smelling and feeling better about myself.

The bus was almost ready to leave, so I got something to eat, and boarded to my seat.

It was such a long and tiresome drive, but there was nowhere for my return. I continue on my journey.

Journey on a Bumpy Road

Even though my seat was not comfortable, I tried to sleep as much as I possibly could. I was more concerned about what my experience would be when I got to Florida.

After driving for a long time, I notice the signs along the highway indicating the amount of miles to my destination in Florida. I was filled with trepidation. When the bus got closer, the driver announced that when we get to Gale there will be one hour wait, so all the passengers would have to have to exit from that bus which would be serviced, and then board another bus that would be coming.

After waiting for a long time I grew impatient. As I waited I strolled around inside of the bus station. During that time a slightly brown skinned man came to me and asked where I was going, I told him Florida. He then said to me, "You have another forty minutes before your bus gets here," I asked him how he knows that. The man told me that he checks everything that happens around that Greyhound Bus Station, because he works for the government.

The moment he uttered the words government to me I soon realized that I had to get away from him, because I was an illegal alien, so I had to be very careful how I converse with him. He wanted to know about me, I told him that all my family lives in Florida, but I had come to visit a boyfriend who beat and treated me badly, so I ran away from him, leaving all my belongings.

That man insisted on talking to me. Each time I walked away from him, he followed after me. He asked me if I was hungry, which I was, but I told him no.

Soon after he came to me smiling, and asked if I would like for him to drive me around to see how beautiful the city of Gale was. My response was no, because I did not want to miss my bus. He told me that he would get back early for my bus. Still I refused his offer.

I began to take that man into deep thought, wondering why he was so determined. I wanted to get away from him, because his action somehow seems strange to me. He insisted on buying me a hamburger and coke from the cafeteria, which I accepted.

While I sat down with him to eat I noticed the redness in his eyes, and a very strange look on his face. I had to find a way to get away from him.

I kept eating, but my eyes and mind were searching for a place to escape from him.

I looked across the bus station; I saw a table where four older white people sat. Three were ladies, and one man. One of the seats was vacant. I did not know what I was going to say to the white people, as I never sat close to any white Americans before. I think for a good minute with the hamburger and coke in my hands. I then took a good look at that man who told me he worked for the government. I made one quick run to the table where the people sat.

When they saw me come they were all frightened. I was almost out of breath. Immediately I said to them, "That man, that man, wants me to go drive with him and I don't know him." The people then turned around and looked at him, and then they told me to sit and calm myself down.

The strangest thing was that, the moment the people turned and looked at him, he got up immediately from his seat, and quickly exited the bus station like he was running. While I sat with the people, I explained to them what had happened. One of the ladies told me to throw the hamburger and coke into the garbage and she would buy me more; which she did.

I did not ask them about their destination, but told me that my bus would be leaving before theirs arrived. They were very kind and sympathetic to me.

When my bus arrived and I was ready to get on board, the man in their company gave me $10.00. They all told me to be careful. And said to me, "God bless you."

I boarded the bus and was on my way to my cousin Val and friends who lived in Florida.

CHAPTER THIRTY-THREE

Arrived in Florida

Late one night I arrived in Chancy Florida on the Greyhound Bus from California. I telephone Val and told him that I was there. He said he was very tired from working that day; and gave his address, and then told me to take a Taxi to his home.

The Taxi driver was a man. It seems there was more than one street which had the same name which made it difficult for the driver to find Val's house. After driving for a while he realized that I did not know where I was going, so he drove into a park and told me that he was tired of driving around with me for nothing, and I needed to pay him. I asked the driver what he meant. He explicitly told me that he needed to get intimate for his time, because he believed I had given him a wrong address; or there will be no one to pay him.

I started crying loudly. Soon other vehicles drove by which seems to have gotten him scared. He then said to me. Never mind, he would find my friend home and take me there. When I got to the house I told the driver to blow his horn. Val came out and paid the Taxi driver, and invited me inside his house, then told me to come and lay down in the bed. I told Val I was dirty and needed a bath, but I had nothing else to wear. He gave me a pair of his jeans shorts, a pair of underwear and tee shirt, and then directed me to the bathroom. I took a shower, went to bed and slept beside him.

It was now daylight, and he had to go to work. We did not talk very much, because he was in charge of the workers for the grove, so he had to be there very early. When I got up no one was home. I became very famished, but I was afraid to eat anything, because I did not know the people who lived there. I hastily made a cup of coffee and had one slice of bread and butter to eat.

I felt bored, so I looked around the house to see if there was anything I could do. The house was not dirty, but could use some straightening up, which I did.

I had no idea when I would be able to get another suit of clothes, so I washed what I had worn with bath soap on my hand and hung them on the line in the backyard to dry.

Being alone all day, I sat on a chair at the back of the house; there I prayed, giving thanks to God for bringing me across the border to America.

It was now evening. Soon I saw a lady enter the house, and not very long Val and two other people came home. I heard Val calling me. To my surprise I was greeted by a group of men who came and congratulated me for coming to America the way I did. After talking with them I got up and went inside. Surprisingly; there was a lady by the name of Millie who I knew from my home. She hugged, and welcomed me, and said to me. "The same way you tidy the house, I hope you got yourself something to eat." I told her that I had eaten and drank a cup of tea. Millie was in the kitchen preparing dinner, she told me to look into the refrigerator and fix whatever I wanted to eat.

Later that evening Val and a friend I knew named Lenny told me that I should come with them to go shopping. They gave me $40.00 each, and took me to the department store. I was surprised to see how low the prices were. While shopping, Val told me it would be cold, because ice was on the trees and ground, so I should buy warm clothes because the next morning he would be taking me to work in the grove to load the orange bins. I bought quite a few outfits and personal items and had money left over. On my way back from the store, Val told me I came at the time when he was alone at home, but it would not be possible for him to accommodate me, because he had a girlfriend who was hospitalized and would be home soon; but told me that both him and my other cousin Lenny had discuss about my coming, so a room had been prepared for me, and the rent was already paid up for two week. Val told me that after that two week ended I would be responsible to work in the grove with them and earn enough to maintain myself. On my way back from shopping I stopped at Val's house and collected the things I had, then went with Lenny to my room. The room was located at the back of the same house where Lenny lived.

The first night I occupied the room Lenny immediately wanted to become intimate with me. I told him that he should give me time to rest my body, because I had been through such hell before I got there, and my body was writhing with pain. He told me that when he gave me that $40.00 to buy clothes to cover my naked behind he did not think about giving me time. Lenny then told me that immigration needs to catch my behind and send me back home. As someone I knew and was friends with, I was so astonished on hearing him say such degrading things to me. I became scared, and wished that I had stayed in Costa Rica.

One day while I was home Lenny told me I should hide myself because his, 'American woman would be coming to see him.' I was surprised because I cared less about his relationship because he was my cousin. The next morning after the lady left I told Lenny that he did not owe me any explanation. From that day our conversation became less than friendly.

The first morning I went to the grove to work I met so many different men; most of them were illegal just like me. I became the center of attraction, because they were all aware of my condition. Val introduced me to the workers and told them that I would be helping them to load the bins. I did not work with everyone, because most of them refused my help.

As the days and weeks went by I did not only load the bins, I had to climb up on a ladder and pick oranges, which was very hard for me to do. As time passed Val and I could not get along because I was not able to work fast enough to suit him. He would curse and tell me that I was acting like I was better than picking oranges. I told Val that I was not pretending, but I had been experiencing excruciating pain all over my body, and especially in the mornings my pain worsened which made it difficult for me to get up. Val told me that I was faking, because white people pick oranges and it doesn't kill them. I told him that colour has nothing to do with pain. The pain got worse, and I started experiencing numbness in my hands and feet, which sometimes lasted for the entire day. Due to that I refused to work, accompanied with the insults I got that brought me to tears.

Lenny started displaying an increased negative attitude towards me. The land-lady, whose name was Miss Daisy, lived in the front section of the house. The kitchen was located close to my room. One day while I was experiencing pain, I lay in my room crying hoping someone would be home to hear my cries. I did not know that Daisy was in the kitchen. I heard a knock on my door, I asked who it was. The voice was that of Daisy. She said to me, "What is wrong with you, and why are you crying"? I told her that I was in pain and unable to get up. Daisy said to me, "Wait a minute, I have another key for your room door, be right back." Daisy came and opened the door and entered. She looked at me and said, "Do you want me to take you to the doctor," I told her I was unable to get up and walk. She assisted me to get dressed.

Daisy took me to a male doctor who was located in Chancy. The doctor questioned me about my pain, he then examined me and told me that I had strained the muscles in my back and abdomen. He gave me an injection and also a prescription. On my way back from the doctor Daisy was very nice to me, she stopped by a pharmacy and bought the medicine.

That evening when Lenny came home from work Daisy told him about my illness. Lenny came to my room and asked me what happened to me, I told him that I had been complaining to both him and Val that I was experiencing pain but you both thought I was kidding. Lenny said he did not believe me.

After I felt better Val and Lenny told me to return to work. I tried working in the grove, but I started experiencing pain again. Because of my illness, neither Lenny or Val and I could get along. They said the pain would go away, but I was scared because my body was not used to doing such an arduous task. Lenny began fussing for trivial things, and said he wanted to help me get on my feet but he refused, because there are other women who are picking oranges for a living, so I have to find a man to take care of me until I get my papers, also give up the room and find another place to live, because he would not be paying anymore rent for me.

At this point I got in touch with one of their friends named Alan and relayed my problem. Alan told me not to worry, because he would accommodate me until I was able to help myself. Few days after I moved my things and went to live at Alan's home.

He showed me the room and told me he lived with his girlfriend but visited to collect rent from the tenants, so I should make myself comfortable. After living at Alan's home for a few days, one night I was awakened by someone moving in the bed beside me. Surprisingly I looked around; it was someone by the name of Paul who was one of Alan's friends. I asked him how he got entrance to my room. He said he had keys to this house, so he came to spend some time with me. That night Paul raped me. I tried to keep quiet, because there were other people who lived in the house and I did not want them to hear because I was ashamed; but he slapped my mouth, and held me down with a pillow.

Paul visits to the house became regular, and always requested intimacy from me. When I refused he would abuse me, by slapping me in my face. One night when the other tenants were absent, he grabbed my hands, dragged me to the room. There he landed me a swift kick to my back, held me down and tied my hands and feet to the bed. I started screaming, but he said it's useless as no one would hear, because everyone was absent, and the music was playing. Paul was very cruel to me that night. He performed his act with a sense of reckless abandonment. When it seems that he got his desire, he pulls the cord and releases me. I was in so much pain, and unable to get up. Paul walked away and left me laying down.

One evening Alan stopped by on his way home from work. I reported to him what Paul had done to me. His reply was, "What he couldn't do his friend did it, and this is America you have to screw hard here to pay your way for room and board." Alan then walked away.

I was home alone so I soaked myself in the bathtub with hot water. I was unable to sleep that night, and several nights following. After that night Paul did not return to the house for a few weeks.

Whenever he visited the house; I tried staying away from him as much as I could. I continue living at Alan's homes, because I had no place to go.

Some days Alan would invite his friends over and asked me to cook for them, when I refused, he ridiculed me in the worst derogatory manners in front of them by saying. "You have no dam papers, so you need to know that just like the other women who came here and had no papers had to pay a price, so you have to screw like a dog for yours, because pretty face don't get it in America."

As time passed Alan told me he would be sending someone to talk with me. The next day one of his friends named Guy visited. Due to the fact that Alan door was always a free entrance to his friends, if I did not open the door and let them in, that would create an animosity between Alan and myself.

When Guy came I opened the door and let him in. Immediately as he entered the house he went directly to the bar which was located between the dining and living room. He poured himself a drink. After Guy sat drinking, I heard him calling me. When I answered, he shouted at me saying, "Come here, I need to talk to you, because I came here definitely to get intimate with you." I reprimanded Guy, by saying to him. "Not because I don't have my papers and no place of my own, I am not trash." Guy did not acquiesce my refusal, he accosted me by the hand and pulled me close to him and slapped me in my face. He then said to me. "We all know you have no papers; I don't think you want me to turn you into the immigration."

I was so shocked on hearing that. He then pushed me to the floor, sat across my chest, took his private and began rolling it on my face, and shouted at me. "If you don't acquiesce my wishes your ass will be back at your home." I prayed for that moment to end. I felt as if he was killing me. After he got up off my body, he slapped me in my face again. Guy then went back to the bar and poured himself another drink, and at the same time cursed me in such derogatory manners. I wanted to get away from the abused. Days after I tried calling the friend I met in California, but because my calls were randomly made I was not successful. I decided that somehow I was going to find someone to help me.

One day I replied to an advertisement in the Chancy newspaper. "Male seeking female companion." I did not know that the man was white as he did not state it in his ad. The day that I contacted him, luckily he was home. He was very polite to me. I told him my name;

his name was Eric. We started communicating on the telephone, and over time we became friends. I told him about some of the problems I was experiencing. Eric became very compassionate to me and offered to help me, but wanted to meet me. He told me that he loved my accent, and would love to visit my home with me. I told him that I was without immigration papers, but when I do receive then it would be my pleasure. He wanted to know how I could get them. I told Eric that I would have to be married to an American citizen. Or be sponsored by someone. Eric said it would be no problem for him marrying me, but he wanted to meet me. We both communicated for approximately six weeks. One day he decided to meet me when my friends were not home.

One day I told Alan that I had a male friend who wanted to meet me. I asked if I could invite him over. Alan said to me, "What type of person is it" I told him that he was a white man. Alan gave me a disparaging look, and then he said to me. "So you have white men now, but you don't want me to be intimate with you. I don't want any damn white man at my house." He got belligerent and began cursing me. Them he shouted.

"Yes! Let the bastard man come, let him come, let him come." After cursing for a while he finally calmed down and asked me when my friend would be coming. I did not tell him the exact time. Eric was very punctual because I had informed him about my situation, so when he came to see me he sat in his car.

While I was talking with Eric, Alan unexpectedly drove his van and parked behind Eric's car. Alan quickly exited from his van and approached Eric. Alan did not introduce himself, but explicitly told Eric to get out of his car because he wanted to talk to him. Eric told Alan that whatever he had to say to him he should say it because he saw no need to get out. Alan got belligerent and started cursing Eric. He said to Eric. "This damn woman is only looking for a man to get her papers." It did not end there. He went on to say. "She is running from immigration and has been hiding in my house." Eric replied. "Maybe some time ago in your life as a foreigner you were also hiding." Alan continued by saying. "This woman is a thief and a piece of trash." Alan degraded me so badly. Eric was embarrassed, and said to me. "It was very nice meeting you, but I am afraid, because your friend is very ignorant, so let us plan to meet another time. Eric said to me. I am going to give you some money to find a place to live. He took his wallet out and gave me three hundred dollars. But before he drove off, he told me I should keep in contact with him and let him know how I was doing.

After Eric drove away, I stood and watched him with uncontrollable tears. I was deeply hurt, and felt that I lost an opportunity which would make my life better. When Eric left I went back to Alan house. Immediately Alan approached me and started shouting, "Is white man you want, not over my dead body." I broke down again into uncontrollable tears. I was so sad and embarrassed. I left the house and sat under an orange tree that was located in the backyard. Alan had two German shepherd dogs which he kept in his back patio because they were bad. Not long after as I sat in the backyard crying, I heard when Alan shouted, "Am going to let the dogs eat your behind." He unleashed the dogs. Immediately the dogs run towards me. My escape was by jumping over the chain link fence and in to a neighbor's yard. That neighbor was not home, so I ran across the street to another neighbor, luckily someone was home and outside.

This neighbor was a lady. When she saw me coming and heard the dogs barking, the lady asked me what was wrong. I told her the problem and how I was treated. The lady then invited me in. She was compassionate to me, and told me not to go back over there. She then called her husband who was in the bedroom watching television. He was a tall and slender dark complexion man. She introduced the both of us, and told me her name was Maggie. Her husband did not talk very much to me, but told his wife that she was the boss. Maggie encouraged me to go and get my things and come and stay with them. She said to me, "You are a good looking person." Maggie told me that she had seen me in the yard several times and wondered what was going on, because it was known to her and others that the house over there was like a brothel. I told Maggie that I was new to the area, and was not aware that such things were being said. After talking with Maggie, I decided to go and get my belongings. I watched to make sure Alan had chained the dogs back before I went.

Alan was still at home. When he saw me come and take my things, he grabbed them from me and told me that if I dare walk out of his house he would call the immigration on me; and then said to me, "Sit your behind down." I was afraid so I decided to relax and make another plan. The money Eric had given to me was kept secured. One day when Alan was gone to work I went and told Maggie what had happened. She was so sad, but encouraged me to try and find somewhere distant from her home, fearing Alan would call the immigration if he realized that I was living close to him. I was so disappointed for not being able to live at Maggie's home. In tears I left and said goodbye.

Maggie saw my tears as I was walking away; she called me back and held me in her arms. Maggie said to me, "Don't cry, God will send someone to help you." She asked me if I had any money, I told her no, because I did not want her to know. Maggie invited me inside and said she did not want her neighbors to know her business. She gave me sixty dollars, and said she did not have very much, but that would buy me something to eat. She gave me her telephone number to keep in touch with her. I told Maggie thanks, and then I left.

Not being familiar to the area I continued living at Alan's home, and worked in the grove for a few days only, because it was such an arduous task for me. I decided that somehow I was going to get away, because I became tired of being abused by different men. I made friends with some of the workers, and relayed my problems to few of them. One day one of the workers named Nathan told me that I could come and stay with him until I got myself together. I became scared, wondering if I would have to experience the same abusive conditions, but I wanted to get away from Alan. I thought about Nathan's offer for a few days before I accepted it.

One morning I left Alan's house with my belongings and went to meet Nathan on the van, and drove with him to the grove. Nathan did not have his own transportation so he rode in the company's vehicle. I helped him work until evening came to go home. I boarded the van accompanied by Nathan with my bags in my hand. All the workers stared at me mockingly. I sat next to Nathan, but he did not give any response to the different gestures.

I went home with Nathan.

Nathan lived in an old wooden rooming house with other men. His room was located close to the kitchen and the bathroom. The kitchen and bathroom was very unsanitary, but I had no choice. Nathan room was not clean, it had a foul smell. After we settled down, Nathan told me he was going to take a bath, and when he was finish he would clean the bathroom for me.

To my surprise, I looked around his room and saw so many roaches. After Nathan return, I went to the bathroom to take my bath. The bathroom was also infested with roaches. The floors were broken, and roaches came from the cracks in the wall in numerous amount. I was terrified at the roaches. I told Nathan about the condition of the bathroom and asked him for some newspaper to lay on the floor, because there was no rug so he gave me some newspaper, but said to me, "You have no place to go, you have no damn papers, and living like a damn blasted fugitive. You should be glad you get a bathroom to wash your stinking behind, because when you came to America you did not have a pot to piss into." I felt so bad, but I took the newspaper from him and laid it on the bathroom floor.

While taking my shower I wondered if I had jump from the 'Pot to the fire.' I got dress I went back to Nathan's room, but he was already in the kitchen cooking. I tried to relax and make myself comfortable and went to the kitchen and offered my help. The kitchen was also infested with roaches of many sizes, and even smelled like roaches. They crawled from the stove and refrigerator and to the counter.

For dinner he made chicken and rice. After cooking he took a plate from the cupboard and told me to get something to eat. I was so skeptical about eating, but I realized I was homeless, so I decided to go along with the situation, and 'shut up.' I took the plate and began washing it in hot water and soap; Nathan got irate and began cursing me. He said to me. "You nasty heifer, what you do, scorn me." I gave no response, but continued washing the plate. I fixed my dinner and sat down in the kitchen to eat. It was very difficult to digest the dinner. After dinner I cleaned up the kitchen and went inside Nathan's; room, he was sleeping. Nathan had a small black and white television, I turned it on. Shortly after he awoke and said to me. "You are too blasted clean and Highty Tighty for me." He had a folding chair in his room; I asked him if I could sit on it. He said, "Yes Miss Highty Tightly." I sat down and watched TV.

It was getting late. Nathan was already in bed sleeping. I wanted to sleep but was afraid to lie down because small roaches were crawling around the room. My sleeping position part of the night was sitting on the chair with my legs stretched to the edge of the bed. Later that night Nathan woke up and saw me sitting on the chair, he asked me why I was not laying in the bed. I told him that a roach was crawling around in the room. He began cursing me in the most derogatory manner. I was so ashamed that I cried uncontrollable. Nathan grabbed my hands and threw me to the wall and said. "What kind of hefting Misses Queen that I have in my damn room. Don't let me blood up your mouth." Being afraid I, 'Shut up.' I went back to sitting in the chair until morning. When he awoke that morning he told me to get my things so he could take me back to the grove and dropped off me so another man could pick me up. When the van came to take him to work, he did not give me the chance to carry my things, he took them to the van. The moment I approached the van the other workers laughed at Nathan, and said, "Sister come stay with me, I won't hurt you at all." Soon as we got to the grove, Nathan took my things and threw them out. This time the workers did not ridicule me, but showed compassion. Nathan then walked away, and collected his sack and ladder and went to work.

I collected my thing, and sat down under an orange tree feeling so melancholy, crying, and not knowing where to go. There was a convenient store which was located not far from the grove, I went and bought something, and went back to the grove. There was also an old shed where the workers would go to take a break, I secretly took my things and hid then inside. The shed had few compartments so no one would know I was there unless an extensive search was made.

I looked around and found old cardboard, old clothes and orange sacks. I quickly took them to my hiding place. The grove was located close to a large lake. After everyone was gone, I waited until it was dark, and took a bath, and then went back to the shed and had something to eat. I also secured food for the next day. I did not want to be seen by anyone, so I ran as fast as I could to get out of sight.

It was night, but I could still see the ripe oranges on the trees. I got some that would last me for the next day.

During the night as I laid to rest, I heard a vehicle coming towards the shed and stopping, but I remained quiet. I heard men's voices which sounded like some of the workers. One of the men was an employee named Lewis. He came inside the shed with a flashlight which he shone around, but he did not see me. I heard when they said, "Let's go she is not here." That night I lay down but it was very hard for me to sleep, because it was dark and scary. It seemed that I might have fallen asleep; because I was awakened by the sound of workers as they were coming off the bus to work the next morning. I was hoping that I would wake up to get away, but I overslept. Being domicile in the shed; and as the days went by I had feelings of suicide. Fear of being recognized, I remain secluded in the shed, and use the bathroom at night in the bushes.

The food supply I had was finished leaving me famished with only oranges. While taking a bath by the lake I saw fishes laying on the sand. I found an old pot sitting in the corner of the shed; I took it to the lake and washed it. I did not have a knife to clean the fish. I took a piece of stick to take the guts out and washed them, and made a fire with dry sticks to cook the fish. I had to be careful eating, because the only light I had was from a lighter. Soon after, I covered the area where I made the fire, so it would not be noticed. After engorging the fish I began experiencing a weakness in my stomach. I made some hot water and squeezed an orange into the water and drank it. Moments after, I regurgitated and felt better. I was now living in the shed for five days.

One day I heard one of the workers' names Harry come inside the shed and call my name. I was afraid to answer, but he insisted that I answer him. To this point I answered Harry. He said to me, "Come here I am not going to hurt you, I know this is where you have been, I want to help you." My replied to Harry was, "Get the hell away from me, let me stay and die, because you being my own country people are so abusive and wicked to me." Harry insisted that he would not hurt me. He told me he knew how I felt, but he wanted to talk to me.

I said to Harry, "don't come close to me, talk from where you are"'" Harry then said to me. 'Don't be foolish', I don't want you to sleep in the shed anymore, because there are lots of snakes that come from the lake. In my ignorance, even though I felt like I was dying, I shouted, "Let the dam snakes kill me." Harry came inside the shed where I was laying, he looked at me and said, "My God you are going to die darling, come home with me, I am not going to hurt you, let me take you to the doctor." Harry told me he had a girlfriend who visits him, but he would tell her about my condition, so I could sleep on his sofa.

After a few minutes, Harry collected my things, and then lifted me from the shed to his car, and drove me to his home. I was so weak Harry lifted me to his apartment, and placed me on his sofa to lie down. While laying down, and being unable to stand, Harry helped me to the bathroom to take a hot bath. The bath tub was not clean, but at that point I did not care, because I had experienced the worst there was, so I was more than thankful that Harry came to my rescue. After taking a bath, he told me that he would boil me some herbs with frankincense and myrrh to drink which should help me feel better, if not he would take me to the doctor. After drinking some of the concoction Harry gave me I regurgitated. Harry then said to me. "That is very good; because gas fills you up while staying in the shed and has nothing to eat." He gave me another cup, which made me feel much better. Harry made beef soup for dinner. While I was eating I heard my stomach growl loudly. Later that evening I experienced excruciating pain in my stomach, but as the evening preceded the pain decreased.

Harry gave me a sheet and pillow and told me that the sofa was a bed, so I could sleep on it. I tried to sleep, but I began experiencing pain in my back and stomach. During the night it became unbearable so I called Harry and told him. Harry took hot water and salt and sapped my body, and anointed me with Bengay, then gave me a cup of hot water with peppermint oil to drink. I went back to bed that night and slept. I was awakened the next morning by Harry; he wanted to talk to me before he went to work. I was feeling much better and was able to get up and walk. He was so glad that I felt better, and told me to make myself at home, and eat whatever I wanted; but I should not answer the telephone, should incase his girlfriend calls. Harry lived in a one bedroom apartment in Chancy.

After Harry left for work I tried to call the friend I met in California, but still after many efforts I was unsuccessful. I started wondering if he had given me the right number. I drank some more of the tea that Harry had given me, and also made breakfast. As the days proceeded I was much more improved. I wanted to take a bath, so I tried cleaning the bathtub. I looked into his kitchen cabinet to see where the salt was. To my surprise he had, several spiritual supplies. I fill the bathtub with hot water to which I add some of those ingredients. I soaked myself in the bathtub until I almost fell asleep. After I got out of the tub, I drank another cup full of tea, and then lay down.

Although Harry told me that I was welcome to partake of whatever he had to eat, and also watch the television, I was still reluctant, and hoping that I don't experience another trauma. Harry came home from work and brought dinner from Kentucky. He told me that he knew I was sick, and even though I was not related to him he refused to treat me like a dog, because he had sisters. I became elated about the compassion he showed to me. He said he would accommodate me until I got on my feet. Harry told me about his girlfriend whose name was Terri, who was an American, and visited him on weekends, but said I should not worry myself, because my presence would not create any problem.

After living there with Harry for a few days, I finally met his girlfriend. She was very cordial to me. A few weeks went by and the friendship between Terri and myself got sour. I discovered that she was a very loquacious person. There are times when she visits I pretend that I was ill to avoid her many questions. Oftentimes she made surprising visits during the days, and at nights, which was no problem to me. Each day that she visited Harry was at work, and I probably would be reading, or resting. I Told Harry about her visits during the days, and the many questions she had been asking me. He accosted her about it, which got her very upset.

One day while I was home cooking I heard a knock on the door, I looked through the window; it was Terri. I opened the door and let her in. She appeared very angry. I asked her what was wrong. Terri said to me. "I came here to beat your behind, because you are going with Harry." Immediately I started crying. She said to me. "You don't talk to me, every time I come here you always leave the apartment or you are always reading some darn book." I told Terri that I have been through a lot which I don't want to talk about. She asked me if I did not have another place to live instead of living at her man's apartment. I told Terri no, but I would take my things and go sleep in the street. I took my things and put them outside. Terri was larger in body than I was. She spared me no mercy, by hitting me with her fist, also kicking, cursing, and pushing me outside. Passersby stood and looked at me, but said nothing. I took my things and put them under a tree that was located in front of the apartment where Harry lived, and then I sat down and waited there until He came home from work.

Coincidentally, that day Harry came home from work early. Terri was still inside the apartment. When he drove up and saw me sitting under the tree, he made a sudden stop and asked me why I was sitting there with my things. I told Harry what Terri had done to me because she felt we were having an affair. Harry got into a vicious rage, and asked me, "Where is she now." I told him she was inside the apartment. Harry said to me. "I know when I am going to die, because while I was at work it's like something kept telling me to go home."

Harry got out of his car immediately and went to his apartment. Shortly after Harry invited me to come inside. Terri was sitting on the sofa. Harry told Terri that she should apologize to me. Terri started crying and said, "You wretched foreigners' are too slick; always keeping everything private, I don't like you all." Harry had a disgruntled look on his face. I told Harry that I am going to find a place to stay, or stay on the street corner, as not to cause any problem between them.

Harry accosted Terri and said to her, "If it was one of your own people it would be alright, but each time I try helping one of my own you run then away." On hearing this I became surprised, knowing that Harry was such a kind person. Terri then apologized to me, but I told her I would not change my mind about leaving, because what she had done, she would probably do it again.

Few days passed so I got in touch with Len who also worked in the grove. I told him what had happened to me, he said I should come and stay with him, because he had two beds in his room, so I can sleep on the other one. He gave me direction to his home, and told me where the key would be. He and I were platonic friends while working in the grove. We had lots of conversations, and shared our lunches. During the time when I had problems with Alan he invited me to come and stay with him, but I was skeptical because his front teeth were all missing. I thought about Len's offer for a few days, and hoping that maybe things would be better for me.

Len was illegal like myself, and lived in a rooming house. Because he was very kind to me I decided to swallow my pride and accept his offer. One evening when Len came home from work; opened his door and saw me, he became so elated. Immediately he lifted me up, and said. "You should have been with me all this time." I replied, "But you are illegal and cannot help me." He told me that we can work something out together. He had to go shopping and took me along with him. I looked at his mouth, but tried to ignore it. Len bought whatever I needed. On returning the other tenants who were from the Island were home in the kitchen preparing dinner. When they saw Len and myself entered the kitchen they began smiling. Len introduced me to then. One of the men's names was Lanny and the other was Neville. Lanny said, "So you are not going to cook with us this evening since you have a wife now." Len's response was, "Nothing changes man, everything remains the same, I just need her to get familiar with everything. Len told me to go ahead and cook since I wanted something different to eat.

After dinner, Len, Lanny, Neville and myself sat in the kitchen and had a long talk. After talking with Lanny, I discovered that we were related by my mother's side of the family. It was getting late, so we said goodnight and went our separate ways. That made me feel more comfortable; and as time passed I would partake of the meals which Lanny prepared. I went with Len to his room, and then took a shower. Returning from the bathroom; to my surprise there was a pink negligee laying on the bed, I asked Len when he bought it, he said when I accepted his invitation. I said to him, "What if I did not come." Len replied. "I did not think you were fooling me." Living with Len made me very happy because he was very kind to me. The only fly in the ointment at that time was because we were both illegal aliens.

As time passed I decided to accompany him to the grove to help him work. Len did not have his own vehicle so he relied on others for transportation. While working with Len I came in contact with, Val, Nathan and Harry. Lanny was also working in the same grove. Only this time no one approached me in any disparaging manner. But as time passed, one day while Len and I were at work Nathan visited the area where we were. He approached Len and myself and began talking to me in derogatory manners. Len was in the tree picking oranges. Immediately Len came down from the tree. He accosted Nathan; they both got into an altercation. Nathan told Len that I was nothing but a courtesan. Len told Nathan that he was very wicked, and abusive to me. Len threatens Nathan. "If you ever return and mess with my Queen I will push my machete in your gut, because you are just a bird like all of us." Nathan walked away and never bothered me again.

Lanny was very kind to me; and because he loved to cook I did not have to unless I wanted to. After a period of time the relationship between Len and I grew stronger, so we decided to find someone to help us with our Immigration papers, which meant getting married to a citizen. Len contacted an American guy named Barry, who was also employed in a grove. Len told me that after talking with Barry, Barry agreed to help me.

Few weeks went by. One day Len told me that he met a lady named Ann and told her about his situation. Len said Ann had a likeness for him and wanted to have an intimate relationship with him; and also would like the both of them to get married, and be a family. I told Len that he should not let me stop him, because I could not help him.

As time passed Len began spending nights and weekends with Ann. I was miffed about it but I was not in a position to help him. I asked Len if Ann knew about his living condition; and with whom he lived with. He said yes; with his cousin together in a rooming house. Even though Len was involved with Ann, he did not deprive me of anything.

One day Len told me that Barry wanted to talk to me. Barry and I had a pleasant conversation. Barry told me that he saw me working in the grove but was afraid to talk to me. After talking for a while, Barry left, but said he would see me the next day. The meeting between Barry and I became regular. On some of his visits he brought me gifts. One day Len was home when Barry visited and brought a bucket of chicken from Kentucky, which included mashed potato with gravy, coleslaw and a large Pepsi's. Len was inside his room watching TV. I told Len that Barry came and brought food, and invited him to join us, but he refused. When Barry left, I went inside to talk to Len. He was very disgruntled; and said to me, "So your man gone now." I gave no response, not wanting to say the wrong thing. During the course of the evening Len fussed with me for the simplest thing. Then he said to me grudgingly, "Don't think that Barry wants you, because he told me that he only wants to get intimate with you." I reminded Len that he had a woman who you sleep with almost every night; and that we made an agreement to get someone to help us. He became angry about what I said. That night Len slept on the floor. I did not hear when he left the next morning for work, but as usual he left money for me in the room on the dresser.

One day I relayed the situation to my cousin Lanny, he was turned off, and said Len was afraid, because he told Barry a lie that I was his cousin, and not his fiancée. Lanny told me that Barry had great likeness for me so I should ignore Len's behavior.

I did not go to the grove to work for a long time, but because Len was having an affair with Ann he was unable to help me financially. I told Barry that I would return to work at the grove, so he invited me to ride with him. In the mornings Barry would make breakfast and bring for the both of us. Somehow the news got to Len ears so he did not visit Ann regularly as before, but remained domicile at home with me.

Len started to quarrel with me almost every night for trivial things. I was getting very unhappy. He had no telephone; the only person who had one was Neville. I still wanted to get in touch with my friend in California; but was never successful.

Neville's room was locked so I was unable to use his phone. My only option was to use a knife to open his door, which I did. When I was in my country I had a pal who lived in Tennessee who I kept communication with. One day I called and talked to her. After realizing that I had access to Neville's telephone, I spoke to her regularly.

The relationship between Len and myself took a downward turn because of the jealousy he displayed. I was still friends with Barry. At a certain point in time I told Barry that I was without immigration papers. Barry said he would marry me because I was a very intelligent and nice looking person, but he needed money to get an apartment for us to live. I did not discuss that with Len. One evening Len was home and Barry visited. Everyone was seated in the kitchen playing dominoes, Barry came and joined us. As we sat and played, Barry said to me, "Honey I am leaving, because I have a class to attend, see you in the morning." That night when Len and I retired, he did not say anything to me. During the night he woke me up and got belligerent in a way I had never seen him before, and demanded intimacy with him immediately. He was totally oblivious to my response, and threw me to the floor where I was being bludgeoned, and ravaged in the most inhumane manner. I began crying, because I felt such terrible pain like he was about to kill me. Lanny's room was located next to Len's. I shouted, "Stop Len, you are killing me." Len said to me. "Yes, I smoked some ganja and came here tonight because you are a piece of crap, that's what you are. And not over my dead body you are getting any papers."

I was in agony, I tried getting away from him. I was naked, but I quickly reached for the door and knocked on Lanny's door. I shouted loudly, "Lanny opened the door; Len is trying to kill me." Luckily he was home. When Lanny opened the door and saw me, he quickly took my hands and pulled me inside his room and locked his door. Seeing my nakedness, he immediately gave me a shirt and brief to put on. I told Lanny what transpired between Len and I; he was very upset about it. I went ahead and slept in my cousin's bed.

It was difficult for me to sleep that night because I was experiencing excruciating pains. My cousin Lanny told me if I continue experiencing pain, he would get me to the doctor. The next morning there was a knock on the door, when Lanny answered, it was Len, and he wanted to talk to Lanny and myself. Lanny told him he would talk to him later that evening. Len then said to me. "The door is not locked."

I was experiencing terrible pain. My cousin gave me money to see the doctor. There was an older man named Mr. Williams who was a taxi driver in the community. After everyone was gone, I got dressed. I went to his home, but he was already gone on a trip. I told his wife that I would like for him to take me to the doctor; she said she would let him know when he returned. When he returned he took me to the doctor. I told the doctor what Len had done to me. After the doctor examined me, he told me that the tissue was torn badly in my private area. He gave me antibiotics and pain medicine, and told me that I should arrest Len. I inform the doctor who was also a foreigner that Len and I were both illegal aliens. The doctor said to me, "Well go home and pray."

When Len came home from work that evening he saw me lying in bed and asked me what was wrong. I told him I was in pain and Lanny gave me money to see the doctor. I showed him the medications the doctor had given to me. Len was ashamed and held his head down. That evening he was very apologetic, but that did not faze me, because I was hurt externally and internally. He asked me how much money Lanny had given me, I told him, so he gave me the money to return to Lanny.

Because of what Len had done to me, the relationship between both him and Lanny took a downward turn. As the days went by I became apprehensive living with Len. I told Lanny that I wanted to leave but I did not have enough money either for a job. And not having a Social Security number to work made things difficult for me. Lanny said to me, "Don't worry yourself, I will find another room so you can come and stay with me, as long as you give me little bit of that thing." I was so astonished, I felt like I wanted to regurgitate. I gave no response, but remained calm.

One day when I was home alone, I opened Neville door and called Muriel in Tennessee, this time I relayed the whole situation to her, Muriel told me to get away. I told her I had no place to go unless I go and sleep with another man. Muriel said to me, "You don't have to go through all of that, you can come and stay with me and my family." Muriel said Lanny, who was my family, was a slack man and I need to get away from them all. I did not have enough money, but I decided somehow to get some. I called the greyhound bus station and inquired about the fare and schedule which I gave to Muriel; and told her when I would be arriving. Although Muriel was generous to me I did not want to be broke when I got to Tennessee.

That evening when Len came home from work, he was very nice and apologetic to me. I told him that I wanted to go shopping the following day for personal items but did not have sufficient funds; so he gave me money. I fabricated another story and asked Lanny for money. I told him I was experiencing the same pains again, and I was out of medication, which was a lie. He said to me, "Don't worry I will help you." He gave me one hundred dollars and said to me, "Go fix up you self, because we are going to have a good time." I smiled and walked away.

The next morning when everyone was gone I called Muriel and told her that I would be leaving and the time of my arrival. Muriel told me that the weather was cold, so I needed a jacket. I did not have any jacket; the only jacket that was available belongs to Len. I took the jacket; and got all my things packed. I called a local taxi and quickly got away fearing someone would accidentally come home and discovered that I was leaving.

I boarded the greyhound bus with all haste to Tennessee.

CHAPTER THIRTY-FOUR

Trip to Tennessee

It was very cold in the morning when I arrived in Tennessee from the greyhound bus. My friend Muriel was very sympathetic about my situation, and invited me to come and stay with her. I had never met her in person, but during the time we corresponded we exchanged pictures. Muriel was unable to meet me at the bus station, but her daughter Sara who Muriel described to me came to get me.

While the bus was approaching the station I started looking to see Sara. At the bus stop I exited and collected my baggage, then began walking around the bus station. Just as I got to the entrance I saw someone standing who fit the description of Sara. I stopped immediately and said to her. "Are you Muriel daughter Sara?" She said yes. I did not have to introduce myself to her because she knew who I was. Sara immediately stretched out her arms and hugged me. I had several baggages, so she helped me to the car.

Sara drove a big long black car. When Sara started the car, I became frightened, because the engine was very loud. I did not say anything to her because I did not exactly understand how to talk with an American accent, I just looked at her and smiled as the car drove off. Muriel was home when I got there. She was very glad to see my arrival. She hugged and kissed me; and took my things from the car. Not very long after Muriel's mother and other members of the family were there to greet me. Muriel could not spend much time because she had to return to work, but before she left she introduced me to her family, and showed me where to put my things, and where

I would be sleeping. Not everyone I met resided there, but they continue to spend the rest of the day.

Muriel's mother's name was Rose; she prepared a big dinner, which includes several American dishes. Because I was not familiar with American cooking I was wondering if I would enjoy the meals. While Rose was cooking I watched her use the kitchen towel to wipe her face and mouth, and at the same time using the same towel to wipe the dishes and utensils. I was turned off by her actions, but I try not to let that bother me. After dinner was ready, Rose said to me, "Come and fix a plate, because you should be hungry coming from so far." I went ahead and fixed myself a big plate. I was very skeptical about eating, because of the different taste in food. But I sat and had a sumptuous meal. Rose lived on another street which was a few blocks away from Muriel's home. After dinner Rose told me she wanted to get acquainted with me; she remained until Muriel came home from work.

It was late when Muriel arrived. When she came in and saw me, she said, "You and Rose are still up." I said, "Yes." After sitting and watching TV for a long time everyone was now ready to retire in bed. The room had two beds. The larger bed was shared by both Kay and her son, the smaller one I slept on.

As the days went, Muriel and I got more acquainted, and became better friends. I did not have very much clothes to wear, because most of the clothes I had in Florida were worn in the grove so they were mostly spotted. One day Muriel decided she would take me to the Outlet to buy clothes. I did not have much money so I became hesitant to go. I told Muriel, she said that would be no problem because she had planned to give me money. I asked Muriel what type of store she was taking me. Muriel said to me, "Girl, this is a second hand store; you can get good things for twenty five cents." I said to her, "Say what." Muriel told me that was where she buys her clothes, because she had no help, and had to be very frugal with her spending. We all went to the outlet. I was so surprised, because I had never gone to a second hand clothing store before. The store was so organized and clean, and the price ranges from twenty to fifty cents. I found clothes that were new, and in very good condition. I bought so many different outfits. The trunk of the car was full. I was now able to go out, and also attend church with Muriel on Sundays.

Muriel had an uncle named Danny. She told me she informed him about me, and probably he and I could work something out pertaining to receiving my immigration papers; because he was very nice, and would take me places, which would allow me to get out and meet other people. I was taken by her suggestion.

One day I was home when Danny visited, Muriel had a garden behind her garage where I was weeding. All of a sudden I heard a male voice calling my name; I looked around to see who it was. It was a tall man who appeared to be in his sixties. I said to him, "Who are you?" He answered and said to me, "Oh, I am Danny, Muriel's uncle, didn't she told you I was coming by to meet you." I said to him, "Yes she did." My hands were dirty, so I told Danny I was going to wash my hands to sit and talk with him, but Danny said to me," You don't have to get all that sophisticated, because I do gardening also." I still insisted that I had to wash my hands, which I did. Danny was standing beside the garden. Muriel had some chairs inside her garage, when I returned from washing my hands, Danny said to me, "Hang on; let me fetch two chairs from the garage." Danny and I sat outside and talked, but we had difficulty understanding each other because of the accent. Danny kept looking at me; I asked him what was wrong and why he kept staring at me. He said to me, "You are a good looking woman, but you talk really funny." I was turned off immediately. I said to him, "I have problems understanding you, because you talk funny also." He did not like when I said that to him, so he became very defensive. We both sat and talked for a long time until it was late that evening. Danny promised that he would return the next evening and take me for a drive so I could get a glimpse of Tennessee.

One evening Danny took me to a local club and introduced me to his friends. And as time passed he took me to the dog track. I always look forward to those moments which were very rewarding to me. Overtime Danny told me that after talking with his friends about me, someone told him about a man from the Island named Johnny Boy, and would like for us to meet.

Few days passed, and Muriel told me about a friend named Hart who lived about six blocks away from her job; and said she told him about me coming from Florida. Soon Muriel introduced us on the telephone. As time went by, Hart wanted to meet me. One day while Muriel was on her way to work she took me to meet him. After several visits we got acquainted. I became bored, because Hart and I had difficulty communicating, so I decided to leave. I walked to Muriel's job and waited until she was finished working.

As time passed Hart and I became platonic friends. He was very kind to me. His many gifts to me were appreciated. Because Muriel and Hart were friends, she told him I did not have proper immigration papers, and hoped my association and friendship with Hart would help me.

To my surprise; one day I receive a letter from him containing money. In the letter he stated that he likes me very much, and wanted to do something nice for me. I was astounded, and words were not adequate to express my thankfulness. Deep within me I did not like him that much. I wanted to call and talk to Hart, but I hesitated on how I should approach him, and what to say, because he was an older man, and I was very reluctant because of my prior experiences. One day I received a telephone call from him asking me why I had not called and told him thanks. I told him that I was preparing myself to call him, but because of my accent made it difficult to communicate with him. Hart said to me, "Yes, you talk funny anyway, but you are a good looking woman, and just learn to talk like an American."

Hart continued to send money without me asking. One day Muriel said to me, "Hart is a good man, because he gives you money, you need to give him a chance." I said to Muriel "I don't like him that much to have an intimate relationship, and first thing, you are the person who is pushing for a relationship, why can't you let me make a decision." Muriel said, "Child don't look at the quality of the man, look at the money and your papers." I did not want to get intimately involved with that older man.

As time went by, Muriel told me that some of her families would be visiting for a weekend so I would have to go and spend that weekend at Hart's home. I told Muriel that Hart and I are only friends. Muriel's response was. "I have been lying to him, telling him how much you say you love him." I hate the fact that I was forced to get involved with Hart. Having no choice, and no other place to stay in Tennessee the only alternative was to comply with Muriel.

I contacted Hart and told him that I would be coming to spend the weekend with him. The next day being Friday, I packed my bag, and Muriel took me to his home on her way to work. Hart's home was not very clean; it had such an obnoxious odor. Also Hart himself was not very clean. I offered to clean his home that Friday evening. It was late when I got finished. Hart asked me if I was able to cook, I told him yes. He showed me where his groceries were kept. I made steak, rice and vegetables for dinner. Hart criticized me by saying, "That's the way people from your country cook steak with all that darn onions." He went ahead and ate dinner anyway. I felt very bad about what he said. This made me resented him more.

After dinner I lay down on his sofa and watched television. Later that night I was awakened by a naked man standing over me. I was so frightened that I shouted loud. To my surprise; it was Hart. I said to him, "Why are you doing this to me." Hart said to me." I need for you to see that I am a man." Having no place to go I ignored him, and said I was not feeling very good so I lay on the sofa, but fell asleep without realizing. I was so terrified, but I tried to remain calm, because I was alone with him at his home.

Morning came; so Hart asked me if I wanted breakfast. I told him that would be nice. He said he had things both in the refrigerator and cupboard. I wanted to make breakfast for him, but it was very difficult for me to cook for this American man, because remembering how he criticized the meal that I had prepared the night before gave me a feeling of apprehension. He requested that I make grits, eggs and toast. I told him that I had never cooked grits before. Hart then addressed me by saying, "How the hell do you think you can live in American because this is what the American people eat here for breakfast." I ignored him and went ahead and made him eggs, toast, coffee, and orange juice.

The morning went by, it was almost noon. I observe Hart playing with his private area. I started getting scared. I wanted to spend the rest of the weekend due to the fact that Muriel relatives were visiting. As I sat on the sofa I heard Hart shouting, "I need lunch now." When I looked around he came and stood before me and said. "I need to go to bed with you now." I said to Hart, "Couldn't you approach me more decently." He said, "Hell no; you are in my house."

Hart suddenly grabbed and forced himself on me. I screamed, but he slapped my face and said. "You need to give me some enjoyment, if not am going to urinate in your face." Because I did not acquiesce to his order; He pointed his private to my face, and urinated all over me. Immediately I grabbed one of his dining chairs and hit him. That caused an uproar which alerted the neighbor.

There was a knock on the door. I opened it quickly; it was a man and a woman who identified themselves as Mr. and Mrs. Foley. They inquired as to what was wrong. I immediately reported the incident. Mrs. Folly said, "Hart had always encounter problems with the women he associates with."

After talking with the neighbor I realize that Hart was not a safe person for me to be around. The neighbor told me to get away because I was a nice looking person. I asked the neighbor if I could finish the weekend with them, and they said yes. I packed my bag and went to the neighbor's home. While at the neighbor's house I called Muriel and told her what had happened. She said that I was lying because she has known Hart a long time and he is a good man. The neighbor overheard the telephone conversation between Muriel and myself and intervened. After the neighbor had spoken to Muriel she was very surprised on hearing about Harts behavior towards me and was apologetic to me. The neighbors were very kind to me.

When the time was fast approaching for me to leave I was very sad, but Mrs. Foley gave me her telephone number, and told me I could always call and talk to her, and regret that her home was so close to where Hart lives, because that prevented me from visiting her. I was so disappointed, because I had just met those people. I felt such positive energy being with them than with Muriel.

Monday morning Mr. Mrs. Foley while on their way to work took me back to Muriel's home. When I got there she was home. Muriel expressed her regrets introducing me to Hart, and that she did not have any idea he was such a bastard. She also said, "I was trying to set you up with Hart because you have no immigration papers; I thought he would be able to help you."

Later that week Danny visited and asked me about my visit with Hart. I told Danny what had happened; and informed him that I still needed help, but was afraid to face another negative situation. Danny was so disappointed, and said to me that he was separated from my wife, and a divorce was not something he had in mind, because he has a vast amount of assets between him and her, if not he would marry me; but said he would try to find someone to help me. The next day Danny returned and told me he was good friends with the owner of the club he visited; and after he relayed my situation the owner decided to hire me part-time. I was excited on hearing that. Danny told me to get dressed and go with him to meet the club owner.

The owner's name was Larry who I had met a few times before when I visited with Danny. Larry explained to me the nature of my job; also wanted to know if I would be willing to work immediately. I told him yes. Danny heard the conversation and told me he would return to take me home after work.

After working there for a few days, one day while in the kitchen I heard Larry telling some of the male customers that I was a nice lady, but I have no American papers; but if he was not married I would not be able to slip away from him. I was surprised, because I had no idea Danny had given all my information to Larry. After hearing Larry's conversation, I began to wonder if he had my best interest. Larry was very kind to me. When Danny was unable to transport me to work he did. One day Larry told me that he was enamored very much with me, and would like the both of us to become intimate; and said he would set me up with a nice man to get my papers. It was during that time I met and befriended Ronnie. Larry still wanted to become intimate with me.

One day while on the job I was accosted by Larry. He told me that I have to become intimate with him for setting me up with Ronnie. I did not acquiesce to his request. A struggle ensued. I said to him, "Aren't customers here, he said no, and furthermore I was planning for you, so I locked the doors." This struggle continue, which ended up with him raping me in the kitchen. I felt like I was victimized, but having no papers also knowing that the owner knew my situation I remained quiet. My plan for revenge was to become a kleptomina. Each day I went to work, because I had access to cash, being a kleptomaniac was my modus-operandi.

I was getting very tired and disgusted, because I was being pressured by Larry. I became very fond of Ronnie. Overtime Ronnie and I became close friends. I did not tell him what had transpired between Larry and myself. Over time after collecting a few hundreds of dollars I quit the job. Larry was not very happy about me leaving, but told me I could always return.

Ronnie and I began spending a lot of time together, but during the relationship I discovered that he was using drugs heavily. He wanted me to join him, but I was afraid, because he took both needles and any drugs that he could have gotten. Whenever Ronnie took drugs, he became very weak and lay in bed for several hours. I started to wonder if I had done the right thing when I got involved with him.

Ronnie and his sister shared a house together. I spent a lot of time with him. One day while I was home alone with his sister, she said to me, "I really don't want my brother marrying you and help you, because I don't think I would like someone from another country as my sister-in law." From that day I saw her as a nemesis, and did not visit Ronnie anymore.

One day while I was home Ronnie visited. He wanted to know why I did not call him. I relayed to him what his sister told me. Ronnie said he never discusses marriage to her, but made it known to her that I had no legal American papers. He told me that he would not turn against his sister, so it's best for him to stay away from me.

Danny was my rock when I am faced with problems, so I got in touch with him and told him what happen. He told me that the man who he was trying to contact, he was expecting result anytime. I became very sad, because having no papers was my greatest barrier. I refused to return to Florida, because the condition there was not better than being in Tennessee.

After a few days, Danny told me that he met Johnny Boy, and after telling him about me; Johnny Boy became very elated and said to him, "If she is a foreigner and have any kind of problems I am the person to help her, and that I would do." Danny made arrangement for Johnny Boy and myself to meet. I waited for that day to come, because I was getting frustrated. He was an elderly man. When he saw me immediately I saw the smile on his face. He did not wait for any introduction, but immediately he said, "Is this the woman you have told me about. My, she is a good looking person, I have to help you baby." Johnny Boy got out from his car and hugged me. He was a very big and strong man. We all went to a restaurant and had dinner. Danny told Johnny Boy that he was welcome to visit me at home. We both exchanged telephone numbers. Overtime, Johnny Boy and I became friends. He told me that he came to America at an early age, but later on in life as he got older, he got married, and made changes in his life. Our platonic friendship was one of a father and daughter relationship. Johnny Boy was now aware of my condition, so he decided to make all the necessary efforts to help me.

The first mission with Johnny Boy was for me to obtain my social security card which I was successful at. He took me to quite a few places to get jobs. I got a part-time job for four hours daily at a small office as a typist. Because my salary was insufficient, he suggested that I need more help; so he signed me up at the local clinic to get medical insurance. Johnny Boy was very kind to me. He knew the place where help was available, and took me to get food and clothes. I took the bus to work, but Johnny Boy would pick me up daily, because the job was close to where he lived.

Johnny Boy encouraged me to save whatever money I could to get an apartment; which I did. The friendship between Johnny Boy and I was something I look forward to daily. His love and compassion to me knew no bounds.

Muriel had a family club and held a meeting every Sunday. I became a part of it. Muriel was the treasurer; I contributed what I could afford. Johnny Boy soon told me about an American lady named Debra who was his friend, and wanted me to meet her. One Sunday afternoon he took me to meet her. As time passed I met Debra's families, I soon became friends with them and visited regularly.

Johnny Boy took me to meet other friends. I was so happy, because everyone Johnny Boy introduced me to were congenial and welcomed me with open arms. Muriel and her mother Rose started resenting me. I could not understand why, because I was very kind to them, but because I was trying to eke things for myself, I was always absent from the home.

The neighbor whose name was Mitch, and lived across the street from Muriel and I became very good friends. On one of my visits Mitch told me that a few days ago while he was washing his car Rose told him that he should not get entangled with me because I was going around looking to find an American man to marry to get my immigration papers. He also told me that Rose had been trying to get information to send me back to my country. Mitch said he asked her why she was so bitter against me. Mitch said she told him that since I came to Tennessee I have been meeting a lot of people and don't spend much time with them. Mitch said he told her, "Maybe she is trying to get herself together." Her response was, "Get what self together, she doesn't fit to be in America, and as a matter of fact I will go to Miles City and get her fixed real good." Mitch told me that Rose doesn't like me and was very jealous, but I should just hang on until something breaks for me.

As the friendship between Debra and myself grew, she informed me about selling cosmetic products for a company. She gave me the information, so I contacted the company and received catalogues from them. The first day I started going to different homes in the neighborhood, the people I met welcomed me, and like the products. As the weeks went by my business became very successful, which made me feel happier with myself.

Rose would fuss with me for trivial reasons, and at times she would ridicule me in derogatory manners. But I totally ignored her because I had no place to go. Not very long after I started experiencing headaches which worsened at night. I told Muriel about it, I also relayed it to Johnny Boy, and what the neighbor told me. I started wondering if Rose might have done something evil to me.

One night I had a dream that there was someone sleeping under my bed. The next morning when I woke up I decided to search my bed. When I undressed the bed I saw that there was a cut into the mattress at the same area where I lay my head to sleep. I pushed my hands inside the area and found a package. I looked to make sure there was no one close to see me. I quickly took the package out, hid it and made up my bed. Everyone was watching TV, so I tried to seize an opportunity to get away from the house to call Johnny Boy. I put the package into a bag and left the house as fast as I could, because I wanted to find a place to go and look through the package. The neighbor was home. I knock on his door and told him I needed to talk to him immediately because I found a package into my mattress. I told Mitch maybe Rose was right when she said she would go to Miles City and fix me, because I have been having terrible headaches every night, with a feeling like I'm going to die. The neighbor opens his door and let me in.

Mitch was very anxious to see what the package contained, but insisted that I go to the backyard to open it. Mitch said to me, "I don't want what that witch does to you come back on me, so take the mess outside." I contacted Johnny Boy while I was at Mitch's house and told him what happen. He told me that he would be coming over to get me. Inside the package contained lots of roots with hair wrapped around, my handwriting and my name along with my picture. Mitch was so shocked when he saw that. He said, Maybe she had been putting root on him for years which caused him all those problems he had. Mitch told me that he went to see a lady once who told him that the problems he had with his marriage stemmed from the neighbor sending bad spells to them, because of jealousy. He said at that time he was very doubtful, but he believes it now.

Not long Johnny Boy came. Not wanting anyone at home to see me leaving the neighbor's house, I got through the back of the neighbor's home and ran down the street. It was then Johnny Boy came and got me.

While driving along with Johnny Boy I showed him what was inside the package, he became irate. Johnny Boy told me that I should tell Muriel about what I discovered, but I was reluctant. That night when I slept at Johnny Boy's home I had no headaches. The next morning being Saturday Johnny Boy took me back to Muriel's house. But before he left he told me that he was going to have a talk with her. I wanted to discourage him, but he insisted. I opened the door and told Muriel Johnny Boy wanted to talk to her. She was surprised, but went anyway. Johnny Boy informed her about the headache I had been having, and also about the package I found stuffed into the mattress which contained personal items belonging to me. Muriel wanted to see the package, which was in the trunk of the car. Johnny Boy showed it to her. I reminded her that her mother had told me she was going to fix me up at Miles City. Muriel believed us, but it was hard for her to believe her mother would have done bad things to me. Johnny Boy and Muriel talked for a long time, then he told us goodbye and left.

Few days after Muriel confronted Rose about what happened. Rose said to her in my present, "This little wretch needs to go back home, because we are very nice to her, and we have no reason being nice to this foreigner when we have other family members who need our help." Muriel said to Rose, "This is my choice to help her, so let me be me." Rose got up and walked away and went home.

I started spending most of my time with Johnny Boy and his friends. After staying away for a few days, I return home. One night while I was home a few members of the family visited. I was in my room laying down and watching TV; everyone was in the living room talking. I did not join them because I was not invited, and I could not understand what they were saying. While in my room, all of a sudden a young man opened the door. I was astonished, and inquired who he was.

The man said; you selfish wretch, I want to beat your behind. I asked him who he was, and what I did to him or anyone in the house, but had problems understanding each other's accents. I am also worrying about my family at home, so I sit by myself and cry. The man attacked me, and began to fight me. Quickly I pushed him away and ran outside. He came after me, and then suddenly everyone who was inside the house came out behind him. He shouted and said to me. This is my aunt's house and if I can't live here you cannot, you need to go back to your poor country. He began hitting me, but no one tried to stop him. I had to defend myself, so I picked up a brick and hit him on his shoulder. All of a sudden some of the family shouted, "Why you hit my cousin, why, you wicked brut. Seems one of the people who accosted me was his wife; she grabbed me and began beating me with her shoes to my head.

I did not know that Mitch was at home, because his car was not parked at the usual place in the front. He came out and shouted, "Not because the woman is a foreigner, don't kill her." Muriel was home when they attacked me and ignored everything, but when she realized that Mitch came to defend me she came out and said to me, "Did you tell him about the package? I said yes." She was shocked. Immediately Muriel told the families to stop cursing and beating me; because Rose was the one who had done me wrong. That did not stop them from cursing me. That night I went to the neighbor's house and slept on his sofa.

As the days went by I became very restless and wanted to leave. I could have stayed at Johnny Boy's home, but I was afraid, even though he was very nice to me, I thought about the many good starts which ended badly.

One day I met a lady named Fay; she and I became friends. I told her about my problems, she offered to help me so one day I planned to visit her at home. It was then I discovered that she was gay. Her doors were open to me. Fay told me that I could stay with her and she would take care of me, but I was put off by the fact that she was gay. I did not insult her offer, but stopped communicating with her regularly.

I did not want to return to Florida, so I made every possible effort to stay in Tennessee. One day while I was selling my products, one of the homes I stopped there was a man working on his car, he placed an order with me, and also said to me, "I love your accent, where are you from?" I told him. He said to me that he went there many years ago. His name was Bill. He gave me his telephone number and told me to call him. I was reluctant, but after a few days I did. He was very glad to hear from me. Over time we made friends. He invited me to go riding with him in a boat on the River. I was excited, but also reluctant, because I had not been to any place like that, before, but I accepted the invitation.

While I was on the trip I met a guy from the Island name Alee. He told me that he was on an assignment from another state but gave me his telephone number and told me to keep in touch with him. I was so excited to meet another person from my country. Alee and I became friends. Because of my association with him I met other people from my country.

Somehow things started to make a positive turn for me, but having to stay at Muriel's home was my only problem, also my income was not sufficient to pay rent for an apartment. I contacted my friend in Florida and asked if I could return. I informed him that I had received my social security card and should be able to get a job. He was very surprised as to how lucky I was, and told me that it would be better for me, because when I return to Florida I would get a job in no time. Val told me that he was friends with someone who would get me hired at a hotel.

I was still trying to avoid returning to Florida. As the days went by, Rose made things unbearable for me. One day she said to me, "As long as you live I am going to make sure you have a hard life." This threat made me want to get away quickly. The friends I made and met were unable to house me. The only door that was open to me was Johnny Boy home, which was a one bedroom apartment. His girlfriend visited him regularly, and I did not want to invade their privacy. Fay was a lesbian who was very nice to me, but that was not my path; so my only choice was to return to Florida.

When I told my friends that I would be returning to Florida, they were all disappointed, and wished they were able to accommodate me.

There was a lady named Lorna, she was very kind to me, but because her sister and her husband were visiting from another country at that time she was unable to assist me; but gave me money, and told me to keep in touch with her and let her know how I was doing.

Connie was among the group of people I met; she was very kind to me. She took me shopping, and told me she did not have enough cash, but was able to treat me using her credit card, and told me to get whatever I wanted. That night I called Alee and told him about my plans, he told me that he would come by to see me and give me some money, because we may never see each other again. Alee came as promised and gave me money.

It was so hard saying goodbye to my friends, but I had no choice. I had to face Muriel and let her know that I was leaving. She was not happy about what had happened. Muriel said to me, "I hope what my mother had done to you did not cause you to go away, because everything just started looking good for you." I broke down into uncontrollable tears. Muriel told me that she was very sorry that I planned to leave, but hope things work out for me. I contacted my cousin Val and told him that I was returning. He encouraged me to come, and told me he would have a vacant room for me, and that in no time I would get a job. I packed my things and boarded the Greyhound bus and went back to Florida.

CHAPTER THIRTY-FIVE

Return from Tennessee

After a horrifying experience in Tennessee I decided that it would be prudent to change my place of residence. The thought of moving back to Chancy Florida had an ominous air about it, but given my present condition I had no option but return to Florida.

Val had previously told me that he would have accommodation for me, and my mind became focus on Val's promise; but somewhat I had a feeling of ambivalence about his promise. When I arrived in Florida and contacted Val, he appeared quite sincere. He took me to the house and showed me the room that I would be occupying, also gave me the key. Before he left, he said to, "Don't worry because you have legal Social Security card that plenty Island people down here have it hard to get." Then he left.

The following day I met the other occupants of the house, everyone were congenial to me. It was not very long after arriving in Florida that Val got an application for me to apply for a job at a hotel. During the time I waited Val took me to apply for a food stamp, which I received immediately. Val gave a shout of exaltation and said, "Boy, you lucky like hell."

As I waited to be hired at the hotel, I went to work in the grove. Val felt good about me, and relayed the new to everyone about how smart I was. This news which Val propagated caused jealousy primarily among some of the Island farm workers. The consternation which some of the workers were secretly harboring because of my progress became very apparent when one of the workers from the Island confronted me with hostility, and said, "How the hell you just came here and get Social Security Card and Food Stamp, when I come here before you." One day while I was at work the same worker who had previously tried to publicly myelin me confronted and said, "You blasted courtesan." Then he slapped me in my face.

In approximately six weeks I was hired as a housekeeper at a hotel in Chancy. My salary was less than $2.00 per hour but I felt better than working in the grove, and also moving away from all the viscous slangs that was directed towards me. Because I lived close to the bus stop, it was easy for me to get to work daily.

The men who lived at the house where I lived were single and illegal; who were always visited by different women. Because of that I met quite a few American ladies who as time passed became my friends. As time passed they invited me to visit with them to an International Club. I refused because I did not have clothes for that occasion. I gave the invitation a good thought, and then I prepared myself to go with them. After several visits I met a man from one of the Islands named Storm; we later became friends.

Some nights Val would visit me, and bring me gifts which include food and money. During his visits he sat in the living room with everyone and watched the television before leaving. On one of Val's visits he told me about a white man who was an apple farmer that he had worked for in the northern state who would be interested in meeting a nice foreign lady. Val told me that I would be the perfect person for him. He promised to get in touch with that man so he and I could communicate. Those visits with Val sometimes lasted until very late at night.

As time passed Storm and I became platonic friends, and occasionally he would visit me. During Storm visits he and the other tenants would sit down and have a few beers, and play dominoes. One day while I was home Val came to visit. Everyone was home. Val accosted me in the present of the tenants, and said he wanted to talk to me immediately. I could not understand why he was behaving in such a manner. He told me that the plan he had to set me up with that white man up north I should forget about it, because he brought me from Tennessee to Florida and gave me a place to live, and also help my behind, and the only man who was allowed to come to the house and see me or go to bed with me should be him alone. I said to Val; but we are supposed to be cousins. He got belligerent and told me to get the hell out of his dam house. I was so ashamed. I wanted to return to Tennessee, but it was not possible so I decided to get in touch with Storm.

Each day I went to work I was in tears. Some of the employees who saw my cries showed compassion to me. There was a white couple by the name of Lily and Brent, who I became friends. During our friendship they became aware of my problems. They lived in a trailer; and told me if I should encounter any difficulties finding a place to live they would accommodate me. One afternoon while I was having my lunch break one of the workers told me that I had a male visitor. I was hoping the visitor was not Val. Surprisingly, it was Storm. I was so glad to see him. After we greeted each other I told him what had transpired. Storm immediately told me that he lived alone and was able to provide accommodation for me in his living room which had a sofa bed I could sleep on. He told me to get my thing ready, and he would come late that night to get me. Storm suggested that he wanted it to remain very secretive about providing accommodation for me at his apartment.

The first few days living with Storm was very pleasant. When he came home from work we would cook, eat and play cards, and exchange stories about events in our country. It was now Friday and I had gotten my first pay. My check that week was $33.00. Storm wanted to know what my salary was, and requested that I gave him half to pay for my accommodation. One day he told me that the only woman he allowed to live in his house and don't have intercourse with was his mother and daughter. As the days went by things became unbearable for me. I did not have enough money to find a place to live, and I refused to get back in touch with Val. Each week that I work, Storm took approximately all of my salary, which was a paltry sum. One night while I was sleeping I felt him lying beside me. He told me that he needed to get intimate with me if not he would put me in the street. A struggle ensued, between the both of us where he ended up raping me. I started screaming which caused him to get upset because the neighbors were alerted. Having no one else, I swallowed my pride; and the next day I made efforts to get in touch with Lanny to find out if he knew of any affordable vacant room. After many efforts to contact Lanny I was successful. I informed him about my problems. Lanny told me that a room was available where he lived, that was renting for $30.00 a week. Although my salary was not that much I was prepared to sacrifice and move away from Storm. Lanny met with the landlord who was from the Island, and told him that he and I were related. The landlord lowered the rent to $25.00 dollars weekly. Lanny and I later met with the landlord, and so I rented the room.

Each day on my way to work I took some of my belongings to the room. One Friday when I got paid I decided that I was not going to give Storm any more money; I told him that I had found a private room to rent, so I would be moving out and requested his help. Storm was not very pleased about it. He told me that the only reason why he would help me was because he did not want me to make any more noise to call the police and probably charged him for sexual abuse. That Friday evening as I drove in his car with him, he told me he was not taking me exactly to the house, but would drop me off a few miles, so I would have to walk the rest of the way. I was very thankful, also disappointed. I told him, thank you. Storm drove off at such a speed causing dust to flash all over me. It was a long walk for me to carry the things in my hands, and on my head. When I got to the house Lanny was there, he asked me how I got there and I relayed the story to him. Lanny said to me, "How the hell a good looking woman like you catching so much hell seems like somebody put a spell on you." He told me that if I was hungry which I was he had left dinner in the kitchen. After eating we both sat down and talked. It was getting late, so we went to our rooms.

I was not earning very much on my job, but on my days off I went with Lanny to work at the grove to supplement my income. It became very strenuous for me. Lanny suggested that I should wash and iron his clothes for him, and he would pay me. I thought of it being a good idea so I took the offer. Lanny paid me a paltry sum of $30 weekly, which was enough to pay my rent. I felt very happy, because I was working and had my own accommodation. I met and got acquainted with quite a few people. Not very long the job became slow and I was laid off. I continue doing the domestic chores for Lanny, and some days I went to work with him in the grove.

I soon became friends with other people which caused me to gain employment at another hotel working as a dishwasher. Not long after working at the hotel my scope of friends increased. Everyone on my job liked me, especially the male workers. Usually when I had no dishes to wash I assisted the workers in the kitchen. Later I was promoted from a dishwasher to a kitchen helper. Soon I became friends with one of the chefs whose name was Louis. He told me that he had a house in which he rented one room to a lady from the Island name Lynette; who was employed at Disney. As time passed Lynette and I became friends. She was very nice to me. I grew to like my job, because I got along with everyone. I met other men from the Island who I also became friends with.

There was an American lady named Lora who I worked with. As time passed I became dependent on her for transportation to work when no one else was available. After I was promoted from a dishwasher to kitchen helper she was not very pleased. Most of the people who worked there were from the Island, but the person who allowed me to get the promotion was a white American man. One day Lora accosted me on my way to work and told me that after that day she would not be taking me to work, because she was not going to be a gal for me and the other employees. I asked her what made her so angry. Lora told me that I was spending time talking with the men in the kitchen because I was looking for food. I was astonished to hear this. I told her that I was surprised she was so jealous, because we both were getting food from the kitchen to eat, and also to take home so it had to be another reason.

To my chagrin; Lora told me that she should be the person who got the promotion, not me. I was shocked. I started crying. When I went to work the next day everyone saw that I had a sad look on my face and inquired what was wrong. I was reluctant to tell anyone, so I decided not to keep it secret.

I told Louis what Lora told me. He could not believe it, and attacked her. Louis told Lora that he was the person who suggested to the other white chefs who was an American to transfer me to the kitchen because of my cleanliness, and was helpful to them. She felt so ashamed. That night when I was finished working, because Louis did not live very far from where I lived, I asked him to take me home. Overtime Lora refused to let me travel with her to work. Louis held jobs at other places; on the days when it was not possible for him to take me to work I had to be absent. Because I had no dependable transportation I had to stop working.

Remembering that Lynette told me that she was employed at Disney; I got in touch with her and told her that I was not working and in need of a job. Lynette told me she knew someone on her job who does hiring, and she told them about me. Lynette contacted that individual. Words came to me in a few days. I was hired to work at Disney.

My finances now took an upward turn. The tips I made sometime gave me more earning than my salary. I was better able to send money to my mother for my children.

Working at the Hotel gave me the opportunity to meet some celebrities, and other important persons.

My search to meet someone to get my papers continued. I met Liz who was also employed at Disney, we both became friends. During our friendship I found out that she was my neighbor. One day while at work she told me she would be having a barbecue and invited me to attend and meet her families. I met her cousin named Gregg who was an American and lived on her street. Over time we all became friends. Gregg and I got better acquainted and later we became platonic friends. I also met his brother who lived in another town. Occasionally on weekends Gregg, myself and his brother would attend local clubs where we met and had fun. Over a period of time I had gotten to like Gregg very much. He was very smart and intelligent which I was fascinated by. We both started dating each other; I fell in love with Gregg and wanted to be with him. As time passed we spent numerous times together. One day he told me that he would like to visit with me in my country. I told him that my documents were not appropriate to travel. Gregg asked me what it would take for me to obtain then. I told him I would have to be married to a United States Citizen. Gregg's response to me was. "I will think about this here."

I did not see or hear from Gregg for approximately three weeks. One day I decided to visit him. I entered his home from the back entrance. When I went there, to my surprise I saw him sitting in the backyard under a tree reading the newspaper. Gregg was very surprised on seeing me. He said to me. "What the hell are you doing here?" I was so terrified of hearing this coming from him. In response I said to him. I have not seen you for a few weeks, and thought that you might have gotten ill. He said to me, "If I am sick is none of your business." I walked away in uncontrollable tears.

Feeling so hurt, and wondering what could have transpired between us causing Gregg to display such a negative attitude towards me. When I went to work the following day, during lunchtime I told Liz that I wanted to talk to her about what had happened between Gregg and myself. She told me she did not want to interfere in my business if not she would have told me that Gregg told her I was a nice person, but he did not want to get hooked up with any illegal alien. She said Gregg willfully used the back entrance of his home, and visited her and her mother at nights just to avoid seeing me. I felt so bad and started crying. Liz told me not to worry because she would talk with him.

Few days after I had spoken with Liz. One evening after I came home from work Lanny told me that someone was at the door delivering flowers to me. I was wondering who that person was. I went to see for myself. It was a young man. I took the flowers. There was an attached envelope. On it was written. "From Gregg, I am sorry babe." I took the flowers and threw it in the trash. Two days after I received a phone call from Gregg. He asked me if I received the flowers. I pretended I knew not what he was talking about, and said to him. "Which flowers?" He asked me if I had not received flowers a few days ago. I told him no. Anyway he told me that he would check into it and come over to see me soon. Each time Gregg asked me about the flowers I told him a lie. I wanted to make him feel just as bad as he made me feel.

One Friday afternoon he came to see me and took me shopping, and gave me money, which he always did.

Over a period of time our relationship grew stronger. One day he asked me if I would like us to get married. I told him whenever he was ready I would be. We both had a loving relationship. I tried to make myself happy, but also had myself in a state of readiness, just in case he pulled another fast one on me. I soon became pregnant. I told Gregg about it. He seems to be very happy. During that time he told me that since we are thinking about getting married and will be starting a family, we need to consider getting a home. I thought it would be a great idea.

I did not have much money, just the job I had at Disney. I told him that I would talk to a man I knew who was a realtor. After contacting the realtor, he told us we would need three thousand dollars to be qualified. I told Gregg about it. He told me not to worry because he would work something out between him, his brother, and myself.

As the weeks went by I became more pregnant and started getting ill which caused me to be unable to function on my job. One day Gregg asked me if I wanted to really have the baby. I told him that it was not my intention to have an abortion. It got to the place where he fussed with me for the simplest things. Because of that his visits became just few of many. I became frustrated. Each time I call Gregg on the telephone he would talk to me in derogatory manners. One day he came to visit me, and said he wanted to have a serious talk with me. I was prepared to have that dialogue with him. Gregg told me I was a nice person, but he had to tell me the truth. He said to me. "I don't want any damn immigrant in my family, so you better off having an abortion."

I became saddened on hearing that news. I told Gregg that I was very sorry for the way he felt about me. I tried holding back my tears, because I did not want to break down before him. He then left.

As the days went by it became more difficult for me.

I was so thankful that I had met Lynette who helped me to get a job. I contacted a few places about having an abortion, and the cost. I made the appointment for the days that I would be off from work.

Mr. Williams who was an elderly man I knew lived on the next two streets from where I lived was a taxi driver. I told him that I would be going to the doctor and needed his service for a few hours. I made arrangement and had the abortion. Few days after I went back to work, and after a few weeks not seeing Gregg, one night I heard a knocking on my room window, I asked who it was, the voice in response was Gregg. I asked him what he wanted. He told me that he wanted to talk with me. I let him in. Gregg asked me if I already had the abortion, I asked him why he became interested. He told me that he really loves me, but wanted a relationship without a child. I said to him, but I am still an illegal alien. He said yes, but I was a good person. I told him to leave, and as he was leaving, I took the glass of water that I had in my room and threw into his face. I told him that I was not a doormat, and will not allow him to wipe his feet on me anymore.

I knew that I would have difficulties sleeping that night. I knocked on Lanny's room door and told him that I would be taking a sleeping pill and asked him to wake me in the morning before he left for work.

I got to the place where I did not want to be involved with anyone. I started a saving account with the intention to return home to my country. But in my mind I was hoping I met someone to help me.

Lanny became my tower of strength again; because of the support he gave me. I continue on my job, and the people I met while at Disney made me happy. As time passed I made other friends and moved on; and faced life with all its fury.

CHAPTER THIRTY-SIX

Vale

During the time I resided in Chancy, I met and became friends with a man from the Island named Eric who introduced me to a couple named Jack and Jill, who lived in Vale. Our meeting was pleasant. They expressed such generosity to me, which endeared me to them.

My friendship with Jack and Jill grew stronger so I confided in them. Overtime I told them I was an illegal alien and I was employed at Disney. Jill told me she was also employed there as a cook, and also was a permanent resident in America, so she didn't have to hide like any 'darn bird' from immigration. I was turned off by what she said to me, but I tried to ignore her. Because of the friendship between Jack, Jill, and myself I asked Jack to introduce me to a nice American man to help me. Jack's response to me was, "As a matter of fact I know someone who would suit you quite well."

Few days passed, I got a telephone call from Jack telling me that he contacted a friend named Bob. Jack told me that after describing my appearance, Bob was very excited to meet me. Jack said to me, "I am going to tell you the honest truth, this man doesn't look that good, but he is a hard worker who will spend his money on you, because he is a fool when it comes to women. You know how we foreigners are skeptical, but we know how to fix men up, and you need to get your papers."

I said to Jack; "What if after meeting this guy we get to like each other what's going to happen? Jack said, "All you need is your damn papers, you don't need to take these blasted, no good American and build them up." Having second thoughts about Jack, I began to wonder if he was responding with jealousy.

Few weeks went by. One day after a telephone conversation with Jill she invited me to come and visit her on one of her days off. During the visit I asked her if she had any information about Bob, she said yes. I sat on her couch and waited. Jill went to her bedroom and shouted to me saying, "Let me tell you this, I am going to give you Bob number, but if the both of you start going together and he begin to spend money on you, don't you act like you are better than I am." I said to her. "Why do you have to think so negative?" Jill did not reply, but had such a disgruntled look on her face. Handing me a piece of paper with the phone number; she said to me. "It is only because I am sorry for you why I even think of giving you Bob's number, because I have families in my country who I want to help come to America." I told her thanks, and that I will always be grateful.

I spend the rest of the day with Jill. I did not appreciate her attitude towards me; but I pretended, for fear she would call the Immigration and get me deported. My only way home was to wait until Jack returned. It was late when he came home. The moment Jack entered the house, Jill greeted him by saying, "I gave her Bob number, so I hope she don't forget us because she get American man." They both took me back home in their truck.

One evening Jack visited me and said Bob was wondering why I haven't phoned him. I told Jack that I was very confused and needed to get my head cleared. Jack said, it's very hard to find a man who will work, and furthermore he wants to meet you. I told Jack that Bob can expect a call from me soon.

One day I phoned Bob, he had a deep southern accent which was difficult for me to understand. He wanted to know why I took so long to contact him. I told him I needed time to make my own decision.

I had a feeling of ambivalence when the time came for me to meet Bob, which caused me to become nervous. Not having his own transportation made it difficult, because he was dependent on Jack or other friends.

When I saw Bob, I was not surprised, because Jack had already described him to me. Bob really needed a makeover. I tried not to be skeptical, because I needed to get myself straightened out. Bob seems to like me the first time he saw me, because he would not take his eyes off me. We had a platonic friendship for a long period of time before we got intimate.

Because I did not work weekends, Bob and I planned to spend some time together. The first weekend we spent together he gave me a few hundred dollars; the next morning which was Saturday Bob got in touch with a friend who had a car, and asked him to take us to Jack and Jill's home. Jill was in the kitchen fixing breakfast. I went and greeted her. Not very long after talking with Jill, I was approached by Jack. He came into the kitchen shouting at me. "Boy, you really messed up, because I set you up with Bob, and he told me he gave you couple hundred dollars." Immediately I got so upset, but kept very calm because of my situation. I said to Jack, "What about the money." Jack told me that he thought I was going to give him some. I got into a rage and ran out from the kitchen and went outside to Bob who was sitting on the porch. I ask Bob why he told Jack that he gave me money. Bob said to me, "That isn't about anything." I said to Bob, "Why you talk so much." I went back inside the house and said to both Jack and Jill. "It seems you set me up with Bob, and if I had known that you were pimping me I would not have you introduce me to anyone. I would have given them some money, but not the way they approached me. I went outside and told Bob that I needed to go back home. I saw a strange look on Bob's face. He asked me what was wrong. I told him that he was too much of a chatterbox. Bob said that he did not mean anything, and if he knew it would have caused a problem he would not have told Jack anything, but Jack insisted to pry in his affair. Bob then called one of his friends to transport us back to the hotel.

Quarrelling with Bob was nonsensical. I continued to spend the rest of the weekend with him, and then went back home. I did not want to continue the friendship between Bob and myself, but because I was an illegal alien I wanted to get my papers so I could help my children, and make a better life for myself.

Due to the altercation between Jack, Jill and myself I wanted to avoid them, but because they knew my situation I swallowed my pride and continued communicating with them.

Bob resided in Vale. He suggested that I move and live with him, but I refused because his apartment was shabby, and infested with roaches exacerbated by his unkempt attitude. It was then Jack and Jill encouraged me to come and live with them. They lived in an old two bedroom board house, which was located close to the road; and told me that I could occupy one of their rooms until I got myself together.

I was still employed with Disney as a housekeeper, and Bob was employed as an orange picker. Disney was a long way for me to go to work. And not having reliable transportation made it difficult. Jill and I worked different shifts, but because Jack was well known in the community he contacted someone named Merle who worked close to the hotel that I was working. She provided me with transportation, so I traveled daily with her to work. I was very fortunate because Merle and I had the same days off.

One Saturday while I was home, Jill was gone to work, I was lying in my bed reading a book, and Jack came and knocked on my room door. I got up to see what he wanted. I opened the door; Jack was already standing at the door, his pants lowered with his private part exposed. Jack said, "I wanted to talk with you a long time, but because I could never catch you by yourself." Jack pushed me back and said. I want you in the room. He pulled my hands and dragged me into the bed, and then said, "Come give some of what you have between your legs." Jack said to me, "I picked you up, got you a man, and now you are doing well, at least you can show some appreciation." I told him that I was not going to be intimate with him. Jack said to me, "If you don't give me some I will call immigration on your behind." I felt like I was going to vomit when he said that to me. I 'shut up' immediately and said to Jack. "I hate you for wanting to do this to me, but if I acquiesce to your desire you are going to keep it between us, he said yes."

As time passed I became uncomfortable living with Jack and Jill, but it was Hobson's choice. Somehow I had to find a way to let Bob know what was happening to me.

One evening I was feeling sad so I visited Bob crying. He asked me what was wrong. I told him that I would love to tell him, but he was such a loquacious person." Bob said to me, "So what happened this time?" I told Bob how I regret moving to the town of Vale, I should have remained where I was; and if I had enough money I would get my own place. Bob continued to ask me what was wrong. I said to him. "Am going to tell you what happened and you better not take it the wrong way, and also promise me you will not let it slip from your flipping mouth." I went ahead and told him how Jack had threatened me, causing me to become intimate with him. Bob got irate about what Jack had done to me and wanted to shoot him, but I told him not to, because they probably would call the immigration on me; so I was going to find another place to live. Bob became dissatisfied and unhappy about me moving away, so he suggested that I move in with him. I was reluctant in accepting Bob's invitation, but he was more like a shield of protection for me with regards to my status.

Bob told me that there was another empty room which was available downstairs of the apartment where he lived, so he would contact the landlord about renting it for me. With Bob's insistence, I Spent a few days with him, and encouraged him to clean his apartment. He was very grateful about my offer, and joined in to help me. In a few days the room was rented.

Because I had such a morbid fear that Jack and Jill would report me to the immigration I was afraid to let them know that I had gotten my own place, so I asked Bob to talk with them.

Bob told me that he was not hiding because Jack and Jill cannot harm me, and if Jack tries to turn me into the immigration he would threaten him. Bob said Jack had been a kleptomania on his job to maintain a lifestyle which involved other female associates; so much so that he was known as the 'village ram.' By revealing his nefarious acts Bob was sure that would cause him so much shame and destitution that he would be forced to return back to his country.

One evening when Bob came home from work he got in touch with one of his friends to collect my things. Jack and Jill were both home. I knock on the door. Jill answered, and opened the door with a disgruntled look on her face. Her response was, "So you never stop until you take over the man. And you must remember that you have no damn papers; and although the man is American, you both are not married yet or file any papers, you can still get deported."

I pretended as if I was not upset with Jill, and talked to her politely.

I told Jack and Jill that I will be always thankful to them, but I just need some time to get myself sorted out.

I did not want Jill to realize that she was the nemesis in my life. I told her that Bob was very jealous, and wanted to get a place for the both of us.

While I was collecting my things, Jack picked up one of my bags, gave it to me. He then whispered in my ears. "You should have let me go to bed with you before you move in with the man. But if you fly high or low, even if I have to rape you again I will, if not I will mess you up in a way where you will never get any papers in America."

I gave no response.

When I got home and settled down. I related to Bob about Jack's threat. This time Bob and I decided to move me away, because he was worried that one day when he came home from work he would receive news that I am caught by the immigrants.

Bob and I now decide to occupy my room which was larger in order to cut down our expenses to fund our traveling.

Bob was very kind to me, but he was an alcoholic. I went to bed smelling like liquor and woke up with the same smell. I did not want to get angry with him because he was very good to me.

I continue to maintain my job at Disney. One day while I was working I was visited by the supervisor. She told me that I should get my personal belongings from the cart and come with her to the office. When I got to the office, she told me that my service was no longer needed, because she has gotten information which proved that I was an illegal alien. I became so astonished. Suddenly I felt such a weakness in my stomach to the place where I was unable to walk to my locker to get my things.

As I said goodbye to my co-workers, I saw the disappointed look on their faces, but they were unable to help me. I was forced to give up a job that I had gotten to love so much. The lady who took me to work was still working. Waiting for her was very long, but I had no choice. It was a hot and sunny day. I stood under a shaded tree and waited. My tears and my perspiration were flowing uncontrollable. I tried not to let Merle recognize that I was upset. When the time was fast approaching for her arrival, I hurriedly went back to the hotel bathroom and washed my face, and put my makeup on. Not long after Merle came. I did not tell her what happened that day, but informed her that I would not be going to work the next day, and I would call her.

That evening when I got home from work I went straight to bed. Bob was not yet home; as usual I always got home before he did.

I was experiencing excruciating pain in my head and shoulders. When Bob came home he was surprised to find me lying in bed and did not prepare dinner. He asked me what was wrong. I told him what happened. Bob got very belligerent; and wanted to vent his fury on both Jack and Jill, but I explained to him again that I was an illegal alien, and feared what they would do to me. Bob said to me, don't worry because his job was seasonal, and soon he will be going on the apple season up north to work, so we will get away from them. Bob's plan was to marry me, and put a big rock on my finger, then take me to meet his folks who lived in Louisiana. I really wanted us to be married for my safety, but he wanted to save enough money to show me off to his families, so he decided to wait until we went up north and were settled, and had a better earning power.

The orange season had now ended, so Bob made plans for us to go to the northern states to pick peaches, apples or whatever fruit were available. I was unable to take all my things, so we disposed of them in the garbage. Even though I had an acrimonious relationship with Jack and Jill, I did not hold a grudge, as I did not have any real families in America with whom I could contact in case I had a problem, so I maintained good communication with them. The day before Bob left; I informed Jill that Bob was planning to go up north to pick fruits. She asked me if I was going, I told her that Bob is contemplating leaving me; so I probably would have to stay until he was able to send for me.

Jill said to me in a sarcastic manner, "That man not taking you with him." By this we had already made plans with the Phone Company to disconnect the service two days after I was gone.

Our bus was scheduled to leave the next evening. I was in such a hurry to get away from Jack and Jill. When the time finally came for me to leave I was so glad. Bob and I boarded the bus to South Carolina.

CHAPTER THIRTY-SEVEN

Travel Up North to Pick Fruits

Because of the many threats I received about deportation by Jack and Jill I decided and went away with Bob.

When Bob and I got to South Carolina we had to find lodging. In our search I got very frustrated because the places that we found were in dilapidated condition.

I began to cry because I did not know that I would be taken into such indigent condition. Bob was accustomed to the condition because he had traveled the areas before.

I became very disgusted about the housing condition and was turned off. Because of my dissatisfaction Bob got very angry with me. I said to Bob, "I am going to find my way to the public highway and ask for help." Bob immediately grabbed me by the hand and dragged me to the ground, he landed a swift kick to my stomach, and said to me yelling. "You blasted people from other countries always acted like you better than other people. I took you here with me to save you from having your so-called country friends who wanted to deport you back home. If I lay in a mess you have to do the same darn thing, if not I will beat your bloody behind." Bob then left me and walked away.

After receiving several blows and slaps in my face I sat on the ground. Soon after I got up and walked further on the road hoping to meet someone to help me.

The place was located in the country. I did not know the name of the town, but I knew we were in South Carolina.

As I continued walking I saw Bob coming to the direction where I was.

He had a disgruntled look on his face. I told him that I wanted to use the toilet.

Bob said to me, "If you want to defecate, go in the darn bush." He then walked away and sat on the side of the bank further down the road.

It was such a lonely road. I did not have any toilet paper but the bag which I had gotten from the store.

I did not care because I was not going to defecate on myself.

I was forced to use an open field, using the paper bag for toilet paper.

I did not know my way around. I was also afraid that Bob would continue abusing me.

It was now evening so I sat by the side of the road. Not very long I saw a brown car driving towards my direction. Immediately I got excited, hoping they might be someone who could help me, or maybe it's the contractor who Bob would be working for.

The closer the car got I realized that there were three black men in the car which included the driver. When the car got to when I sat the driver stopped the car. Bob was sitting some distance from where I was, he got up and came beside me. The driver greeted me. I realized that he was from the Island. Immediately I saw when his eyes 'pop' open. That gave me such a relief knowing I met someone like myself with whom I could communicate with. One of the men was American, but the other two were from the Island. After we introduced ourselves I realized that they were also looking for work on the farms to pick fruits.

I did not let them know what had transpired between Bob and myself because Bob was standing close to me.

The driver of the car's name was White. He said to me, while staring. "Damn it, this was where you stayed; no it could not be, with your nice looking self. Come with us, let's see if there are any better places around here." White took us to Newt North Carolina and found living quarters at a motel and, away from the dilapidated and unsanitary condition where Bob wanted me to live. I felt much more comfortable.

We all became good friends, and found employment on the same farm in South Carolina.

White was our only means of transportation, so he would take us to different farms to work.

We had our meals from the restaurant daily, so I suggested to everyone that it would be better if we had a stove, and being a woman I would cook for everyone, which would cost less.

Everyone was in agreement with my idea and bought a stove. We were better able to save money.

As time passed jealousy arose between Bob and myself because I usually sat and talked with the men.

Even though I explain to Bob that they were our friends, and our only means for transportation, that did not stop the jealousy.

One night Bob got into a jealous rage because he wanted me to go to the bar with him in my dirty clothes, I refused. Bob began cursing me. This time I was not afraid of him as before, because I hadn't met and made friends.

The following day White told me that when he took Bob to the store, and while shopping he saw Bob bought a long knife and a six pack of Old Milwaukee Best Beer. I pretended I didn't know about the knife.

That same evening when Bob returned from the store, I saw a change in his disposition, because he was very quiet while he sat drinking his beer.

I tried talking to him, but he gave no response.

I became very suspicious as to the reason for him buying the knife.

It was now time to go to bed, as my friends were also ready to sleep.

Bob still sat outside drinking his beers.

I started getting nervous. I got up and told my friends that I was scared, because since Bob had returned from the store he has not spoken one word to me.

White told me that the door would be left unlocked just in case they were asleep and Bob tried to attack me.

No sooner as I returned from talking with my friends and went to bed I was attacked by Bob with a long knife. Quickly I escaped and ran to my friend's room.

Luckily they were awake that night.

I became hysterical, because I saw no reason for such behavior.

Not long after Bob came and knocked on the friends door crying.

White went outside and talked to him.

I overheard Bob telling White that the reason why he wanted to kill me he felt that I might leave him for one of you guys.

White told Bob that we are all good friends, and because we are actually from the same country we talk about our experiences. Bob told White that he was sorry, and said that I should come to bed. Being afraid of Bob, I slept on the floor in my friend's room that night.

Bob was always invited to join in our conversation, but he refused by saying, "You are all the same kind of people so you sit and talk with them."

Bob tried to apologize to me many times but, remembering how he treated me before meeting White and his friends; I had to sever the relationship. I had no place to stay but with my friends. My friends all occupied the same room. There were not adequate sleeping quarters for me so I was accommodated by sleeping on the floor.

One day we went shopping, Bob came with us, as he had no other means of transportation. On returning home Bob asked to come and spend the night with him. I told him that I did not trust him. Bob got belligerent and vented his fury on me. He then took a knife from his bag and tried to cut me, other people saw him, also a man who was sitting in his van. When he saw that Bob was about to cut me, he took his pistol out and fired a shot in the air. Bob got scared and started running away. At that moment I came to a decision that he was dangerous for me to be around.

I was now forced to stay with my friends, as going back to Florida was not my intention, also I had no place there to stay, and was afraid of being deported by Jack and Jill.

After the peach crop was over my friends decided to go further north. We stopped at a camp in Virginia to pick apples, but after several days the work ended; so we saw no reason to stay and decided to leave.

White was in control, because he knew most of the areas; he decided that we would travel to Maryland. We began another journey in search of work, and stopped in Hastin.

We found a camp where work was available, picking tomatoes, beans, and cucumber.

The accommodation was limited, so I had to share living quarters with White. The room had a single bed with inadequate space, sometimes I had to share a bed with White, or slept on the floor. This continued for a while.

Working on the farm was very difficult for me. I started getting ill, by experiencing pain in my back, and swelling in my hands and feet.

Mr. Allen was in charge of the camp and the workers. I informed him that I was unable to report to work due to my illness. Mr. Allen told me not to worry because as a migrant worker I was qualified to receive medical help and food stamps. Mr. Allen saw that my condition was grave. That same day he took me to get a medical assistant. I was unable to work for approximately two weeks.

Having no income but food stamps White began to fuss with me daily.

One day he told me that even though we both are from the same country he is not going to tolerate me laying up in the bed while he has to go out and slave himself without getting even a little wife from me.

I did not like White to become intimate with him. I respected him as my brother. I had no place to go, exacerbated with my illness. I was now forced to become intimately involved with him.

After recuperating I return to work. Picking tomatoes was not very easy, I had to be fast.

I was unable to pick fast enough to fill my basket so I stole from the other workers. That had become my modus operandi throughout the entire season.

Work had gotten slow, because the season was almost over. As usual White was the decision maker, so he told us that he would get in touch with the farmer he had worked for in New York.

After several telephone conversations, White told us to get ourselves ready because in a few days we would be on our way to New York to pick apples. I was so excited about going to New York. It didn't matter where; just knowing I would be going to New York was all that matters to me.

It was a long drive, and the car was heavy laden.

White was unable to read, so he was dependent on my help. As we drove along I became tired and fell asleep, so we got lost and found ourselves on route to Canada.

Realizing that we were on the wrong highway we tried to turn around. It was too late, as there was no outlet. White got very angry and started cursing me. He told me that I had no right falling asleep because it was because of him rescuing me why the American man did not kill me.

I became very scared being an illegal alien. While White was driving. I asked him to stop the car and let me out hoping that I would find an escape route as a pedestrian, but he cursed at me and kept driving. As we drove along I saw a car with two men dressed in uniform. The driver immediately looked at us and quickly turned the car around and followed behind us then signaled us to stop.

After stopping, the officers approached us and inquired about our destination. White told the officers that we were going to New York to pick apples but got lost. The officers told us to come along with them. We were now escorted by the immigration to the border.

I became very sad, and began crying. At this point I thought White would have shown me some compassion, but he spoke to me in such a derogatory manner. I wanted to open the car door and escape, but was afraid if I did I would kill myself.

We were now held and questioned by the Immigrations. My friends got scared, except Harry who was an American.

I had no legal documents so I was held in custody.

White and his other friend Stanley had no problems because they were permanent residents. White acted very aggressive and told me that I was responsible for the problems they were having. He said to me.

"I should have let Bob kill your behind in South Carolina, but all I did was pick up your crosses."

Journey on a Bumpy Road

He immediately stretched his hand and slapped me in my face, but one the immigration officer pulled me away.

After the investigation I was taken by an officer to a room where I was held into custody.

Surprisingly; the officer came and showed compassion to me. He said that my friend was very unkind to me, and he would have let me go, but there were other officers involved. He then left.

After waiting a long time to be processed by the immigration I was incarcerated at Manning.

During my incarceration all my belongings were taken from me. The immigration officer who was assigned to me was very kind.

One day when the officer came to visit me I asked him if it would be possible for me to get a book from my bag to read. He said he saw no problems. I got my bible and started searching for different scriptures. I remember reading Psalms, but became fascinated with 119 which I read three times daily accompanied by chanting, Eli, Eli, Lama Sabastini, "My God, My God why are you forsaken me." And praying that the US Immigrations would have compassion on me." The next day I was visited by the officer. He spoke to me with such kind words. I began crying, and told the officer that my fiancée was waiting for me to join him in New York; because we had planned to go to New York to pick apples and earn money to take me back to meet his family and get married. The officer asked me where my fiancée was born. I told him Tennessee. The officer's response was, "Oh, he is an American." The officer told me that he would see what can be done to help me, and would return later that day to see me.

On his return, he brought me a hamburger and coke. He began visiting me, and on each visit he brought me something to eat.

One day the officer asked me if I had any money in the bank to bond myself out to avoid deportation. I asked him how much money I needed. He told me $500.00. I was astonished on hearing this coming from the officer because I was placed in jail to be deported, but my prayers and supplication to God was working for me. I told the officer 'yes,' the money was in the bank in Florida.

He asked me if I had someone to get it for me. I was not sure if Jill would have done that for me. I explain to the officer the relationship between Jill and myself, and the threat I received from her to deport me. The officer told me not to worry, because he would take care of it for me.

I gave the officer the information and he contacted the bank. The money was wired immediately to the bank in Manning.

The following day one of the guards at the jail came and told me to get ready, because I will be released in a short while.

I never understood, and I never questioned anything. While I was in jail my cell door was the only one that remained open. I was allowed to sit out and watch TV. I made friends with other inmates. Before I was released one of the ladies who I communicated with told me about her charges. I wrote a few scriptures and gave it to her to read.

I was released and taken by the immigration officer to the bank, and then to the immigration office at the border where I signed a few documents, and paid for my bond to be released.

I had agreed to go back to Tennessee with my fiancée to get married.

But among everything I knew that my faith was at works for me.

I was released on bond with the date set for my hearing.

I was not worried about that as I know God was working on my behalf.

The officer offered to transport me to the bus station. I told the officer that I would take the bus, because I did not want to be fenced in anymore.

My wishes were granted. The officer showed me the bus that would take me to the Greyhound bus station in Manning.

White had told me they would be going to a Stewart in New York. When I got to the bus station I inquired from the receptionist who was a lady where Stewart was located and if the bus goes there. She told me that I would have to take the bus to Chester and then take a taxi from there to Stewart.

I boarded the greyhound bus to Chester New York. When I got the Chester, I came off the bus and took a taxi.

The driver was a man; he asked me for my destination. I told him that I would like to go to Stewart and find the camp where my friends who are farm workers stayed. I did not know the risk I was taking.

The taxi was metered, and it was a long drive to Stewart.

The taxi driver took me to several places, but I was not successful.

My money was finished, as the cost for my travel took all I had.

While I was driving along with the taxi driver he told me that the owners for the taxi company he worked for were from the Caribbean, and he was also friends with other Caribbean people.

I told the driver to take me back with him to Chester since he was returning and let me sleep on his porch or basement that night, then in the morning I would like for him to take me to his friends. He told me he would.

On my way back the driver stopped at Kentucky and bought a two piece chicken dinner.

After we drove off, he asked me if I was hungry. I told him yes, but I had no money because I paid it all to him.

The driver broke off a piece of chicken and a piece of biscuit and gave it to me. He then said to me. "You bloody Caribbean people, you don't deserve any Kentucky Chicken, because in your country all you eat is filth, you do not use to eat any good food." I was so hurt and embarrassed, but I remained calm.

The driver took me to his home.

But before he invited me in, he told me that I should wait outside because he did not want me to bring any bad luck into his house. I waited outside.

Not long after he came and sprinkle a strong smelling liquid across the doorway, and told me to walk backward three times, and then jump over the threshold, and into the house.

He stood and watched me. After honoring his wishes, he invited me in.

When I got inside his house, he stopped me again and told me to wait a little because he did not want me to come any further until he was sure I was a clean woman. The man directed me to the basement.

As I waited there, he brought me a bottle of Clorox and a pail; and showed me where the water was, and then told me to wash myself with the Clorox, and when I was finished I should let him know.

Smart as I was, I washed myself with the water and soap that was laid beside the faucet, and when I was ready to call him I poured some of the Clorox on the ground where he could smell it when he approached the basement.

When he came, he pushed his head down to the basement. After smelling the Clorox, he said, now he doesn't have to worry, because he's having a clean woman in his house tonight.

That night my sleeping accommodation was on his couch.

As I lay to sleep, I was awaken by him trying to rape, and abused me.

It was hard resisting as I was threatened by him, telling me that if I did not acquiesces his desire he would call the immigration on me; which I regret telling him my situation.

The fear of him calling immigration forced me to obey his wishes.

I cried the entire night.

When morning came I asked him if his promise still stands. He said he was afraid as I may tell those lies on him. I told him I would not do that, because I don't want him to call the immigration on me. I said that to get away from him.

On his way to work he took me to one of the men from the Caribbean named Vince, also an elderly American man named Terry. He told them I had no place to stay so he kept me at his house the night before. Also fabricated a story saying I did not like Americans; and wanted to find other country people.

After the introduction, I immediately told them everything that he did to me.

Vince got in a vicious rage, and pulled out his machete and slapped him.

The man got into his car and drove away quickly.

I explained to Vince and Terry my situation, they told me that they were taxi drivers in the city, and knew where the different camps were located, because they had taken many people from the bus station there on the apple season. After relating my situation to them; Vince and Terry decided that they would both take me to Stewart.

They were successful in finding my friends.

CHAPTER THIRTY-EIGHT

Living at the Camps

It was early one afternoon when I arrived at the camp in Stewart where my friends were; when they saw me come, they were all astonished by my appearance. White was picking apples from a tree that was located close by, shouted and said. "Kiss my granny foot, not in my life I ever heard or seen anyone got caught by the immigrations and was freed having no papers."

I told them that I read my bible and prayed.

Vince and Terry were very happy that I had found the friends. Terry told me he was also part owner for the taxi company; he gave me his phone number including $150.00, and told me to get in touch with both him and Vince if things didn't work out for me. They told me goodbye and left. I stood and watched as they drove away, with tears running down my face.

My friends were all living at the camp. Having no place to go White gave me accommodation to sleep on the floor in his room. As time passed White became very abusive to me.

There was another man named Neville who lived on the other side of the building on the camp; he overheard the many altercations between White and myself. One day Neville told me that he realized I was badly treated by White, accompanied by sleeping on the naked floor. Neville told me that he had an extra bed in his room, and would accommodate me. I accepted Neville's offer.

After living in the camp for a while, I became the cook and domestic worker for everyone. Some days I would pick either cherries or plum.

When that season ended I began picking apples.

It was very difficult for me, because my back, hands, fingers and feet were always in pain. At nights I had to soak myself into hot water with apple cider vinegar, Epsom salt, and alcohol.

Because the majority of the men at the camp were from the Islands most of the meals included dumplings' which was difficult at times for me to make because of the excruciating pains in my hands. I was very unhappy, but I wanted to earn money to help myself.

White and the other friends decided to move from Stewart to another camp in Comfry because the season almost ended.

I continue living with Neville, who later became very abusive to me. Exacerbated by the fact that the season, and his earning had decreased, the abuse worsened. I wanted to run away, but had no place to go.

I contacted White and the other friend, although White was abusive to me, but I had nowhere to go.

White invited me to come and stay there and cook for them and I would be paid. I accepted the offer.

I was feeling much better, because it was a different crowd of people who oftentimes laughed and made fun with me.

White soon met and became involved into a relationship with someone, so it became very difficult for me to share the room with him freely. During the visitation of his female friend I had to sleep in an old wooden chair on the porch outside.

As time passed, there was an American man named Frank who I cooked for, and lived in the same camp. He saw my condition and told me that the room he occupied had two beds, so I should sleep on the other bed. I was very apprehensive, because of my past experiences; but also appreciative for his kind offer to me. As time passed I accepted Frank's offer.

One day when everyone was gone to work I was alone at the camp.

I saw a dark color green van drive into the yard. I did not know what to do. In my mind I thought it was the Immigrations. I was actually having a panic attack.

Planning my escape had me pondering as I did not want to be caught.

Immediately an idea came to me. But while I was thinking I was shaking.

I took the pillows from my bed, and then I went under the spread, laid flat on my stomach. I covered myself and placed the pillows close to me, hoping I would not be recognized. I laid there for a while. Not very long after I heard the van drove away.

I got out of bed and ran down to the farm and reported the matter to my friends who told me it was not the immigration, it was the utility van that came to check the light meter. They all laughed at me. Over time the person who was in charge of the camp took me to receive food stamps because I was a migrant worker. I did not have to spend mine because I was the cook and there was more than enough food for me to eat.

Frank started locking me out of his room. I could not understand why because I was very nice to him.

I spoke to the other workers about it. I was told that he did not like the fact that I always cover myself with a sheet from head to toes, and always sleep through the nights, and never lay in the bed beside him.

Frank started to talk to me in derogatory manners, and told me to leave, as he was not prepared to accommodate me any longer. Having no place to go I ignored him.

Frank began wetting my clothes, and would curse me badly.

That didn't seem to satisfy him; so he eventually threw me out.

I ended up sleeping in the back of one of the workers' vans.

I was offered sleeping accommodation by different men, but I had to pay an ultimate price for it.

I became very tired of sleeping with Tom Dick and Harry to survive, so I decided to do something to end my condition; I got in touch with Vince and Terry in Chester. I explained to Terry what was happening to me. After talking with Terry, he told me not to worry, but give him a few days because he would find a place for me to stay so I can come to Chester and get a job.

I was getting very impatient and frustrated as the weeks went by, not hearing anything from Terry.

Surprisingly; one day I was at the camp, all the workers were home.

That day Terry drove up, he came out of his van and told me boldly to pack my things and come because he found a place for me to live; and I was too good looking for a woman to be going through so much abuse. I got my things and left with Terry.

On my way to Chester with Terry, he told me that if he had met me a few months ago he would have made me his lady, because he was trying to find a nice woman, but whatever he can do for me he would.

He told me that he rented a room from one of his friends for $25.00 per week. Terry gave me $200.00 dollars, and told me to pay my rent for the month, and promised that he and Vince would assist me until I found a job.

CHAPTER THIRTY-NINE

A Change Must Come

It was on a Saturday afternoon when I arrived in Chester New York. Terry introduced me to the landlord who was an American lady named Mae, and her husband Jack who was from the Island. Mae appeared to be cordial.

After our meeting, Mae took me to my room which was located upstairs in the back of the house.

After settling in for the night I saw no need to waste any time. The next day being Sunday I bought a newspaper. In search of a job I found one as a live in babysitter.

My starting salary was $100 weekly.

I was glad because I would be able to pay my rent for another month.

The following week my employer whose name was Dawn decreased my salary to $80 with an excuse that she had to pay her rent.

As the weeks went by my salary continued to decrease. I confronted her about it. She told me that because I eat from her she made a deduction.

I got very irate because when I first started she explained that she would pay me more if she got home late at night, which she always does.

I continued working with Dawn until I found another job.

Because of my association with Terry, Rally was one of the people I met, who was also owner for the taxi company.

I explained my jobless situation to him. Rally told me he knew about a job that was available and would get back to me.

While I was working with Dawn I decided to inquire about Roger who was my son's father. I was told that he lived in New York, not realizing that New York was a large State.

In my search I met someone from my country by the same name.

We began communicating.

During the many conversations I had with that man I oftentimes wonder if he was the person who I was looking for. He told me where he came from, and was also familiar with all the places I knew. His voice sounded similar to that of my son's father, but still I was not certain, because it was so many years since I had seen him. Still I continue to communicate with him. One day unexpectedly I received flowers from him, and then a few days after I received a card containing money. I was still in doubt wondering if I was doing the right thing. After several weeks he decided to meet me, but each time the meeting was planned he cancelled it, which continued for a while. I started having doubts about him so I suggested to him that our meeting would be best later in the evenings.

Having doubts, I told Dawn about meeting him one night, but I wanted to make the arrangement when she was home. She agreed.

One Friday night I invited him over to meet me. I stood beside the window looking to see if that was my son's father, because even though I had not seen him for many years I felt that somehow I would remember him.

When he approached the front porch I realized that he was a total stranger. A feeling of apprehension came over me, I became reluctant to meet him, but because I was not home alone I opened the door and invited him in. He greeted me by saying, "You are a very nice looking person." We sat down and talked for a long time, and then he took me out to eat and brought me back home.

As time passed we continued communicating. I was not very excited to meet him like I did at first, because during one of our conversations he told me that he was not that Roger; but he was trying to meet a lady from his country. I was turned off because of his dishonesty.

Over time, one evening he invited me to his home to have dinner with him which he had already prepared.

I had a strange feeling that he had done something to the dinner.

I told him that I had already eaten. Immediately he got belligerent and started to beat on me.

I was unable to escape the onslaught because he had the doors barred. He then dragged me into a bedroom and continued beating me, then began to tear my clothes off, assaulted, abused me, at the same time shouting at me "You think you are better than me, that's why you don't want me."

I replied, "You should not have lied to me." He continued to slap me in my face, and kicked me. When I tried to scream he slapped me more, and spat in my face.

I was in pain. I wanted to get away. Not long after he left the house and went outside to his car. Immediately I took his telephone and called Terry and told him what had transpired. Terry told me that he would be there to get me.

I had to plan an escape route. Not long after the telephone rang, as soon as he sat down I quickly ran to one of the doors, kicked away the board that he used to bar the door, and ran outside. He came running down the street after me, but when he realized that he was not fast enough to catch me he got very angry. I quickly ran away from the street where his house was located and hid under bushes that were located alongside another street and waited for Terry. Soon Terry came to my rescue. I was beaten and bruised all over in my face and arms. Terry seeing my condition took me to the hospital in Chester, where I received medical treatment.

At the hospital I was asked if I wanted to press charges. I asked the attending nurse if I would have to go to court, she said yes. Knowing I was an illegal alien I told her no.

Terry waited until I was treated then he took me back to Dawn home.

While I was being treated at the Hospital I met another man from the Island name Randy. We spoke, and then exchanged phone numbers. After a period of time we communicated and became platonic friends.

During our many conversations he told me he wanted to meet a nice woman from the Island even if she did not have her permanent residency.

I was moved by what he said, because I was in that position and needed someone to help me; but although I was contemplating on moving away from Dawn home and would have loved to meet someone to help me, I became ambivalent.

We continued as platonic friends for quite some time, but as time passed we got intimate.

Randy suggested that I move in with him because he loves me very much and would like us to get married. I was very excited, but I told him we need more time to get to know each other. He kept insisting that I move in and live with him. I liked Randy very much, but I wanted to make my own decision. I would visit and spend weekends with him, but return to Dawn home.

One day I decided to surprise him, so I moved my things and hid them under his bed.

One evening when he came home, after we both had dinner I told him I had a surprise for him. He asked me what it was. I told him that I hope he will be excited. He kept asking me what it was; I said to him, "What was it you wanted me to do".

Immediately he got belligerent and said to me. "You did not move in."

I said yes, because you wanted me to move in.

He immediately got very mad and told me if I don't leave he would call the immigration on my behind because he had his 'right out' lady.

I was so hurt; I thought I was going to die. I could not believe that he had become so cruel to me.

It was late that night. I called Terry immediately and told him what had happened, and asked him to come quickly, or send a taxi. Terry came just immediately, and in time before the authorities came to Randy's place.

Just as Terry got me and drove to about three blocks we met both Immigration and Police cars approaching. We had no reason to stop.

Terry took me that night to Dawn home.

The following day Dawn asked me why I came back. I told her what had happened to me, but I did not mention to her about my immigrant status. She was very disappointed, and said to me, "Randy looked so calm."

I was very scared that he would probably send the immigration to Dawn home, because he knew where I used to live.

I was deeply hurt and was unable to eat.

Dawn told me that the accommodation would be for a short time because she was planning to move. I told her I would work something out for myself.

Few days after I contacted Rally and told him what had happened to me, I also inquired about the job he was seeking for me. Rally told me that I contacted him just in time because he was planning to see me on Friday of the same week to take me to meet with the employer; which was taking care of an elderly white lady.

Rally took me to meet the lady. The moment I entered through the door and the employer saw me. Without questioning she hired me immediately.

On that job I worked five day as a live-in companion aide, and was off on weekends.

Having no place to stay, and because Dawn was moving I asked Rally if he could help me find a place to stay. He told me yes, because the room his niece once occupied was vacant, so I was more than welcome.

I was very happy with my new job which gave me more earning power.

Rally told me that he would not charge me to live there because that room was used to accommodate foreigners, also his family. I was then able to start saving.

I wanted to get my papers, but having no one to sponsor me I had to get married.

I met another man from the Island named Winston, who was a taxi driver.

We became friends. Overtime I relayed to him about my situation as an illegal alien.

He appeared to be considerate, and told me that I was a nice looking lady who would make any man a good wife.

One day I went to visit him, after spending the day. He told me that he would marry me, but I would have to be a courtesan for him.

I told him no.

He told me that his ex-wife who lived in Connecticut was a prettier person than I was used to do that for him. I told him that was she, but not this woman.

He then took his finger and stuck me very hard in my forehead, leaving a mark which is obvious to this day. I immediately called a taxi and left his house and went back to Rally's house.

I continue to maintain my job. One day Rally suggested that I give him my salary to save weekly since I had no social security number to take out a bank account. He was not privy that I had one. I told him I was capable of keeping my own money.

Because I refused to give him power over my finances he became disgruntled and looked at me disparagingly, and also ridiculed me as the days went by.

Normally he took me to work, and picked me up on my weekends off. But refusing to give him access to my finances that all changed; so I started to take a taxi, or the bus wherever I wanted to go. That did not matter to me.

One day at work I gave my patient laxative, which I usually give her once a week.

Normally she would alert me when she needed the bed pan. I heard her calling me, I thought she wanted me to give her the bed pan. When I got to her, not realizing, immediately she grabbed my hair and dragged me towards her, took her hand and rubbed her feces in my face. When I realized what she had done, I asked her why she had done this to me. She said to me." You little black little wretch".

Immediately I picked the telephone and called one of her sons who lived close by. When he came over he was very upset about what his mom had done to me. He took me to the bathroom and washed me off, then he got his mother all cleaned up. From that day and onward she would curse me for trivial things.

I wanted to work, but I also wanted to leave as I was tired of the abuse I received from her. Each time I reported to the families about the ways she treated me but they all ignored me.

One day two of the families came to visit her. That day gave me the opportunity to pack my things and leave.

News came to me approximately three week after that they had found another lady to take care of her, but she was very unhappy and refused to let that lady touch her or eat from her. Somehow her daughter got in touch with me and relayed the condition about her mother; and that it was urgent that I return; because her mother yearns for my care, because I was a better caregiver.

Shortly after I made arrangements to meet with the families.

During our conversation I realized that the patient had not taken a bath for almost three weeks because she refused having her new caretaker touch her and that the family was not competent to assist her.

What made it worse she wanted no one to touch her but me.

That day in question I went to the patient bedroom; she had such an obnoxious odor.

The moment she saw me, her eyes popped wide open. She immediately apologized to me that she was very sorry, and expressed that she wanted my return. I told her if I return she would have to increase my salary.

Her response was whatever I needed, because I was the only person who understood to take care of her.

After meeting, and discussing with the family they agreed to increase my salary; and wanted me to start working immediately.

They stood and watched me as I took care of their mother.

They were in total shock to see someone small in stature was able to take care of their 300lbs mother so easily.

My employer's behavior soon changed somewhat; because she behaved much better with me than before. I continued going backward and forward from my job to Rally's home where I resided.

As time passed the patient got very ill so she was placed in a nursing home.

I became unemployed, and was domicile at home every day.

Rally started to address me very disrespectfully because I refused to go to bed with him; and would talk to me in derogatory ways.

Oftentimes he told me that he would rather have a different foreign woman in his house anytime, because he doesn't have to beg her to go to bed with him, their clothes would be off quicker and in a blink.

Locking the door to avoid me having entrance was one of the punishments he gave to me.

The president, and main owner for the taxi company whose name was Charles and I became very good friends. He was also one of the persons who I would talk to when I was in deep distress. I informed him about Rally's behavior towards me.

Charles told me that he would deal with that matter because Rally had no right locking me out. We all came to this country with nothing and have stood up to help each other, and furthermore the place doesn't belong to him.

Charles told me that he had provided that place with available room to accommodate foreigners who had no papers; neither a place to live.

The next day Charles reprimanded Rally about his treatment towards me.

I continue residing there. I was unemployed, but my search for a job never stopped.

I met an elderly man named George who was another friend of Terry. He was a homeowner and had rental properties.

On a few occasions I visited with him.

Although Charles spoke to Rally, he still continued to address me in derogatory ways, so I was getting very Leery of his attitude towards me. I told George that I was seeking a vacant room, but at that time his rooms were all occupied. I contacted Dawn, because I did not know many people in Chester.

She invited me to come back and live with her, because she was in need of someone to be a company for her son until I found a place.

Dawn told me that her sister needed a babysitter for a few hours weekly.

I took the job and was paid $50 a week.

I did not complain because I had no place to live. Dawn's sister brought the baby to the home on her way to work.

After babysitting for a few months, Dawn requested for me to pay her $100.00 each month for rent. I was totally astonished, because even though she allowed me to live with her until I found a place; I offered my service to her, by doing the domestic chores at her home. Dawn was a business owner, so I usually go to her place of business and help as a janitor, asking nothing in return.

I refused to pay Dawn rent so she got very belligerent with me, and then told me that I need to find another place because she doesn't want any foreign woman in her house. Also expressed to me that she came from Mississippi; and she would put roots on me. Dawn told me that she knows that foreign people work roots, but it's not as effective as the roots in Mississippi.

She told me to leave and she would find one of her own American to take care of her sister's baby.

It was in the winter and it was snowing terribly. I had no place to go.

I packed my things and took a taxi to George's home. When I got there he was home. I explain to him about my circumstances and what Dawn threatens me to do. He invited me to come in.

George said I was very lucky, because two of his tenants had moved out a few days ago. I asked him the cost for the room per month, he told me $80.

I paid him for the month, and had enough money left to last me until I found another job.

I then started to feel comfortable having my own room.

My main concern was to secure a job. So I searched the employment section of the newspaper.

Serendipitously; I found another live-in job with the Morgan's to take care of their mother. This job gave me a sense of security and brought me much happiness.

I was well loved and appreciated by the Morgan's, and was treated like a family member.

After working with them for some time her daughter Jo wanted me to meet someone to go out and have a good time.

I met a guy named John who lived in Pennsylvania. We had a long distant platonic friendship, but as time passed; he invited me to visit him. John bought the ticket for me to come and see him. There was another lady named Rena who was also employed with the Morgan's on the weekend when I was off.

The day when I was to fly to Pennsylvania Rena was late coming to work. Jo got very aggressive. When Rena arrived, Jo told her boldly that the next time I had to go away and she arrived late, she would be fired.

Mrs. Morgan burst out into a big laughter.

While working with the Morgan's I was offered room and board, but I kept my room that on my days off I would have a place to call home.

After a period of time I met George families, they became fond of me.

As times went by I felt like I was in a family setting.

Overtime; one weekend night when I was sleeping in my room; not being privy to what was happening I did not hear the door open.

I was awakened by George standing over me with an erection.

I was so shocked because I respected him very much, and never expected him to behave in such manner to me. He had always been very calm and nice to me.

I asked him what he was doing in my room.

He told me that he wanted some of the nice body I have locked up inside the room. I told him to get out, but he told me that he knew I had no papers, and if I was smart enough I would not let him call the immigration on me.

I had no place to go, and furthermore I was so comfortable and I was afraid that he would really call the immigration on me.; my only option was to acquiesce his desire.

As time passed I became dissatisfied and did not want to continue living at George home any longer. I knew if I had told my employer what was happening to me they would offer me help, but because they were white I did not want to impose on them.

I got in touch with Mae, the landlord whose home I first lived when I went to Chester. I inquired if she had any more vacant room, which she did. I immediately packed my things and began moving. This was done secretly; fearing George would stop me. I finally moved back to the first house I lived in Chester.

Not long after Mrs. Morgan died so I became unemployed again, but I had enough money to pay my rent for up to six month until I found another job. I went ahead and paid Mae $600.00 for six month. Mae was very thankful, and told me that she was in need of that amount immediately.

Living there was not where I wanted to live, but I made myself comfortable.

Mae was very congenial with me. She would offer me food, and told me if I was in need of anything I should not be afraid to ask her. Her Jack husband was an alcoholic.

Mae would often complain to me about her husband's unfaithfulness.

Because she shared such a secret with me, we developed a friendship.

One night I was gone to bed. I was awakened by a knock on my door. When I responded, to my surprise it was Jack. I asked him what he wanted, he did not reply, but staggered himself into my room and threw himself on my bed in his drunken state.

I told him that I was going downstairs for his wife to come and get him.

He told me that he came personally to go to bed with me, and said it's been a long time since he haven't been with a woman from his country.

I told him to leave, but he got into a rage, and began fighting me.

I ran quickly downstairs and reported him to his wife.

After I told Mae what Jack had done, he told me that I could not live at his house unless he slept with me, because I was not his daughter. That night he and his wife got into a big altercation which involved the police.

I continued to live there until I found another job, which caused me to be away from home. When I was away at work everything was ok.

But when I return on the weekends Jack would curse me very badly.

I remember Terry told me about another man by the name of Rick who came from the Caribbean, and had rental property. I got in touch with him and met him. And as time passed I got more acquainted with him.

One day I asked him if he had any vacant room for rent. Luckily he had.

The cost was $30.00 per week.

I immediately rented the room.

Somehow Jack discovered that I was moving out. He violently accosted me and gave me a swift kick down the stairs.

This caused me terrible pain, because I was bludgeoned, and was in blood.

I was unable to mount back up the stairs to get the rest of my belongings.

The taxi driver who was transporting me to my new residence knew me and was a witness to the incident; he showed compassion and took me to the hospital.

The driver then called Charles and relayed to him what happened to me.

Charles told him to see to it that I was taken care of and that he would be rewarded for his time.

After I was treated at the hospital I was transported back to collect the rest of my things.

Mae came and showed compassion for me, and told me she was sorry for what her Jack had done to me.

She helped to put my things together and took them to the taxi.

I then told her thanks and drove away in the taxi.

I was now settling in my new residence.

After living at my new residence for a few weeks Rick the landlord refused to take rent from me. Each time I gave him rent he would push it back under my door.

I became apprehensive because I did want to experience the same situations as I did before.

On my days off I clean his house, wash his clothes and sometimes offer to cook meals for him.

Rick started displaying generosity to me, and told me that he appreciated all the things I have been doing for him.

One day I was at home, he was upstairs in his bedroom, because all the bedrooms were located upstairs.

I heard him calling me, and said he had something to show me.

I told him that when I am finished with what I was doing I would come to him.

Soon as I went upstairs he told me to sit down on the stairs because he had something to show me. He immediately came from his room with a book in hand. I was wondering what it was.

To my surprise it was a book containing pornographic pictures. I asked him where he was going with it, he told me he wanted the both of us to look through it and tell him what position I love as he was able to perform everything in that book. I told Rick that I was not interested. He was very turned off by my refusal.

Although I was displeased with Rick's approach towards me, I continued living there and did the domestic chores in the home.

As time passed, one Saturday while at home I was attacked by a woman who identifies herself as Rick's lady. She addressed me by saying that it seems as if I came to take over Rick's home. Being surprised; I asked her what she was talking about.

She told me that she had never seen anyone rent a room, also clean the landlord's house, and washes their clothes.

In response I told her that I live there, use the kitchen, and the bathroom, and also sit in the living room, so definitely I found it very difficult looking at dust and dirt. She asked me why I had to wash his clothes.

I told her that he advised me to use both a washing machine and dryer, and that kindness goes both ways because Rick and I are foreigners, so why shouldn't I show appreciation.

The lady continued with her accusation. She finally realized that I was of a different temperament, and was not guilty of her accusations; and then told me she was sorry. She wanted to make friends with me, but I told her no, I was just a tenant there, and that is what I would be until I leave there. And the sooner the better it will be for me. Rick continues to refuse taking rent from me.

I had a friend in Detroit who I had to visit. I told Rick that I would be away for a weekend. He said that I was a grown woman who was free to do what I wanted.

After the weekend has ended I returned home. To my surprise I was unable to open the door and wondered what had happened.

I sat on the front porch for a long time and waited until Rick came home from work, which was very late that evening. I asked why the door was unable to be opened. He told me that he had changed the lock. I asked him why.

Rick told me that he was not aware that I had a man. I said that I didn't know I was supposed to tell him about that. He then opened the door and let me in.

Rick was very angry; and displaced a bellicose attitude with me, which I could not understand why.

I asked him for another key because I had to go to work, and usually return home before he does. He became very disgruntled, but he gave it to me.

As the days and weeks went by, Rick's attitude changed towards me.

He would fuss with me for trivial things, and address me in many derogatory ways.

Soon I began getting scared, so I decided to move away.

I contacted Jo and told her my problems; she was very saddened about how I was treated by everyone because I was illegal; and told me that her daughter Ann had an apartment but is hardly there because she spent most of the time with her fiancée. Jo also told me that Ann wanted to rent half of the apartment. Jo encouraged me not to worry because both she and Ann would work something out for me. Jo gave me Ann telephone number to keep in touch with her. I was so happy, because I would be moving some distance away from the people I knew.

Because Ann's apartment was not ready I contacted another friend and found a room that was located a little distant from where Rick lived.

As the days went by I started packing my things.

One late evening after I returned from work I started taking my things outside so when the taxi came I would be ready. Rick realized that I was moving.

He got into a vicious rage and asked me where I was going, I told him that I was leaving because of his behavior, and also the derogatory ways he addresses me.

He told me that if he doesn't want me to leave I could not.

I told Rick that I was not his lady, and he has no legal right to keep me.

Rick threatens to call the police and immigration on me. I told him to go ahead.

Luckily I had already called for the taxi which was expected anytime.

While I was waiting for the taxi the police arrived.

Rick told the police that I was moving out with his rent. I informed the police that when I first moved in and rented the room from him I paid him, but after the first few weeks ended and I offered him rent he refused it. I told the police about his actions and behavior towards me; and that it seems he wanted me for his lady, but I did not have that in my mind, as he was an older man who could be my father.

The police told Rick that he has no right to stop me from moving and should let me have all my belongings.

Rick immediately told the police that I was hiding from the immigration as I had no papers. The police response was they were out doing police business not immigration work. One of the police officers said to me, "Hurry up and leave, your friend is very wicked."

Immediately I heard the taxi blowing the horn for me.

Before I left I heard Rick use the phone as he called another set of police and told them to bring the immigration as he was holding an illegal fugitive.

Just as I was finishing putting my things in the taxi and we drove off, I escaped being held by officers.

The taxi driver knew me; and was very compassionate.

When I got to my new place, he helped move my things in my room.

I had a sleepless night because I was deeply hurt.

As time passes by and I continue to live at this new place.

My employer and patient Mrs. Morgan became ill and was admitted to the hospital. Due to that I spent more time at my new place.

A few days after; I got words from Mrs. Morgan's daughter, Jo that her mother had passed away. I had to spend the night there as my week had not ended. That night while I was sleeping; in my dream I was attacked by a man spirit who was dressed in a black cape.

He held me down in the bed and was reaching for a whip to beat me. He kept holding me down, I was unable to get away.

I kept struggling in my dream, until I was awakened.

When I woke up my room was very hot like the furnace was turned up. I went downstairs to Mrs. Morgan's room, it was also very hot.

There was no cool place in the entire house. It was 2am that morning.

I called Jo and told her what happened to me.

She told me she was sorry, and as a matter of fact I should not have slept there that night; and also said she did not think her father spirit would be there. Jo told me to call a taxi and go home, and don't spend the rest of the night there.

I got some of my things and left, because I knew I would be able to get them another day when Jo was there.

After Mrs. Morgan's funeral Joe invited me over to her home.

She gave me money and gifts which surprised me.

I also got the rest of my things.

It was very sad for me to part with the Morgan's because they were treated like family. We cried for a while then we all parted. I was now again without a job.

Jo told me that my reference from her would be no problem. Jo and her family and I continued as friends during my tenure in Chester.

The following week I placed an ad in the newspaper. Soon I found another live-in job taking care of an elderly lady.

That job paid me more money than I was paid from Mrs. Morgan, but that did not change the fact that the Morgan's were my friends.

My room was located close to the main road. One day I looked out my window and had a clear view of Rick walking down the street and was looking directly at my room.

I was wondering if he had inquired and found out where I lived.

I decided to find somewhere and move away very quickly, because I was afraid of his threat.

I got back in touch with Jo that same day and told her what Rick had done to me and I was afraid that he would call the immigration on me. Jo told me that I was too nice a person to be hurt by others, because her mother would not like that to happen to me.

In no time Jo called me back on the telephone and told me that Ann agreed for me to occupy the house, and that she would leave the keys in the mail box with instructions; so I could start moving immediately.

I was so glad. I told Jo thanks.

I got some clothes immediately, took a taxi and went to Jo daughter's house. It was a one bedroom, living room, kitchen, bathroom, and a patio with access to the basement. It was fully furnished; all I needed was my clothes and food. I felt so good about where I was welcome to live, because it was located in the suburb of Dowey.

I spent the night there and went to work the following day, and for the rest of that week.

When I came home from work for that weekend I told my landlord that I had found another place and was moving. I was now living a long distance from where Rick lived.

Living at Dowey was very exciting for me.

I had fun on my weekends off by going to garage and yard sales. I was not worried about meeting Rick, because I was not in touch with anyone he knew. My life was more private, and my means of transportation was by taking a taxi, or buses.

This new job gave me more independence. I was making more money, and was now able to have a saving account. I had my own telephone, and went shopping just like other people did. I felt such peace and happiness.

My friendship with Charles continues, and because he was affiliated with one of the Caribbean clubs, I would attend on weekends when I was off at no cost. Most times I was treated as one of their guests.

I met and became platonic friends with quite a few people. I was earning money which gave me some independence, and I did not want to get involved with anyone who probably would abuse me again and interfere with my happiness, so I did not push any effort.

I maintain the friendship I had with Charles, and the few people I felt comfortable with having no families here in America.

I continue communicating with Jack and Jill in Florida, even though they were so unkind to me. Jill would oftentimes call and ask me for money which I usually send to her. But each time I sent money to her she wanted more; which forced me to fabricate stories to my employer about having a major crisis in my family.

This was done constantly. Jill often called and told me that the immigration were looking for me. I did not understand that as long as my address or location was not known I would not be affected. I thought I was paying her to shut her mouth from turning me over to the immigration.

My new employer Mrs. Hays and I got along very well.

Many late afternoons she would invite me to come to her room and watch TV. Sometimes she told me stories about her younger days. Some nights she asked me to massage her body with lotion on a regular basis.

As time passed Mrs. Hays became generous to me. She did not only increase my salary, but gave me money and time off to go shopping.

One day she told me that I was a good looking young lady; but she did not like the clothes I was wearing, and especially whenever I came to her bedroom room at night.

One night as I was massaging her body, she dragged my hand onto her private part, shouting, "Rub me very hard".

I became frightened. She held my hand down, forcing me to masturbate her.

I was very surprised at her because she was in her late 80's.

I return to my bedroom with an indescribable feeling.

On awakening the next morning I was so frustrated; I made breakfast, but I felt very ashamed to face her. She got up early, which she never usually did and came to the kitchen. She greeted me with a big smile and gave me a hug. I had the worst shock in my life.

She then told me I should not worry about making dinner because she would order what we wanted.

I started to refuse visiting her at nights, and whenever I visited I explained to her the areas of her body I would be massaging.

Her generosity continued; and always told me the massages made her feel good.

I kept working with her, because I was afraid I would not find another good paying job because of my situation.

As time passed Mrs. Hays requested my social security number. I became afraid, because I did not understand that giving her my social security number would not affect my immigration status.

Being fearful I decided that somehow I would have to get away.

I contacted Jill in Florida and told about what Mrs. Hays requested from me, but Jill told me she had no idea about things like that.

I started getting scared that maybe this would cause the immigration to locate and deport me.

At nights when Mrs. Hays called me, and I did not answer, she came to my room and ordered me to accompany her back to her room.

I became disgusted and wanted to find an escape route from her, but did not want to leave her alone.

One day I got into an argument with her and told her that I would leave.

She realized that I was very upset, and told me that she was only joking, and said all she wanted was for me to come and massage her body at night.

I told her that massaging her body was ok, but she always drag my hand to her private parts, and I was not a lesbian and I don't intended to be one.

She told me that she was a millionaire and could help to become whatever I wanted in life. I told her it does not matter how rich she is, that was not my path.

I was so sick and tired of Mrs. Hays, so at nights I would call a taxi and leave.

Somehow she discovered that I was absent at nights and started getting very angry with me. One day she told me boldly, "I am in love with you." I felt like I was going to vomit. At this point I decided that I definitely had to leave, as I was not going to submit and acquiesces her desires.

I got in touch with Mae and told her that I was planning to leave the job, and asked her if she was able to work, her response was yes.

Mrs. Hays got very angry and decided to replace me. She placed an advertisement in the newspaper. Immediately I told Mae about the ads, and she responded to it.

While Mrs. Hays was interviewing Mae she asked me to come and sit with her. After the interview was finished, she told Mae to wait in the kitchen.

Mrs. Hays wanted my opinion about Mae. I pretended that I did not know Mae. I told Mrs. Hays that Mae was very mature and seems to be a wonderful person who would be the perfect person to take care of her. Mrs. Hays invited Mae back inside and told her that she was hired.

I was now ready to quit this job and get away.

I told Mrs. Hays that I was returning to Florida because I was very lonely living in Chester.

Mae was now prepared to take my job. This was what Mae wanted, because of her husband's treatment towards her; and she wanted to get away from home.

My plans became final so I told Mrs. Hays goodbye.

It was very sad; I saw tears fall from my employer's eyes.

I now became domicile at home with a feeling of relief.

Luckily I had money saved so I was able to take care of my bill for a few months until I found another job.

I contacted Charles and my other friends and started visiting the club again.

After being home for a period of time, I decided to go job hunting, hoping to find another job that would pay cash and not use my right name.

I found another job to take care of an elderly lady. My earning power was not that strong, also I was not able to save any money, but I was happy to be working.

Approximately four month after my employer died which was so unfortunate for me.

I placed another ad in the newspaper and found a job, working for three days per week. That job paid less than the one I had before; but I tried to maintain myself.

My employer named Moe; she was very nice to me.

She would offer me dinner to take home, and sometimes made an extra pot so I would have food for another day.

As time went by the job turned out to be beneficial to me.

Moe and her husband James were sometimes absent from home once a month. During that time she had to hire someone through an agency to take care of her mother which was costing her an enormous amount of money, as she stated. One day she asked me if I would be able to take care of her mother when they were away and she would increase my earnings. I told her yes. I was so happy, and always looked forward to their absence.

As time passed Ann wanted me to take over the entire house that she rented. I was forced to pay a bigger rent so I decided to rent the bedroom upstairs and occupy the living room hoping that would give me extra money for rent, and other bills; and also thought that the renter would be an American Citizen who would probably help me to get my permanent residency.

In no time I found a renter.

My tenant name was Leo, we later became friends.

Usually when he came from work in the evenings I was making dinner.

Leo always likes the smell of my cooking and oftentimes asked me for some. Because I prepared my meals somewhat differently I was hesitant to offer him.

I kept having excuses, until one evening I gave him some. It seems that all I did was to put butter at the cat's mouth. Leo requested that I make dinner for him in the evenings and he would supply whatever I needed, and also pay me. I thought about it especially knowing I would be rewarded.

I took the offer which intensified our friendship. We then became friends so I told him quite a few things about me.

Over a period of time we became intimate, during which I became pregnant.

Leo was not happy about my pregnancy. That reminded me about the experience I had when I lived in Florida and became pregnant; and was forced to have an abortion. It was during that time my friend had just come to visit me.

When she came to me she was pregnant. I was very mad about her state of pregnancy, owing to the fact that we both had been through so much difficulties. I told her boldly that she should not allow another baby to interfere with her life, because for many years she wanted to come here. I had no immigration papers, but that was not my concern, I was her friend.

I gave her money and she had an abortion.

Overtime Leo and I started having an acrimonious relationship; I could not understand what had transpired to cause the problems.

One day in question I accosted him about the problems we had. He told me that one day when I was at work he became intimate with my friend, and that quite a few times when he called home from work and spoke to her, during the conversation between them she told him that I was no good, because I was only using him to get my papers. I could not believe that she was so deceptive to me.

I did not fuss with her, because I love her as my friend. I tried to ignore what Leo had told me, and also I tried to avoid any confrontation between us because I was afraid that if that happened either of them would call the immigration on me.

One day when I came home from work Leo moved out.

I felt very bad because I was pregnant, and had no one to help me.

I made several telephone calls to Leo's job, and left messages but he refused to communicate with me. As time passed, one day I got in touch with him. He told me that after talking with my friend he realized that he did not want me.

I continue to let her live with me, because I really like her.

I told my employee what Leo had done to me, she was very compassionate.

She encourages me to have an abortion and go on with my life.

I made arrangements to take a week off and have my friend work in my stead.

Leo told me that he would not return, so in a few weeks I had an abortion. I encouraged my friend to apply for food stamps and welfare, because I was not in a position to take care of her until she found a job.

I introduced her to the friends I knew and met.

One day I contacted Randy who had called the police on me after inviting me to live with him, not realizing it was a foolish idea, and took my friend and myself to visit him. After spending some time at his apartment I started reminiscing about the night of the incident when Randy called the police and immigration on me. I felt like it was happening all over again to me.

I could not stay there any longer; I quickly removed myself from his apartment leaving him and my friend.

It was a long walk to the main road as he lived in the suburbs, but I continued walking until I got a taxi and went home.

After remembering what Randy did to me, and what Leo told me about my friend, I felt very uncomfortable, and betrayed, so I told her to leave.

As the days went by I became confused, and frustrated, and was sorry that I let her leave, but that was too late. I blamed myself for introducing her to Randy, but I wanted her to meet other people, and someone to help her. When she left I broke down into uncontrollable crying and experienced terrible nightmares.

One day I visited Mae and told her my problems. Mae was very understanding, and encouraged me.

My friend was now gone, so I was back to living alone.

My employer Moe and her husband James had to go away, so they wanted me to work extra days and nights.

I was very happy, because it increased my earnings.

I began to pack barrels to send for my family. And also send money.

The house that my mother lived in was unfinished. Overtime, as my mother and I communicated I asked her how much money would be needed for the completion of the house that had started between her and my brother Roy.

In a reply from her, she refused my offer; and said she did not want me to return and own anything there. I felt such rejection coming from my mother as I usually did.

My search to meet someone to get my papers never ceased.

I had a friend named Tony who was one of the taxi drivers for my friend Charles. I asked him to introduce me to someone who would help me. Tony told me he would have to be careful because I was a nice person, but said he was involved into a relationship if not I would have no problem.

Tony told me that his brother's name Ray was single, and that he would introduce him to me, and hope things work out between the both of us, and also help me to get my papers.

A few days went by and I met Ray. Overtime we communicated by telephone and became friends. After a long friendship we became intimate.

Ray was employed at a hospital in Chester. Every week before he got pay he promised to assist me financially, but when the weekend came I never saw him.

One Monday evening while I was home he visited me. It was getting late and I wanted to go to bed. I asked Ray what time he would be leaving, he told me that he would be spending the night. Ray had no clothes to change into, so I asked him what he will wear. Ray told me he had clothes in the basement. I could not understand what he meant. I asked him how he got entrance to my house, because I did not give him a key. Ray told me that one day when he came to visit me found my door open so he went back home and brought extra clothes, which he hid in the basement. I was astonished, and got very angry, but I tried to remain calm.

As time passed, one day I felt ill and told my employer that I had to leave earlier. That day to my surprise, when I went home I heard music in my house, I could not understand, because I was positive that I left no music on.

The closer I got to the house the louder the music sounded.

As I opened the door and approached the stairs I also heard voices. I started wondering what the devil was going on. I slowly open the door.

To my surprise when I opened the door and went in, the voices were coming from my bedroom. The bedroom was upstairs, and the living room and kitchen was located on the lower level. When I went into the kitchen I saw food that was already prepared. I got very scared, but bravely I approached the stairs to my bedroom.

To my chagrin, I saw Ray and another woman in my bed. I was totally astonished, because I did not give him any keys for entrance.

I quickly went downstairs and got water from the refrigerator, ran back upstairs and threw the water on the both of them.

They became frightened and got into a rage with me. Ray presumptuously asked me what I was doing there, and who gave me keys to come in, I became belligerent, and hit him with a chair.

I asked him how the hell he got keys to enter my place, he gave no response. The woman started quarreling with me and wanted to know who I was and why I came there. I told her to get dressed, get out of my bed, and let us have a talk. Ray quickly took his clothes and ran.

After she got dressed I sat down and talked to her. She told me that Ray told her he rented a house from a lady who lived in Massachusetts, but came by very seldom to collect her rent.

I asked her how long she had been coming here, she told me three times weekly. The woman told me that Ray took her to my place and made her believe it belonged to him, and that she was his only lady.

I inform her that I was the lady he is talking about, and I live here. I threaten to call the police, because I did not give Ray keys to my house. I told her I was his lady, but I work almost every day, only this day I felt ill why I came home.

I was going to call the police, but I called his brother Tony who was my good friend.

Luckily Tony was working close to my area that day.

When Tony came I told him what Ray did by presenting the evidence. Tony was very berserk. Ray was sitting on the back patio. Tony asked Ray how he got keys to my house. Ray told Tony that one of my days off I asked him to go to the store. That day I gave him the keys because I was busy cooking.

Ray said he took a taxi and quickly went downtown and had another set of keys made. Tony became miffed and cursed his brother Ray, and said to him that each time he tries to introduce him to a nice person he always embarrasses him.

Tony took the keys and returned them to me. I told Ray to leave.

I was very hurt and upset about what Ray had done.

That same night the phone rang and it was Ray telling me he was sorry. He continued to call me every night but I refused to converse with him.

One night I was awake when he came knocking on my door.

Because it was late, and I did not want to alarm my neighbors, I let him in. Few minutes after Ray came in he started to quarrel with me. I asked him what the problem was. Ray told me that I messed up his plan, because the girl was going to set him up to get money. I told Ray that was not my concern, and I don't want him to rob any money and remain at my place.

Ray took his leather belt and bludgeoned me so badly; then said to me, that I need to go back to my country because you damn people are too darn sophisticated, and he had a great mind to let them send me back home. Ray then left.

I was in blood and unable to walk. I scramble to the telephone and call Charles and report what Ray had done to me. Charles came immediately and took me to the Hospital.

I was questioned by the doctor and nurses at the hospital, but I told them a lie, due to the fact Ray had threatened me; I was afraid they would send the police after Ray, and if I had to attend court my immigration status would be discovered.

I was given an injection and antibiotic and sent home.

I told the owner of the house that I had a problem with Ray, so the owner changed the locks for me.

I was still afraid that Ray would meet me somewhere and harm me.

Because Moe and I had such a good friendship I relayed my problems to her, but I did not tell her about not having my papers.

I asked her if I could spend a few nights at her home. Luckily at the moment she and her husband were planning a vacation for two weeks. That was perfect planning.

I counted the days, and hoping the vacation time for my employer would begin.

I contacted Charles and told him about my fears. Because I usually leave for work early in the morning, Charles arranges for one of his taxi drivers to take me to the bus stop downtown. Returning from work was no problem because there was always someone around.

Moe and James were now on vacation.

I was very happy because I did not have to worry about meeting Ray.

I contacted Tony and told him what Ray had done to me; he was not very pleased, but encouraged me. Tony told me not to worry because he would assist me financially.

The following day I spoke to Tony's mother. She was very sorry about what Ray had done to me.

They both thank me for not calling the police because he was once in prison and served many years, and would probably return.

Ray's mother told me she would look at my hospital bill and pay it for me.

After returning home from the hospital Tony and his mother came and visited with me.

Tony's mother told me she thought I was not being truthful to her and wanting money, but after she saw my condition, and the medical report from the hospital she apologized for having bad thoughts about me.

Tony believed me, because he never covers up his brothers wrong doings.

Tony and his mother took me to the grocery store and bought enough groceries that would last me for about a month, and gave me $200.00; and said if I needed anything I should call them. They both left.

Tony and I continue to communicate. He always made sure I had money, and took me whenever I had to go places.

Tony encouraged me to save my money, just pay my rent, and he and his mother will help me with whatever I needed.

I was glad for the offer but I never imposed it on them. Even when I did not call, Tony and his mother would call and offer me help. I did not refuse because they took my refusal as an insult.

Getting my papers was the most important thing to me, but I was afraid that maybe I would experience the same situation with another man.

I got to the place where I became very frustrated by the many letters I received from my mother telling me that if I don't come and look about my children she would let the embassy know where I am so I would be sent home to take care of them

There was nothing I could have told my mother to make her understand how difficult it was for me having no one to sponsor me to get my papers.

I wrote and told my mother that I was already going with different men to find help, so I did not know what else to do, because I was only able to send whatever money I could afford, so it was entirely up to her to make whatever choice she wanted.

I mentioned to her that when things had been going good for me and I offered her money to complete the house she refused.

Moe's mother died so I became unemployed again, but she was very nice to me. Moe told me that she would not be able to pay me the full amount like she did before her mother died, but she would like for me to continue working for her two days of the week, and when I found another job I should also have those days available for her.

I accepted her offer, as little was better than nothing.

As the weeks went by my job search increased. I placed an ad in the newspaper. Someone replied. I was interviewed and hired.

This job was taking care of another elderly lady for three days weekly.

My earnings were not much, but no other jobs were available to me.

This new employer family took a liking for me. I was given gifts which include clothing, food, and whatever I needed.

I was welcomed in a very pleasant atmosphere which made me feel very good. Over time that lady died.

It was very sad for the families. They asked me to continue working for them for a few days, which I did. They were very kind to me, and gave me one month's pay with good wishes.

Being unemployed I got very frustrated. I wanted to get my papers to be able to help my children and families, but in my mind I thought that probably getting involved with a woman would be a better solution for me.

I bought a singles magazine and replied to an advertisement.

I struck up a friendship on the telephone with a lady who lived in Minnesota.

During our continued communication she made several financial offers to me. I thought about them, but in my mind I did not feel that was my path. She sent me an airplane ticket to visit her. That threw me off the worst.

I called her on the telephone and told her I don't think that would be right for me, so I was returning the ticket.

She told me to cash it and take the money. I told her it would not be appropriate to take her money.

She told me that I was the only honest person she ever met.

We continued communication for a long time, but as time went by I cut communication off totally.

I decided that somehow I will have to get someone to help me, so I seek out spiritual help.

I read an article in the newspaper about a man who lived in Illinois who said his work was guaranteed by uniting people together for love and marriage. I got in touch with him by phone.

He told me that he would give me something that would allow any man who got close to me to like, love, and want to marry me.

Immediately I mail the money he requested from me, because I was desperate to get myself together, so I could be able to get a better job and go to school. After I received the package from that spiritual man, I did as I was instructed.

One day while I was home and the phone rang; it was Leo wanted to come over and talk to me, and said he was very sorry for how he treated me.

I was not prepared to get involved with him again, but because he said he was sorry, I decided to invite over.

That evening when Leo entered through my door, he approached me with such a pleasant smile on his face, which I have never experienced from him when we first met.

After talking for a while, he had to leave, but promised he would return the next day. When he returned, I asked him if he could marry me and help me, he told me yes. I was now making wedding plans. I called the spiritual man and told him thanks for what he had done for me, and that I was planning to get married. Few weeks after we got married. The following week Leo and I began living together.

Not long after I found a job taking care of another elderly lady who lived alone.

Leo was also working and supporting me, so I was now able to start sending money to my mother for the children.

Leo introduced me to his family. Oftentimes they would invite me to go out with them.

I was very uncomfortable, because they were all American, and it was difficult for me to understand the accents.

On weekends they would visit the clubs. I attended with them, but not regularly.

Leo's sister-in-law named Jade and I develop a friendship. But one day while we were in a conversation, she told me that she didn't think I fit into the family, because I was a foreigner.

I told her I thought she had accepted me. She said it's not about accepting. I was a different nationality. I did not talk to Jade for a while.

I became pregnant for the second time for Leo. This time he told his brother and wife Jade about the pregnancy.

One day Jade telephone me, she asked me why I did not tell her that I was pregnant, I told her that I was not yet ready to talk about it.

She said to me, "That mean you going to have a funny talking baby." I told Jade that was the reason why I avoided talking to her, because she always ridicules me, and I refused to accept it.

As time passed whenever Leo had to talk to his families or anyone on the telephone he would either go into the bathroom, or wait until I was in the bathroom. One day I questioned him about it, he replied to me in a very disrespectful manner.

Most nights when we went to bed I discovered that Leo carried an obnoxious odor. Because of that I refused to have intercourse with him; which caused him to get angry with me and abused me, by slapping me in my face, and degrading me.

I came to the realization that maybe he is not taking a proper bath. One day I made a hole in the wall that gave me a clear view into the bathroom. In the evenings when he came home from work

I usually spy on him. I witnessed Leo turn the shower on and let it run, then stood by the sink and wash his face and then wipe himself with the wash rag.

I was so mad on discovering that he was only taking bird baths.

One evening I decided to take a shower with him.

He got very mad with me, and started slapping me in my face, and told me that he did not invite me to take a bath with him. I told him that as his wife and I thought it would be exciting.

Leo said, "To hell with you being my wife, it's the worst thing he did marrying a darn foreign woman." He said he didn't know why he didn't stay where he was, because he did what he wanted.

I said nothing, but took my shower and left him standing in the bathroom.

The relationship did not get any better, no matter what I did. I wanted to obtain my residency; and even though he was not a very clean person I tried to ignore the situation. There had been times when I visited him down in the town of Chester, or other places, each time he saw someone who was not very good looking, or not neatly dressed he would say to me. "There go some of your own people, that's the way you look, like a piece of trash." I usually felt so embarrassed, but I ignored him.

I became unable to maintain my job because of the problems I encountered with the pregnancy. On several visits to the doctor I was told to stay off my feet and stop working, which would be better for me and the baby.

When I relayed the information to Leo, he became very disgruntled on hearing about the doctor's order.

That did not stop Leo from being abusive to me, also during intercourse; even though I cried that he was hurting me, which seemed to only intensify his action.

One day Jack called and told me that he was on his way to pick apples but had to stay at the greyhound bus station in Chester overnight because there were no buses available to take him to his destination until the next day. I invited him to come and spend the night until the next morning.

I told Leo about it.

The next evening when Leo came home from work Jack was already gone. I realized that Leo was very upset. I asked Leo what was wrong. Leo's response was. "You know, it's bad enough having another man in your house, but it's darn bad having another ugly foreigner in your house using your kitchen utensil and sharing your bathroom."

Leo then told me that he did not want any other foreigner to come to his home again, if not I would have to leave or he would.

As the days went by Leo became aggressive and cruel toward me.

Because of my illness I was forced to stop working. That made him angrier, and as the days went by he quarreled with me regularly.

One day surprisingly; when he came home from work, he packed his belongings and told me that he would never return so I should find my own country man to help me.

I became frustrated, having no income and was faced with my bills.

I contacted Mae and told my situation to her. She promised to check some things for me to get help.

One of the places was an organization. I later contacted them myself. I was offered a place to stay during my pregnancy, but was told when the child was born I could not remain there; I would have to either give the child to them for adoption or leave.

I was leery about getting involved with that organization, so I contacted Jill in Florida about my condition, she told me to come and stay with them until I had the baby and was able to get on my feet.

I decided to relocate to Florida, but had to get rid of my furniture and household belongings. Some I gave to Mae, and the others I had a garage sale.

I was about five and a half months pregnant.

After I sold everything I decided to leave for Florida. Mae encouraged me to remain and let the organizations help me, but I thought Jill would be compassionate to me because of my kindness towards her accompanied with my state of pregnancy. Before I left Mae said to me, "I hope you never look back and said you are sorry you left Chester."

Few days before I left Chester I spent most of the time with Mae. Her son named Son who lived in New York was visiting her.

Mae relayed my situation to him. Son was so saddened about how I was treated, but told me he would be there to help me because of my kindness towards his mother. Son gave me his telephone number and $100.00, and told me to keep in touch with him.

Later that day we all said goodbye. Mae and I were in tears. She wanted me to stay. I regret leaving her, but I had already made my mind up.

I boarded the flight and went to Florida.

While I was in Florida I contacted Leo and informed him of my whereabouts.

As time passed we continued to communicate.

My baby was approximately seven months old.

Leo told me that he would find a place for us, and promised we would have a better relationship. Not very long I returned to Chester and joined him.

The apartment was located on Wheel Ave in a very dilapidated condition and had an obnoxious odor.

I had to get the place all clean, and purchase furniture along with whatever was needed to make the apartment look livable.

It was during the winter, we had to take the baby along with us each time we went shopping. We did not have much money, because Leo salary was paltry; and I had to make ends meet. I would collect cans and bottles and sold them for extra money. I was unable to buy a stroller, so I confiscated one of the shopping carts from the grocery store and took it home where I had it hidden behind the back of the apartment. That I oftentimes used for a stroller.

Things were very hard for me because I was unemployed and did not obtain my immigration papers.

Washing was very difficult, which was done on my hands. The clothes were hanged in the bathroom and through the house to dry. Sometime I became very tired and experience excruciating pains in my hands.

I had to shop for the cheapest things at the grocery store, so I was not able to make big dinner on Sunday's.

Each time I cook Leo made me felt ashamed. He ridicules me by saying things like. "How you know how to cook meat and you never eat meat in your country."

Most evening when he came home from work I stayed in the bathroom, because of the embarrassment at the dinner table.

Not long after I discovered that he would urinate in the bed.

I encouraged Leo to see the doctor, because he might have a problem with his bladder. He got very defensive and would fuss with me. Because of that I always sleep in a wet bed at nights, unless I slept on the floor.

Leo usually plays with his private part openly before the baby and myself. I talk to him about it; he told me that he has done that with the other women, so who the hell I was for him to please me. I became very unhappy and decided not to wait much longer. I ask Leo to take a day off work and take me to the immigration in Notbury to file for my residency.

While Leo and I sat at the immigration office in the waiting room, he told me he was doing me a favor because I had his child, but being I was a foreigner he did not give a damn.

On one occasion I had to face the immigration judge because I was on deportation. While we sat there I witnessed a man who was seeking information about deporting someone whose papers he had filed and received their alien card. That man told the immigration officer that his wife caught him cheating with another woman and that he had the right to do whatever he wanted, because he helped her including her children to get their alien cards. He told the officer that he wanted her to be deported, so he can be a free man.

The officer invited the man in, and told him that they would have to talk about that.

On our way home from the immigration, Leo cursed me in the most derogatory manner. He then addressed me by saying. "You darn foreign women are all ugly leeches."

When we got home he said to me, "Now, I am going to look at a woman tonight and you better not say a word if not your tail will be back in your country."

That night he went out and returned very late.

When he came home he began to quarrel with me, and told me he got him some good American sex, and that was better than what he had been getting from me. I went to bed in tears.

The landlord was from the Island, and was the pastor for a large church.

He and I got acquainted. I relayed some of my stories to him; he invited me to visit the church, which I did. I asked him if he could help me to find a cheap room to rent. He told me he would get back to me. Sometimes I would attend church which made me feel a little better.

After a few weeks I contacted my landlord in reference to what I spoke to him about, he told me that he did not hear about any vacant room, but he had a friend who lives alone and needed a nice looking lady. I was so shocked on hearing that coming from the pastor. I told him that I would call him about that. I never spoke to him again.

I tried to make myself happy, because I wanted to make the marriage work, and also to get my immigration papers, but the way Leo threatened me about deportation I was always wondering if I should continue with the marriage to him.

I started feeling very unhappy, because Leo never had anything good to say to me, he degrades, and was always displeased about what I did by criticizing and talked to me in derogatory manners. I became afraid when evening came, and he came home.

One morning when I woke I was inundated with urine in the bed. I told Leo that I would go to the pharmacy and get something for his bladder. That evening when he got home from work I showed him that I had bought him cystex. While he was having dinner I gave him the bottle and told him to read the instructions. Leo being ignorant did not take the time to read anything; instead he began cursing me, and said that I was giving him something to kill him. He then said, "I hear that you foreign people like to put roots on people, but your root isn't nothing compared to American roots, because I will make sure you walk and eat your own mess."

That morning when he left for work he never returned.

I did not want to return to Florida, but I had no other choice.

I packed my things, boarded the greyhound bus and left Chester.

While in Florida I received a letter from the immigration that I should come for an interview.

I contacted Leo and asked him if he would go with me to the interview and help me to get my papers.

He said. "I have already told you I am not going to help you."

I cried and begged him to help me even for the child's sake.

A few days went by and I had not contacted him.

One day I got a telephone call from him telling me that he would help me for the child sake.

I told him that I would let him know when I would be coming to get the direction for where he lived.

A few weeks went by and I went to Chester. Leo accompanied me to the immigration to be interviewed. After the interview I left, and returned to Florida.

CHAPTER FORTY

Return to Live with Jack and Jill

Although I had feelings of apprehension about Jack and Jill; I kept a line of communication open with them, because I had no place to go in case a problem ensued. And because I had gotten married to an American citizen, and was pregnant I saw no reason to be apprehensive; although during that time my husband and I were separated, I felt better secured with myself from deportation. I was approximately six months pregnant, and facing difficulties. After discussing my situation with Jill, she invited me to return and live with her and Jack.

It was evening when my flight arrived at Chancy Airport. While I was walking through the lobby I heard my name being called, but somehow I ignored it, and as a matter of fact I was not sure as to what I was hearing. When I came off the airplane I did not recognize Jill standing with the other people who were waiting for their friends or family, so I headed straight to the baggage claim. At the baggage claim I was greeted by Jill and two other ladies, one of which was white. Jill then said to me, "Didn't you hear your name call to meet your party at the ticket counter." I said, "No, maybe because the people were talking I could not hear."

I asked Jill why she wanted me to meet her at the ticket counter. She said, 'So we all could go to baggage claim together.' Jill then helped to get my baggage and took them in the car. After my baggage was in the car, Jill said to me, "Wait, I forget to do something." Jill and the white lady immediately walked away and left me standing with the other lady. The lady introduced herself to me as Jen, and Jill had told her about me, but she did not tell her that I was such a nice looking person. Not long after Jill and the white lady came back, and we all got in the car and went to Jill's home.

Reminiscing the condition of the house and the situation between Jack and Jill and myself, I became fearful, and uncomfortable, but because I was pregnant I tried to relax myself from fear of deportation by Jack and Jill.

The room I had once occupied was still vacant, so I assumed my residency. The following day Jill went out and I was home by myself. Later that day the white lady who I met at the airport came to visit and wanted to know if Jack and Jill were home, I told her no. She said to me, "As a matter of fact I came to see you." I asked her what the reason was. She expressed that she would like to borrow $200.00 from me. I was surprised, because the only person knew I had money was Jill. I said to the lady, "I don't know you, I only met you at the airport, plus I don't know your name; and I don't have any money but $50.00 until my husband sends me money." The lady became disgruntled and walked away, then slammed the door; and drove her car away at such a fast speed. When Jill came home I told her that the white lady came and asked me for money. I told Jill I had no money, just enough until my husband sent me some that week. Jill also gave me a disparaging look.

Living in Vale was not a bed of roses. The house had gotten older, and was infested with fleas which were numerous in the days, but worse at nights. Jill tried different products to get rid of them but had very little success, somehow the fleas disappeared.

Almost every day Jill accommodated several men at her home. Most of which were from the Island, playing dominoes and other games. On weekends she would prepare large meals to entertain them. Sometimes I tried to watch them play but I was always given a disparaging look from either Jill or some of the men. One Sunday afternoon as I was stood on the porch watching the men play domino Jill ridiculed me in front of the men by saying, "Don't bother look any man here, because Island men don't father American man baby, so go sit don't and try to go back to your husband." Immediately tears fell from my eyes to my face, then I began crying. The men looked at me and said to Jill. "Don't do the woman like that; all of us come from other countries." One of the men said, "Baby mother if I did not have a woman I would take you because you look like a woman with class." Jill became very angry.

Immediately I was over taken by such despair. I felt like running away, but I had no place to go; and being pregnant did not give me much choice but to remain in the condition until things changed between my husband and myself. I did not have any friends, or anyone I could talk to, I found comfort daily by reading the bible. I was sad all the time. The backyard was populated with quite a few trees, some of which were oranges.

During the days I spent my time sitting under those trees, reading my bible, praying and also crying. Because of that I experience weakness in my body.

After living with Jill for a few weeks I started having feelings of apprehension, and unable to identify it. One day while I was home alone one of the men who visited the house name Adrian came to visit. He asked me where everyone was, I told him that I was alone. Adrian said to me, "As a matter of fact it's you I wanted to talk to." Adrian began talking to me. I listened to what he said; and after hearing what Adrian told me I began telling him about the feelings I was experiencing that Jill might want to mess me up because she knew my situation. Adrian told me that Jill made it known that her reason for calling the immigration to deport me was to collect $500.00; but because I was pregnant she postponed her plan until another time. I was very astonished when Adrian relayed that information to me. I told Adrian that the reason why Jill accommodated me was because she knew I had a little money, because actually everyday she borrows from me and whenever she feels it's all gone she will get me deported. Immediately I started crying. Adrian said to me. I am glad you are a woman with good sense and are able to see things for yourself. He told me that he came to offer his friendship to me. After talking for a while Adrian told me he had to leave, because he works at nights and wanted to get some rest. He told me goodbye, then he drove away.

As time passed I experienced that same feeling of apprehension living with Jill; I wanted to run away, but I knew nothing about that town, and was not close to any public transportation made it very difficult for me. As time passed, one day another man who also plays dominoes at Jill house name Clive came to visit. I heard a knock on the door. I moved the curtain to see who it was, he shouted to me and made a sign with his hand and said, "Come here I need to talk with you." I quickly opened the door and went outside to him. Clive told me that Jill was malevolent towards me; because I was such a nice woman, and she wants to mess me up. Clive told me that both he and Adrian had a good talk pertaining to me. He said Adrian likes me very much, and if Jill realized that Adrian were friends with me she would feel threatened and leave me alone. I told Clive that I like Adrian as a person who I would share a platonic friendship, but not for a relationship. Clive said to me, "Yes I understand that, but the man also likes you, so take the opportunity before Jill tries to mess you up." I told Clive that I would give it some thoughts. Clive then gave me a paper containing Adrian telephone number; and told me that I should call Adrian immediately since I was alone so that he could help me. I asked Clive to stand outside and let me be aware when Jill or anyone else was coming. Clive was very cooperative.

I called Adrian on the telephone, he seemed very glad to talk with me, and said whatever I wanted him to do for me I should not be afraid. I did not refuse Adrian's offer, because I needed someone to protect and help me.

Over a period of time Adrian and I struck up a platonic friendship. As time passed, in the evenings after work Adrian usually came to visit me; and would invite me to go for a drive with him. Jill became angry about my association with him, and would curse me in the most derogatory manners; but Adrian would ignore her. One late evening when I was home alone with Jill; she reprimanded me by saying. "Don't you ever think Adrian wants you, because you are not good enough for him?" Jill would ridicule me for trivial things. Over time and for my own safety I struck up an intimate relationship with Adrian; because my back was against the wall. Soon he began teaching me to drive, which was done at nights on the side roads located beside the groves. Adrian and I started spending more time together. Jill was not happy about the relationship because she had always been the nemesis in my life, but Adrian was more determined than I was not to let Jill separate us.

Journey on a Bumpy Road

I was over seven months pregnant so I decided to see a Gynecologist. My only way of finding one, was by way of a telephone directory, because Jill refused to inform me about anyone. During my search I found a doctor who was located in Chancy. Adrian told me that I should not worry about the distance; just make the appointment to match his days off.

My only means of receiving my mails was having them sent to Jill's Post Office Box. Although I was separated from my husband he usually sent money for me weekly to Jill's Post Office Box. Three weeks went by and I did not receive any money from him. I had no way of contacting my husband but by calling his sister-in law. I telephone his sister-in-law and gave her the telephone number to Jill's house with strict instruction as to the time he should call me. Few days after my husband called. I asked him why he hadn't sent any money to me. He told me that every week he sent money, because he had the receipts as evidence. With a feeling of ambivalence, I told him that I would get my own letter box immediately, because I had a feeling Jill was taking my money. After I had spoken to my husband; I asked Adrian if I could use his Post Office Box; he told me I was free to do whatever I wanted. I got back in touch with my husband and gave him my new address.

As time passed I told Jill that I had to get my own Post Office Box, because there are times when I wanted to check for my letters and she was gone to work, or is not at home. Jill got berserk; she had a fork in her hands as she was cooking. Jill said to me, "You nasty vagabond you, if I never want you to use my Post Office Box you could not use it, now you telling me you have your own, you bastard. I feel like pushing the darn fork in your gut." I quickly ran outside, and away from her.

Being afraid I walked away and went and sat by a grove, which was located close to a few houses and a little distant away from Jill's home.

That grove was located close by the road where actually everyone drives, so I decided not to return to the house until I saw someone I knew that would be going to visit Jill.

After sitting for a long time I saw a car that resembled Clive's car coming in my direction. I looked to make sure my eyes were not fooling me. To my surprise it was Clive. I quickly got up and positioned myself so he would be able to see me. When Clive saw me, he made a sudden stop and asked me what was wrong. I relayed the problem to him. Clive said to me, "It seems Jill is getting mad in her darn head, so I will talk with her."

I was afraid to go with Clive, but he assured me that she could not hurt me, because she knows that he doesn't play, and he knows how to assuage her. When Clive took me home he questioned Jill as to the reason why she acted the ways she did to me. Jill told Clive that she doesn't like me. Clive said to Jill. "Well tell her to leave instead of wanting to hurt her." Clive continued to dialogue with her, soon after she became calm. Clive invited me to come inside and have my dinner. I was hungry, but was afraid of being close to Jill. Clive spent a long time with Jill and I; it was late that night when he left.

Adrian had to work that evening until the next morning so I did not see him. When he came home the next morning and visited me, I told him what had transpired between Jill and myself. He was very angry, but insisted that I hold on until I gave birth to my baby, because he has not yet gotten his divorce and did not want to take me home with him, because the house he lived in was once shared with his wife. Adrian made it possible to spend a lot of time with me, and would drive me to different places.

One morning Jill asked me to loan her $300.00. I told her I had to go to the bank to get it. I was not working, and refused to spend any more money, because I had already given her quite a bit. I told Jill that the money was in the bank. I did not have the money in the bank, but I realize that I was being used. I got in touch with Adrian and told him that Jill wanted to borrow more money from me and I had a feeling she would not return it. Adrian said to me, "Your vibes are always right." Adrian encouraged me to go to the bank, to open a joint account and secure the money I had; which I made a concerted effort to do. When I returned home Jill was in the kitchen cooking and singing, she appeared very happy. I interrupted and told her that I was unable to get money from the bank because it was deposited into CDS and if I made an early withdrawal I would have to pay a penalty. After relaying the information to Jill, immediately she ceased from singing and got into a rage. She said to me, "You nasty wretch; I need to let them deport your meager behind right now."

The rest of the day was spent in confusion, and trepidation; because each time Jill saw me she cursed me in the most derogatory ways; and told me, "Don't even eat my freaking food. Go and eat filth." From that moment onward whenever Jill cooked she refused to give me even a modicum of her meal to eat; but I continued to display kindness to her.

Jack was away from home. After his return the condition at home remains the same. Owing to that I continued sitting in the backyard under the trees, as usual in uncontrollable tears. Sympathy was the last thing that Jill would have shown to me, but cursed me more.

As the friendship between Adrian and myself continued; one night he and I went driving so he began teaching me to drive. While driving we were approached upon by two police cars. Adrian says to me, "They are going to give him a ticket for allowing me drive with no license." I got very nervous wondering if I would be taken to jail in my state of pregnancy. The police gave Adrian a warning and told me that it is important for me to get a driver's permit so that I would be able to learn to drive safely. I inquired among the people who I knew, but was unable to get one. There was a lady named Lena who came from one of the Islands. I asked her if she had a book that I could borrow to study for my driving permit. Lena told me yes, but I have to pay her $50.00 to borrow it. I thought that was so wrong, but I had no choice; because of Adrian's work schedule he was unable to take me to get one from the driver license office. I paid Lena for the book because I was desperate to learn to drive.

Approximately one week of reading and studying I went and got my permit. One day I was approached by Jill, she asked me how many questions I got right, I said to her, "I got them all." Jill surprisingly said to me again, what you did to get your permit, because she went more than one time and never got them right, because she doesn't know anyone who had ever gotten them all right the first time. I told Jill that my good luck came from reading my bible and praying. Jill said to me again. How when I read my bible and pray God never answers her. My response to her again was. "It seems that somehow

God is in sympathy with me for the suffering children I left abroad at home." Jill became disgruntled, and gave me a disparaging look, and then walked away and spit at me.

One day I was home alone. There were quite a few telephone numbers that were written on the calendar hanging in the kitchen. I took a peep to see if any of the numbers listed were related to anyone who visited the home that I could talk to. Jen number was listed. She was the black lady who accompanied Jill and the other lady to the airport.

In askance I call to see if she was home, and not become upset about me calling her., but when Jen realized that I was calling, she got excited and said to me, "Girl I would have done anything to talk with you, but every time I came to Jill's house, she is always up under my tail."

Jen told me Jill asked her to accompany her to the airport to pick me up because I was coming from New York with money; and Jill wanted to get it from me, and then get you deported; but she encouraged Jill not to deport me, because we all came here from our country to better our lives. But Jill insisted. Jen asked me if I did not hear my name call on the intercom; but I told her no. Jen said that Jill had summoned the immigration to come and pick me up; also the reason why Jill asked me if I did not hear my name call on the intercom was that she and the immigration were waiting to pick me up at the customer service desk.

Jen told me she don't know what was walking with me, and what kind of spirit I have, but she was so glad that I was not a fool, and that the sooner I get away from Jill's house the safer I will be, because Jill was still planning to let the immigration send me back home. I told Jen thanks for the warning.

Few days went by. One morning I was home alone. I had a premonition that something was going to happen. The front door is usually locked with a padlock from the outside. Somehow my mind told me to lock the front door with the padlock and remain inside the house in case someone came to the house it would appear that no one was home. So I did. Not very long after placing the padlock on the front door, and returning through the back door, I saw a green car that was driven by a white man stopped in front of the house on the other side of the road. The writing on the side of the car was written in bold letters, so I recognize the words 'Border Patrol.' Suddenly the man came out of the car wearing a white shirt, green pants and a badge and knocked on the front door. I became very nervous, but I stood beside the window in a state of panic and looked at the man. He looked at the door, and then he walked away and got in the car then drove off. I watched to make sure he was gone. Immediately after the man left I called Jen on the telephone and reported to her what had transpired. Jen told me that earlier that morning Jill called and told her she was going to call the immigration office because she was in need of money and that she could get $500.00 to send to her families at home. Jen said she told Jill if she didn't like me, and did not want to accommodate me she should tell me to go. Jen told me that Jill addressed her by saying. "You not my darn friend and you have your papers, and the only good thing she saw for me was to go back home and eat filth."

Jen told me she was sorry for me, but if she had lived in another city distant from Jill she would help me; but I need to continue praying and ask God to protect me until I have my baby and get away from her, because she is a 'nasty bastard.'

The Monday of the following week I was home. Late that evening the telephone rang. Jack called and told me that Jill was in the hospital due to a car accident she sustained. Late that night Jill came home wearing a collar around her neck. The next morning I went to a phone booth and called Jen and told her what happened to Jill. Jen told me she knew, because after she came home from work that night, Jill called and told her that she had an accident. Jen told me that Jill had an appointment with the immigration; she was going to meet with them to accompany her to the house to pick me up; she said it was at that moment she met into an accident with another driver. Jen encouraged me to continue reading the bible and pray God is going to deliver me, because of Jill because she was very wicked to me after all the nice things I had done for her. I talked to Jen for a while then I went back home.

The accident that Jill had sustained caused her to become ill for a while, and because she had difficulties ambulating I assisted her, and also with preparation of her meals. Although I was hurt about the things she did to me, I had sympathy for her.

Adrian was now divorce and was trying to find another place to move away from the house he and his ex-wife shared together. I did not feel good within my heart to leave Jill in her illness when Jack was gone to work during the days, so I stayed and helped her until she recovered. Over time she recovered.

One day I was home, but sitting in the backyard at my usual spot. Jill was also home. Sometimes before she goes out, she would look in the back yard for me and let me know she was leaving. That day in question after I had finished cooking and cleaning the house, I took my bible and went and sat under the trees. After sitting for a long time, I got up because I wanted to use the bathroom. I tried opening the door but realized it was locked from the inside. I looked to the front of the yard where Jill's car usually park, but it was not there.

There was nowhere for me to enter the house, but through the window. I did not know how long she would be gone, either if she had gone on another trip to the immigration, so I wanted to get dressed, and also get my pocket book in case I needed to escape. The window was not very strong, and could be open easily from outside; I tried my luck and was successful. I went inside the house, got dressed, got my pocket book, and quickly got out of the house. Lena did not live very far, so I decided to visit her.

When I got to Lena's home she was there. I knock on her door. When Lena saw me, she told me to come in quickly, because she did not want Jill to be driving by accidentally and saw me.

After visiting with Lena for a few hours, suddenly Jill came to visit Lena. When Lena saw Jill approaching her house, Lena told me to hurry to the back room and hide under her bed, because she was afraid that Jill would mess her up with witchcraft. During Jill's visit with Lena they both got into a dialogue. I heard when Jill said to Lena, at the same time pounding on Lena's coffee table. "No matter how much she read her bible and prays, and no matter where she go, or what she does I am going to make sure she never get her papers in this country." Jill told Lena that she had willfully locked me out of the house. When I heard what Jill was saying, my belief was confirmed that she had a strong dislike for me. The visit with Jill and Lena did not last very long.

Lena did not want me to leave immediately, fearing Jill might not have gone home directly, so I waited until it was late that evening. I went home and pretended I had no idea about what had transpired at Lena's house.

The time was fast approaching for me to give birth to my baby, so Adrian spent a lot of time with me. One day while Adrian and I were shopping at the department store I began experiencing labor pains. I inform Adrian as to what was happening. Shopping for the baby was done, so my bag was already packed. Adrian rushed me to the hospital. I was checked in and examined by the nurse who told me that I was close to giving birth. In the delivery room I was given an epidural. After prolonged labor I had the baby, which was a girl. Adrian could not stay with me during the entire delivery, because he had to go to work, but that next morning he was at my bedside. After visiting with me for a while Adrian left. That evening he told me Jill wanted to visit me. Adrian informed me that I should not let her see neither me nor my baby, because she may put a bad spell on us.

The next day while I was still in the hospital the nurse told me that a lady was there to see me who told her she was my aunt. I told the nurse I had no aunt in America, and I would not see that lady. I told the nurse to tell her anything to get her away.

I peeped out my door, I saw Jill sitting in the waiting area. I quickly got back into my room so that she would not see me. My stay in the hospital lasted for four days because I had a tubal ligation, and I was also experiencing excruciating pains.

When I got home from the hospital I was in pain, and experiencing weakness in my body, so it was difficult for me to stand on my feet to prepare my meals.

At home Jill had prepared her usual meal, which consisted of yam, coco, dasheen, cornmeal dumpling, and salt mackerel. She offered me some. I should not have eaten any hard food after just given birth, but I was very hungry, so I had some to eat. The following day I became very constipated and thought I was going to die. Adrian took me to the doctor. The doctor asked me what I had eaten, so I told him. The doctor told me that it seemed as if that lady did not like me and wanted to hurt me, why she gave me that food to eat, knowing I had just given birth and had a surgery. I was sent home with strict instruction from the doctor pertaining to my diet.

One day while Jack and Jill were absent Lena came to see me and wanted to know how I was doing, I told her about the difficulties I was having. She told me when she returned home she would give her husband dinner to bring for me later that evening. The meal was not to my liking, but it was better than what Jill would have given me to eat. As the days passed I was feeling better, and getting stronger.

I told Jen that I had given birth to my baby; we kept our communication very private. One day surprisingly Jen came to visit and brought clothes for my baby. Jill got very angry when she saw what Jen had given to me. Jen said to her, "Why the hell you don't give the woman a break." The hatred that had been directed to me from Jill knew no bounds, and did not get any better, but worsened, but I had to wait until Adrian had found a place to live.

Few weeks passed and Adrian finally found a room for us. The room was in a dilapidated condition, very unsanitary, and carries an obnoxious smell. I was very uncomfortable; but wanting to move away from Jill's house I was prepared to do whatever cleaning and disinfectant that was necessary to make myself comfortable. Soon after I got the place ready I told Jill that I would be moving, she gave me a disparaging look, and began cursing me, but I ignored her, and began taking my things and put them outside on a couch that was located on the porch. It was difficult for me to carry the things and baby in my hands at the same time. I wrapped the baby into a blanket and placed her on the couch, so I would be able to move my thing more easily and quickly. Immediately after I put the baby down on the couch, Jill came and took up the baby and carried her inside. In my mind I thought maybe because I was leaving she wanted to spend some time with the baby. All of a sudden I saw when Jack came and placed the padlock on the door and locked it.

While he was locking the door, I heard him mumbling to himself, "Let me go to the store and buy some sugar." Still I had no negative thoughts about Jack and Jill. Jack walked towards the direction where the store was located. Not long after Jack left, a police car drove up. The officer came out of the car and walked into the yard. Immediately Jill came out of the house with my baby in her hand. The officer said, "Where is the woman who abandoned the baby." Jill's response was, "See her standing there." I was so astonished. I told the officer the difficulty I had moving my things out, so I lay the baby down on the couch. I told the officer that I would not have abandoned my child, because the child gave me legal right to this country. Immediately Adrian drove up. I asked him how he knew I had a problem. Adrian said that while he was laying down, just like something told him to come and see me now.

The officer asks Adrian what he was doing there. Adrian said to the officer, "This is my old lady, and where she is I will be there."

Adrian then asked the officer what was the problem. The officer told him that he had information that I had abandoned the baby. Adrian told the officer that it was untrue. He informed the officer about the wicked things that were done to me by both Jack and Jill. Adrian told the officer that he had been trying to find a place for me to move away, but was not successful until a few days ago. The officer looked at me and shook his head, then he told Jill to return the baby to me, and then he drove away. Adrian went ahead and packed my things into his car. We then drove away and went to the new place.

Jill did not know where I lived; and I did not want her to know, because I was still afraid that she would have me deported.

After living there for a few weeks, one day Adrian told that he received news from Clive that Jill found where we lived, and said she is going to 'mess me up'. Adrian then decided to get another place that would be distant from Jill. We found another place in Chancy. In no time we move away quickly from Jack and Jill.

My baby had gotten older so we relocated back to Vale. Jack and Jill did not live in that community anymore.

We rented two rooms from Mrs. Moore, which was located on the main street. She was also the owner of other houses which she rented to others in the community.

The house I lived in was a rooming house which was occupied by other people most of which were immigrants who were also illegal aliens, including me. As time passed, and although I was unable to understand their accent we made friends with each other.

There was an older American man who lived next to my room named Chad. Chad and I became friends. He was very generous to me. I did not like living at Vale because it was located in a bucolic setting but I had no other choice. There were times I could be seen walking along the road with my baby, or sitting down under a tree in a melancholy mood. Lena did not live very far from me, but my visits to her were few. There were quite a few orange trees that were located in the back yard and beside a utility shed, beside the landlord house which was located in the same yard. During the times when I was in a melancholy mood I would also sit under those trees with my daughter and read my bible.

After a period of time I got a job working at the same factory where Adrian was employed. I had no one to babysit for me, but because Adrian and I did not work the same shift we made arrangements that matched our work schedule. I started out cleaning the trash from the orange bins, until I was later promoted to operating a machine. This job gave me a little earning power, and gave me the opportunity to meet other people. I told Lena that I was working at the factory. She got very disgruntled, and said to me, "How the hell you have no papers and get work." I said to Lena, "When God is on your side he open doors for you." When the holidays came around I would prepare a large dinner and entertain my neighbors who were also my friends.

When weekends came around Adrian invited his friends over to drink. I was not pleased about their behavior, because they spoke very loudly and disrespectfully to me. I told Adrian that I did not approve of his friends visits, because they were very disrespectful. Adrian said to me, "They are my cursed friends, so if you don't approve of them get the hell out, or I'll call the dam immigrations on you."

As time passed I decided that it was important for me to learn to drive and get my driver license to become independent, and go places by myself. Adrian helped to teach me when he had time. Other times I got the help from my immigrant neighbor named Sily.

Sily was employed at Disney and was home during the days, so he was available to help me. I asked Sily what was the cost for helping me, but he said he would not charge me as I was a nice person, and we are friends. Over a period of time while Sily was teaching me to drive, one day he drove off the main road onto an unpaved road which led to the grove. I asked Sily where he was going; he said that he found a good place where I would be able to practice parallel parking and backing up with no interruption.

As the car drove along I started getting scared, because the further along Sily drove the trees became tickly forestry. Immediately I told Sily that I did not want to go any further, but he got very irate and then drastically drove into the groove. I began screaming at him. Sily immediately took a gun from under his car seat and said to me, "Shut the shit up, I took you here to give some." I was so shocked; I did not know what to do. Sily then open the passenger side door of the car. The moment I saw him, he turn around to open the door, immediately, I grab the gun from his hand. We both now change position, which he did not like very much. I ordered him back into the car and demanded that he take me home.

Sily was very scared. He kept begging me not to shoot him, but that was not my intention, I wanted for him to take me home. Being afraid that Sily might hurt me; when I returned home I did not return the gun immediately.

Because Chad was my trusted friend; a few days after I told him what had transpired between Sily and myself. Chad was so sympathetic towards me, but was very mad about my experience; and said as friends; Sily should have been more respectful to me. I told Chad that I was afraid to return the gun to Sily, and also I did not want Adrian to know what had happened. Because Sily and I were illegal aliens I refused to report him to the police, fearing everyone who lived in my building would be caught by immigration Chad promised he would have a good talk with Sily and straighten things out for me.

Two days after I spoke to Chad I heard a knock on my door. When I opened the door and looked out, it was Chad. He invited me to talk with him inside his room. To my surprise when I entered Chad's room Sily was sitting there. At that moment I was not afraid, because I felt Chad had things under control. Chad expressed to me that he had spoken to Sily about his situation, so he decided to get rid of the gun, and promises he would not hurt me. I gave Chad the gun, and told him to destroy it for me. I said goodbye and left Sily sitting there. I did not dialogue with Sily anymore because of what he had done.

My concerted effort was to obtain my driver license to give me a little freedom.

There was another immigrant name Jake who used to teach me, but due to his work schedule made it difficult. One evening when he came home from work I told him that I did not complete my driving lesson, and asked if he could help me. Jake told me his only day off was on a Sunday which was the only time he had to visited his families who lived in Evans Beach. Jake wanted to know what else I needed to do that would prepare me for my driving test, I told him. Jake agrees to help me with a cost of $35.00 an hour. I told Jake that I would get back to him.

My job had become very slow because the orange season was almost finishing, but I decided that by any means I would sacrifice the money for my driving lesson. Not very long after I contacted Jake and told him I would be ready whenever he was available to teach me.

Jake said to me, "Are you sure you can pay me? I said yes." Jake said to me, "Boy you foreign women are something, even when you cry; you always have a little money tied and put aside." I told Jake it's not only foreign women who have done that, everybody has to sacrifice for rainy days. Jake then said to me, "I was just playing with you when I told you $35.00." In response, I told Jake that it doesn't matter, because I need to get my driver license.

On the third Sunday after practicing I was able to back up and parallel park. But that Sunday after I was finish with my practice, on my way home Jake said to me. It is a long time he been watching me and wanted me to give him some of my body. I said to him, "What". I told Jake that I would not do that. While on our way home, Jake placed his hands between my legs. I got very irate and began cursing at him. We were a long way from home, but were also on a busy street. Jake then pulls to the side of the road and stops. He said to me, "You walk home from here." I got out of Jake's car and began walking. As I walked along I came to a service station. I knew Chad's telephone number; Adrian was working and I was unable to contact him. Usually on Sundays Chad was always visited by his fiancée, but because we were good friends I could call him anytime I was in trouble. A telephone booth was located at the service station; I called Chad and told him what had transpired between Jake and myself. Chad was surprised, and was also very angry. Not very long after waiting Chad came and got me, then took me home. Chad was like a father, brother, and everything to me. Although I was of a different nationality made no difference, he was always there for me.

While Chad and I were driving home he said I should let Adrian know some of the things that were happening to me, so I decided to tell him when I got home. That evening when Adrian came home from work I told him about the negative experiences I had been experiencing to get my driver's license. Adrian told me the reason why he wasn't interested to teach me to drive was because of him being jealous that as a good looking woman if I got my license I would be able to meet other men and probably leave him.

I lashed out in anger toward him. I told Adrian he had been a hindrance to me by keeping me back, especially knowing that we are both from the same country, and have my starving children there. I relayed to him what Sily had done to me. Adrian said, "I thought that all of us who lived here were friends, because we actually eat from the same pot." I said to Adrian, "It takes a friend to screw up a friend."

One day Adrian asked me if I had enough confidence to take the driving test now. I told him yes. He suggested that we go driving and if he saw that I was capable of driving he would take me the next morning when the Driver License Office opened, which would be on a Tuesday to get my license. Adrian myself and my daughter went driving. He was surprised about my good driving. The following Tuesday Adrian took me to the driver license office to get my driver license, and I was successful.

Adrian decided to confront Jake about what he had done to me, and also requested that he return the money. Jake was miffed, because I told Adrian what he did. I had paid Jake thirty five dollars quite a few times. Adrian told Jake that he did not want him to return it in increment, but to avoid any more commotion; Jake went ahead and paid back all the money I gave him. Overtime, one day Jake apologized to me; and said if I ever need a favor I should let him know. I was now able to drive.

One day I drove to Lena's home to see if she was there. I wanted her to see that I was improving myself, as she did not know I had got my driver license. When I got there she was home. I got out of the car and knocked on her door and told her that I had gotten my driver license. Lena immediately gave me a disparaging look, and then said to me, "Look how long am trying to get someone to teach me to drive, and you come to this country after me and get your license." I said to Lena, "We don't have the same luck, but in time you will succeed." I then left and went back home. I realized that Lena was very jealous about me, so I did not visit her very much.

Being able to drive; some days I would take Adrian to work and keep the car.

Because the orange season had ended I was not working anymore, Adrian income was not enough; I needed help for my daughter, so I applied for food stamps and welfare for her which was granted. Having no one to verify for me I asked Lena. Lena's expectations were that I would give her some of the food stamps that I would receive for my daughter. I told her that the amount I would be getting was just enough to get food for her. Lena displayed a bellicose attitude towards me, and called me a liar.

I continue to maintain the relationship with Lena, although I knew she was jealous of me; I ignored her because in reality I had no one to call for assistance.

Whenever she was dressed and in the company of her friends she pretended like I did not exist because she had her permanent residency, but I was more fortunate than her. That caused her to direct negative things towards me.

When Adrian was gone to work I usually take my daughter and go driving, if no place but to the department stores and look around. Because of that I started meeting people. I met a Lady from the Island named Betty. Over a period of time Betty and I exchanged telephone numbers, and we became friends. She was employed at the same factory I used to work, but during the time I worked there we scarcely met each other, because we worked different shifts. As our friendship grew I told her what Jack and Jill had done to me. She was very surprised that I was associated with them. Betty told me about the malaise that Jack had done to her which had caused her an enormous amount of misfortune in her life. Betty expressed to me that he was a very wicked man. Overtime as Betty and I continued our friendship continued, she did not know that I was Adrian's fiancée, but heard that she was a lady from another country. Betty told me that Adrian has been telling my business to other people. Many things Betty told me she heard the other men spoke about were things I told only to Adrian. Betty told me that Adrian was also involved into a covert relationship with another lady who he had been giving my jewelry and money to. I was miffed on hearing, but I promised Betty I would not reveal any of that information to Adrian but make some changes at home.

The orange season had begun, so I got my old job back. After working for a period of time, one evening on my way back home from work a lady who was driving a truck ran the stop sign and we had an accident. Immediately a young man who was passing by knew me, went and told Adrian who was at work what had happened to me. Adrian came and assisted by driving me home because I was nervous. As the days went by I began to experience excruciating pains, and was unable to return to work, so I had to see the doctor and was given three weeks off work, after which I went back. It was very difficult for me to perform my job, but I wanted to save enough money to buy a car for myself. As time passed I was unable to work, so I informed the doctor about my condition. The doctor advised me to refrain from anything strenuous for about three months which would help me to recuperate more quickly.

The season was almost over so in a few weeks I was laid off from the job.

The accident that I had sustained contributed to my illness which caused me to experience pain in my lower abdomen and during intercourse. I explained my condition to Adrian, but he showed no compassion. At nights I was awakened by him in a berserk attitude. When I refused he would curse me. One late night in question Adrian woke me up and told me that he wanted a woman to satisfy his desire. I told him that he needed to give me more time to get well. Adrian said to me at the same time knocking his private organ against the wall, "See it here I am red hot and ready, if not get the hell out of my place." I broke down into uncontrollable tears.

The next morning I went and sat on the porch with my baby crying. I did not realize that anyone was at home. The couples were also immigrants. The wife did not speak English, but the husband did. The husband came and sat on a chair next to me. He told me that he and his wife heard me crying. Because it was an old wood house you had to talk softly because other tenants could hear your conversation. He began talking to me, and told me that he heard what Adrian said to me the night before. He was in sympathy with me and said, "Why did he have to talk to you so loud, knowing other people live next door and can hear your business. And why was he so nasty to you." I was surprised when my neighbor said that to me. He also said to me, "You are such a nice woman; you need a nice man who will respect you." The man asked me if I had any families or friends to go and live with, I told him no. He suggested that I should try and get me a live-in job, but I pointed out the condition to him pertaining to my daughter. The neighbors and I soon became very good friends; and made sure my daughter and I had food to eat.

I was becoming very unhappy and wanted to go away, but because I had no papers, and having my daughter I could not sleep on the street. I had to endure the condition. During those years; I wished I had known about shelters. I would seek refuge for me and my child.

Adrian would talk to me in the most derogatory ways. I became so ashamed because the neighbors always hear when Adrian cursed me; which was done late at night when I did not acquiesces his desires. One day I sat down and had a good talk with Chad about the abusive treatment I was receiving from Adrian. Chad told me that he was seventy years old and he has lived to see many things. He told me that the things that I put up with, one day God is going to free me. I sat and cried day and nights.

The landlord was an American lady. During the times when I was in deep distress I would sit under the trees in the back yard with my baby. But whenever I saw the landlady I would quickly get away, fearing she would disapprove of my presence there. One day as I sat under the trees I was approached by her. She told me that she doesn't like foreign women. I told her that I haven't done anything wrong to her. She paused for a minute, and then she said to me.

"But you don't talk like the others." I said to her. "It's because you have only met certain type of foreigners." There were several ripe orange and grapefruits on the tree. She told me that I should not be afraid to pick fruits from the trees for me and my daughter because they are going to rot." I said to her, "Thank you ma'am." Although she gave me permission to enjoy the fruits, each time I always asked her permission. Over a period of time the land lord and I develop friendship.

One day while I was sitting at my usual spot in the yard she handed me a plate that was wrapped with aluminum foil, and said to me, "I have seen you sitting there daily, but today I saw you crying from my kitchen window. I don't know if you are hungry, or something is wrong with you, but take this. I brought you some pork chops with rice and greens." I took the plate from her and told her thanks. She also invited me to come over and sit with her when I was not having good days. I took the invitation and visited her.

The landlady started asking me questions about why I was not working. I did not want to let her know I was illegal, I told her that I was waiting on the immigration who would be sending my work permit, because the old one had expired. She encouraged me that whenever I got money that I should invest into CDs and also buy saving bonds and put away, but at that time I had no money as I was not working. Few weeks went by, and the landlord told me that she needed someone to help with her domestic chores; and if I did she would take me to the bank to purchase savings bonds with the money I earned from her. I gladly accepted the job. I worked four hours daily for three days weekly. I was paid a paltry sum of $75.00 weekly. From that $75.00 I bought saving bonds for $37.50cents, which I could afford. This job did not last for very long, because after a period of time her family came to visit with her, which lasted for a long time.

The landlord had grown to have a very strong likeness for me and told her families about me. When they came to visit she would invite me over to meet with them. They were very appreciative of me taking care of their parent's home.

One night Adrian and I went to bed; my daughter was asleep in her crib, surprisingly Adrian got belligerent and started to kick me off the bed, and then started kicking me in my belly. My daughter was awakened by my cries. Everyone who lived in the building were either asleep, or working. Seems the neighbor who lived close by heard the noise and got upset with Adrian's behavior, and began pounding on the wall and shouting. "Stop beating the woman because she doesn't want to be intimate with you." Immediately Adrian stopped abusing me, but my daughter was crying like she was in agony. I got up from the floor and took her into my arms, but she held me so tight crying, and at the same time screaming, "Mama, Mama, Mama." My daughter was only one year and a few months old. She then pulled herself from my arms, and ran into the kitchen, on returning she had a knife in her hand. I tried taking it from her but I ended up cutting my hands. Finally I took the knife from her, but that did not satisfy her, she took her bottle and a shoe and hit Adrian in his face. It was very difficult for me to sleep that night. My daughter spent the rest of the night crying.

The next morning Adrian had to go to work. I was so anxious for him to go, so that I could talk with my friends. As soon as he left I went and knocked on my neighbor's door. They felt so sorry for me, and wanted to help me, but they were not in a position to do so. I did not want to tell the landlord about my problems because I had already told her a lie about my immigration status, so I decided to seek help from other places.

I continue visiting the doctor for treatments. Because of my illness which was caused by an automobile accident I also had an attorney to represent my case. Not financially able to maintain myself I had to remain in the relationship with Adrian. Adrian was abusive to me. I had not gotten a divorce from my daughter's father who was also abusive to me, but I contacted him hoping that we could get back together, but he told me explicitly that he don't want any foreign women in his life because you people are too high class and perfect for him, and he was not prepared to change to live his life to be like a dam foreigner. I came to the realization that I had to fend for myself.

With no money in hand I became promiscuous and lived the life of a courtesan with my neighbors and friends; and at the same time making inquiries to meet someone to help me.

One day at home Adrian was at work; he called me on the telephone and said he had someone interested in me. I was surprised. That evening when he came home from work, he brought a man I had never met. Adrian introduced me to the man and said, "I know you are not working and need money, but this is my buddy, I told him about you, so he is willing to sleep with you for $500.00. I was sitting on the couch. Immediately I got up and said to Adrian in the presence of his friend. "Get this dog away from me." You as my own country man should present something better to me. You are nothing but a dirty scoundrel.

As the days went by I developed more dislike and disdain for Adrian and want to leave. Not very long after I received money for my settlement, Adrian became extremely nice to me, and encouraged me to buy a car, but I was reluctant, because the relationship between us was very abusive; and having no papers, either a job I realized that he would be using me. My decision did not meet his approval and so his attitude towards me worsened.

It was not my intention to Marry Adrian; and I did not want to spend any money until I met someone to help me, or maybe if I was caught by the immigration, I would not return home broke.

The supervisor on the job where I used to work was my good friend. He was a fisherman in the community and surrounding areas. One day he told Adrian and myself that if we had a truck he would sell large containers of fish to us at a lesser price so we could help ourselves. Adrian and I decided on doing so. I then decided and bought a pickup truck. The week after we bought the truck, I planned to contact the fisherman and let him know that we were ready to take up his offer. That did not happen as planned. Adrian got one container of fish, which were actually given away. When I questioned him about it, he told me that he can't manage to do that kind of work because the fish smell is going to make him stink. I accosted him angrily, because we were not the only people selling fish to make extra money.

The divorce from my husband was finalized. Adrian thought I was going to marry him, but I refused with an explanation that marrying him would take a long time for me to get my papers because he was not a citizen, but a resident. Adrian was unhappy about my decision, but I cared less. That was not the reason. I had such an abusive relationship with him, so I did not want to tie myself to him by marriage.

The abusive and promiscuity had become an integral part of my life. It has been said 'that when the student is ready, the teacher will appear.' The teacher came and I became very disgusted and made concerted efforts to free myself from the rigors of that woodwork. Doubting myself that because of my condition no escape route could be found. One day I had a conversation with Chad. He told me that at the rate I was going he knew that I would one day find someone to help me.

Soon I became disgusted about how bad my life had been; as an illegal alien. I came to the decision to get either the worst American man instead of my own country kings. Not that the Americans did not abuse, or treated me badly. But the most bad treatment and abusive life I had experienced; surprisingly, came from my own country folks. One day I looked to God and said a prayer, "Lord you brought me through the border of Mexico, but I know that you are not yet finished with me, I have more things for you to do for me. This time I need for you to send me a man. Not someone only to marry to get my papers. Someone who doesn't cause me to be a compulsive liar. Someone who doesn't abuse me, someone who I don't have to cheat on. Someone who would respect and help me. Someone simple, and honest to me." Few days passed and I discussed the matter with Adrian; he was disgruntled about the idea of getting someone to marry me. As a matter of fact I did not want to pay anyone, because my intention was to marry someone, and get away from him.

One day Adrian told me he had spoken to one of his friends about my situation, and that friend agreed to help me, but I was very hesitant about his friend. I remember that I had spoken to James who was an American sometime ago and asked him if he would marry me; and help me obtain my residency. His response was, as a matter of fact he needed a 'foreign woman.' He agreed to help me, so I decided to get in touch with him. I told Adrian about the conversation James and I had about helping me; Adrian also decided to get in touch with him. Adrian then said to me. Are you sure James will help you, because he has several women, and also has a bad reputation, because he had been in and out of jail; so he was not a decent man. I told Adrian that I was not interested in a relationship with him. I just needed my darn papers.

As the days went by Adrian would curse me using profane language, sometime when I prepared the meal he would throw it away and said to me, "I know if you had your papers you would not be living with me." I told Adrian that I did not appreciate the treatment I had been receiving from him, so I intend to seek help in any areas that would be available for me.

Adrian was not pleased with my response, but I was very unhappy living with him, also knowing we both came from the same country I expected better support from him. One Sunday I drove to the store to buy a newspaper. To my surprise I met James. I was so happy to see him. I reminded him about the conversation we had when he told me that he would marry me, and asked him if he had changed his mind, he said not at all. I gave him my telephone number, and told him that I was ready and available. I was elated after meeting James. When I returned home I told Adrian that I met James and spoke to him about helping me, and that he agreed. Adrian got very belligerent and said to me, "Is American man you want, you nasty wretch? I am going to frigg it up." After such an altercation I decided that somehow I would have to talk with James. Coincidentally, one evening James called. I told James that I did not want to just marry him for my papers; but I wanted to get away from Adrian. James' response was that he liked me very much, so that would be no problem. At first Adrian was happy about me getting someone to help me, but after I found someone on my own, he displayed an unsavory attitude towards me. I spoke to James and told him just to make things pleasant for me; he should try talking to Adrian and convince him that his plans were only to help me.

James and I had made our plans. I told him that we had to live together as husband and wife, but if we could not get along we go our separate ways. We both decided to get married.

One day James and I went and did the necessary test that was required to obtain a marriage license. It seems the closer it got for me to get married Adrian got more belligerent with me, but I was determined that his ignorance was not going to stop me.

Few weeks after James and I decided to get married. He contacted a pastor who had been his friend for a long time. The wedding was supposed to take place at the pastor's home, but because we were running late the pastor asked us to come to the church and get married, we agreed. We both got married at a Baptist Church.

After the wedding I took James with me to visit Lorna who was my friend and lived in Chancy to share my good news. She was so happy for me. We got there just in time for her dinner. She told me to fix my plate. Soon as I took the plate in my hands it fell to the floor and broke in two pieces. Lorna immediately shouted, "Lord my God, your problems are over, but you and your husband are going to have a lot of problems. You need to pray, pray, pray, but you are going to get your papers." She gave me another plate. James and I then sat down and had dinner. Before we left Lorna's house, James looked around her house and said to me, "I am taking you from that man, because you foreign women know how to cook and keep a house looking good. "Lorna looked at us and smiled. We both left and I went back home to Vale.

It was late that evening when I returned home. Adrian babysits my daughter because I had no one else. He gave such a disparaging look, but I had experienced worse from him, so I did not let that discourage me. It then became clear that Adrian did not want me to get someone to help me. One day Adrian told me that he was sorry that he did not get me deported when he had the chance. I became angrier knowing that he was such a nemesis to me.

I got in touch with James and told him what happened and encouraged him to look for an apartment that he could afford. James did not have any money, neither a steady job; he was also very careless and irresponsible. But I decided to take my chances. Soon we found a place to live. The financial burden was dependent on me; so I paid the rent also the security deposit to secure the apartment. James and I then got the apartment all fixed up and ready to occupy. I had to plan an escape route to move away from Adrian. I told Adrian that James said he would not be helping me unless we lived together like man and wife; if not he would personally have me deported; because

I am the woman he had been dreaming about. It was a very hard pill to swallow, but I was very tired of the many physical, mental and abusive treatment I had been receiving, and the profane language that Adrian told me, because I had no papers. Adrian did not accept my decision very well. But I fully decided to step out into the water with God holding my hands.

Each time I packed my things to leave Adrian would throw them into the garbage, or either burn some of them. One day I got irate and told Adrian that I need to get my life together because all I have been doing is living the life of a courtesan to make ends meet, and had him believing it's his money I was saving. I said to him; what could be saved from the paltry weekly income, when we have bills to pay, put food on the table, also gives you spending money. Do you ever think about it? Well! That is what I had been doing, to make ends meet. Now I am very tired, so I have to move on to better my life.

Adrian immediately shut up, he said to me, "You were doing all that up under my nose and I did not know." I told him that I wanted us to sell fish to supplement the income, and your response was; you are not going to stink up yourself to please me. So having no papers I had was to find a way to help myself in order to help my children. I Said to Adrian, "All you have done was just drive around and show your teeth making people believe you have money, when I was basically living the life of a courtesan." I told him that if he ever try and stop me again I would walk away and leave everything. Because for real I am lawfully married to an American who really likes me, so neither him nor anyone else cannot deport me now. And that I would be taking the truck, because the money that bought the truck came from my promiscuous lifestyle. He had to go to work, so the next morning. I got in touch with James and told him he should come, because I would be ready to leave. When James came, I packed my things into the truck and left with my daughter to my new residence in Chancy.

I felt a great relief moving away with my daughter from such a draconian condition. James was not working, but I still maintained my job at the factory; but after working for a while my job ended. Not very long James found a job as a large equipment operator for a company. The salary was not very much, but we supplemented it by collecting aluminum cans, on his job site, also along the roadways; which usually works well, especially when he had a short pay week.

Few months after I got in touch with Lorna and told her that James was ready to file for my permanent residency. Lorna gave me information about an Immigration Consultant named Mr. Gordon whose office was located in the city; and said I should contact him. I made an appointment to meet with him.

Our first meeting was very cordial. During the conversation he appeared vet genuine; which made me feel complacent, with a sense of trust. I got the necessary documents that he required. Weeks and months went by. One day I contacted him about the documents he had filed for me. Mr. Gordon told me that the papers were being processed; so I should be receiving a letter very soon.

Not hearing from Mr. Gordon for quite some time. One morning I was home, my husband was gone to work. I heard a knock on my door. When I looked out, I saw the Immigration Consultant standing, and holding his briefcase in hand. I became overwhelmed with joy that he brought me good news.

I gladly open the door and let him in. To my chagrin; as he approached me, he said he came to go to bed with me. Not wanting to acquiesce his desire; Mr. Gordon told me that I should be nice to him because in his hands he held the key to my permanent residency.

I tried resisting, but he forced himself on me. A struggle ensued, where he ended up being intimate with me.

Before Mr. Gordon left he told me not to worry anymore because my papers would arrive in no time.

Time passed, and not hearing from the Immigration Consultant I visited him at his office in question about my immigration status. He told me to expect a letter in the mail in a few days; also he would be representing me.

When I received the letter from the immigration and told him, he refused to represent me; and said it was not his job.

James and I took the appointment letter to the immigration. We were denied having no one to represent us.

Returning home I contacted Mr. Gordon and reported the matter to him. His action to me was abhorrent. I became so embarrassed; I could only walk away in uncontrollable tears.

After being abused and cheated of my money by Mr. Gordon I suggested to James that we should take another chance and go to the immigration. We were turned down at each attempt. This causes us to become discouraged; because James wanted to visit with me to my country to meet my children, and families.

As time passed I heard about amnesty that would qualify me as an illegal alien to gain my residency, and would also later give me the opportunity to become an American citizen. I investigated and found the information to be true.

I began preparing all the necessary documents that were required. Soon I received my work permit, and as time proceeded I obtained my residency.

A once melancholy person, suddenly became very happy; as I anticipated my trip to see my children and families, after being absent for many years.

As time passed some of the children came to visit me, and later James helped them to become permanent residents.

After a few years I became a United States Citizen, and also attended Technical Colleges; which gave me such feelings of accomplishment. 'That was one of my main goals.'

Over time I discovered that James was illiterate and doing drugs heavily, also had a bad upbringing without proper parental guidance. He sometimes became verbally abusive when he wanted money, or whatever he could get his hands on to support his habits. I actually lived the life of a prisoner at home, fearing what he would have sold for drugs; which had caused such financial strain in the home. But realizing that he had been a hard worker, with good intentions; spiritually I became very aggressive, and as a tower of strength for him to overcome the drug habits he once entertained.

Over time James and I started attending church. I was soon ordained as an Evangelist; and James was appointed as a Deacon. Those were the halcyon times that I had experienced, being used by God, with the Holy Spirit.

During my evangelistic years I was invited to London to minister to families. I also had the opportunity to visit my friend on the train from London to Wales where she lived.

Although I was a spiritual person, the marriage between James and myself had been very difficult, because we encountered many obstacles; including spiritual and physical; but we stood and fought and prayed together; and later became home owners.

Overtime; and after many traumatic experiences we decided to relocate to another state. James requested a transfer from his job, and was successful. Soon after we sold the home we once owned, and then James, myself and my daughter relocated to another state.

Few years after relocating; we bought another home.

We met and made new friends; who were genuine to us.

My sojourn was very difficult but I have learnt that life is not a bed of roses. And any flowers that ever bloom had to go through tough dirt.

As difficult as things have been for us both over the years, and now; James and I are trying to live and enjoy a quiet life.

www.ingramcontent.com/pod-product-compliance
Lightning Source LLC
Chambersburg PA
CBHW052100280426
43673CB00070B/25